W9-BQM-397

Ḥabad

KANSAS SCHOOL OF RELIGION
UNIVERSITY OF KANSAS
1300 OREAD AVENUE
LAWRENCE, KANSAS 66044

JUDAIC STUDIES SERIES

Leon J. Weinberger, General Editor

BM 755
.S525 F69
1992

ḤABAD

The Hasidism of R. Shneur Zalman of Lyady

Roman A. Foxbrunner

KANSAS SCHOOL OF RELIGION
UNIVERSITY OF KANSAS
1300 OREAD AVENUE
LAWRENCE, KANSAS 66044

The University of Alabama Press
Tuscaloosa and London

Copyright © 1992 by
The University of Alabama Press
Tuscaloosa, Alabama 35487–0380
All rights reserved
Manufactured in the United States of America
designed by zig zeigler

∞

The paper on which this book is printed meets the minimum requirements of American National Standard for Information Science-Permanence of Paper for Printed Library Materials, ANSI Z39.48-1984.

Library of Congress Cataloging-in-Publication Data

Foxbrunner, Roman A., 1947–
Ḥabad : the Hasidism of R. Shneur Zalman of Lyady / Roman A. Foxbrunner.
p. cm.—(Judaic studies series)
Includes bibliographical references and index.
ISBN 0-8173-0558-0
1. Shneur Zalman, of Lyady, 1745–1813. 2. Hasidism. 3. Habad. I. Title. II. Series: Judaic studies series (Unnumbered)
BM755.S525F69 1992
296.8′3322′092—dc20
[B] 91-26040

British Library Cataloguing-in-Publication Data available

To Constance

In loving memory

Contents

Preface / ix

Transliteration and Spelling / xi

1. Teachers and Teachings / 1

2. Man in God's World / 58

3. Ethical Ways and Means / 110

4. Torah and Commandments / 137

5. Love and Fear / 178

6. Conclusions / 195

Excursuses / 203

Notes / 221

Glossary / 289

Selected Bibliography / 295

Index / 301

R. Shneur Zalman of Lyady (Courtesy of Kehot Publication Society)

Preface

The Hasidic thought of R. Shneur Zalman (RSZ) of Lyady (1745–1813), known as Ḥabad Hasidism, has had and continues to have a major influence on Jewish life throughout the world. ("Ḥabad" is an acronym of the initials for the Hebrew words *Ḥokhmah, Binah, Daʿat*—wisdom, understanding, knowledge). This book, based on all the extant teachings of RSZ, systematically presents that thought and analyzes its underlying theological, philosophical, religious, and ethical concepts. The focus is on axiology and on three broad questions: What were RSZ's criteria for religioethical perfection? What did he want his followers to believe, know, feel, and do in order to aspire toward that perfection? What were the attitudes and values he sought to inculcate with this end in mind? Because RSZ's Hasidism was an outgrowth of the Hasidism of R. Israel Baal Shem Tov and R. Dov Baer of Mezhirech, their teachings and previous scholarly interpretations of these teachings are also examined and analyzed. The pre-Hasidic roots of RSZ's Hasidism are analyzed only on those occasions and to the extent that such analysis appears necessary fully to appreciate RSZ's view.

In examining a passage or group of related passages from RSZ's teachings, my immediate purpose is to answer two questions: Considering, whenever possible and relevant, what and with whom RSZ studied, the men he admired, the audience he was addressing, and the fundamental values he shared with similarly educated contemporaries, what does he mean to say and how does it relate to what he says elsewhere? For the sake of brevity, I have generally refrained from unfolding my analysis of the sources cited in the notes. A conclusion or series of conclusions will often be fully supported, however, only when all or most of the sources cited are combined and analyzed. For the same reason I have omitted from the text a number of interesting and sometimes significant points and apparent contradictions, all of which may be uncovered by consulting the sources cited for that purpose.

Chapter 1 presents a survey and assessment of the scholarship relating to R. Israel Baal Shem Tov and R. Dov Baer of Mezhirech, as well as a general introduction to RSZ's teachings and their salient characteristics—syncretism, tension, and paradox. Chapters 2 and 3 attempt to set forth the foundations of RSZ's Hasidic thought. The titles of Chapters 4 and 5 reflect the broad religioethical categories that RSZ himself recognized; that of Chapter 6, the Conclusion, speaks for itself.

I am grateful to Professors Isadore Twersky, Sid Leiman, and Leon Weinberger for their helpful comments and suggestions; to the Memorial Foundation for Jewish Culture for its generous support; to all at The University of Alabama Press who contributed to transforming manuscript into book with admirable courtesy, diligence, and ability; to Pamela Ferdinand for her masterful copyediting; and to my father for enabling me to pursue the graduate studies that eventually led to this work. It is dedicated to my late wife, who enabled and encouraged me to write it. During her tragically short life she warmed and illumined the lives of many, and mine most of all.

Transliteration and Spelling

Key to Transliteration

(omitted for first letter) ʾ	א	m	מ
b	בּ	n	נ
v	ב	s	ס
g	ג	ʿ	ע
d	ד	p	פּ
h	ה	f	פ
ṿ	ו	ts	צ
z	ז	ḳ	ק
ḥ	ח	r	ר
ṭ	ט	sh	שׁ
(for consonant) y	י	ś	שׂ
kh	כ	t	תּ
l	ל	t	ת

Note on Spelling

"Zaddik" and "Tsadiḳ" (or tsadiḳ) are deliberate variants (see Glossary).

"Mitsṿah" is used rather than "mitzvah" when its Ḥabad connotations are intended.

God's attributes are capitalized—e.g., "Will," "Pleasure,"—when they denote kabbalistic reifications.

"Love," "Fear," and "Service" are capitalized when their specifically religious connotations are intended.

1

Teachers *and* Teachings

Rabbi Shneur Zalman (RSZ) of Lyady believed that his religious ethics were those of Rabbi Israel Baal Shem Tov (the Besht), whom he considered his spiritual "grandfather," and Rabbi Dov Baer, the Maggid of Mezhirech, whom he revered as his primary master of Hasidism. He considered the Maggid's teachings to be essentially elaborations of the Besht's. Although he also studied with, and was influenced by, other members of the Maggid's circle, he saw only the Besht and the Maggid as his true religioethical mentors; they were for him the ultimate authorities on Hasidic thought and conduct, and he saw himself as third in the single line of succession of Hasidic masters.[1]

Consequently, to understand his Hasidic thought in context, one has to determine how he understood the Besht's and Maggid's thought; to what extent he adopted their teachings, to what extent he modified them, and to what extent he may have departed from them. While other literary and personal influences will naturally be considered in the course of this study, it is primarily the teachings of the Besht and the Maggid that concern us in this chapter. Since these teachings have been the subject of considerable scholarly attention and debate, and it is not at all clear what they really were or how they should be interpreted, it is first necessary to undertake a survey of the previous work in this area. Having established what the key doctrines of the Besht and the Maggid were and how they may have been understood by RSZ, it will then be possible to analyze what he does with them. Having determined, as far as possible, how these doctrines affected the Jewish world to which RSZ belonged, it will then be possible to determine how he, in particular, assimilated them. This chapter, in other words, is intended as a general introduction to RSZ's teachings.

Until quite recently, the study of Hasidism has had an unhappy history. From H. Graetz's vilification to S. A. Horodetsky's glorification, with a pause for E. Zweifel's apologetics, the common denominator was impressionistic evaluation rather than careful analysis (see Excursus A). S. Dubnow's influential history, *Toldot ha-Ḥasidut* (1930), was no exception in this respect. What distinguished Dubnow from his predecessors was a more systematic approach to Hasidism as a significant historical phenomenon with personalities, places, dates, books, important events, and trends of thought that required identification and description. For obtaining such information within the context of a cohesive historical narrative, *Toldot ha-Ḥasidut* remains a valuable work. But for an understanding of the ideas and success of Hasidism within the context of Jewish intellectual history one must look elsewhere, for this is not Dubnow's forte.[2] Moreover, his attempts in this direction are invariably colored in Haskalah pastels. Consequently, we are expected to believe that the rise of Hasidism stemmed from a popular revolt against precisely those factors in Jewish life that moderate Maskilim found particularly objectionable. The movement is represented, in effect, as a kind of Hegelian (or Fichtean) antithesis to a decrepit Rabbanism, soon to be superseded in its turn by the final synthesis, presumably Dubnow's own nationalistic version of Haskalah.[3]

After delineating the abject political, social, and economic conditions of eighteenth-century Polish Jewry, Dubnow deprecates the communal leadership of the period and concludes that Jewish complaints against its high-handed, autocratic ways were responsible for the demise of the Council of the Four Lands (Ṿaʿad Arba Aratsot).[4] This assumption lends credibility to his claim that the traditional gap between the intelligentsia and the masses widened at this time, a claim that, incidentally, forms the basis of B. Z. Dinur's sociological explanation of Hasidism's genesis.[5] The insensitive communal leaders, Dubnow argues, combined with a narrow-minded rabbinate and an otherworldly kabbalistic elite to make the people's lives miserable. The rabbis heaped extreme "religious" (i.e., halakhic) demands upon them, even going so far as to transform Shabbat, the day of joy, into a day of distress. Interested only in the form and not in the spirit of religious practices, they buried prayer—ideally a free communion between man and his Maker—beneath a mound of petty legalisms. Their bitter opposition to secular studies, particularly philosophy, added intellectual confinement to these religious shackles, while the extreme ascetic demands, gross superstitions, and comminations for the most minor religious infractions in kabbalistically oriented *musar* works made the inner world of Polish Jewry at least as wretched as the outer. The "dry formalism" of Torah-study and mitzvah-fulfillment was a woefully inadequate antidote for these oppressions. What was needed was a warm, simple, anodyne approach to Judaism based on faith and good cheer, an approach that would anesthetize the troubled mind while reviving the faint heart. What was needed was Beshtian Hasidism.[6]

What is the historical validity of this scenario? The complaint that many communal leaders were insufferably arrogant autocrats had been reverberating in Jewish communities and religioethical works for centuries,[7] but neither Dubnow nor Dinur have shown or attempted to show that the injustices they perpetrated became considerably more intolerable, or that the discontent they generated was significantly greater, in pre-Hasidic Poland. In fact, it is hard to imagine a more tense and unpleasant relationship than is revealed in the confrontation, in 1576, between the people of Lvov and their communal leaders; and H. H. Ben Sasson has shown that this relationship was hardly an aberration in sixteenth–seventeenth-century Poland.[8]

Similarly, there did of course exist in Jewish society, as in all literate societies, a social gap between the scholars and the less educated; but it has yet to be demonstrated that this gap widened appreciably, if at all, during the first half of the eighteenth century. According to Jacob Katz, the gap did not, in fact, widen, but the lower caliber of rabbinic incumbents made it more difficult for the people to accept their leadership.[9] But even this assessment is questionable, and on the basis of Katz's own data. Although he cites evidence for progressively lower qualifications demanded by communities of rabbinic aspirants, he also cites evidence for progressively longer contracts and greater salaries.[10] These latter two developments may indicate merely a consolidation of the rabbinate originating at the top, but they may indicate also, at least to the extent that the communal oligarchy was responsive to communal sentiment,[11] an enhancement of this institution in the eyes of the people. Indeed, R. Jacob Emden tells us that the early eighteenth-century rabbis of Poland-Lithuania were highly esteemed by Jewish communities in Germany and were often chosen over local candidates to fill incumbencies.[12] It seems probable that the communities of Poland-Lithuania therefore tried to encourage them to stay by lengthening their contracts and increasing their salaries. Such competition for their rabbis could not fail to impress even the simplest of Polish Jews.

The ascetic demands of kabbalistic ethical works of this period were indeed extreme; the beliefs and ideologies they expounded are often unacceptable and even oppressive to minds influenced by a different socio-cultural milieu. But their unprecedented proliferation, especially during the early eighteenth century, and explicit statements by some of their authors point to the existence of a receptive audience.[13] An attempt to explain this phenomenon would require separate treatment, but one important factor was undoubtedly the legacy of the Ḥaside Ashkenaz,[14] whose ascetic religious ethics and demonology were embraced by the sixteenth-century Lurianic kabbalists of Safed and their ideological heirs in the following two centuries. Transmitted through preaching, influential ethical works such as *Reshit Ḥokhmah, Shene Luḥot ha-Berit,* and their popular condensations, as well as through the original literary vehicles, *Sefer Ḥasidim* and *Sefer Roḳeaḥ,* this legacy included a deeply pessimistic worldview in which continual, joyfully accepted suffering, both physical and mental, was a sine qua non for religious perfection; in which the essential attitude cultivated comprised adamant withstanding of all physical temptations (i.e., pleasures) and absolute fortitude in surmounting all obstacles that this world perversely presents, in order to attain the beatitude of the next; in which the religious life was concomitantly seen as continuous warfare against the hostile gentile environment without, man's instincts within, and demons everywhere, so that the only hope for survival was constant, anxious vigilance, and the only hope for victory was total concentration on the battle at hand. The weapons were prayer with the proper *kavanot* (meditative devotions), intense asceticism, and zealous fulfillment of both the explicit and implicit directives of *retson ha-Bore* (the will of the Creator).[15] Needless to say, not all of Polish Jewry was equally influenced by these ideas, but all of its members did live in a religious world suffused by them. It was, moreover, a world where—despite the inroads of Sabbatianism[16]—Torah-study, mitzvah-fulfillment, and a positive orientation toward halakhic thinking and conclusions, no matter how apparently restrictive, still reigned supreme.[17] What was distasteful to Dubnow in the twentieth century was still sacred to his forebears in the eighteenth.

On the other hand, hostility to secular studies in pre-Hasidic Poland was far from universal. It is or should be a commonplace that, ever since the first stage of the Maimonidean controversy in the early thirteenth century (and to a lesser extent even earlier), Jewish scholars had been polarized over the permissibility and value of these studies, with various degrees of compromise usually predominating.[18] Important for our period are the major antiphilosophy diatribes penned by R. Meir ibn Gabbai a few decades after the Spanish Expulsion. The widespread conversions in Spain during the last century of the Jewish community's residence there were most frequently attributed to religious and moral corruption engendered by the pursuit of rationalistic philosophy.[19] Some even saw the Expulsion itself as divine retribution for this misguided quest for alien enlightenment.[20] Ibn Gabbai carried these beliefs to their logical conclusion, and most if not all of his very influential *ʿAvodat ha-Ḳodesh* (written in Turkey, 1531) is either an explicit or an implicit repudiation of the Maimonidean approach to Judaism, with all nonkabbalistic speculation included in the indictment. He is the most recent, well-known author cited by the even more influential R. Isaiah Horowitz (1565–1630) in his censure of philosophy, and it is again ibn Gabbai whom R. Joel Sirkes (1561–1640) mentions as his authority for its reprehensibility.[21]

Nevertheless, although their individual postures varied, many other notable rabbis who flourished or influenced Jewish thought in Poland during the sixteenth to midseventeenth centuries shared a fairly positive attitude toward secular studies and philosophy. These included R. Moses Isserles (1525/30–1572), R. Solomon Eidels (1555–1631), R. Abraham Horowitz (Isaiah's father, 1550–1615), R. Eliezer Ashkenazi (1513–1586), Maharal of Prague (1525–1609) and his brothers R. Bezalel and R. Sinai, R. Mordecai Yaffe (ca. 1535–1612), R. Yomtov Lipman Heller (1579–1654), and R. David Gans (1541–1613). In a class by himself in this respect was R. Joseph Solomon Delmedigo (1591–1655), physician, philosopher, mathematician, astronomer, and avid student and popularizer of the sciences in general.[22]

Nor did the broad spectrum of positive attitudes to secular studies change significantly during the next century. Although the cultural climate in Poland-Lithuania deteriorated drastically after the massacres and upheavals of 1648–1658, by 1740, when R. Elijah of Vilna was twenty and the Besht was winning his first followers, most major communities had largely recovered. Those that were centers of learning before 1648—Vilna, Minsk, Pinsk, Cracow, Posen, Lublin, and Lvov, to name a few—had regained that status, and their scholars were again pursuing their studies in whatever direction their interests led them. As H. H. Ben Sasson puts it: "Jewish cultural and social life in the second half of the seventeenth century and in the eighteenth continued to a considerable extent along the lines developed in the great era of the sixteenth and first half of the seventeenth centuries. Recent research has shown that Pinsk, a community in the east of Lithuania, recovered from its troubles more completely and at greater speed than had been known before."[23]

In fact, as early as 1661, students who had fled to Germany with their families were returning to Poland to study Talmud. One of these, Tuvia b. Moses Cohen (1652–1729), finding conditions still inhospitable to intellectual pursuits, returned to Germany to take up medicine and the sciences at the University of Frankfurt an der Oder.[24] He continued his studies in Padua, the usual destination of aspiring physicians from Poland-Lithuania.[25] In Venice, in 1707, he published his illustrated encyclopedia, *Maʿaśeh Ṭuvyah*, on philosophy, astronomy, cosmography, geography, botany, and medicine, plus miscellaneous information and speculations on other fields. He admired and was admired by several of the leading rabbis of his generation, who shared his broad intellectual interests. One of these was his stepbrother, R. Yair Ḥayyim Bacharach (1638–1702) of Germany, who met and may have been influenced by Delmedigo.[26] A man of immense rabbinic erudition, author of glosses to Maimonides' *The Guide of the Perplexed*, and a reverent student of kabbalah, Bacharach also confessed to a love for all the sciences and displayed considerable knowledge of mathematics and astronomy in his *responsa*.[27]

Tuvia's brother-in-law, R. Moses b. Solomon Friedman, Rabbi of Lvov, wrote to Bacharach after 1679, praising Bacharach's works, describing him as a man great in "Torah and *ḥokhmah*" (wisdom), and offering him assistance in obtaining a prestigious rabbinate in Poland,[28] obviously feeling that a scholar of such broad learning would be perfectly acceptable as a Polish communal leader. Bacharach's daughter married the son of his rabbinic counterpart in Bohemia-Moravia, R. David Oppenheim (1664–1736), a bibliophile whose famous library contained scores of books and manuscripts in the fields of philosophy, astronomy, mathematics, medicine and other sciences, history, poetry, grammar, rhetoric, belles lettres, and polemics, plus dictionaries and reference works in both Semitic and European languages.[29] That Oppenheim not only owned but also encouraged the writing of such works is clear from his approbation for *Maʿaśeh Ṭuvyah*, which he apparently wrote while the book was still in progress. Needless to say, he eventually acquired a copy for his library.[30]

During this period, too, R. Zevi Hirsch Ashkenazi (1660–1718) was receiving halakhic queries in Altona and Amsterdam from all parts of Europe.[31] According to his son, R. Jacob Emden (1697–1776), Ashkenazi knew six languages and had studied the sciences. He had established his reputation as the head of the yeshiva (*klaus*) of Altona, where for nearly two decades scholars from Poland-Lithuania flocked to him to advance in both their religious and secular studies.[32] Emden himself, despite his opposition to Greek philosophy and works based on it, strongly favored the study of the sciences, particularly medicine, read books on many secular subjects, and was on generally cordial terms with Moses Mendelssohn (see Excursus B). His archnemesis, R. Jonathan Eybeschutz (1690/95–1764), was also a man of broad secular learning and an admirer of the young Mendelssohn, but, unlike Emden, he also valued the study of philosophy.[33]

Lithuanian rabbis were writing grammatical works and advertising their knowledge of mathematics and logic.[34] Johathan b. Joseph of Ruzhany (Grodono province) moved to Germany and wrote a series of astronomical books and commentaries (e.g., *Yeshuah be-Yiśra'el* [Frankfurt, 1720]).[35] R. Eliezer of Krasnik (d. 1769), originally from Vilna, was eulogized as a great scholar of "Torah, Sifra, Sifre, Tosefta, philosophy, the seven sciences, [both in] the revealed aspects and the secrets."[36] R. Yeḥi'el Heilprin (1660–1746) of Minsk was using Gans's wide-ranging *Tsemaḥ David* to write his chronicle, *Seder ha-Dorot*.

As in previous periods, the lines of communication between Poland-Lithuania, Bohemia-Moravia, Austria-Hungary, and Germany (as well as the Netherlands and Italy) were open and humming. There was a continual flow of scholars, and therefore of scholarship and scholarly interests, between Jewish communities in these lands. While still rabbi of Nikolsburg (Moravia), Oppenheim was offered the rabbinate of Brisk (Lithuania), and though he declined,[37] he apparently felt that the city and its environs now came under his jurisdiction.[38] R. Ezekiel Katzenellenbogen was brought from Lithuania to be rabbi of Altona and its sister communities, and, as noted above, Emden informs us that this was only one example of the German preference for Polish-Lithuanian rabbis.[39] Conversely, Polish communities were quite amenable to hiring rabbis from Western Europe, and Emden's father ended his career as rabbi of Lvov. Additional evidence for the intellectual interrelationship of Jewish communities in Europe during this period (1660–1740) may be adduced from contemporary responsa (of, e.g., Bacharach, Ashkenazi, Oppenheim, and Emden); the biographical data contained in the many *haskamot* to Bacharach's works;[40] his introduction to *Ḥavot Ya'ir*; Ashkenazi's Polish-

Lithuanian pupils; Tuvia Cohen's correspondence with his former countrymen;[41] and the curricula vitae of such leading rabbis as Jacob Joshua Falk (1680–1756), born in Cracow, went on to become rabbi of Lvov, Berlin, Metz, and Frankfurt, and Jonathan Eybeschutz, who studied in Poland, Moravia, Prague, Prossnitz, and Vienna, and went on to officiate in Prague and Germany.[42]

Thus, while much of the secular scholarship of this period was taking place outside Poland, any native Polish scholar with a modicum of intellectual curiosity could avail himself of the educational opportunities in Jewish communities elsewhere—and many did so. Some eventually returned to Poland; those who did not kept in touch with their families and fellow scholars, so that on the whole the Jewish intelligentsia of Poland in 1740 was hardly less secularly enlightened than it was in 1640 or 1540. If Polish Jewry as a whole was not receptive to secular learning, it was no less receptive than Joseph Delmedigo claims to have found it in 1620–1625. And if there were notable exceptions in Delmedigo's day, although he claimed there were none and that even in Italy he found only one,[43] the same was true a century later.

By then, however, a new subject had been added to the curriculum of most scholars. Lurianic kabbalah began circulating in Europe by word of mouth early in the seventeenth century.[44] Manuscripts began to trickle out of the Holy Land primarily after Hayyim Vital's death in 1620,[45] and subsequent decades saw the trickle become a flow and then a mighty river that inundated Jewish thought and often submerged other intellectual interests. This form of kabbalah was a fresh and exciting development that also had an insurmountable advantage over other fields of study: Its teachings were, according to its exponents, divinely revealed.[46] These other fields were never completely abandoned, however, and by 1740, when the new kabbalah had been acclaimed for over a century, its relative novelty and allure were just beginning to wane. The Gaon of Vilna, for example, would soon maintain that not all of Luria's teachings were revealed to him by the prophet Elijah.[47] Moreover, the image of kabbalah in general had been somewhat tarnished since it had become the basis for Sabbatian ideology and propaganda.[48] Consequently, the Lurianic tide began to recede, and those submerged areas of interest began to reappear. In Germany, for instance, Maimonides' *Guide* was republished for the first time in nearly two centuries (Jessnitz, 1742), "with the tacit approval of the chief rabbi of Dessau; the cost of printing had been defrayed by a relative of the chief rabbi; and the reading of proofs had been supervised by Aaron Hirsch, a member of the Beth Din."[49] And in Poland-Lithuania, the works or words of such early Hasidic masters as R. Pinḥas of Koretz, the Maggid of Mezhirech, R. Abraham "ha-Malakh," R. Menaḥem Mendel of Vitebsk, R. Menaḥem Naḥum of Chernobyl, and RSZ, as well as of their archopponent, R. Elijah of Vilna, attested in varying degrees to the positive value they attached to philosophy, to some of the sciences, or to both.[50]

Thus, although there is, as we shall see, some validity to Dubnow's analysis of the religious problems that confronted eighteenth-century Polish Jewry, his maskilistic interpretation of Hasidism should be largely rejected, and the first truly significant attempt to explain the rise of Hasidism, analyze it from within, and relate it to previous trends in Jewish thought must be dated no earlier than 1941 and located in the last chapter of Gershom Scholem's *Major Trends in Jewish Mysticism.* There and in a subsequent paper on the Hasidic doctrine of *deveḳut* (cleaving to God), Scholem introduced most of the major themes around which the historical study of Hasidism has since centered. In effect, he defined the essential problems to be Hasidism's relationship to Lurianic kabbalah on the one hand and to Sabbatianism on the other. Under these rubrics he masterfully discussed topics such as the popularization of kabbalah; the new emphasis on psychology rather than theosophy and on ethics rather than metaphysics; the "neutralization" of Sabbatian messianism; the adaptation (or adoption) of Sabbatian terminology, emotionalism, and specific customs; the relation of the Sabbatian-type prophet to the institution of the Zaddik; the centrality of the deveḳut doctrine and the doctrine of elevating profane (literally: "alien") thoughts. Alleged pantheistic tendencies in early Hasidism were also analyzed. These issues were then taken up in greater detail by Isaiah Tishby and Rivkah Schatz-Uffenheimer, and particularly by Joseph Weiss, who devoted a good part of his career to the study of Hasidism.

With scholars of such caliber working in the field, one would expect to find by now a solid foundation of reliable data and substantiated conclusions regarding the teachings of the Besht and the Maggid on which further research may be based. But this is not the case. As far as I can determine, the themes just mentioned were approached before the most basic literary questions concerning early Hasidic works were satisfactorily answered: attribution,[51] reliability of quotations, and internal consistency. Major Hasidic works published until around 1815 (when the founders' disciples were still alive), which should have been carefully studied and, ideally, compared with extant manuscripts (see

Excursus C), were apparently either partially examined or superficially perused, with hardly any attempt made seriously to address these problems.[52]

With respect to the Besht's teachings, the works of his Boswell, Rabbi Jacob Joseph of Polonnoye, contain at least four hundred statements that this disciple claims to have heard directly from his master, along with many others that he variously identifies as being either at secondhand, or "in the style of my teacher," or "according to his method," or as possibly inaccurate in some way.[53] The consistency and precision with which he distinguishes between these categories suggest that his direct quotations are the most reliable examples of what R. Israel Baal Shem Tov actually taught. This does not mean, though, that these are examples of what he actually said, since it is highly unlikely that anyone took notes while he spoke. If subsequent custom is any indication, the Besht's homilies were generally delivered on Sabbaths and holidays, when writing is prohibited. Moreover, these occasions, even on weekdays, were not lectures—they were inspirational experiences during which sitting with quill, inkwell, and notepaper would be completely out of place. At best, the conscientious disciple would try to retain as much as possible of what he heard[54] and record it as soon as possible, translating the original Yiddish into Hebrew. The dubious faithfulness of these translations was already recognized by RSZ but has generally been ignored by students of Hasidism in their analyses of Hasidic thought.[55] Scrutinizing the language and terminology of Hasidic homilies, even those of Rabbi Jacob Joseph, can reveal much about the disciples who authored them but little about the masters who delivered them. Only by comparing many homilies and aphorisms on the same theme and by devoting particular attention to the contexts of the often cryptic aphorisms can we hope to arrive at what the Besht and Maggid actually meant to convey.

We must also bear in mind the rather hazy and disjointed style in which these teachings were originally articulated. The master did not consciously arrange his thoughts beforehand but spoke, ideally, under the divine inspiration of the moment. "I will teach you the best way of pronouncing Torah," the Maggid once told his disciples, "which is as follows: not to be aware of oneself, but as an ear hearkening to the way in which the 'World of Speech' speaks within one. It is not he himself who speaks. As soon as he hears his own words, let him stop."[56] According to R. Ze'ev Wolf of Zhitomir, the Maggid generally took his own advice, and there are indications that the Besht, at least occasionally, did likewise.[57] The results were homilies in which thoughts were tenuously strung together by subconscious associations, in which the terminology apparently lacked both clarity and precision, and which sometimes soared into mystical realms unintelligible even to the Maggid's most astute disciples.[58] There is therefore no doubt that in addition to translation, each transcriber of these homilies often also supplied, unconsciously, perhaps, originally unarticulated connections between thoughts and a significant measure of interpretation; that he retained primarily those parts or elements of the homilies that struck a responsive chord on his psychic harp; and that what he wrote does not necessarily reflect the main thrust of what the master actually said or intended to convey.[59]

These reservations are least applicable, however, to R. Jacob Joseph's works, which carefully and conscientiously distinguish between what the author actually heard directly from the Besht and secondhand or putative Beshtian teachings. Since such distinctions were important to him, it is safe to assume that he also took pains to transmit the directly heard teachings as faithfully and with as little editorializing as possible. These works therefore comprise the largest and most reliable repository of the Besht's authentic teachings.[60] The analects in *Keter Shem Ṭov,* which purports to be a collection of all the Besht's teachings found in R. Jacob Joseph's works, are neither complete nor completely reliable. The editor writes on the title page that he also collected Beshtian teachings from *Likuṭim Yeḳarim,* but there is nothing in these passages—which are slipped into the middle of *Keter Shem Ṭov* without any warning—to warrant this attribution.[61] In fact, there is every indication that almost all the teachings in *Liḳuṭim Yeḳarim* derive from the school of the Maggid, with the possible exception of a few sections expressly attributed to the Besht.[62] Among these sections are four numbered paragraphs prefaced by the words: "Tsaṿaʾat me-Rabi Yiśraʾel Baʿal Shem Ṭov." These words, followed by the first part of the first paragraph, comprise the beginning of the anthology misleadingly titled *Sefer Tsaṿaʾat ha-Ribash* (The testament of the Besht). Far from attributing the entire volume to the Besht, this title simply continues a tradition dating back to the Gaonic period whereby works not given another title by their author or original editor are referred to by their opening word(s). In our case the compiler (or publisher) himself apparently resorted to this expedient, and, as in *Liḳuṭim Yeḳarim,* the only sections that even he attributes to the Besht are those prefaced by such attribution: 16 out of 143.[63]

Another collection of purported Beshtian teachings published before 1815 is the small anthology by R. Menaḥem Mendel of

Przemyslany, or R. Meshullam Feivush of Zbaraz,[64] *Darke Yesharim*, also known as *Hanhagot Yesharot*. Joseph Weiss identified the author, R. Menaḥem Mendel, as the leader of one of the more "radical," popularistic groups of Hasidim on the periphery of the central movement. These groups were allegedly composed largely of ignoramuses who devoted themselves primarily to the quest for ecstatic religious experiences. Weiss saw R. Menaḥem Mendel's disciple, R. Meshullam Feivush of Zbaraz, as the main propagandist for his master's non-Beshtian ideology, believing him to be the man behind the publication of *Darke Yesharim, Tsava'at ha-Ribash*, and the editor of *Likuṭim Yeḳarim*, all three of which were intended to serve as counterpoises to the "orthodox" version of Hasidism contained in the works of Rabbi Jacob Joseph and the Maggid's disciples.[65] Manuscripts examined by Z. Gries,[66] as well as a study of the relevant published sources using the method outlined above—that is, comparing the contents and contexts of all the teachings on the same subject without overemphasizing the formulations in a few selected passages—do not bear Weiss out (see Excursus D). *Darke Yesharim* is simply an anthology of mostly Maggidic teachings, which should be analyzed in conjunction with the other sources. Since Rabbi Menaḥem Mendel was one of the Besht's older disciples, it would not be surprising if he, like Rabbi Pinḥas of Koretz, did, in fact, consciously part ways with the master on several issues. To determine whether and how he did, however, one would have to be reasonably certain that his formulations are not merely variations of genuine Beshtian teachings cited by Rabbi Jacob Joseph or by the Maggid (through his disciples); and even then, considerably more corroboration would be necessary to conclude justifiably that these differences point to the existence of discrete, non-Beshtian groups of early Hasidim.[67]

The problem of attribution is considerably mitigated for the anthologies of Maggidic teachings and has recently been addressed by R. Schatz, Z. Gries, and A. Kahn.[68] But the question of reliability is at least as serious, since, as Gries has shown, manuscript evidence seems to indicate that not only did the Maggid's disciples edit his teachings, but some may have intentionally or unintentionally omitted certain exhortations they did not find congenial, notably with regard to the importance of Torah-study.[69] Nor is their internal consistency less problematic. On the contrary, one finds apparently conflicting statements concerning the three central doctrines—the Zaddik, deveḳut, and elevation of profane thoughts—as well as different approaches to such traditional values as Torah-study, prayer, *kavanah*, Love and Fear, and asceticism.

Consequently, before passing judgment on the relation between the doctrines of early Hasidism and Sabbatianism or even Lurianic kabbalah, one must isolate the various approaches to these themes that are explicit or implicit in all the extant Maggidic sources and all the authentic Beshtian teachings. Only then can one attempt to determine which may have been emphasized by the Besht, the Maggid, or both; which are relatively insignificant; which may have been underscored only occasionally; and which crept into the transcriptions by way of the transcriber's or copyist's personal inclinations. Such a comprehensive analysis has never been undertaken, although Gries has made important bibliographical strides in this direction. What has been done is to assume, primarily on the basis of historical factors found outside Hasidic sources, that certain very plausible relationships do exist, and then to search the sources for the evidence.[70] Not surprisingly, such evidence could not possibly elude the diligent researcher (see Excursus E).

Moreover, besides addressing the literary and expository problems, to succeed in understanding the religious world of eighteenth-century Hasidism one must enter its universe of discourse: the Bible and major commentaries; the Talmud, commentaries, and codes; the major Midrashim; the *Kuzari*, the *Guide*, Albo's *Sefer ha-ʿIkarim*, and influential homiletical works;[71] the Zohar and major post-Zoharic kabbalistic works; and the major works of Jewish ethical literature and contemporary ethical teachings as reflected in ethical works published from the late seventeenth to mideighteenth centuries. The *paideia* of every passable Jewish scholar—and all the masters and transcribers of early Hasidic teachings certainly qualified for at least this category—included all of these, though obviously there were differences in extent and profundity of knowledge, as well as in the specific ways the texts were interpreted. None of the disciples who were instrumental in disseminating the masters' teachings came to them without a creditable mastery of this curriculum (as is evident from their works),[72] and it was obviously with this in mind that they were addressed.[73] The homilies we possess, particularly those of the Maggid, were formulated with a tacit and legitimate assumption that certain fundamental values, ideas, and practices were common knowledge and commonly accepted.[74]

It is, of course, possible to do a laudable phenomenological study of any aspect of Hasidism without constant recourse to these works, but such an approach will satisfy neither the intellectual historian nor the discriminating lay reader who would like to know what these phenomena, and the teachings they reflected, actually meant to their originators; why they succeeded in rapidly captivating much of European Jewry; and how they were related to pre-Hasidic and contemporary modes of religious thought and behavior. It will also generally lead to distortions whenever such questions are discussed. Completely untenable conclusions will be drawn, such as R. Schatz's statement that early Hasidism considered remorse for sin to be a major sin itself. The absence of traditional motifs will be seen as highly significant; unremarkable variations of old concepts will be described as new or even "radical"; and true innovations will be either missed or misinterpreted.[75]

On the other hand, a study of Hasidic and pre-Hasidic sources alone will not enable us to explain satisfactorily the particular combination of social and religious modes and concerns that distinguishes early Hasidism. Its socioreligious and ideational backdrop may be illumined by contemporary ethical works, as B. Z. Dinur and M. Piekarz, respectively, have shown.[76] Its often hidden axiological roots may be uncovered by referring to the other components of the paideia mentioned above, as Z. Gries has attempted to show with respect to *Tsavaʾat ha-Ribash*.[77] The work of these scholars can provide us with an understanding of Hasidism's founders' historical role as pioneers of a religious revival among the masses. But the Besht, the Maggid, and their inner circles also comprised elite brotherhoods of mystics, whose teachings flowed not only from cognitive sources but also from their immediate religious experiences. These experiences were worked into interpretations of the sacred texts (as in the homilies), articulated as apothegms in which familiar terms were filled with new meanings[78] and reflected in religious postures and practices that set these circles apart from nonmembers.[79] Such groups, whether Jewish, Moslem, or Christian, often exhibit certain common characteristics that complicate the search for specific historical and intellectual filiations.

Consider, for example, a certain movement of mystical pietists divided into several groups, each centering around a spiritual master. Each master emphasizes a different aspect of the movement's ideology. Some are learned mentors, others quite ignorant; some are elected by their followers, others inherit their positions. All possess various forms and degrees of supernatural power, such as prophecy, mind reading, thought control, healing the sick, and performing other outright miracles. Among them are men who pour honey from empty jars, bring forth fire from plain grass, levitate, walk on water. God speaks to them clearly, teaches them Scriptural interpretations and divine secrets, allays their fears. Their day begins in the middle of the night, when they rise to pray and study with great joy. They are great ascetics and so totally immersed in the divine service that they are often unaware of their surroundings.[80] They seclude themselves regularly for introspection and meditation, and these periods of solitude are instrumental in producing or sustaining their charismatic powers.[81] Their prayers possess creative potency,[82] and they sway dizzily when reciting them or when studying the divine words, unable to restrain their ecstasy. According to their disciples, after the masters took a few morsels of their meal, the leftovers were filled with their blessing.

They taught that the ideal activity is continuous invocation of God's Name—that is, complete absorption in the Divine; even the sacred rites tend to distract man from true awareness and constant remembrance of God.[83] The first step toward this goal is self-nullification—the annihilation of one's ego—through intense concentration on God's absolute unity. This means that despite His absolute transcendence, literally nothing but God exists, the world being only an imperfect manifestation of the Divine. From our limited perspective we are separate from Him, but, in truth, this is merely an illusion. The divine Breath must continuously bring the universe into being; if it were to cease for an instant, the cosmos would revert back to its true state of nothingness. In absolute terms, therefore, everything is sacred and nothing profane, because everything partakes of the Source of sanctity. To believe that any aspect of reality is autonomous from the Absolute Reality is tantamount to polytheism.[84]

The devotees of this movement attributed all their thoughts, feelings, and actions, including all their spiritual achievements, to God's grace. "I do not move of myself," wrote one, "but am moved by Him. I do not work of myself, but am used by Him."[85] Dancing and frequent ablutions were essential features of their religious regimen. They strove to cultivate indifference to public opinion,[86] to conceal their virtuous actions from the public eye,[87] and to progress steadily along the path to spiritual perfection that their masters illumined for them. They criticized religious philosophers for attempts to rationally investigate the supernatural, but the most frequent targets of their disparagement were legal scholars and jurists. These were portrayed as self-seeking materialists preoccupied with mundane legalisms, petty hairsplitting, and their own public image. Uninterested in attaining sanctity, these scholars naturally deprecated those who made sanctity their goal.[88] The jurists, for their part, denounced their denouncers for their (alleged) antinomistic doctrines, lax observance of certain religious practices, and departure from traditional forms and formulations of communal prayer.[89]

This movement, except perhaps for its asceticism, may justifiably be identified as eighteenth-century Hasidism; it is, in fact, thirteenth-century Sufism.[90]

Such phenomenological parallels call into question the assumption of historians that such Hasidic phenomena as dancing and gestures during prayer are related to Sabbatianism.[91] As far as I know, there is no way to determine to what extent such phenomena had specific historical connections and to what extent they developed internally through the inner dynamics of such mystical brotherhoods. What we can know with a fair degree of certainty is what the Besht taught, what the Maggid taught, and to what extent their teachings were adopted or adapted by their disciples.

As indicated above, these teachings, even when truly innovative and based on mystical insights, were also outgrowths of a common paideia and were embedded in commonly known texts. As Scholem has observed, almost every mystic "bears within him an ancient heritage. He has grown up within the framework of a recognized religious authority, and even when he begins to look at things independently and to seek his own path, all his thinking and above all his imagination are still permeated with traditional material."[92] It is in this context of traditional ideas that the central doctrines of the Besht and the Maggid must be analyzed to determine how they affected the ethical thought of RSZ, a man completely steeped in these ideas.

What are some of the notable findings that such an analysis yields? Let us begin with what one does not find: One does not find an "obsession"[93] with deveḳut in the sense of an emotionalistic communion with God. Neither in the Besht's nor in the Maggid's teachings does one find dicta implying that this kind of deveḳut has now become the first rung of every man's ladder of ascent.[94] Instead, one finds the word *deveḳut* used frequently, to be sure, but differently in different contexts.[95] With respect to Torah-study it is used in at least three senses. Occasionally it is interpreted to mean protracting the utterance of each word, thereby "clinging" to it;[96] occasionally it means clinging to the divine light that inheres in each letter of the Torah;[97] and occasionally it means spiritualizing these physical letters (and oneself) by "attaching" them to the power of thought and mentally elevating them to their supernal source.[98] Another Beshtian dictum omits the word but apparently refers to a fourth way in which it is used: to study with Love and Fear,[99] that is, consciously to prevent Torah-study from degenerating into an academic exercise.

Students of Hasidism have concentrated on the second and third uses cited above and have asked the obvious question: How is it possible simultaneously to concentrate on understanding the abstruse dialectics of a Talmudic passage and on the metaphysical qualities of its individual letters? And they have arrived at an equally obvious answer: It is impossible. Some, ignoring other Beshtian formulations to the contrary, point to one in which Rabbi Jacob Joseph quotes his master's advice to minimize Torah-study time on Sabbath in order to maximize deveḳut time.[100] Others, ignoring this statement and another like it, attribute the dichotomy between deveḳut and *talmud Torah* to one of the Besht's more-radical disciples.[101] The master himself, they insist, actually emptied Torah-study of its intellectual content and substituted the emotionalism of letter-deveḳut for its immediate purpose.[102] He had little difficulty in making this transition, the theory goes, because he studied little more than the aggadot of *ʿEn Yaʿaḳov*, which require no great intellectual effort anyway.[103] This despite our possessing his explicit exhortations to study and comprehend fully the four sections of the *Shulḥan ʿArukh* in their entirety and to study in general with both comprehension and fervor (*hitlahavut*).[104]

Besides failing to account for all the Beshtian statements on this theme, these interpretations are based on the extremely unlikely assumptions that the letters in question are the letters of the Talmud and, in the case of the second theory, that radical currents of thought were so strong among the Besht's disciples that they would accept a doctrine that summarily repudiates two thousand years of Jewish tradition concerning the nature of *talmud Torah*. The mystical tradition from which the Besht's teachings clearly derive confers cosmic significance upon the letters of the Pentateuch only. These alone were the letters with which God created the universe; which constituted various combinations of His Name(s); in which His divine light was concealed; the precise configurations of which were enormously significant; the "crowns" of which could generate "heaps upon heaps of halakhot"; each of which corresponded to one of the 600,000 root-souls of Israel; and the omission of one of which therefore halakhically invalidated a *Sefer Torah*.[105] These were the letters that individually, and particularly in certain combinations, contained vast spiritual potencies, the study of which, according to R. Moses Cordovero, constituted the highest level of Torah-study.[106] It never occurred to anyone to ascribe such importance, or any intrinsic importance, to the individual letters of other sacred texts. Such an ascription would have absolutely no halakhic or kabbalistic foundation. With respect to the Talmud it would contravene the very nature of that corpus, which is a compendium of the oral tradition, primarily the Oral Law, put into writing only as an exigent measure.[107] Although there are statements indicating that superficial study also has religious value, no one I know of suggests that reading Talmud without comprehension satisfies the halakhic obligation of *talmud Torah.*[108] To read the Pentateuch (with the intention of studying it) without comprehension, however, was generally accepted as a lower level of *talmud Torah* requiring the appropriate *berakhah.*[109] One could therefore readily fulfill the *mitsvah* of Torah-study on this level while engaging in a quest for deveḳut through contemplating the soul and source of each letter.

This specific doctrine is a Beshtian innovation. It differs from Abraham Abulafia's technique of letter combinations, which was not necessarily connected with Torah-study.[110] It also differs from the traditional form of deveḳut—that is, contemplative communion—which can be combined with almost any activity. This general deveḳut doctrine had been taught since the rise of kabbalah in Provence[111] and would obviously appeal to the Besht's mystically inclined personality. There is no indication, however, that he was any more preoccupied with it than was R. Isaac the Blind of Posquières and his disciples, R. Ezra and R. Azriel of Gerona in the thirteenth century.[112] The Besht's teachings give this impression only because they articulate for the first time and in striking detail the problems encountered by a human being living among fellow human beings who strives to transcend his human limitations and ascend to the divine. Like Baḥya ibn Pakuda, but unlike Maimonides, the Besht believed that with great effort and determination every man could engage in necessary mundane affairs without breaking off contemplative communion.[113] Like Maimonides, but unlike Baḥya, he taught that once this level is attained, all those affairs become sanctified vehicles for divine service.[114] In the interim, however, man faced a protracted, depressing struggle with his very humanity, and it was inconceivable that this struggle had no inherent value but was only a necessary means to the end. After all, the same unitary Creator is directly responsible for both man's present weakness and his potential greatness; His divinity permeates every thought, feeling, utterance, action, and created thing in the universe; and there is no reason to assume that one facet of creation is essentially superior to another. While the divine light is clearly and directly irradiated only by those facets relating to selfless Torah-study and mitzvah-fulfillment, it is nevertheless present, although distorted and refracted, in the others as well. Man's supreme mission is to redirect this distorted light, thereby revealing the essential unity of creation within the absolute unity of Creator.[115]

In more concrete terms this means redirecting, through the appropriate form of deveḳut, profane thoughts and prohibited or undesirable activities, so that they, too, will clearly reflect their supernal Source. This is accomplished by mentally clinging to the refracted divine light that vivifies the given endeavor, and guiding it back through its profane medium until it coalesces with its original emanation.[116] "Profane loves," for example, are sublimated by concentrating on the *sefirah* of *Ḥesed*, the source and vitality of all love, and mentally guiding it out of its profane medium back to its sacred origin.[117] Business dealings and other neutral activities are elevated by concentrating on appropriate *yiḥudim*.[118] The exact nature of these is not elucidated, but presumably they, too, involve contemplation of the sefirah corresponding to a particular activity. In the case of conversation, the Hebrew letters into which the utterances may be transliterated are connected with the appropriate sefirah and thereby elevated and, if necessary, transformed from evil into good.[119]

Of special concern were profane thoughts during prayer,[120] the ideal time for ideal deveḳut. Like all kabbalists who preceded him, the Besht ascribed unlimited powers to concentrated thought.[121] Pure, properly channeled thought was, after all, the sole vehicle for conscious deveḳut, and deveḳut of the microcosm means deveḳut of the macrocosm and the consummation of creation. But a distinguishing feature of Hasidism, as has often been observed, is its transformation of Lurianic theosophy into an instrument of "psychological analysis and self-knowledge."[122] Whatever else concentrated thought may achieve, the Besht, far more than any of his predecessors, was immediately concerned with how it affected the worshipper himself. "Man in his entirety," he proclaimed, "is where his thoughts are."[123] If they are in the upper worlds, so is he; and if they descend to the realms of *ḳelipot*, they drag him down with them. But since God is truly omnipresent; since the Zohar and particularly R. Isaac Luria taught that even those realms are really prisons for sparks of divinity that can be liberated through the proper *kavanot*;[124] and since the Besht believed that Providence ushers into man's mind every single thought he has[125] (and consequently the Besht extended the doctrine of divine sparks to include thoughts and emotions), it followed that profane thoughts were only divine messengers in disguise, and their message was clear: Remove our prison garb and set us free.[126] By freeing them the worshipper also frees himself from his earthly shackles and returns to his Heavenly Father. The means for liberating profane thoughts was, for the Besht, the same as for purifying any other profane or impious activity: deveḳut. The mind sublimates them by attaching itself to their vitalizing divine sparks and returning these to their source. The essence of the original thought is thereby elevated while the thought itself degenerates into the harmless, lifeless shell it really is.[127]

This doctrine is thus a variation of the Besht's deveḳut-Torah synthesis, but whereas the letters of Torah are sacred vessels containing the rays of the Infinite Light, the letters of profane thoughts harbor divine sparks but they themselves are worthless and must either be discarded or recombined to form holy *tsirufim* (combinations). The Lurianic idea of "purifying the sparks," often mentioned in formulations of this doctrine, is combined with a new emphasis on Hebrew letters as receptacles of divine effulgences and the Besht's belief in divine providence extending to individual thoughts. All three elements are integral components of the doctrine, and there is no basis for subordinating them to a tenuous argument for Sabbatian influence.[128] In fact, despite valiant efforts by prominent scholars, it can be stated unequivocally that no conscious link has ever been established between the Besht's teachings and the tenets of Sabbatianism (see Excursus F). Every Beshtian doctrine, emphasis, or custom may be compellingly analyzed in terms of non-Sabbatian religiointellectual developments, contemporary ethical teachings (as M. Piekarz has shown), and common religious phenomena manifested by various brotherhoods of mystics at various times in history. The most that can be said, as A. Rubinstein and M. Piekarz have suggested,[129] is that Sabbatian ideas were "in the air" and may have been picked up by both Hasidic and non-Hasidic leaders without their being aware of the origins or original significance of these ideas. In any case, the rather narrow quest for Sabbatian influences on certain Hasidic doctrines has obscured many prominent, innovative Hasidic teachings that have no Sabbatian overtones at all, and that, when considered in conjunction with the alleged Sabbatian adaptations, may shed a different light on the issue.

Before taking up these teachings, however, we should return to the various meanings of deveḳut in the dicta of the Besht and the Maggid. The four uses cited above, relating to Torah-study—with the possible exception of the simple, mechanical prolongation of each word—point to meditative practices only. Their purpose is to spiritualize the act of study and the student by means of the latter's most potent spiritual power, the power of thought. There is no indication that the student should aspire to achieve ecstasy or rapture. Even formulations repeating the Zoharic exhortation to study "with Love and Fear"[130] fall far short of this demand and insist only on a fitting emotional posture while studying. Frequently, of course, deveḳut *is* used to connote some state of ecstasy or rapture. Generally the context is prayer, but at least two references are made to such a state outside of prayer as well. One claims prophetic insight, the other automatic speech, for a man attaining this level of deveḳut.[131] Still other formulations regarding deveḳut in prayer apparently use the word as synonymous with kaṿanah,[132] but there is nothing to support the generalization that emotionalistic deveḳut completely supplanted Lurianic kaṿanah.[133]

A more detailed study of Maggidic teachings yields additional uses. In *Liḳuṭim Yeḳarim* alone we find deveḳut to mean a general but constant awareness of God's presence;[134] a more specific and intense consciousness of His presence everywhere, particularly in all "holy acts";[135] a simple but permeating feeling during prayer of actually addressing Him;[136] fiery enthusiasm (hitlahavut) in fulfilling the commandments;[137] and contemplation of the great Love and Fear that are His due.[138] The only ideological innovation to be found in these demands is the call for hitlahavut, a term that abounds in Hasidic works, that occurs rarely in earlier literature, and that apparently connotes an unprecedented degree of religious emotionalism. A second innovation regarding deveḳut is the Maggid's assertion, according to the editor of *Or Torah*, that even a simple man can attain the ecstatic form of deveḳut during prayer, "for this level is not contingent on a man's actions."[139] Such a statement could not have been made by the Besht, who, as far as the sources indicate, did not share the Maggid's preoccupation with ecstatic self-nullification.[140] In fact, when the Besht repeats the traditional kabbalistic directive to pray (not for one's personal needs but) only for the *Shekhinah*, he expressly limits it to "the worthy," whereas the multitude is to pray "ki-feshuto"—in the simple manner.[141] Obviously, then, he would not advise, let alone exhort, the latter to ascend toward the even more rarefied atmosphere of ecstatic deveḳut. Similarly, even the Maggid does not demand of every man this form of deveḳut outside of prayer, and when it comes to elevating profane thoughts, our simple man is expressly disqualified.[142]

The mystical elite, however, are expected to strive for the continuous contemplative communion that Maimonides attributed to the Patriarchs and Moses. Any lapse of deveḳut can be due only to the intrusion into the mind of something other than God. Such a thought automatically assumes that its object exists, and for the Maggid, as for the Sufis, this was tantamount to idolatry.[143]

This acosmistic belief, coupled with an intense, vivid feeling of God's nearness, also resulted in a new approach to the old problem of the nature of evil. Like all Hasidic innovations it was generated by taking selected traditional ideas to their logical—but nevertheless surprising—conclusions. The author of the Zohar had contented himself with observing that "there is no [entity on the] 'other side' that does not contain a fine, small ray from the holy side,"[144] although he goes on to cite one exceptional category that is completely evil. R. Isaac Luria had taught that sparks of holiness—actually, "parts of divinity"—were scattered throughout the world as a result of the "breaking of the vessels."[145] These sparks are embedded, as it were, in everything with which a commandment can be performed, from the bread over which a blessing may be said and which provides energy for Service, to a halakhic problem giving rise to contradictory solutions. Any type of physical matter halakhically utilizable for a mitsyah and every intellectual obstacle to the proper understanding of Torah exist only for the sake of man's extracting the holy sparks from them by fulfilling the mitsyah and surmounting the obstacle. This is the realm controlled by *Ḳelipat Nogah*, "the translucent (metaphysical) shell," so named because it is a potential vessel for the divine light. Its domain consists of entities and activities containing an admixture of good—the sparks—and evil—the matter of the physical entity itself or an improperly motivated neutral activity. Prohibited matter, however, such as forbidden foods; and prohibited activities, such as lewd thoughts, slander, and neglect of Torah-study, contained no holy sparks. This is the domain of the three "impure shells," which are completely opaque and impermeable to the "indwelling" divine light. They exist only by virtue of a tenuous contact with the "encompassing" light, from which they draw sustenance.[146]

The Besht apparently found this ontology unsatisfactory. He knew that nothing could continue to exist unless continuously permeated with a divine influx contained in the letters of speech with which God calls it into existence.[147] Since the three impure ḳelipot are real entities, there was no reason to assume they could sustain their existence merely by some tangential contact with the encompassing light. Surely sparks of the indwelling light lurk deep within them, forlorn captives of arrogant jailors laboring under the delusion that they need only the encompassing light to survive.[148] Surely the Zoharic dictum—"No place is free from His presence"[149]—which the Besht not only knew but constantly experienced,[150] must include the realm of these ḳelipot as well. Moreover, the Children of Israel were, after all, the King's beloved firstborn son, who, having left his Father's palace, now seeks to return.[151] It was inconceivable to the Besht that a compassionate father would place totally hostile forces in his son's path for the sake of testing his loyalty.

These considerations and experiences, among others, led him to conclude that, in truth, nothing can be absolutely evil, and every evil phenomenon or reprehensible act may and should somehow serve as a stepping-stone to the good.[152] Evil thoughts, utterances, emotions, even evil actions and men are not obstacles but opportunities, not adversaries but allies. The wicked exist so that the righteous may have a vivid basis for comparison and derive pleasure and encouragement from the contrast.[153] Awareness of a certain sin in others stimulates the righteous to seek its inevitable reflection in the mirror of their own souls in order to perform the appropriate *tiḳun*.[154] Physical desire can be transformed into spiritual desire for God;[155] physical pleasure can be utilized to imagine the infinitely greater spiritual pleasure of the righteous.[156] As for the evil inclination itself, the Zohar had already compared it to a harlot appointed by the King to seduce his son. Although she carries out her mission faithfully, she earnestly hopes to fail; for she, too, loves the prince and wishes him well.[157]

As with many of the Besht's seminal concepts, the Maggid extends this well beyond its original dimensions. The Besht may have concurred, but we possess no explicit statement by him, as we do by the Maggid, investing idolatry itself with holy sparks.[158] Another statement, this time drawing a logical conclusion from the description of creation in Vital's *'Ets Ḥayyim*, attributes even greater sanctity to these sparks than to the sparks inhering in the higher levels of creation.[159] A third dictum, based on the Maggid's own insistence on the ontological primacy of divine pleasure (to be discussed presently), explains the necessity of evil in terms of this pleasure principle. Since "continuous pleasure is no pleasure,"[160] and only frequent changes from a less to a more pleasurable state can satisfy God's desire for pleasure from human goodness, it is necessary for an opposing force periodically to arrest the righteous man's steady progress. The contrast between his lapse from goodness and his subsequent reinvigorated ascent produces the requisite increment in divine pleasure.[161] The inevitability of sin is thus transformed from an admission of man's weakness into an integral and positive element in God's purpose for creation. To sin and then return is to transform the sin itself into a means for increasing divine pleasure.

It would be a mistake to interpret this—or any Maggidic teaching—as attenuating the onerousness of sin and opening the door to religious anarchy. Nowhere does the Maggid imply the desirability of intentionally sinning for the sake of repenting or for elevating sparks.[162] Nowhere does he negate the importance of sincere remorse for sin or adopt a "nonchalant attitude" to it.[163] These misconceptions flow from accepting hypothetical assumptions concerning Sabbatian influences and from ignoring both unarticulated traditional values and contemporary religious problems. If these pitfalls are avoided, a study of the Maggid's teachings on sin will reveal his real aim: to discourage depression and foster a confident, buoyant approach to religion. Not remorse for, but morbid preoccupation with, sin is his subject. Like the Besht, he repeatedly discountenances religious self-consciousness and incessant introspection (see Excursus G), because, for the deeply pious, the usual concomitant emotion is a stifling and often incapacitating depression.[164] An approach to sin emphasizing human frailty as its ontological basis[165] tends to have the same effect, particularly on mystics aspiring to deveḳut with the Divine. Looking at sin as a potential test that can theoretically always be passed[166] does not improve matters, because in the real world everyone frequently fails, from the righteous plagued with profane thoughts to the wicked unable to restrain their passions. Indeed, one of the features that made Hasidism so enormously appealing was its frank and sympathetic treatment of this eternal chasm between the ideal and the real.[167]

Any doubt that depression was one of the major problems facing sensitive religious leaders of the time may be dispelled by perusing contemporary ethical works. Reading the very influential *Shaʿar ha-Melekh* (Zolkiew, 1769),[168] for example, one is plunged into a world of unremitting gloom, pessimism, and oppressive piety. The author, R. Mordecai ben Samuel, was the rabbi of a Galician community, a contemporary of the Besht, and clearly the type of fire-and-brimstone preacher against whom many of his teachings were directed. The book is divided into sections according to festivals and fast days; by far the longest sections are devoted to the Seventeenth of Tammuz, the Ninth of Av, and "Eulogy for the Righteous." The festival of Sukot is completely omitted, obviously because "the time of our joy" was incompatible with the central themes of the work—weeping, worrying, self-mortification, and despondency. Every possible occasion for critical self-scrutiny accompanied by sorrowful self-mortification is exhaustively expatiated upon. Lengthy quotes from the Midrash and particularly the Zohar, complemented by even lengthier homiletical interpretations and parables to support his exhortations, are interspersed with vituperative diatribes against the religious laxity R. Mordecai perceives everywhere. He castigates his congregants unsparingly for types of behavior that are halakhically neutral and perfectly natural: failure to suppress the desire to manage one last meal before a voluntary fast; failure to undertake and complete such fasts on certain occasions, such as each of the Ten Days of Repentance; smoking on public fast days; failure to devote such days entirely to weeping and mourning; completing a Talmudic tractate during the Nine Days—even in the regular course of one's studies—and subsequently partaking of meat and wine during the traditional *seudat mitsvah.*[169] These and similar infractions of the laws of asceticism and sorrow are not merely decried but are described as singularly heinous offenses marking their perpetrators as rebels and reprobates. Even the Sabbath was to be, for the truly devout, a day of tearful mourning—despite clear halakhic statements to the contrary.[170] Not surprisingly, the author also found cause to criticize some members of his flock for attempting to avoid his sermons.[171]

When not lamenting his people's sorry religious state, R. Mordecai bemoans their tragic fate. The note of utter hopelessness and despair sounded throughout this work is extraordinary. "At all times and at all hours," he observes, "they [the gentiles] come and fall upon us."[172] The constant fear of persecution is beyond endurance. "Often we say: 'death is preferable to our life'; days have come, about which we say: 'we do not desire them.' . . . Behold, God is testing us to determine whether we truly cling to Him, and He abandons us [to the gentiles], for in these times we are abandoned, and anyone who wishes may lay claim to us. . . . [T]herefore every man of Israel must zealously sanctify his thoughts [and be ever prepared] to sacrifice his life for the sanctity of the Name."[173] And in another passage: "God has left us and we have been forgotten by Him, as it were. . . . [W]e must not question His ways, but rather worry about our many tribulations."[174] Again and again he mourns the massacre, particularly at Uman in

1748, of innocent children and many great scholars, which was then compounded by plague and pestilence.[175] Again he pays lip service to the traditional credo "not to question His ways" and then proceeds to do just that. His attempts at theodicy are feeble and half-hearted. Most of these deaths, he maintains, were intended to separate the dross from the gold, the illegitimate from the legitimate offspring. The exceptions were probably descendents of the wicked suffering for their ancestors' sins.[176] In addition, these seemingly senseless and endless persecutions serve useful religious purposes. They increase weeping "so that the measure (lit., bottle) may be filled with our tears."[177] The death of the righteous strikes fear into the people's hearts and inspires them to pray that the departed souls may be atoning altars for the survivors.[178] It also inspires ever-salutary fasting and repentance, and though the Accuser retains his power to impede their effectiveness and continues to separate the people from God, self-mortification can help silence him, because it symbolizes the adverse circumstances of this bitter *galut* (exile) that cause them to sin.[179]

The founders of Hasidism—the Besht and the Maggid—saw more clearly than many of their contemporaries that well-intentioned dispensers of despair such as R. Mordecai were sapping the religious vitality of Polish Jewry. The works of such authors were often popular, to be sure, but their effects were counterproductive. Gloom, guilt, and interminable fasting—"God does not want these,"[180] they taught. The sources do not indicate, however, that they countered this worldview by plying their followers with an amalgam of "popular pantheism," blind optimism, insensible faith, mindless emotionalism, and mystical anarchy.[181] Because the Besht's teachings often took simple forms—the story, the parable, the anecdote, the aphorism[182]—simple folk among his contemporaries may have drawn such simplistic conclusions. Because these individuals constitute the majority of any popular movement, they were the ones who projected the living, if not the literary, image of Hasidism still widely accepted today. It is quite clear, however, that the more scholarly followers of the Besht, and particularly of the Maggid, did not understand their masters' teachings in this way. Such disciples of the Besht as Rabbi Jacob Joseph, R. Meir Margoliot, R. David Heilprin, and the Maggid; such disciples of the Maggid as RSZ, R. Menaḥem Mendel of Vitebsk, R. Levi Isaac of Berdichev, R. Aaron Samuel ha-Kohen, and R. Samuel Shmelke Horowitz—these men collectively brought to bear upon their masters' words over a century of diligent scholarship and an unquantifiable degree of intellectual ability and acumen. According to Schneersohn tradition, while both the Besht and Maggid brought their teachings home to general audiences through stories and parables, the Maggid taught his scholarly disciples in a far more intellectualized form,[183] and it is very probable that the Besht had a somewhat similar arrangement. It was not pantheism or anarchy or simple faith[184] and optimism that attracted these scholars and nourished them intellectually and spiritually for a lifetime. Nor would charisma alone account for their devotion to the masters and their teachings. Clearly the Besht and Maggid succeeded in creating an environment of considerable intellectual, as well as emotional, appeal within the framework of the traditional values and ideas accepted by these disciples.

In opposition to the tearful, fearful, breast beating advocated by leaders such as R. Mordecai, the Besht and Maggid recommended a buoyant, self-confident approach to Judaism. Sin was still nefarious, heartfelt remorse still a sine qua non for *teshuvah*, but the exaggerated preoccupation with one's failings, whether imagined or real, was to be shunned like sin itself. In opposition to the principle of despondence implicitly preached by such leaders as R. Mordecai, the Maggid emphasized the principle of spiritual pleasure.[185] Divine pleasure, he taught, is the life force pulsating throughout creation, which itself exists to increase that pleasure and to provide the righteous with the pleasure they derive from guiding creation to its consummation. Some homilies compare the pleasure God derives from puny man's Service to a mighty monarch's enjoyment of a talking bird. Others emphasize His need, "as it were," of man's devotion and the pleasure He takes in satisfying Israel's desires. Spiritual pleasure is seen as the legitimate goal and most desirable concomitant of Torah-study, mitzvah-fulfillment, and deveḳut; indeed, it actually elevates the commandment performed to its supernal source. Its corollaries are enthusiasm and joy in Service, and a continuous, conscious desire to know God. This knowledge consists not of intellectual apprehension, which is impossible, but of the pleasure derived from being with Him and of the desire itself to attain this pleasure. Knowledge of the Divine, in other words, is not cognitive but affective, and its contents are suprarational desire and sublime pleasure (the two integrants of the psychological sefirah of *Keter*, which corresponds to the divine *Ayin* and transcends even Ḥokhmah. Of the two, pleasure is higher in the supernal hierarchy, corresponding to *ʿAtiḳ Yomin*, the first sefirotic manifestation of Divinity).[186]

As noted above, the Maggid's emphasis on spiritual pleasure is related to his teaching on the ontological need for evil in order to provide periodic increments in divine pleasure. This idea, in turn, reflects another striking innovation of eighteenth-century Hasidism: a positive appraisal of diversity, change, and related values such as striving, growing, overcoming. A basic assumption of Platonic and Aristotelian philosophy, which had permeated Jewish thought primarily through Maimonides, was that a serene, self-sufficient, eternally changeless state of being is the supreme form of existence. The paragon of this state was accordingly identified as the Supreme Being, whom Aristotle described as continuously engaged in serene self-contemplation. Being absolutely perfect, He needs nothing and desires nothing. The supreme form of knowledge, indeed the only knowledge worthy of the name, consists of the eternal truths constituting His nature. The ideal life is one spent contemplating these static truths and, when necessary, applying them to practical behavior. Because there is only one truth, "there can only be one ideal of perfection common to all humanity, one standard by which all customs and actions must be measured."[187] A man living continuously according to this univocal, eternal law—variously dubbed universal, general, or natural law—will be truly happy, which means "he will have the attribute of permanence . . . and he will remain happy throughout his life."[188] Pure contemplation is theoretically the loftiest activity, both intrinsically and because it is the most continuous, the most self-sufficient, the most leisurable, and the most pleasurable.[189]

Pleasure itself is described as "something whole and complete," not, as some asserted, "motion or coming to be."[190] It is not an independent feeling, but rather contingent on the activity it completes. Continuous pleasure is therefore impossible only because men, unlike God, are incapable of continuous activity.[191] After death, however, the disembodied intellect can attain this "condition of enduring permanence" and "remain permanently in that state of intense pleasure" that Maimonides identifies as *ʿOlam ha-Ba*.[192] There the righteous leisurely enjoy the tranquil beatitude of a steady influx of divine knowledge.[193]

Unity, uniformity, continuity, self-sufficiency, serenity, harmony, symmetry, immutability, and lucid rationality—these are the keynotes not only of Greek epistemology, theology, ethics, and legal theory but also of Greek psychology and cosmology.[194] Plato's soul aspires to a continuous, harmonious interplay of its three parts so that its true unitary nature may be revealed. Its separate virtues are actually parts of one whole virtue, the essence of which is knowledge.[195] Aristotle urges men to aim for a symmetrical equilibrium between their psychological extremes.[196] Similarly, the spherical earth is suspended motionless at the exact center of the universe, which itself is self-contained, self-sufficient, and shaped like that most symmetrical of all forms, the circle. In Plato's words: "[The Creator's] intention was, in the first place, that the animal [i.e., the universe] should be as far as possible a perfect whole and of perfect parts; secondly, that it should be one, leaving no remnants out of which another such world might be created; and also that it should be free from old age [eternal,] and unaffected by disease [incorruptible]. . . . Wherefore he made the world in the form of a globe, round as from a lathe, having its extremes in every direction equidistant from the center, the most perfect and the most like itself [i.e., symmetrical] of all figures; for he considered that the like is infinitely fairer than the unlike."[197] In this universe the eternal sun, stars, and heavenly spheres move with absolute regularity in eternal, perfectly spherical orbits. The planets, too, must travel in such orbits, and any observed deviation only indicates a temporary, but still circular, aberration.[198] These cosmological assumptions and their astronomical corollaries were universally accepted until the beginning of the seventeenth century and were not universally rejected by astronomers until its last decades. Popular notions, of course, did not change until still later.[199]

The primary presuppositions of Greek thought listed above were the tinted glasses through which many of the most influential Jewish thinkers after Maimonides viewed Judaism. Biblical and aggadic intimations concerning man, Creator, and creation were, if at all possible, allegorically interpreted to conform to these values. *Aggadot* that could not be fitted into this Greek mold were either declared unauthoritative "poetical conceits" (*Guide*, III, 43) or, more frequently, tacitly ignored. The three pillars of Maimonides' theology—God's existence, unity, and incorporeality—along with their religious superstructure and philosophical foundations are firmly embedded in the bedrock of these assumptions. Nor was Maimonides an iconoclast in this respect. Critics questioned his methodology, but hardly anyone would dispute his conclusions and suggest that God could conceivably need, desire, feel, or otherwise undergo any change in His eternally static state of self-sufficient perfection. Pleasure, suffering, (feeling) compassion, love, and anger are clearly beneath His imperturbable dignity.[200] In His creation, too, perfection and goodness are synonymous with immutability; privation and evil with corruptibility.[201] Since "the works of the Deity are most perfect," they must also be "permanently established as they are, for there is no possibility of something calling for a change in them."[202]

This applies, however, only to all the specific forms, which are "perpetual and permanent," whereas matter, which necessarily exists to complement these forms, is the sole source of evil because of its corruptible nature.

> All man's acts of disobedience and sins are consequent upon his matter and not upon his form, whereas all his virtues are consequent upon his form. For example, man's apprehension of his Creator, his mental representation of every intelligible, his control of his desire and anger, his thought on what ought to be preferred and what avoided are all of them consequent upon his form. . . . [T]here are individuals who aspire always to prefer that which is most noble and to seek a state of perpetual permanence according to that which is required by their noble form. They reflect on the mental representation of an intelligible, on the grasp of a true opinion regarding everything, and on union with the divine intellect which lets overflow toward them that through which that form exists.[203]

A man whose matter never entices his form to sin is accordingly superior to one who must occasionally struggle to overcome such temptation.[204]

The Torah, too, speaks not to variegated individuals differing not only from each other but even from themselves at various periods; it addresses itself rather to the uniform needs of the naturally stable majority and "pays no attention to . . . the unique human being."[205] Its commandments are just and perfectly wise because they are equibalanced and therefore perfect and eternal.[206] In its wisdom it teaches that divine providence extends only to rational beings; "providence is consequent upon the intellect and attached to it. For providence can only come from an intelligent being, from One who is an intellect perfect with a supreme perfection than which there is nothing higher. Accordingly, everyone with whom something of this overflow is united will be reached by providence to the extent to which he is reached by the intellect."[207] But what makes intellect "a supreme perfection than which there is nothing higher"? It is nothing but its unique ability to unite with necessary, permanent truths and thereby become eternal and immutable itself.[208]

The foundations of Maimonides' religious philosophy became, to a great extent, the foundations of Jewish religious thought. Although the details and implications of this philosophy were endlessly debated, its Greek presuppositions were almost universally accepted by philosopher and kabbalist alike. The pietism of Bahya's *Ḥovot ha-Levavot*, which adumbrated the pietism of Abraham Maimonides and was quite compatible with this philosophy, was also extraordinarily influential, particularly after the Spanish Expulsion.[209] Ethical works, to the eighteenth century, generally gave the impression that the ultimate good and the truly pleasant were associated with a state of serene, spiritual equilibrium. Although man lives in a world of change, he was expected to strive to approximate that state as closely as possible, and the ideal situation was one in which man was sheltered from as many mundane vicissitudes as possible. Asceticism was an indispensable aid in this quest because, among other things, it enabled him to slough off most of these distracting, unsettling encumbrances and simplify his life by minimizing the normal variety and intensity of physical experiences. Only in this way could his mind maintain the requisite equanimity and his soul the requisite purity for continuously contemplating his religious mission and, according to the kabbalists, the sublime symbolic concepts corresponding to his daily religious acts and biologically necessary activities.[210] The pious masses condemned to a turbulent life among the slings and arrows of outrageous fortune looked longingly toward such steadfast *perfecti* for religious role models. The more ardently they looked, the more achingly aware they became of their spiritual inferiority—a feeling generally reinforced by their models' written works, if not their spoken words.

It was not the gap itself that distressed them, nor even their superiors' condescending attitude. These were accepted as part of a divine order in which hierarchy, not equality, was the governing principle. The Neoplatonic gradation of being was complemented by clear-cut religious hierarchies: saint-scholar, (pious) scholar, literate, barely literate; *Kohen, Levi, Yiśra'el*; Talmudist-Kabbalists, and Talmudists who claimed to have "no business with the esoteric."[211] Unlike the chronic ill will engendered by social distinctions based on wealth and power,[212] the relative standing of individuals according to these categories never rankled.[213] Whoever stood closer to God naturally merited greater reverence and was perfectly justified in recognizing this fact. What did apparently agitate and depress the conscientious common man was his own spiritual debility. Surely he should be able somehow to extricate himself more and more from his worldly entanglements and serve his Maker in purity. True, it is His will that he labor for his livelihood while struggling with his materialistic instincts in a discordant world hostile to religious aspirations; but surely he is expected at least partially to transcend his humble station in life and rise to a higher plane of existence. Yet he was unable to do so.[214]

While the Besht and the Maggid did not, of course, repudiate the religious ethics of Maimonides and Baḥya,[215] they did, in effect, repudiate their Greek philosophical postulates. The founders' own theology was hardly new, however. It was, rather, an extension of the prophetic and aggadic view of God that had been eclipsed for centuries by these Greek ideas. Like Judah Halevi, but going far beyond him, the Besht and the Maggid[216] rejected the God of Aristotle and returned to the God of Abraham.[217] God's perfection, they intimated, consists not in eternal, changeless self-contemplation but in a dynamic fullness of being (used as a verb, not a noun) that becomes progressively more perfect and encompasses every imaginable change and diversity, including emotions and even contradictions. A dialectical tension reverberates within Creator and creation, because contradictory yet complementary modes of being are pitted against each other in a constant, Heraclitean struggle for ascendency. In the sefirotic realm, limitless Ḥesed is forever opposed by limiting *Gevurah*; in more personal and more characteristically Hasidic terms, God's self-sufficiency is opposed by His recognizing that He is actually incomplete without us,[218] and His gaze is therefore ever directed toward us. As our Father—the Maggid's favorite image[219]—He loves us unconditionally, is saddened by our failures, shares in our joys and sufferings.[220] As our King, He really does take pleasure in our Service and become angry at our lapses into rebelliousness. As the supremely sensitive Being, He responds to every nuance of every Jew's condition, appreciating his limitations, understanding and allowing for his foibles, empathizing with his particular plight. The cosmos is not a serenely persistent, immutable result of His original will to create, but a vibrant, dynamic manifestation of a continuous succession of pulsating divine wills that vivify it.[221] The lush, colorful, variegated world of phenomena and feeling is not an obstacle to be avoided, a test to be passed, a temptation to be suppressed; it is an opportunity to be exploited for Service. Just as the interaction of every man with this world is distinctive, so must his form of Service be distinctive—there is no single ideal for all men. Since this interaction varies from time to time, and particularly since time itself is renewed every moment, each man must constantly adapt his Service to the changing world.[222] The connotation of change was thus transformed from instability to progress.

What was a valid form of Service yesterday may be invalid, and is certainly insufficient, today. Every generation, too, requires new ideas, new approaches, new interpretations of the Torah.[223] The Besht and Maggid believed that their generation required, among other things, that the steady light of reason be superseded by the flickering flames of hitlahavut and desire,[224] and that fear of sin be overshadowed by vigorous, positive action.[225]

This metamorphosis of diversity and change into positive values affected every area of religious thought. The resultant emphasis on individuality spawned a new subjectiveness in which one's own pyschological and emotional processes were minutely scrutinized. Not surprisingly, the most fascinating processes were those relating to one's ability and proclivity to change, and the problems most frequently discussed, although not necessarily articulated, were: How does the mind generate new ideas? How can it effect changes in the natural course of events? What role does change play in man's battle with evil? What is the significance of those apparently inevitable fluctuations in religious devotion that affect even the most righteous of men? In response to the first two questions the Maggid taught the doctrine of self-nullificatory identification with the supernal Ayin.[226] In response to the third the Besht taught that evil occasionally dissembles as (i.e., changes its form to give the appearance of) good, and that man must (often) camouflage his good intentions (i.e., change their appearance) in order to overcome his Evil Inclination.[227] And in response to the fourth he taught the doctrine of *ḳaṭnut-gadlut*,[228] alternating lower and higher states of spiritual receptivity that, together with his incessant struggle for continued spiritual progress, require man periodically to redouble his efforts in order to return to the state from which he fell and then ascend still higher.[229]

Related to the latter idea is the Besht's teaching regarding the periodic "fall" of the Zaddik.[230] In the state of ḳaṭnut a Zaddik loses the immunity from sin resulting from his deveḳut during gadlut, but it is still inconceivable that he would succumb to even the most ethereal form of evil—a profane thought. A Zaddik's thoughts are, by definition, always with God even during ḳaṭnut; how, then, does it happen that they occasionally descend to the realm of the profane?[231] Although the Besht clearly appreciated the positive value of change and the desirability of continuous spiritual striving, he could not accept them as ends in themselves. Teleological explanations were still the most psychologically satisfying, and since eighteenth-century Jewish thought still revolved around the interrelationship of the Zoharic triad—Israel, Torah, God[232]—all basic existential questions had to be answered in terms of a purpose involving one or more of its members.

According to kabbalistic tradition, each member individually and all three together were a mystical organism in which isolated developments were impossible. Any change in one part of the body mystic, no matter how slight the change or how insignificant the particular part directly affected, reverberated throughout the entire system.[233] In answering our question, the Besht took this concept to its logical conclusion. Since the Zaddik's profane thoughts cannot be due to any inherent flaw, they must reflect a weakness in some other member of the body of Israel. Because he is the head of this body, the Zaddik's involuntary mental sin is generated by the people's actual sins,[234] much as feelings of guilt after committing a crime occasionally cause headaches: Although the hands performed the act, it is the head that suffers.[235]

But this was still not satisfactory, because it explained only the cause but not the purpose of this phenomenon. A final teleological component had to be supplied, and this was the Besht's conclusion that the Zaddik's profane thoughts are intended to signal him to activate deeper powers of devotion and thereby reverse the adverse organic process initiated by the people. By elevating these thoughts he elevates himself—for a man is where his thoughts are—and restores the entire body to health.[236] The people, to be sure, are still expected to do wholehearted teshuvah themselves,[237] but whenever they flag the Zaddik steps into the breach. Similarly, they are certainly expected to pray themselves for their needs and desires, but because he is ever responsible for their welfare, the Zaddik must, in the course of his prayers, always descend to the level of their basic material needs and elementary religious problems in order to supply the former and mitigate the latter.[238] The true Zaddik, like R. Hanina ben Dosa, sustains the world both materially and spiritually.[239]

This analysis of the Zaddik's periodic fall is based on the few statements concerning the subject that Rabbi Jacob Joseph attributes directly to the Besht. Similar but hardly identical doctrines regarding the preacher's need voluntarily "to descend" in order to raise his audience, the Zaddik's occasional need actually to commit a minor sin in order to raise the people, and their various ramifications, were promulgated by Rabbi Menaḥem Mendel of Bar, R. Jacob Joseph himself, and other members of the movement.[240] Although the differences between these teachings and the Besht's authentic views are fairly obvious, they deserve to be spelled out. First, the Besht's Zaddik falls only involuntarily; second, only in thought; third, his fall is a natural—to the extent that sin is natural—periodic phenomenon and not at all a daring, dangerous leap into the abyss; and fourth, the organic relationship causing this fall should affect every Jew in a similar way. Unlike the Zaddik of R. Jacob Joseph and R. Menaḥem Mendel of Bar, who must possess extraordinary qualifications to be allowed to undertake this hazardous descent (and who therefore does indeed resemble the Sabbatian superman), the Besht's Zaddik is only a special example of the spiritual interdependence of all Israel.[241] This was a doctrine, in other words, born not of flirting with sin, as Joseph Weiss maintained,[242] but of a profound sense of mutual responsibility.[243]

Nevertheless, it was obviously the Zaddik, not the average man, who occupied center stage in the early decades of the movement. Partially, of course, this was due to the subjectivity of the early masters, who aspired to join or felt they had already joined the ranks of these religious perfectionists. But this does not account for the unprecedented fascination with the Zaddik's almost unlimited cosmic powers, an aggadic motif[244] greatly emphasized and embellished by the Maggid and many of his disciples. The awesome grandeur of the Zaddik as mighty spiritual potentate clearly captivated them and their followers, and this intense preoccupation with contemporary, visible heroes is another novel development that cannot be satisfactorily explained in terms of presumed Sabbatian undercurrents. The adulation of an absentee messiah or the megalomania of a Jacob Frank can hardly be considered adumbrations of the ramified hero worship of Hasidism.

Standing back and viewing this phenomenon in the context of the movement's other ideational innovations, however, reveals a familiar pattern. The new emphasis on God's immanence; on diversity and change; on sensation, emotion, confident action; on subjectivity, organicism, optimism,[245] individualism; on intuition and the unconscious as supreme sources of knowledge;[246] the new consciousness of the contrast between man's greatness and weakness; the fascination with (religious) genius, energy, power; the shift of values from metaphysics to psychology, from the world to man; from being to becoming, actuality to potentiality; from achieving, or, in the case of God, comprising, a state of serene, uniform perfection to an ever-restless striving for a dynamic, ever-increasing perfection encompassing real contradictions in constant dialectical tension—these features of eighteenth-century Hasidism were also the distinguishing features of a contemporaneous intellectual revolution in Europe known as romanticism.[247] Needless to say, there are no known historical connections between the two movements, but it seems clear that the same intellectual upheaval that emerged toward the end of the eighteenth century in European literature, philosophy, and art was simultaneously shaking the philosophical foundations of Jewish religious thought on that continent.

Turning now from the world of ideas and the men who consciously influenced and were influenced by it, we come to the world of the common man, which, as ever, was directly influenced by men, not ideas. Many thousands were swept up by the extraordinary magnetism of one Zaddik or another. But this did not mean, as S. Ettinger has asserted, the abandonment of the rabbi's "charisma," generated by knowledge and tradition, for that of the Zaddik, generated by his supernatural powers.[248] Competent scholars were still the only possible authorities on halakhic matters for both Hasidim and their opponents. If the Zaddik happened to belong to this category, Hasidim naturally preferred to consult him, although with all his pastoral duties he could not possibly be expected to devote much time to adjudication. If his strengths lay elsewhere—a fact that could not, in those days, long remain undiscovered—his followers had no choice but to take their halakhic problems to the local rabbi. In either event the people flocked to the Zaddik for something the rabbi did not and had never been called upon to provide: a deep, warm, fatherly concern less for their religious problems as devout Jews than for their personal problems as human beings desperately striving to be devout Jews.[249] The belief that his understanding and compassion were complemented by an ability to mitigate or even alleviate these problems—an ability resulting not from some mystical or magical knowledge but from personal sanctity—naturally made him an irresistibly appealing type of popular leader. The masses were attracted not by rarefied and unarticulated theoretical claims to supreme religious authority based on his direct contact with God, but by his obvious willingness to embrace them with empathy and to do everything in his considerable power to help them survive economically, cope emotionally, and flourish spiritually. The rabbi's primary role was to issue rulings, the Zaddik's to proffer blessings. Feelings toward both ranged from reverence to awe, but only the Zaddik was the object of a boundless and generally blind religiofilial love, and therefore beyond criticism. Questions concerning the *kashrut* of a purchased chicken were still submitted to the rabbi, but one's anxiety about where the next chicken would come from was vouchsafed to the Zaddik. The rabbi still officiated at marriages and divorces, but only after the Zaddik's aid had been enlisted to bless the former and prevent the latter. The much admired feeling of solidarity and brotherhood among the Zaddik's followers was a direct outgrowth of this Zaddik-Hasid relationship. The Zaddik was the father of an extended family in which all his followers were siblings sharing his values, his spiritual bounty, and often his table. Fraternal rivalry was unnecessary because his benevolence was believed to be more than enough for all.

This outline of the common man's internal response to the Zaddik is based on the impression one gets from disparate sources: *Shivḥe ha-Besht*, the autobiography of Solomon Maimon, contemporary polemical literature, and the letters of the movement's early leaders,[250] beginning with the Besht himself. His well-known letter to R. Gershon of Kutov reveals a mystic who was preoccupied with "incessant and spiritually heroic efforts" to "nullify the accusations" and defend his people against adversity.[251] Needless to say, it was the common man, rather than the sheltered scholar, who generally stood in greatest need of his efforts. This was the man to whom many of his teachings were addressed and who became the mainstay of the movement he founded.

Yet the Besht's disciples, as well as those of the Maggid, were not, it seems, particularly impressed with the intrinsic spiritual worth of their humble charges. For Rabbi Jacob Joseph of Polonnoye they were gross matter (*ḥomer*) created to be transformed by and into the Zaddik's form (*tsurah*) and constantly threatening to reverse the process.[252] For R. Abraham Kalisker they were coarse simpletons whose religious edification must be limited to the inculcation of humility, fear of God, and faith in the Zaddik.[253] For R. Elimelekh of Lyzhansk they were satellites of the Zaddik, whose spiritual role completely overshadowed theirs.[254] For Rabbi Levi Isaac of Berditchev they were supremely worthy objects of compassion, ever-innocent defendants in their trials of adversity, whose case he was always eager to plead. But they remained mere objects to the Zaddik as subject: He prayed for them, blessed them, and defended them because they were his hapless brothers, religious and existential weaklings who meant well and whose Father appreciated such concern for his still-beloved children.[255]

But for one of the Maggid's disciples the common man was much more. RSZ portrays the simple, devout Jew less as an object for the Zaddik's benevolent concern than as a subject possessing unique spiritual potential. Unlike the scholar who can slake his innate thirst for God at the wellsprings of Torah, the simple Jew is the Bible's burning bush, smoldering with an eternal flame of desire for the Divine. God's first revelation to Moses, who was the prototype for all true leaders of Israel, consisted of a lesson in leadership: He and his successors were empowered and expected to fan this flame in the heart of the common man to burn with the greatest possible intensity, particularly during prayer.[256] The leaders were to help channel this amorphous desire into the Love and Fear[257] that are requisite for the zealous fulfillment of God's will through the practical commandments.[258] RSZ located the source of this desire in a spark of Divinity that is innate to the soul of every Jew and is the ontological basis for the commandment to love one's fellow (Jew) regardless of his external religious stature.[259]

The metaphor of the simple Jew as the eternally burning bush was articulated in a homily RSZ heard from the Maggid in the Besht's name. Yet it was recorded by, and apparently only by, the Maggid's disciple, of whom one would have least expected allegiance to such democratic notions, a man who was by nature an intellectual aristocrat of the first order. Moreover, he was the only disciple to record several other Beshtian teachings on the essential equality of all Jews before God and the dialectical relationship in the spiritual hierarchy between the simple and the scholarly.[260] This apparent anomaly is only one of the many problems concerning RSZ's Hasidic thought that have never been adequately analyzed. The single full-length attempt at analysis published to date is volume two of M. Teitelbaum's *Ha-Rav Mi-Liadi u-Mifleget Ḥabad* (Warsaw, 1913), in which RSZ's abilities as a philosopher, scientist, grammarian, and stylist are assessed from the blinkered perspective of a Graetzian Maskil. Any aspect of RSZ's work congenial to the "scientific" criteria of such an enlightened one is noted approvingly; any deviation therefrom is duly lamented, often with a magnanimous mitigative reference to RSZ's benighted intellectual environment.[261] The question Teitelbaum obviously had always before him was, what "contribution" did RSZ make to the refined, rational culture of Western Europe? Apparently attempting to demonstrate a breadth of learning far beyond the ghetto mind, he packed his work, particularly the footnotes, with gratuitous parallels and tidbits of erudition[262] that reveal much about Teitelbaum but nothing about RSZ. Apparent inconsistencies and general tendencies in RSZ's thought are explained by puerile psychologizing or simplistic generalizations.[263] Apparent stylistic problems are addressed by positing certain verbal "penchants."[264] The relationship of RSZ's religioethical teachings to the doctrines of his teachers and contemporaries in the movement is completely ignored. Indeed, the entire ethical core and thrust of his teachings is perfunctorily treated in several brief chapters comprising about one-third of the volume. Each chapter is introduced by a superficial survey of earlier Jewish thought on the subject, consisting mostly of selective quotations and paraphrases. RSZ's speculative, and therefore "higher," teachings, on the other hand, receive lavish and occasionally creditable treatment in the other two-thirds of the book. Even here, though, Teitelbaum is far less concerned with his subject's thought per se than with its philosophical merits for cultured men of refined (rationalistic) sensibilities.[265]

The more recent article-length studies are more objective and analytical but founded on other methodological shoals. Joseph Weiss's characterization of *Ḥabad* spirituality is noteworthy for sweeping statements that are undocumented and untenable.[266] I. Tishby and J. Dan explain apparent inconsistencies in RSZ's thought by facilely positing the existence of an exoteric-esoteric dualism corresponding, not surprisingly, to more-traditional and more-"radical" teachings.[267] This approach is based not on sound textual or historical evidence (as I hope will become clear) but on the assumption that since Hasidism contains not merely new but *radical* ideas—as Scholem has allegedly shown—its most lucid and systematic expositor must also have something to hide and must take particular pains to hide it. Their interpretation and categorization of passages flow directly from this hypothesis, which, as I have argued, is both untenable and unfruitful.

Rivkah Schatz-Uffenheimer goes still further and maintains that RSZ's teachings not only contain radical elements in the antitraditional sense but that the entire *Tanya* is a radical anti-Maggidic manifesto.[268] She reaches this conclusion by highlighting certain selected passages and largely ignoring the ideological context—rabbinic, philosophical, kabbalistic—in which they are implicitly embedded. Working with discrete, naked texts, she substitutes intuition for well-founded analysis, and statistics for a well-integrated understanding of RSZ's thought. Consequently, emphases become doctrines, unremarkable interpretations become daring innovations, novel insights become radical departures, and misconceptions abound (see Excursus H).

By way of contrast, Louis Jacobs's explications of some of RSZ's teachings in his edition of *Tract on Ecstasy* (London, 1963) by RSZ's son, and in *Seeker of Unity* (London, 1956) are estimable efforts. His intended audience is presumably that generally neglected segment of readers that falls between the scholar and the layman, and he doubtlessly succeeds in meeting its needs. Similarly, Nissan Mindel's *R. Schneur Zalman of Liadi*, volume 2: *The Philosophy of Chabad* (New York, 1973) is generally a clear, straightforward exposition of Part 1 of *Tanya*. It may be read profitably by anyone who finds the complex style and kabbalistic terminology of the original too formidable even in translation. Unfortunately, Mindel occasionally departs from the straight path of exposition and takes detours into the thickets of analysis and intellectual history. Since the purpose of his work is primarily didactic, it is not surprising that one emerges from these side-trips with something less than an accurate, objective view of RSZ's contributions to Jewish thought.

Similarly, David Schapiro's exposition of Part 2 of *Tanya*[269] may be useful for clarifying the text (although this particular text is already quite clear). The reader, however, must weed out Schapiro's own purely speculative and occasionally bizarre contributions.[270]

More helpful is Adin Steinsaltz's running commentary to this part of *Tanya*, *Be'ur he-Tanya: Shaʿar ha-Yiḥud veha-Emunah* (Jerusalem, 1989). Similarly, Steinsaltz's *The Long Shorter Way: Discourses of Chasidic Thought*, edited and translated by Yehuda Hanegbi (Northvale, N.J., 1988) is a modern popularization and elaboration of concepts treated in *Tanya*. Here, however, these concepts are used primarily as a springboard for an exposition of Steinsaltz's own (often fascinating) views. This is, perhaps, in keeping with his understanding of Torah-study in general: "It is as though the Torah were the blueprint of the world, and in order to construct one's own building, one would have to draw one's own extensions to the master plan, creating a private version of Creation with all the inevitable errors, erasures, and corrections" (*The Long Shorter Way*, p. 150).

Jacob Immanuel Schochet's *Mystical Concepts in Chassidism* (revised and reprinted in the Soncino edition of *Tanya* [London, 1973], pp. 804–86) stands in interesting contrast to this creative approach. Its avowed purpose is to provide the student of Part 4 of *Tanya*, "Igeret ha-Ḳodesh," with the kabbalistic background necessary to understand that text. In presenting these concepts, Schochet states in his foreword that he "strove to grasp and offer the views and interpretations of R. Schneur Zalman of Liadi."[271] Accordingly, his "basic sources" are "the writings of R. Schneur Zalman of Liadi with abundant references to the original writings of the Zohar and of R. Isaac Luria."[272] The reader will not, however, find these intentions fulfilled. Topics are explained primarily by drawing on an amalgam of kabbalistic sources, references to which greatly outnumber references to RSZ's teachings.[273] It is tacitly assumed that RSZ's teachings conform to these sources. Consequently, Schochet can maintain that analogies, explanations, and motifs barely or never mentioned, and certainly never emphasized, by RSZ are valid interpretations of his views (see Excursus I). Schochet's presentation does, however, retain one important aspect of RSZ's approach to his sources: The possibility of conceptual development during the course of time or of real disagreement on basic kabbalistic themes is never admitted. Conflicts between sources regarded as authoritative (or between passages in the same source) are usually resolved by positing "different levels"[274] to which each source (or passage) really refers. This principle, made plausible by discarding Ockham's razor, guarantees the infallibility of all revered texts and stimulates the interpretative creativity necessary to demonstrate that infallibility. It also removes the sources' authors from the historical arena and places them in the timeless world of metaphysics.[275]

Nor is Schochet alone among modern scholars in disregarding historical considerations. Except for the exoteric-esoteric hypothesis of Tishby and Dan, students of RSZ's teachings have given the impression that they were all of a piece, written as books, and addressed to posterity. That they were predominantly oral, delivered over the course of several decades, under various circumstances, in various styles, to variegated audiences with varying religious needs—these realia have never been incorporated into an analytical framework.

Although a critical, comprehensive biography of RSZ has yet to be written (see Excursus J), many of the relevant sources have already been published. D. Z. Hilman's excellent anthology *Igerot Baʿal ha-Tanya u-Bene Doro* (Jerusalem, 1953) contains much useful and still untapped material. But particularly valuable are the written records of the Schneersohn dynasty. RSZ, most of his successors to the leadership of Ḥabad,[276] and several other members of their families kept meticulous journals. We know this from the journals of R. Joseph Isaac Schneersohn, sizable parts of which were transmitted orally during Hasidic gatherings,[277] transcribed, and then scattered through a series of published volumes titled *Liḳuṭe Diburim* (4 vols., 3rd ed., New York, 1957), *Sefer ha-Siḥot* (followed by the year in which they were delivered, e.g., 5700), *Sefer ha-Maʾamarim* (followed by the year), *Ha-Tamim* (a bound volume [2d ed., Kefar Ḥabad, 1971] of the eight Ḥabad periodicals of that name published in prewar Poland), as well as several pamphlets of various titles.[278] These narratives reveal a man and a family of unusual historical sensibility.[279] The incidents related are almost always dated, often down to the day of the week, sometimes down to the hour. They are related vividly, in detail, with obvious and conscious precision.[280] A teaching or tradition transmitted by RSZ to his son R. Dov Baer, or his grandson R. Menaḥem Mendel, was often transmitted to each successive recipient at the same age or on the same holiday, and R. Joseph Isaac frequently takes pains to supply the date for every link in the chain and to reproduce the words verbatim.[281]

In addition to the written records he inherited, R. Joseph Isaac was heir to and recorded a rich, living, oral tradition. This was reverently transmitted to him primarily by his father, but also by his teacher of many years, R. Samuel Bezalel Sheftel, a disciple of one of RSZ's outstanding younger disciples; by his uncle R. Zalman Aharon, a recipient of many traditions from RSZ's grandson R. Menaḥem Naḥum (ca. 1778–1876); and by other Ḥabad Hasidim who were also only one disciple removed from RSZ.[282] Miracle tales, particularly when not well attested, were frowned upon[283] and appear very rarely. This alone would suffice to place this tradition on more solidly historical ground than such hagiographies as *Shivḥe ha-Besht*.

Yet scholars have refrained, sometimes pointedly, from using this material,[284] while *Shivḥe ha-Besht* has been treated as a valuable historical source. This despite its author's avowed intention to relate not historical narratives but inspirational miracle tales; and despite the fact that the only claim of accuracy he makes refers not to the tales' historicity but to his transcription. While he does indicate that he heard them from "men of truth," it is clear from his introduction that he is far less concerned with their historical truth than with their inspirational value.[285] Still, according to Dinur, Scholem, Weiss, and H. Szmeruk, historical elements may be distilled from them,[286] although we are never informed just how this may be done. Dinur's argument for the historical value of certain stories that serve as vehicles for Hasidic teachings[287] overlooks the author's claim that all the stories carry such teachings.[288] Similarly, the fact that the Besht often taught by parables[289] does not enhance the historical value of the parables in *Shivḥe ha-Besht*. Episodes lacking miracles are only slightly less problematic, since the common avowed aim of all the stories is to glorify the Besht and his colleagues in order to arouse religious awe in the reader. This intention cannot be ignored in light of the "intentional fallacy" because, even assuming such a fallacy exists, it is inapplicable to prose works with a "practical message."[290]

Joseph Weiss characteristically went beyond his predecessors and, based on his scrutiny of several passages in *Shivḥe ha-Besht*, argued for the existence of a circle of pneumatics in pre-Hasidism "which links the declining Sabbatian movement with its Hasidic metamorphosis" and illuminates the Besht's early religious and social aspirations.[291] There is no indication that Weiss ever questioned the historicity of the passages from which these far-reaching conclusions were drawn; nor does G. Nigal in a more recent study that accepts Weiss's conclusions and continues his method.[292]

All this is not to say that *Shivḥe ha-Besht* is devoid of historical value, but simply that reliable means for separating its historical truths from the half-truths and imaginative reconstructions have yet to be found. Consequently, it cannot be confidently used as a source of factual information. It may, however, be profitably used in conjunction with other Hasidic sources to illumine the socioreligious values of early Hasidism, particularly since the inculcation of these values was its author's primary purpose.

On the other hand, there is a category of narratives concerning the Besht and other Hasidic leaders that may be considered as factually reliable as any oral or "traditional" historical source. Since Hasidic traditions can rarely be corroborated by non-Hasidic sources,[293] the criteria for classifying a narrative in this category relate to the narrator himself and to the purpose, style, and tone of the narrative. Narratives related as historical events, that emphasize that fact, that are narrated or transmitted by someone who is characteristically precise in his speech and writing and who exhibits a definite critical sense—such narratives belong in this category. The fact that their ultimate purpose is religious and didactic does not detract from their historicity.

An example of such a narrative may be found in the Midrash commentary *Ḳore me-Rosh*, by R. Aaron Samuel ha-Kohen (ca. 1744–1814), one of the Maggid's more scholarly disciples.[294] R. Aaron, whose works are characterized by a conscientious attention to accuracy of detail,[295] asseverates and reiterates that he is faithfully testifying to what his father-in-law, R. Joel, told him. The Besht had stayed at R. Joel's home, and R. Joel, who was the Rabbi of Stafan, did him the honor of accompanying him to a nearby village. Their wagon passed through a forest; the leaves were rustling and birds were singing. The Besht asked the driver to stop the wagon, listened, and told R. Joel that the trees and birds were telling them they had forgotten something important in town. R. Joel was annoyed, not believing that a contemporary could know such things (cf. Tal. B., *Giṭin,* 45a; *Sukah,* 28a). But it turned out to be true, and they had to send someone to fetch the forgotten item.

However one chooses to explain it, this anecdote belongs in the category of reliable oral traditions that can be used to fill in the historical record. This applies even more emphatically to the biographical Schneersohn tradition, which contains very few miracle tales, is considerably more detailed, and was transmitted not as hagiography, nor even as part of a commentary, but as history. Its primary purpose was to inform and edify, not to impress. Many if not most of the biographical narratives in R. Joseph Isaac's sources describe events in the lives of Ḥabad leaders that they themselves recorded or related to their successor(s). Over and above any didactic purposes he may have had in publicizing them, R. Joseph Isaac (and his predecessors) considered these events important because they dealt with men he (and they) knew to be supremely important. Scrupulous accuracy was therefore essential; not, to be sure, for reasons of scholarly objectivity, but on the contrary, for reasons of axiological subjectivity: Because these men were supremely important, it was equally important that our knowledge of what they did and said, when they did and said it, and all the circumstances surrounding it, be as precise as possible. R. Joseph Isaac's own statements, as well as the tone and style in which he transmitted these traditions, attest to this attitude.[296]

Consequently, although one cannot rule out the possibility that hero-reverence somewhere during the course of a tradition's transmission resulted in some distortions or inaccuracies, R. Joseph Isaac's records are the most detailed and reliable sources for RSZ's biography we possess. This is particularly true for relatively value-free biographical data, such as the development of his homiletic style, the literary history of his discourses (which does not emphasize the faithfulness of the transcriptions), and important dates. Other biographical information is certainly no more tendentious than an autobiographical work, which, when judiciously used, is obviously a valuable historical source despite its author's inevitable bias. The only source comparable to these records is H. M. Heilman's *Bet Rebi* (Berditchev, 1902), which is based on oral family and Hasidic traditions that are not as well attested, and on "reliable books and authors"[297] that are never named. There is no question that Heilman did not have access to (all) the written Schneersohn records and journals that formed the foundation of R. Joseph Isaac's knowledge of RSZ's life. Nor was he privy to many important details that were transmitted from father to son only, down to R. Joseph Isaac. Nor is he in any way more objective, as his introduction alone demonstrates and as is clear from the tone of the entire book.

R. Joseph Isaac was an avid, indefatigable collector and recorder of Ḥabad traditions, and only a small portion of his work in this area has been published.[298] Nevertheless, even this fraction is enough to provide us with the historical context of RSZ's teachings without which valid interpretation is impossible. While some discrepancies may be found when all the published material is compared, these are not sufficient in number or significance to vitiate its essential claim to historicity and reliability. This material therefore allows us to sketch RSZ's intellectual biography and to approach his thought as the product of a living mind, rather than as dead words on paper.

As was the case with all intellectually capable boys of that time and place, the foundations of RSZ's education, both chronologically and ideologically, were the Bible, Mishnah, and above all, Talmud with codes and standard commentaries. It is necessary to restate this truism here because scholarly treatment of Hasidic thought has glossed over its obvious consequence: These works formed the rabbinic substratum with which all ideas subsequently learned had to be compared and were *automatically* (though not necessarily consciously) compared. Naturally, the greater the student's achievements in the study of rabbinic Judaism, the greater its influence on how these subsequent ideas were assimilated. And RSZ's achievements were great indeed. By the age of eighteen (in 1763) he had mastered the entire Talmud with all its major commentaries and codes. By the age of thirty he had consolidated this knowledge sixteen times over and had masterfully re-edited major portions of the *Shulḥan ʿArukh*,[299] integrating text, commentaries, sources, and subsequent halakhic developments into flowing, *Mishneh Torah*–like paragraphs.

Unlike most boys, however, RSZ's early Talmudic studies were supplemented by subjects not usually associated with the educational practice of early eighteenth-century Russian Jewry: (Jewish) philosophy, grammar, and exegesis; mathematics, geometry, and astronomy. While he was introduced to the latter three informally by two brothers who had fled Bohemia and settled near Lyozna,[300] he studied the former three with local savants several hours a day for two years, beginning at the surprising age of seven.[301] Around the same time he was also introduced to Isaiah Horowitz's *sidur* with commentary, *Shaʿar ha-Shamayim*, with which he was thoroughly familiar by the age of eight.[302]

By the age of thirteen he was dividing an eighteen-hour schedule into thirds. Two-thirds of each weekday was devoted to Talmud and codes; the remainder to Bible, aggadah, Midrash,[303] Zohar, other kabbalistic works,[304] and philosophy. On Sabbaths, one-third was spent on Talmud and codes; one-third on Bible, aggadah, and philosophy; and one-third on Midrash, Zohar, and other kabbalistic works. By far the greater part of his time, in other words, was devoted to rabbinic works, and though these proportions and hours undoubtedly varied in later life, this predominance never did.[305]

Among more-recent religious works, the young scholar, like many of his contemporaries, found Isaiah Horowitz's encyclopedic *Shene Luḥot ha-Berit* the most spiritually satisfying. In addition to Talmudic studies, this was the work he regularly taught to a group of disciples in Vitebsk, beginning around 1760, and it was Horowitz's sidur and kavanot that this cloistered seminary used.[306]

After several years of growth in this intellectual hothouse, RSZ resolved to emulate many of his contemporaries and undertake "exile" for the sake of Torah-study.[307] While debating where to go, it occurred to him that his religious development had been disproportionate; the mind had outstripped the heart. He had learned to serve God with his reason, through study and comprehension, but had yet to learn how to serve Him with suprarational desire and will, through prayer.[308] Rumor had it that prayer was precisely the area of concentration at Mezhirech, and in the summer of 1764[309] he set out from Vitebsk, where he had resided since his marriage in 1760.

But at Mezhirech he found something very different from what he had envisioned. Seeking a measured corrective for the overemphasis on cognition at Vitebsk, he found the opposite extreme. Instead of a brotherhood of diligent scholars emphasizing "Service of the heart," he encountered a group of mystics so preoccupied with ecstatic prayer and discussions of the higher world that they barely found time to study God's word as it pertained to the lower.[310] For two weeks he wavered, unsure whether he had made the right decision.[311] It was only the Maggid's demonstration of Talmudic erudition and the rational composure he maintained during his mystical discourses that finally won RSZ over.[312]

A keen judge of character and ability,[313] the Maggid soon appreciated the exceptional qualities of his newest and youngest disciple. He arranged daily sessions between his son, R. Abraham, and RSZ, during which each spent half the time teaching the other in his area of expertise: RSZ taught rabbinics; R. Abraham, kabbalah.[314] In 1770 the Maggid instructed RSZ to compile a new edition of the *Shulḥan ʿArukh*.[315] He entrusted RSZ with, and consulted him on, many organizational details.[316] He set aside regular periods during the week for giving RSZ private kabbalistic instruction and transmitting to him in turn the teachings and traditions he, the Maggid, had heard from the Besht.[317] It is very probable that the Maggid transmitted these in a form he felt would be appreciated by this most intellectual of his disciples, and that consequently RSZ's impressions of the Besht and the Besht's ideology differed significantly from those of his colleagues.[318] It would also be natural for RSZ to emphasize concepts he heard from the Maggid that may not be emphasized in the extant transcripts of Maggidic teachings, most of which are traceable to R. Levi Isaac of Berditchev.[319]

RSZ was particularly moved by the Besht's teachings on the spiritual potential of the uneducated and simple but sincere and conscientious Jew. This was, in RSZ's view, the Besht's single major innovation,[320] and, indeed, a study of the ideational antecedents of the Besht's teachings makes this conclusion very plausible. The greater an eighteenth-century scholar's immersion in these antecedents, the more sensitive he would be to a significant and powerful ideological contribution by a near-contemporary who was rapidly becoming a legend. Since no other Beshtian idea had fewer or weaker roots in earlier Jewish thought,[321] none would be more striking for a scholar of RSZ's caliber. This, coupled with a humanitarian spirit of great compassion,[322] may help explain his predilection for these teachings.

Upon his return to Vitebsk in the spring of 1765,[323] RSZ began to befriend and minister to these common folk and to persuade his reluctant disciples to do likewise.[324] Sometime between 1767 and 1773 the community of Lyozna offered him the position of *maggid* (preacher), which he accepted and retained until his move to Lyady in 1801. He was thus called upon regularly to deliver inspirational sermons to a congregation consisting largely of just such listeners.[325] The religious ferment that was beginning to bubble up in various Polish-Russian Jewish communities around this time was heightening even their aspirations. Judging by the pastoral letters that R. Menaḥem Mendel of Vitebsk and R. Abraham Kalisker wrote to the movement's adherents during the 1780s and 1790s, the common people's primary problem now was how to attain the spirituality for which they thirsted while oppressed with the numbing need to eke out a subsistence livelihood from menial vocations pursued among uncouth gentile peasants. Related to this was their dissatisfaction with homilies and musar teachings that had lost their power to inspire.[326] RSZ undoubtedly attempted to address these problems when preaching to his Lyozna audience.

He continued to visit the Maggid periodically until the latter's death in 1772. In 1773 he spent several months as a disciple of R. Abraham, the Maggid's son and heir apparent. After R. Abraham's death he traveled to Gorodok several times as R. Menaḥem Mendel's disciple[327] and insisted on perpetuating this form of relationship even after R. Menaḥem Mendel emigrated to Israel in 1777, until his death eleven years later. Although RSZ greatly respected the older and very learned R. Menaḥem Mendel,[328] he accepted him as his master primarily for the same reason he accepted the far less accomplished R. Abraham: It was the Maggid's wish that this should be the order of succession.[329] This humility, which permitted him to subordinate himself to men who were, as far as the extant evidence indicates, his inferiors in scholarship, character, and leadership abilities, was one of his outstanding traits.[330]

Like most revolutionary movements, early Hasidism was marked by a tendency toward extremism and militancy. The Besht launched and the Maggid greatly expanded a concerted clandestine campaign to acquire new adherents among the scholarly. Erudite disciples were dispatched to many towns and cities in Lithuania and the neighboring provinces to engage scholars in Talmudic discussions, impress them with the only achievement they found impressive, and win them over to the cause.[331] Less-qualified emotional zealots such as R. Abraham Kalisker had no patience for such subtleties and resorted to ridicule and bizarre behavior to make their case.[332] By 1772 R. Abraham realized he had gone too far and, afraid to face the Maggid, begged and got RSZ to intercede on his behalf through R. Menaḥem Mendel.[333] On other occasions RSZ found himself actually defending the opposition against the Maggid's unyielding antagonism.[334] Nevertheless, he fully shared the Maggid's view of the Hasidic movement as a heroic, embattled group of revolutionaries who had to wage both defensive and offensive warfare to survive. If the Maggid was its general, RSZ quickly became its field marshal. From around 1770 and particularly during the three years after the Maggid's death, RSZ traveled extensively to attract scholars to the movement,[335] using the method outlined above with considerable success. By 1776 he had succeeded in establishing in Lyozna a seminary of about forty young men engaged in a carefully planned, closely supervised course of Talmudic studies. The best of this already select group were divided into two graded classes to whom RSZ delivered Hasidic discourses in private.[336] Compared to what was to follow in Lyady, these were short, undeveloped, often cryptic teachings, actually better described as sermonettes; but compared to the Hasidic teachings the general Lyozna public or even his other disciples heard, they were lengthy, detailed expositions. Even at the very beginning of his career, in other words, RSZ was teaching regularly (on Sabbaths and holidays) on at least three levels to three types of audiences.[337] He would also, from time to time, suddenly emerge from his study to galvanize his disciples with lightninglike inspirational flashes, apothegms that were verbalized bursts of spiritual energy.[338]

Studies at the seminary were disrupted in 1777 when RSZ spent several months accompanying R. Menaḥem Mendel through Russia on his way to the Holy Land and agonizing over whether to leave Russia with him. After his return to Lyozna in 1778, he selected fifteen scholars and reestablished the first of the two classes. Conditions for acceptance were proficiency in Talmud, Tosafot, R. Asher, *Mishneh Torah*, Midrash, *Kuzari*, *ʿIḳarim*, and a respectable knowledge of Zohar. A second, lower class was founded in 1780 and a third in 1782–1783. The members of these *Ḥadarim*, as they were styled, were RSZ's Old Guard, his most devoted, most cherished disciples; they were the chief—indeed, the indispensable—disseminators of his intellectualized brand of Hasidism. It is not surprising, therefore, that he lavished five years of intensive, almost uninterrupted instruction upon *Ḥeder* One.[339]

Various events moved RSZ to schedule additional periods of instruction for some or all the members of this Ḥeder. Some of these arrangements were temporary, others permanent. An example of the former is the weekday session he set aside for them in 1785. An example of the latter are the weekday and Friday night discourses he began to deliver to a handful of disciples and his son, Dov Baer, in 1788. These were occasioned by his future successor's coming of age and constitute a fourth level of RSZ's teachings. In addition, he was exceptionally devoted to his brilliant grandson Menaḥem Mendel, a prolific writer to whom he transmitted privately a wealth of teachings and traditions, all of which were reverently recorded. His grandson's birth in 1789 marked the beginning of RSZ's longer public discourses, the first one comprising the first three chapters of *Tanya*. When Menaḥem Mendel came of age, RSZ repeated for him the discourses he had delivered until that time, so that the grandson became a complete repository of the grandfather's teachings.[340]

From time to time RSZ, like all sensitive teachers, found it necessary to emphasize or moderate certain aspects of his teachings to correct misconceptions or extremist tendencies among his disciples. Upon his return to Lyozna in 1778, for example, he found that those remaining had become a group of secluded, ascetic mystics, and his teachings of that period were directed at redressing this imbalance. Similarly, the years 1799 and 1803 saw (for different reasons) outbreaks of religious emotionalism, and several discourses of those years therefore stress the ascendency of intellectual over emotional fervor.[341]

Mitnagdic slander caused RSZ's arrest and imprisonment in Saint Petersburg in 1798 and again in 1800,[342] but his son and close disciples found ample consolation in the far more intensive instruction they received after each incident. Convinced that the real cause was not earthly slander but heavenly displeasure with his failure sufficiently to elucidate the Besht's teachings, RSZ undertook to rectify his error. Upon his return to Lyozna in 1798, but especially after he moved to Lyady after the second arrest, he began to deliver private discourses of unprecedented length, depth, and clarity. These finally became discursive disquisitions, most often on Zoharic passages and kabbalistic concepts, frequently supplemented by three or four explicatory discourses. He began to permit and occasionally encourage select disciples to unpack the implications of these discourses and contribute explications of their own, some of which he occasionally used to stimulate his own thinking on the subject.[343] His public discourses also grew longer and more complex from year to year.[344] Nevertheless, he continued his early practice of sporadically delivering short, inspirational homilies and apothegms, both to his sons and close disciples and to wider audiences.[345] These and some public discourses now became the main vehicles for teaching religious ethics, while the private discourses dealt almost exclusively with questions of kabbalistic theosophy. In between these two functional categories was a third: public discourses combining the features of both in somewhat attenuated form. Their theosophy is less detailed, their ethical emphasis less pronounced.[346]

The chief transcribers of the Lyady period were apparently R. Dov Baer, R. Moses (RSZ's youngest son), R. Pinḥas b. Ḥanokh Henekh Shick (known among Hasidim as R. Pinḥas Reizes), and R. Menaḥem Mendel.[347] Weekday discourses were recorded as they were being delivered;[348] thanks to the facile penmanship of R. Dov Baer, Sabbath and holiday discourses were generally ready for recopying and dissemination within thirty-six hours.[349] During the Lyozna period Hasidim were adjured to bring with them on their pilgrimages to RSZ all the copies they had made or bought, so that they might be corrected by a specially appointed committee headed by RSZ's brother, R. Judah Leib.[350]

In 1801 the very organized R. Menaḥem Mendel began to record the discourses more systematically, and in 1804 he set aside daily sessions to study them and add, usually in parentheses or otherwise clearly demarcated,[351] his own explications.[352] For the next thirty years he spent a total of thirty-two thousand hours poring over the transcriptions and copies he and others had made; only then did he feel ready formally to edit and compile a collection for publication.[353] *Torah Or* (Kopys, 1836) and its companion volume, *Liḳuṭe Torah* (Zhitomir, 1848), contain, according to R. Menaḥem Mendel, most of RSZ's discourses from the years 1796–1813.[354] These are, however, mostly public discourses, in which questions of religious ethics are usually in the forefront. Collections of the private discourses had already been published by R. Dov Baer in his *Beʾure ha-Zohar* and as a commentary to the prayers in RSZ's revised edition of the prayer book (both Kopys, 1816), *Seder Tefilot mi-kol ha-Shanah ʿal pi Nusaḥ ha-Arizal* (originally published without commentary in Shklov, 1803).[355]

The public discourses R. Menaḥem Mendel chose not to publish, as well as many private discourses, remained in manuscript until 1958, when Rabbi M. Schneerson initiated a program of publication under the rubric: *Maʾamre Admor ha-Zaḳen* (Discourses of RSZ). That year saw the appearance of Volume 1, subtitled *Hanaḥot ha-Rap*[356]—that is, the transcriptions of RSZ's very close disciple, R. Pinḥas Reizes, of discourses spanning about five years (ca. 1807–1812 and possibly earlier), and Volume 2, subtitled *Ethalekh-Lyozna*—that is, discourses contained in a manuscript beginning with the word *Ethalekh,* which were presumably delivered during RSZ's Lyozna years.[357] Volume 3, *Sefer ha-Maʾamarim 5562* (New York, 1964), and Volume 4, *Sefer ha-Maʾamarim 5568*, are, as their titles imply, discourses delivered during 1801–1802 and 1807–1808, respectively. Both are based on transcriptions attributed to R. Dov Baer and were proofread by R. Menaḥem Mendel.

In 1978 a portion of R. Joseph Isaac's library, presumed lost in Warsaw during the war, was acquired by Rabbi M. Schneerson. Included in this collection are hundreds of manuscripts, among them several complete volumes of RSZ's discourses for one or more years of the

Lyady period and about two hundred manuscripts containing discourses from the Lyozna period. Virtually all of these manuscripts have now been published as part of the *Ma'amre Admor ha-Zaḳen* series.

Most of the transcriptions and copies of the Lyady period contain editorial interpolations and explications resulting in significant stylistic differences between various transcriptions of the same discourse. R. Dov Baer's transcriptions in particular are notable for such additions.[358] Although the essential content of the discourse does not vary, its original form has nevertheless become sufficiently blurred generally to preclude drawing any reliable conclusions from wording or phraseology alone. Discourses from the Lyozna period,[359] when R. Judah Leib was RSZ's chief transcriber and when a system for correcting copies was definitely in operation, may actually be more reliable in this respect. However, some manuscripts containing these discourses (dating from 1792) also contain teachings published in collections of homilies attributed to the Maggid or one of his disciples. Also, a comparison of the manuscripts and the published discourses of this period reveals both minor and significant variations between different versions of the same discourse. Consequently, scrutinizing the wording of a single Lyozna discourse is equally pointless, and philological questions can be addressed only after comparing a number of discourses dealing with the same issue. Similarly, in editing *Liḳuṭe Torah,* R. Menaḥem Mendel occasionally combined several discourses on the same theme. Conversely, copyists sometimes copied only part of a longer discourse, giving the impression that that part alone was delivered as a discourse on a given date.[360]

As for precise dating, the general rule is that unless at least one transcription or copy of a discourse contains a date line, it is impossible to establish the date it was (originally) delivered. RSZ (and his successors) periodically repeated certain discourses almost verbatim in order to "purify the air." He repeated others from time to time with minor or major variations and additions. At least one discourse published in the *Seder Tefilot* is a combination of several discourses on the same theme delivered over a period of one or two years. Moreover, during the leadership years of R. Dov Baer and R. Menaḥem Mendel, they repeated or delivered their own versions of many discourses they heard from RSZ.[361]

Most of the elements in this outline of RSZ's intellectual biography and the literary history of his teachings have been ignored in the most ambitious study of RSZ's thought to date. In his unpublished dissertation, "Mishnato ha-ʿIyunit shel R. Shneur Zalman mi-Liadi" (Hebrew

University, 1975), written under I. Tishby, Moshe Hallamish uses the published works as if they, and not RSZ, were the source of his teachings.[362] His general method is to select a theme that he, if not RSZ, considers to be an important rubric and examine what each book has to say on the subject,[363] although a collection such as *Likute Torah* contains variegated discourses spanning nearly two decades. He fails, in other words, to connect *Tanya* and the discourses with the man and culture behind them. The result is a host of misconceptions, misinterpretations, and futile, fallacious, or superfluous speculations (see Excursus K). Overlooking the rabbinic foundations of RSZ's thought almost completely, and largely ignoring its Beshtian and Maggidic roots, much of Hallamish's study concentrates on labeling: Is RSZ a quietist? An activist? A spiritualist? A pantheist? An acosmist? A radical or a conservative?[364] Is he more Lurianic or more Cordoverian? Strings of quotations (interspersed with commentary) from one book are arrayed against strings of quotations from a second book, and so on down the list of books Hallamish chose to use, until some conclusion is reached.

Hallamish accepts and extends the Tishby-Dan exoteric-esoteric theory. In chapter after chapter of Parts 2 and 3 he intimates that in addition to suppressing more-"radical" Hasidic ideas, RSZ omitted from *Tanya* the technical Lurianic explications and refinements of his ideology because these, too, were considered too daring to publish. Following suit, those who edited his discourses for publication are assumed to have veiled ideas that Tishby and Hallamish believe required veiling. This despite the fact that the previous century had seen scores of kabbalistic works, Lurianic and non-Lurianic, of almost every shade of radicalism pour off the presses with barely a murmur of protest;[365] and despite the fact that in 1796, when *Tanya* was published, the publication of Hasidic discourses was the exception rather than the rule. Hasidic culture was then still in its early stage of primarily oral transmission. It consisted of living masters pouring the words of the living God into the ears of their disciples and listeners. Hearing a teaching from the master or even at secondhand from a disciple who reproduced it as faithfully as he could[366] was a permeating experience that textual study could not approach. The fervently spoken word could move emotionally and illumine intellectually as the written word could not; it was therefore valued far more highly.[367] Moreover, even for those among RSZ's followers who had to content themselves with transcriptions and copies of transcriptions, these were in their hands within a few weeks at the most and had a freshness and immediacy far surpassing that of a published volume of collected discourses. In fact, Ḥabad Hasidim proved very reluctant to buy such volumes when they became available.[368] Only when the wellspring stopped gushing—the master died—or when its waters became polluted—his teachings were adulterated by successive recopying—were processing and bottling through editing and publication considered desirable or necessary. In RSZ's case, adulteration of his words was the primary impetus for publication of Part 1 of *Tanya*,[369] and his death the stimulus for publication of the discourses. What to include and what to omit were decisions RSZ and his editors made not on the basis of self-censorship—which, if Tishby and Hallamish are right, they were very poor at—but on the basis of the intended purpose of each work. As Part 1 of *Tanya* was intended to be primarily a book of practical religious advice,[370] details of Lurianic theosophy that had no direct bearing on this advice had no place in it.

Obviously the present study will differ markedly from Hallamish's in its approach, method, emphasis, interpretations, and conclusions. As I have outlined my general purpose and plan in the Preface, it remains only to add here several general observations on RSZ's method and style that may prove helpful in understanding his thought.[371]

Except for the discourses on Zoharic passages, RSZ delivered his homilies and discourses in the discursive, associative style of the Maggid.[372] The usual pattern, particularly in *Torah Or* and *Likuṭe Torah*,[373] consists of a Scriptural, aggadic, or occasionally halakhic problem followed by a chain of themes bristling with Scriptural, aggadic, kabbalistic, philosophical, and liturgical allusions. The problem is used merely as a springboard for the development of these themes, which themselves are linked by psychological, rather than logical, associations: A word, phrase, passage, or concept touches off a memory teeming with parallels and apparent contradictions. Ideas take shape extemporaneously and are generally left only partially developed when a new association is activated.[374] The answer to the original problem is anticlimactic and adds more to the symmetry of the homily than to its substance.

Since man's body is God's corporealized reflection,[375] and his soul is "truly part of God above,"[376] RSZ in his most common analogies passes easily and often imperceptibly back and forth between the sefirotic realm and human anatomy, physiology, and psychology.[377] The latter are assumed to be well understood and therefore serve as the given from which the unknown processes of the Divine may be glimpsed. There is a striking contrast between RSZ's approach to physical phenomena, which purportedly function in ways that are so obvious as to be almost self-evident,[378] and his approach to their analogous supernal phenomena, which function in ways that are so obscure as to be almost incomprehensible. Nevertheless, if it is true below, it must be true above, and vice versa. One need only locate the corresponding elements and remember that the parallel is only "as it were."[379]

The heightened anthropomorphism that this method entailed seemed to trouble RSZ no more than it did other kabbalists. An exception was God's speech—the humanized revelation-symbolism that from the twelfth century had paralleled the *sefirot*-symbolism in kabbalistic works[380] and that receives very frequent and very detailed treatment in RSZ's discourses. Apparently, since all the details of this symbolism are based on human speech, a rare disclaimer was called for.[381] On the other hand, RSZ expended enormous effort in attempting to demonstrate, by various means, time and again, God's absolute transcendence and immutability, as if these qualities were indeed called into question by the abundance of detailed anthropomorphic symbolism he adopted.[382]

This conceptual tension is an example of the most important characteristic of RSZ's metaphysical thought. Scholem has already observed that Luria's doctrine of retraction (*tsimtsum*) added paradox to Cordovero's dialectical understanding of the emanation processes.[383] He has referred to the Lurianic symbols of *Shevirah* and Tiḳun as "the greatest victory which anthropomorphic thought has ever won in the history of Jewish mysticism."[384] He has pointed to the inherent incompatibility of, on the one hand, mystical myth, anthropomorphism, symbolism, and imagery—best exemplified by Lurianic kabbalah—and, on the other hand, the antianthropomorphic philosophical concepts into which certain kabbalists—best exemplified by Cordovero—attempted to transform these pictorial modes of thought.[385] Concerning Cordovero, Scholem has written: "The doctrine of Cordovero is a summary and a development of the different trends in kabbalah up to his time, and his whole work is a major attempt to synthesize and to construct a speculative kabbalistic system."[386]

RSZ's metaphysics—which concerns us to the extent that it is the foundation of his Hasidic thought—goes beyond both Luria's and Cordovero's in syncretism, dialectics, and paradox. It is a comparatively unsystematic synthesis of Cordovero's systematic, conceptual kabbalah; Luria's unsystematic, mythical kabbalah; and eclectic interpretations of rabbinic aggadah. It strives, moreover, to unite Maimonidean rationalism with Hasidic romanticism. By thus (unconsciously) attempting to combine three diverse modes and two opposing trends of Jewish thought, RSZ was attempting the rationally impossible. Yet this should not surprise us, for RSZ was essentially a mystic, not a rationalist; a religious thinker, not a historian of ideas. His primary goal in most of the homilies and discourses was not to educate but to inspire, and sources of inspiration need not be conceptually compatible to be effective.

Our analysis, however, will reveal not only dialectical tension and paradoxes, but a fair share of clear-cut contradictions. Some inconsistencies may be explicable in terms of the audience RSZ was addressing, the concept he was emphasizing, or the internal development of his thought. But most, apparently, are the combined result of his attempt at synthesis; his extemporaneous, associative mode of exposition; and his conviction that all opposing facts and forces are ultimately reconcilable because all are encompassed by God's unity. Since He combines within His unity an infinite variety of opposites, the reality that flows from Him and the thought describing that reality must exhibit the same characteristic.[387]

RSZ's metaphysics therefore combines the dialectics of both Heraclitus and Hegel. It affirms the underlying unity of all opposites as well as the need for their synthesis; the desirability of harmony[388] as well as the creative tension of strife. The discourses interweave reason and intuition, concepts and images, philosophy and kabbalah, halakhah and intimations of antinomism.[389] The consummately rational, exceptionally lucid halakhic author appears to have undergone a Karo-like transformation[390] when delivering these disquisitions. He abandoned the standard canons of reasoning that frown on contrariety, question begging, and other forms of the unwarranted assumption, and embraced instead a kind of transcendental logic that is generally indifferent to such rules.[391] Moreover, as mentioned above, this is a world of thought in which sefirotic aspects and their corresponding entities may be multiplied ad infinitum. On those relatively rare occasions when RSZ addresses a contradiction between statements *A* and *B* concerning a given emanation or faculty, the resolution generally consists of positing that *A* and *B* actually refer to two different aspects of the thing in question—a higher and a lower, an inner and an outer, the source and its projection, its manifestation in a higher world and in a lower. These aspects are, of course, further divisible.

The necessity for this special logic stems largely from RSZ's faith in the divine infallibility of the entire Lurianic corpus as edited by Vital.[392] Since this corpus teems with inconsistencies, and since the letters of its alphabet—the sefirot—have neither a fixed order nor even fixed identities,[393] standard Aristotelian logic is incapable of assimilating it. How, indeed, could this logic cope with a world in which *A* sometimes changes identity with *B*—or any other letter—sometimes precedes *Z*, and generally moves up and down the alphabet according to often contradictory laws of motion?

This mobility within the supernal hierarchy is particularly crucial because of RSZ's preoccupation with hierarchy in general. One of the most frequent questions explicitly or implicitly asked in the discourses is: Which is higher? The objects of comparison may be the four categories of the natural world,[394] two sefirot, prayer and study, knowledge and action, the physical and the spiritual, this world and the next, the righteous man and the penitent, or any pair on the long list of pairs comprising the outline of RSZ's worldview. Probably because of his overriding concern with axiology, few discussions were complete without at least intimating this question, which usually translates into: Which is intrinsically more valuable? Since, on the one hand, everything descends from the volatile sefirot, while, on the other, the Neoplatonic element in kabbalah decreed that everything has a *fixed* place in the hierarchy of being, what was needed was a different kind of logic that could assimilate this tension.

But, as noted, RSZ was not content to limit his speculative thinking to kabbalistic terms. He wanted to incorporate rabbinic and philosophical assumptions and terminology as well, obviously considering these to be merely different approaches to the same truths[395] (with the caveat that human philosophy could only scratch their surface, while the divinely inspired rabbis of the Talmud and the authoritative kabbalists could plumb their depths and scale their heights). Viewed historically, his endeavor is comparable to an attempt to synthesize the physics of Aristotle, Newton, and Einstein. It is true, of course, that he incorporated selectively, but this only mitigates the problem. We are faced with a kaleidoscopic corpus that resists both facile and ingenious attempts at harmonization. Our only real alternative is to analyze that corpus as it appears.

2

Man *in* God's World

The Kabbalistic Legacy

RSZ based his worldview on a set of assumptions he shared with most eighteenth-century Jewish scholars familiar with kabbalistic thought. Kabbalistic theosophy begins with the *En Sof*—the Infinite Being—which is the unknowable and unrevealed essence of God and the emanator of the *Or En Sof*, the Infinite Light that is the actual creative force of the universe. Because it is unknowable, the En Sof is also referred to as Ayin—nothingness—insofar as what cannot be known is, from man's perspective, virtually nonexistent, although in truth it is precisely and only the Ayin that constitutes absolute reality, everything else being a contingent creation or emanation. Since the "nothing" of this Ayin was for the kabbalist the source of creation, the traditional doctrine of creation from nothing (ex nihilo) was thus transformed into a concept meaning creation from God, or, as Scholem puts it, "the emergence of all things from the absolute nothingness of God."[1]

The primary emanations are known as the ten sefirot, which are the stages through which God manifests Himself in His different attributes and also constitute the archetypes of all that exists. The Or En Sof "clothes itself" in the sefirot and takes on their respective character, as water takes on the color of a colored glass into which it is poured. Whether or not the sefirot were actually identical with the Or En Sof was widely debated among early kabbalists. In the later stratum of the Zohar they are seen as vessels or tools that are neither quite identical with, nor separate from, the light they contain, whereas according to Cordovero they embody one aspect that is identical with the light and another that is separate from it.

From the early days of the Kabbalah, these ideas concerning emanation were closely linked with a theory of language. Scholem puts it well: "The process of emanation was described as a kind of revelation of the various names peculiar to God in His capacity of Creator. The God who manifests Himself is the God who expresses Himself. The God who 'called' His powers to reveal themselves named them, and, it could be said, called Himself also by appropriate names. The process by which the power of emanation manifests itself from concealment to revelation is paralleled by the manifestation of divine speech from its inner essence in thought, through sound that as yet cannot be heard, into the articulation of speech."[2]

The successive sefirot that emanate from the En Sof are: (1) Keter (Crown); (2) Ḥokhmah (Wisdom); (3) *Binah* (Understanding); (4) *Gedulah* (Greatness) or Ḥesed (Loving-kindness); (5) Gevurah (Power) or *Din* (Strict Judgment); (6) *Tifʾeret* (Beauty); (7) *Netsaḥ* (Lasting Endurance); (8) *Hod* (Majesty); (9) *Yesod* (Foundation); and (10) *Malkhut* (Kingdom). In later kabbalistic works the sefirotic order often begins with Ḥokhmah, as Keter was considered too closely united with the En Sof to be considered a separate sefirah. The related sefirah of *Daʿat* (Knowledge) was then added after Binah to complete the ten emanations. In addition to this linear order of succession, the sefirot were also grouped structurally in various symbolic forms. The most common grouping was into three triads representing the form of a man:

	Keter	
Binah	Daʿat	Ḥokhmah
Gevurah	Tifʾeret	Ḥesed
Hod	Yesod	Netsaḥ
	Malkhut	

Ḥokhmah, Binah, and Daʿat represent the three parts of the brain; Ḥesed and Gevurah, the right and left arm respectively; Tifʾeret, the torso; Netsaḥ and Hod, the right and left leg respectively; Yesod, the sexual organ; and Malkhut represents either the complete image of man or his female partner, without whom he remains incomplete. This grouping of the sefirot is related to the fact that for the kabbalist, the Scriptural allusion to the arm of God, for example, was not merely an analogy to the human arm, as it was for the medieval philosophers; it was, rather, that manifestation of Divinity that ultimately materialized as the human arm. The triads mentioned above consist schematically of Ḥokhmah-Ḥesed-Netsaḥ on the right, Binah-Gevurah-Hod on the left, and Keter or Daʿat-Tifʾeret-Yesod in the center. Each triad contains sefirot bearing a particularly close conceptual relation to each other.

Since the sefirot were also considered to be progressive manifestations of God's Names, each sefirah was said to correspond to one of these Names. Moreover, various other groupings and parallels were posited by kabbalists, such as the five upper and five lower sefirot; the first three "hidden" sefirot and the "seven sefirot of building," corresponding to the seven days of creation; and, particularly important for RSZ, the three intellective sefirot and the six emotive sefirot.

From the thirteenth century onward kabbalists began to speak of sefirot within sefirot, the idea that each sefirah comprises all the others ad infinitum. Further subdivisions and parallels were posited, such as the "620 pillars of light in Keter" (=God's Will, corresponding to the 613 Biblical and seven rabbinic commandments comprising that Will); the "32 ways of Ḥokhmah"; the "50 gates of Binah"; and the "72 bridges of Ḥesed" (corresponding to the word's numerical value). Cordovero introduced the idea of *beḥinot*—various aspects within each sefirah that help explain its connection to its predecessors and successors. Moreover, in addition to the light emanating from higher to lower sefirah, kabbalists introduced a reflected or "returning" light (*or ḥozer*) from lower sefirah to higher—particularly from last to first—that, on its return path, stimulates the differentiation of still more beḥinot.

For the kabbalist the sefirot were not only the keys to the mysteries of theosophy and cosmology but also to the interpretation of Scripture. Besides relating historical events or commandments, every verse contains symbols of the divine nature and processes. For example, the Zohar takes the first word of Genesis, *Bereshit*, and divides it into two: *Be*, here connoting "with" or "through," and *reshit*—"the beginning", that is, the first word of creation corresponding to the first sefirah, Ḥokhmah. The verse now means: God initiated the process of creation by manifesting Himself in (the sefirah of) Wisdom; the heavens and earth were created through—and indeed were potentially present in undeveloped, undifferentiated form in—His primordial Wisdom. Thus, "creation is nothing but an external development of those forces which are active and alive in God Himself."[3]

According to Luria, since God is infinite, "he was compelled to make room for the world by, as it were, abandoning a region within

Himself, a kind of mystical primordial space from which He withdrew in order to return to it in the act of creation and revelation. The first act of En Sof, the Infinite Being, is therefore not a step outside but a step inside, a movement of recoil, of falling back upon oneself, of withdrawing into oneself. Instead of emanation we have the opposite, contraction [tsimtsum]. The God who revealed Himself in firm contours was superseded by one who descends deeper into the recesses of His own Being, who concentrated Himself into Himself."[4]

Before the tsimtsum, the En Sof contained both the quality of Ḥesed—loving-kindness—and the quality of Gevurah or Din—strict judgment. But, like everything else, Din was still undifferentiated and therefore unrecognizable. The limiting, negating act of tsimtsum caused the quality of strict judgment to crystalize and become clearly defined. For tsimtsum was itself an act of strict judgment that decided how much of the Infinite Light of the En Sof would be revealed and how much concealed. Here, again, Scholem puts it well:

> It must be remembered that to the kabbalist, judgment means the imposition of limits and the correct determination of things. According to Cordovero, the quality of judgment is inherent in everything insofar as everything wishes to remain what it is, to stay within its boundaries. Hence, it is precisely in the existence of individual things that the mystical category of judgment plays an important part. If, therefore, the Midrash says that originally the world was to have been based on the quality of strict judgment, *Din*, but God, seeing that this was insufficient to guarantee its existence, added the quality of mercy, the kabbalist who follows Luria interprets this saying as follows: The first act of *tsimtsum*, in which God determines, and therefore limits, Himself is an act of *Din* which reveals the roots of this quality in all that exists; these "roots of divine judgment" subsist in chaotic mixture with the residue [*Reshimu*] of divine light which remained after the original retreat or withdrawal within the primary space of God's creation. Then a second ray of Light [Or En Sof] out of the essence of *En-Sof* brings order into chaos and sets the cosmic process into motion by separating the hidden elements and molding them into a new form.[5]

The Or En Sof descends through the four supernal worlds—*Atsilut*, *Beri'ah*, *Yetsirah*, *'Aśiyah*—each containing its own hierarchy of ten sefirot that "clothe" the light and progressively coarsen it to the point where our physical world can materialize.

Since the tsimtsum occurred everywhere equally, the resulting primordial space was circular, whereas the second ray of light that then entered constituted a straight line. Subsequently, therefore, all emanations appear both in concentric circles and linear form. "This double-facedness in the process of emanation is typical of the dialectical tendency of Lurianic kabbalah. Every stage in the development of the emanating light has not only a circular and linear aspect but also modes of both an 'inner light' [*or penimi*] within the vessels that are produced [see below] and a 'surrounding light' [*or maḳif*], as well as of *ʿatsmut ve-kelim* ('substance and vessels') and direct and reflected light [*or yashar*—or ḥozer] that are taken from the teachings of Cordovero."[6]

As noted above, although the act of tsimtsum constituted a withdrawal of the En Sof, a residue, or Reshimu, of its presence remains in the metaphysical space created by the tsimtsum, somewhat like the residue that remains in a bottle of oil that has been emptied. Later kabbalists emphasized either the Divinity of the Reshimu or, on the other hand, its "leftover" aspect; that is, the fact that it is what remained after the essence of the En Sof was withdrawn and thus the Reshimu must be not quite identical with it.

The initial configuration of divine light that emanates from the En Sof into the primordial, post-tsimtsum space is known in Lurianic kabbalah as *Adam Ḳadmon* (primordial man), which is both the immediate source of the lights that eventually became the sefirot and the metaphysical archetype of man on earth. The original lights of Adam Ḳadmon were emitted in coalesced, undifferentiated form (*aḳudim*, or bound together) and therefore required no vessels to contain them individually. Subsequently, however, Adam Ḳadmon emitted individuated bursts of light that became *ʿOlam ha-Neḳudim* (the world of dots, i.e., points of light), also referred to by Luria as *ʿOlam ha-Tohu* (the world of chaos). To remain individuated, these lights required vessels to contain and separate them, and these were emanated as the three highest sefirot. When the six lower sefirot, or vessels, were subsequently emanated, however, the lights they were to harbor proved too powerful, and the vessels shattered. This planned cosmic catastrophe, known as *Shevirat ha-Kelim* (the breaking of the vessels) scattered vessel fragments and the lights that still clung to them throughout our material world. The limiting fragments represent the power of Din, the potential source of evil on earth, whereas the lights they contain—the "288 sparks" referred to by Luria—represent the power of Ḥesed, the potential source of good on earth. All the phenomena of this world consequently contain an admixture of good and evil (or ḳelipot—shells), and it is man's task to select and separate the good from the evil, thereby elevating the sparks and restoring the ideal order.

Through fulfilling the commandments and particularly through prayer with the proper kavanot, man is empowered to achieve tikun—a mending or rectifying of the Shevirah and the restoration and reintegration of the original ontological order that was still further disrupted by Adam's fall. As Scholem puts it, "the task of man has been defined by Luria . . . as the restoration of his primordial spiritual structure or *Gestalt.* That is the task for every one of us, for every soul contains the potentialities of this spiritual appearance, outraged and degraded by the fall of Adam, whose soul contained all souls. From this soul of souls, sparks have scattered in all directions and become diffused into matter. The problem is to reassemble them, to lift them to their proper place, and to restore the spiritual nature of man in its original splendor as God conceived it."[7]

According to Luria, man's soul has 613 spiritual parts corresponding to the body's 613 physical parts and to the 613 commandments. By fulfilling all the commandments man achieves the tikun of body, soul, the material world with which he performed the commandments, and, ultimately, all the supernal worlds that respond to man's actions. He has this power because, like God, he encompasses the entire cosmos in his being and, in fact, was created to complete and perfect the creative process that God initiated. "If the *sefirot* in which God reveals Himself assume the form of man, making him a microcosm in himself . . . then man on earth is obviously capable of exerting an influence upon the macrocosm and upon primordial man above. Indeed, it is this which bestows on him the enormous importance and dignity that the kabbalists went to great lengths to describe. Because he and he alone has been granted the gift of free will, it lies in his power to either advance or disrupt through his actions the unity of what takes place in the upper and lower worlds."[8]

Ontology

The kabbalistic legacy outlined above was the foundation on which RSZ built his Hasidic ontology. This ontology, like most of RSZ's thought, revolves around an interrelated series of complementary opposites.[9] The most fundamental polarity is, of course, that which exists between God and the universe. Generally RSZ uses this polarity either to emphasize God's transcendence or, like Cordovero, as a last defense against implications of change or multiplicity in His Essence.[10] On the one hand, His creating and maintaining the universe does not link His Essence to it in any way. On the other hand, although from our limited perspective a real, multifarious cosmos exists apart from Him, from His infinite, all-encompassing viewpoint it is totally nullified within His unity. The higher the existent in the chain of being, the greater its perception of this unity. Occasionally RSZ grasps one antipode to emphasize how God is totally separate from creation, and occasionally he grasps the other to point out that creation is really submerged in God.[11] At least once he reverses himself and explains that the unity of Ḥokhmah of Atsilut with the Godhead, usually described as absolute,[12] is actually only relative and valid only from Ḥokhmah's perspective. From the perspective of the Godhead, Ḥokhmah is merely a discrete garment.[13] Thus, the higher one goes, the more multiplicity one perceives. This is one of many instances in which RSZ uses the same concept in opposite ways. The unity of Ḥokhmah of Atsilut with the Godhead, generally cited to support a panentheistic viewpoint, is used here to support a theistic one.

Closely related to this existential pair is an epistemological one: the hidden and the revealed (*heʿelam-gilui*), sometimes identified with the philosophical potential-actual or substance-form.[14] Usually RSZ uses this to explain how all change, including creation, is only apparent, since everything actual already existed previously *in potentia*. Coal contains hidden fire; a seed contains, in undifferentiated form, the full-grown plant; a drop of semen, the entire fetus.[15] Similarly, in kabbalistic terminology, the ten sefirot of Atsilut were originally hidden in the En Sof, and He had only to reveal them. With respect to His Essence, where all opposites fuse, the hidden and the revealed are one, but with respect to the sefirot and lower worlds, creation is distinguishable from Creator. Thus, the original tsimtsum, which made finite existence possible, constituted concealment and change only from their imperfect perspective, not from His.[16]

In one discourse RSZ reaches this standard conclusion only after suggesting that the act of tsimtsum did not conceal the light but only restrained it from being revealed.[17] In another he insists that God did not actively reveal the Or En Sof, but that it was revealed spontaneously (though voluntarily).[18] Such attempts suggest that the hidden and the revealed are not simply two aspects of the same thing, but that even from God's perspective the transition from one to the other constitutes real change. Indeed, in one discourse RSZ clearly states that there is an unbridgeable gap between them, since what is revealed is never the essence of a thing but merely an emanation from it.[19] Similarly, Atsilut is frequently portrayed as a divine emanation completely separate from its Source—a paradoxical state reflecting its role as the intermediary between Creator and creation.[20]

The idea of such an intermediary is a key element in RSZ's metaphysics.[21] Whereas Zeno of Elea tried to demonstrate the impossibility of motion and plurality by positing that for any two things to be separate, the intervention of a third—or of a part within each of the two—is necessary, and so on ad infinitum,[22] RSZ used the same concept for the very opposite purpose. Disregarding the logic of infinite regress,[23] he posited that for the hidden to become revealed, for Creator to emanate creation and the unbridgeable gap to be bridged, an intermediary comprising aspects of both is necessary. The transition (i.e., the movement) from potential to actual, from unity to a semblance of plurality, takes place within this hybrid existent.[24] The general idea of two opposite first principles requiring, for one reason or another, a third to serve as intermediary, has both philosophical and kabbalistic roots.[25] In addition to all ten sefirot of Atsilut, various discourses identify the intermediary between God and creation as Keter or Ḥokhmah of Atsilut.[26]

Once the emanation process begins, two opposite types of light appear: the transcendent and the immanent, usually referred to by the Zoharic *sovev kol ʿalmin* and *memale kol ʿalmin*, but also by the Lurianic *ʿigulim-yosher* and *makif-penimi*.[27] Sovev is generally defined as the absolutely infinite light of the En Sof that necessarily remains concealed from all finite existents (until "the future").[28] Because the terms used to identify it conjure up the image of a circle, RSZ occasionally takes pains to dispel this misconception. Sovev, he insists, is not spatial: It is, rather, hidden and is therefore said to "encompass" apprehension, that is, to be beyond its outer limits.[29] Elsewhere, however, he does not hesitate to use standard Lurianic symbolism that graphically describes sovev as actually encircling creation; or to link ʿigulim (circles) with the spheres of medieval astronomy (and the Godhead with Maimonides' First Mover); to divide them into upper and lower halves, and to observe that, like a circle, sovev has no gradations but is everywhere equal.[30] Similarly, one discourse emphatically denies that sovev is concealed, insisting that it is actually revealed but undifferentiated light that, unlike memale, does not invest each vessel according to its capacity but rather bestows its emanation equally on all. Another discourse grants sovev an even greater degree of revelation than is manifest in memale. But both go on to explain that this is only from sovev's perspective, not from the perspective of the receiving vessel, which does indeed fail to perceive it.[31]

One discourse compares sovev and memale to, respectively, the force propelling a thrown stone and the power of the fingers moving a pen, that is, to a latent versus perceptible form of the divine presence.[32] Other discourses speak variously of sovev as identical with His Essence (*ʿAtsmut*, or the Godhead);[33] as flowing from the aspect of Malkhut within the En Sof;[34] as everything above Atsilut;[35] as identical with Keter (=Will);[36] with the Will to Will;[37] or, in philosophical terms, with His omnipotence, or with His knowledge that encompasses all existents and is the instrument of His providence.[38]

What emerges despite all the inconsistencies and involved discussions is that sovev is the divine light transcending creation. It is that aspect of God that is furthest and equally removed from all finite being, both physical and spiritual. It alone can therefore give rise to gross matter.[39] And memale, of course, is its opposite: relatively finite, graded according to the recipient vessel it permeates, it is depicted as a line that has a top, a bottom, and all the levels in between. It is the "koaḥ ha-poʿel be-nifʿal," the immanent light that continuously sustains creation, the active creating force as opposed to sovev's detached, passive role. In sefirotic terms it is identified as Malkhut of Atsilut, which descends to create and vitalize the lower worlds.[40]

Sovev and memale are explicitly linked to Luria's worlds of *Tohu* and Tiḳun, possibly the central pair in RSZ's metaphysics.[41] Different discourses describe them in philosophic, symbolic, aggadic, or personified terms. In one discourse Tohu is linked with the word in Genesis and with Naḥmanides' interpretation of it as hylic matter.[42] In others it is variously identified as Keter, aḳudim, *neḳudim*, maḳif, ʿigulim, or Gevurah—this last because of the intensity of its light.[43] It is the primordial realm of unlimited, undifferentiated light whose vessels were too small and too few to contain it and therefore shattered during the planned catastrophe of Shevirat ha-Kelim.[44] It is the original world, which, the Midrash states, God created using only Din—here interpreted by RSZ in the sense of power—before "realizing" its infeasibility and combining Din with *Raḥamim* (mercy, compassion) to achieve a perfect synthesis.[45] But an unlimited emanation also suggests infinite beneficence—that is, Raḥamim—so that we might have expected the aggadic sequence to be reversed: first Raḥamim and then the necessary limitation of Din (used in its traditional kabbalistic sense); and, in fact, RSZ does reverse it in one discourse.[46] Similarly, since Tohu is not merely an emanation but an entire *world* that was destroyed, the aggadah portraying God as a builder and destroyer of primordial worlds is invoked.[47] That the other aggadah speaks of *combining* Din with Raḥamim, without first destroying Tohu, was obviously considered insignificant.

Studiedly avoiding any identification of Din with evil and any intimation of catharsis as the underlying cause for the Shevirah,[48] RSZ prefers to explain it by ascribing to Tohu certain moral flaws. The vessels, but not the lights,[49] of Tohu were guilty of hubris, selfishness, and uncooperativeness. In a word, they lacked modesty. Each felt completely self-sufficient and was totally uninterested in its colleague's situation. They were also small, that is, narrow-minded. Each would accept only its own aspect of the Or En Sof, and this aspect, unmitigated by its opposite, was irradiated in all its infinite intensity. Since the Or En Sof is perfect, in that it incorporates all opposites, the vessels were overwhelmed by its plenitude and shattered.[50]

Tiḳun, of course, as the term indicates, came into being to correct Tohu's flaws. Whereas Tohu is a turbulent world of excess and discord, Tiḳun is an oasis of moderation and harmony. Amorphous, sprawling matter is given definite form, unbridled power (Gevurah) is restrained by compassion, the lights are weakened, the vessels are increased in number and size and acquire the tolerance and self-effacement necessary for cooperating with each other. The strong, wilful character of Tohu is transformed into the meek, pliant character of Tiḳun. The hierarchy of Tohu's elements is reversed as well—what is highest in Tohu is lowest in Tiḳun.[51]

But, one may ask, if the lights are weakened and filtered through more vessels, does this not imply a diminution of the divine presence and therefore a move toward imperfection rather than perfection? According to Luria this does indeed seem to be the case. The divine presence is diminished, and the dross that was hidden in the world of Tohu is thereby allowed to acquire a more discrete existence so that man can confront and purify it.[52] But RSZ, apparently following R. Abraham "ha-Malakh," consistently emphasized *revelation* of the divine light as the final purpose of creation,[53] and he could hardly accept this contrary implication. Also, if self-nullification was, as the Maggid taught, the key to realizing that purpose, surely the world of Tiḳun must be primarily defined by this trait. Yet there was no getting around the fact that the lights of Tiḳun were weaker than the lights of Tohu or that self-nullification was hardly the mainstay of Luria's Tiḳun.

Here, as in many similar instances of confrontation between conflicting theories and assumptions, RSZ resolves the problem by introducing a mediating element. It is true, he reluctantly admits, that the lights of Tohu are weakened, but, according to the Maggid, this is only the result of an overpowering infusion of the Or En Sof through that most self-nullificatory of all vessels, Ḥokhmah.[54] This emphasis on Ḥokhmah's role in Tiḳun is primarily RSZ's contribution and, not surprisingly, it dovetails nicely with his religioethical thought. The "lower seven" sefirot—the emotive vessels—immediately recognize the superiority of this first of the "upper three"—the intellective vessels—and nullify themselves before the light of the En Sof it contains; thus they are able to act in unison. Self-nullification, in other words, is both the prerequisite for, and the effect of, divine revelation. But, one might ask, which comes first? The reason given for the infusion of the unifying Or En Sof is the commingling of the lights of Tiḳun and the resultant "perfect place" (*atar shelim*) for this revelation, a place that lacks nothing because every entity now contains every other entity and that therefore beckons to the perfect light of the En Sof. Yet in the same discourses the reason given for the existence of this perfect place is the infusion of this light.[55] Again, one might be tempted to ask: Since the light of the En Sof is identical with the light originally permeating the vessels of Tohu, is RSZ's explanation not tantamount to asserting that when the light is too strong the vessels break, but when it is still stronger they unite and flourish?[56] According to some discourses, this is precisely the case. The lights of Tohu were so powerful because of their absolute union with the Or En Sof. But they were too dependent on this union, so that when they were forced away from it by being channeled into vessels, they lost control and burst their bounds. "In the future," however, they will reascend to their original status and remain there forever.[57]

RSZ resorts to similar kabbalistic dialectics to explain the relation between Tohu-Tiḳun and *orot-kelim*. Since intensity of the light and inadequacy of the vessels are the salient characteristics of Tohu, while the opposite is true of Tiḳun, one would expect Tohu to be the source of all subsequent lights (orot) and Tiḳun to be the source of all subsequent vessels (kelim). But in several discourses RSZ asserts that just the opposite is true—and for two opposite reasons.

1. The lights of Tohu are identified with neḳudim—points of light that do not interact to attenuate their individual potency and that therefore overpower their respective vessels. By doing so, they, like the lights of ʿigulim, transcend these vessels and become circular, encom-

passing lights, or maḳif. But since encompassing—that is, containing—the lights of Atsilut is precisely the function of the *vessels* of Atsilut, their source must be Tohu. The lights of Tiḳun, on the other hand, are adequately contained and therefore persevere to become the source of all subsequent orot.[58]

2. The lights of ʿigulim, whose source is Tohu, are identified with aḳudim, the emanation stage preceding neḳudim in which all the lights are intermingled, undifferentiated, and "concealed," that is, contained only in potentia in one vessel. Since concealment is a form of limitation, and limitation of the light is the function of the kelim, ʿigulim and, by implication, Tohu, must be their source. The lights of Tiḳun, however, are fully developed and revealed within their vessels, and since revelation is the function of the orot, Tiḳun must be their source.[59]

Thus, while reason *1* attributes kelim to Tohu because of its overpowering light, reason *2* attributes kelim to Tohu because of its concealment of the light.

In his many discussions of the orot-kelim relation, Cordovero essentially exhausted the subject. He explored all four possibilities: The kelim are absolutely united with the orot and therefore equally divine; they are not absolutely united; on one level they are and on another level they are not; they are and are not. At one point or another he reached each of these conclusions, illustrating them by means of various analogies, most often by the body-soul relation.[60] RSZ—or Rabbi Menaḥem Mendel—acknowledges his indebtedness to Cordovero[61] and, not surprisingly, goes virtually no further. The analogies may differ slightly, but Cordovero's paradoxical picture remains unchanged. Like the other ontological pairs, orot-kelim was really an attempt to bridge the gap between Creator and creation by proxy, each member of each pair representing one of the two. Since God is omnipotent, He can bridge the unbridgeable. But how? According to Luria the first step must be self-limitation—tsimtsum—an idea that was adumbrated, although not emphasized or developed, by Cordovero.[62] God through His omnipotence delimits His limitless presence to allow finite realms and beings (to appear) to coexist with Him. His presence is represented by the orot, the containment of that presence by the kelim. They flow from complementary powers within Him—the orot from His power to emanate infinitely, the kelim from His even greater power to restrict that emanation, to make it relatively finite, and thereby to permit the existence of finite existents. In Atsilut and above, the orot and kelim are said to be one with Him and with each other. Yet they cannot be considered identical, for if they were, creation would continue to be impossible.[63]

The same tension appears in RSZ's discussions of the four supernal worlds. The lights and vessels of Atsilut are described as being infinitely higher than the sefirot of the other worlds because they alone are united with their Emanator. But this does not prevent RSZ from insisting that there is a greater gap between Atsilut and the Emanator than between Atsilut and the lower worlds. Thus, occasionally Atsilut is set at one pole, with the lower three worlds at the other, and occasionally it is grouped with them in opposition to the Emanator.[64] Similarly, although Atsilut is described as transcending every created intellect,[65] RSZ spares no effort to make its uniqueness comprehensible.

The principle of opposing pairs applies within the ten sefirot of Atsilut as well. Each has either an opposing-complementary partner or serves as mediator between an opposing pair. Each has an infinite number of opposing-complementary inner and outer aspects and is categorized within one of several pairs of opposing-complementary or mediating groups: the intellective or upper group versus the emotive or lower group (with Malkhut and Keter, the first and the last, as a kind of separate group);[66] and right versus left, with the center mediating. The tension between these aspects, pairs, and groups reflects the innate tension within the Godhead, where the desire to exercise His creative power to its fullest extent—ad infinitum—clashes with the realization that to do so would defeat the purpose of that desire: the actualization of a form of creation capable of assimilating that creative power.[67] But since God transcends and thus unites opposites, He combined the two into a vehicle for creation. In kabbalistic terminology, Ḥesed is opposed by Gevurah, Tifʾeret[68] mediates to combine them harmoniously according to the dictates of Ḥokhmah and Binah as combined by Daʿat, and Malkhut implements the plan.

Whereas Ḥesed is always identified with the infinite abundance of divine emanations and beneficence, Gevurah, depending on the discourse, is either synonymous with the restriction of Ḥesed or with a far more powerful outpouring of divine vitality. Ḥesed, like Ḥokhmah, its senior colleague in the right triad, is "cool," steady and serene. It is a "descending" emanation and is known as or yashar—light emanating directly from the Source. Gevurah is a "hot," pulsating, dynamic emanation surging upward and therefore known as or ḥozer (which in turn is associated with the infinitely powerful or maḳif).

Ḥesed-Gevurah give rise to, or are themselves offshoots of, the emanation-return cycle known as *ratso-shov* or *maṭi velo maṭi*, and symbolized organically by the processes of inhaling-exhaling or systole-diastole.[69] As Scholem puts it: "All existence presupposes a dialectical, two-fold movement; nothing comes into being by a simple one-way action. Everything subsists by the combinations of retraction and emanation. The rhythm of the living God, like that of organic forms, including man, can be described as a double process of inhaling and exhaling. . . . The double rhythm of regression and egression is at the root of everything that exists."[70]

RSZ's discussions of ratso-shov (lit., running [and] returning, from Ezekiel 1:14) indicate that each vitalizing emanation bursts forth for an actual moment of time and then returns to its source. Indeed, it is the duration of this cycle that gives rise to time. Since successively lower worlds are successively more distant from the Source, the time required for the cycle increases, and the minutes of ʿAśiyah, for example, are much longer than those of Yetsirah. At the Source itself, past, present, and future are instantaneous.[71]

As with the other sefirot, the question of whether something reflects Ḥesed or Gevurah depends on perspective, since every emanation is Ḥesed from the beneficiary's viewpoint but requires restraint on the emanator's part to avoid overwhelming the recipient's more limited vessel. In addition, like the other sefirot of Tiḳun, these two are composite configurations (*partsufim*) of all ten. Each is named according to its predominating component, but it has the potential to submerge that one and bring its opposite to the fore. Gevurah of Ḥesed for example, outwardly resembles Gevurah of Gevurah, although its goal is actually Ḥesed. The original tsimtsum and the creation of the limiting vessels of Tiḳun belong in this category, since they were acts of concealment for the sake of revelation.[72] The nature of a divine act, in other words, is determined primarily by its purpose, not its immediate effect.

Turning our attention to the intellective sefirot: Keter, Ḥokhmah, Binah, and Daʿat are inextricably interrelated. Keter comprises a higher aspect, ʿAtiḳ Yomin, identified with the faculty of pleasure, and a lower, *Arikh Anpin*, identified with will. Unlike all other human faculties, which are "inner" powers residing in some part of the body, will and pleasure encompass it; they are transcendent powers whose rays can be beamed anywhere. In one sense, Keter is most closely related to Ḥokhmah, the first flash, or "point," of intellect, and both are occasionally referred to as Ayin (nothingness)—an emanation having no real separate existence, a level so far above human comprehension that it may be considered nonexistent. In another sense, Keter—specifically its higher aspect—is most closely related to Binah, which develops and ramifies the "point" of Ḥokhmah, for only at this stage of understanding is intellectual pleasure fully discernible. In kabbalistic terminology: ʿAtiḳ is present in Ḥokhmah but not revealed until Ḥokhmah develops into Binah. Like Keter, Binah, which encompasses the incipient knowledge of Ḥokhmah, is termed maḳif. And in a third sense, Keter is most closely related to Daʿat and Tifʾeret, since it is what gives them their ability to synthesize opposites. Keter itself has this ability because it commands the absolute respect of the sefirot and convinces them to lay aside their differences and unite.[73] Keter, Daʿat and Tifʾeret are therefore used more or less interchangeably in various discourses.

Similarly, Ḥokhmah and Binah, the "two inseparable colleagues" (Zohar, III, 4a), are often said to possess similar qualities. Both, for example are capable of resisting the ḳelipot because, among other reasons, they were not (significantly) affected by the Shevirah. Like Binah, Ḥokhmah is termed maḳif. Different discourses identify each as the source from which man derives the ability to sift good from evil.[74] But RSZ, following the Maggid and R. Abraham, magnifies the role of Ḥokhmah far more than do Luria and Cordovero. It apparently earned this distinction because of its many important connotations. For RSZ it was simultaneously the highest aspect of divine reason; the sefirah with which the Or En Sof is most closely united; the supernal source of the Torah; the vessel containing the divine spark in every Jewish soul; the instrument of Tiḳun and thus the chief weapon against evil; the essence of self-nullification and thus of the supreme religious virtue; and that human faculty that, by nature, rules the passions (with the assistance of Binah and Daʿat) and thus makes morality possible. It was both the blueprint and the instrument—through Malkhut (= *Ḥokhmah Tataʾah* [Lower Ḥokhmah]), its administrator—for creation and for its consummation.[75]

RSZ frequently identifies Ḥokhmah—used in the sense of reason—with pleasure, alluding to the dual meaning of *taʿam*: reason and taste, that is, a pleasurable sensation. When pleasure is clothed in Ḥokhmah it becomes taʿam. Conversely, pleasure is Ḥokhmah's source, which is why the pleasure is greatest at the moment of an intellectual breakthrough. In other words, over and above its rational aspect, Ḥokhmah is the vehicle for intellectual pleasure, the supreme form of the supreme faculty. In several discourses RSZ glorifies the exquisite pleasure that intellectual apprehension provides, and Ḥokhmah, the faculty of discovery, contributes the initial thrill of that pleasure.[76]

Pleasure and Reason—ʿAtiḳ Yomin and Ḥokhmah—are also closely related to Will—Arikh Anpin—because every desire must, according to RSZ, have some rationale, and the ultimate rationale is spiritual pleasure.[77] It is a commonplace that God's reason for any act—including, of course, creation—often transcends man's intellect and may therefore appear arbitrary or unjust. RSZ insists that there is invariably and necessarily a transcendent reason hidden in the recesses of the divine Mind (*Moaḥ Setimaʾah*), which is also the first vessel for divine Pleasure. This Pleasure, in turn, derives from the hidden essence of the Godhead and is its highest power. In simple terms, God's ultimate motive for acting any given way is pleasure. The reason He derives pleasure from one thing rather than another is unfathomable, as is the possibility for a perfect, changeless Being to derive pleasure at all.[78]

Occasionally the pleasure He derives from man's conquest of evil is described as self-generated by an apparently arbitrary act of will,[79] but generally RSZ appears reluctant to attribute true arbitrariness to God, and one must assume that the act of will is itself rooted in a reason that is linked to divine pleasure. Like the Maggid, RSZ sees evil as a vehicle for increasing this pleasure, since it provides man with the necessary adversary to overcome. Nothing, it seems, increases divine pleasure more than the process comprising: (1) the strife between good and evil, (2) the subjugation of evil, and (3) its transformation into good.[80]

Here, again, the Heraclitean element in RSZ's thought comes to the fore. "All things come to pass through the complusion of strife," said Heraclitus. "Opposition brings concord. Out of discord comes the fairest harmony." RSZ would agree completely. He would fully appreciate Heraclitus's observation that "in the circumference of a circle the beginning and end are common."[81] For RSZ the circle symbolizes sovev, the all-encompassing light where the highest emanations—those closest to the Godhead—and the lowest meet as equals. There is, in fact, a natural affinity between the highest and the lowest extending through all levels of creation. "The feet of Adam Ḳadmon end at the bottom of ʿAśiyah, close to the light of sovev"; or, as he frequently quotes from *Sefer Yetsirah*, "their end is wedged into their beginning and their beginning into their end." God's works, like God Himself, have no beginning or end, that is, no absolute hierarchy. The purpose of any purposeful project, RSZ observes, is conceived first and realized last; the original thought comes to fruition only in the final act.[82]

Although this thought-metaphor simply states the potential-actual relationship between conception and completion, it is subtly transformed when RSZ immediately and characteristically shifts to his more common emanation-garment terminology.[83] The original thought becomes the first and highest emanation or complex of emanations, the first sefirah or supernal world or configuration. The completed act becomes its lowest counterpart. The highest is now not simply realized but *clothed* in the lowest. Because the world of kabbalistic symbolism is a world of individual power centers that interact with each other by encompassing or permeating—clothing or being clothed—it is perfectly natural for RSZ to make this transition from abstract thought process to (symbolically) concrete supernal entities. Indeed, as we shall see, even when expatiating on thought processes themselves, RSZ treats each stage as if it was a concrete entity originating in a specific location and descending from there to reveal itself by permeating or encompassing a lower element in the hierarchy of thought. In our case, since being encompassed implies subordination to the encompassing entity,[84] the fact that the highest is clothed in the lowest suggests that the lowest possesses something the highest does not. It is only for this reason, in fact, that God condescended to create a world infinitely removed from His perfection: He realized that He would be not only a benefactor but also a beneficiary.[85] And this is another reason for Tiḳun's superiority over Tohu, since only in Tiḳun does the lowest sefirah combine with, and contribute to, all its superiors, including the highest.[86]

A thought-process metaphor that simply illustrates the link between origin and outcome has thus been transformed into the same principle of existential reciprocity expressed by or yashar–or ḥozer and ratso-shov. Everything is, or should be, both benefactor and recipient. This holds true, however, for the relation betwen *any* two levels in the hierarchy. As the Maggid's faithful disciple, RSZ required a principle that would specifically link first and last, and he formulated this as: "Whatever is higher descends lower"[87] (i.e., the higher the emanation, the lower it descends). An interesting attempt to explain this phenomenon is found in an early discourse in which RSZ, like the Maggid, equates "high" with incomprehensible or unassimilable. The highest vitalizes the lowest because, unlike its superiors, the lowest can never assimilate this life force and therefore does not expire in the ecstasy of delight it would otherwise achieve.[88] Another discourse explains that the highest sefirah—Ḥokhmah—has a natural affinity for the lowest existent—inanimate matter—because both are characterized by extreme self-nullification.[89] Usually, however, the principle is taken as axiomatic. It is used to explain, among other things, the divine soul's descent into an inanimate vessel of flesh and blood; the superiority of the physical act to the spiritual thought; man's need to sustain himself by eating lower (i.e., actually higher) forms of life and drinking inanimate water; man's being created after the lower creatures; the ability of only the greatest sage to elucidate the most abstruse concepts for the simplest student; the reason that a king (= the lowest sefirah, Malkhut) wears a crown (= the highest sefirah, Keter); the greater humility and greater compassion of greater men (their empathy descends lower); and to explain why the lion, a nonkosher animal, is on the right side of the divine Chariot, while the ox is on the left; beasts are physically more powerful than men; their self-effacement is greater; they taste better; sacrificing them helps expiate sin; bread, although made from the lower flora, satiates more than does the meat of fauna; the reflected heat near the ground is greater than that of the air above it.[90]

Most important, perhaps, it is also used to explain the power of evil. Since the intense lights of Tohu preceded the weaker lights of Tiḳun, and evil resulted from the breaking of the vessels in Tohu, it is clear that those divine sparks still attached to the fragments are far more potent than the lights of Tiḳun. It is, in fact, for this very reason that these sparks remained attached even when the vessels fell to form the lowest realm of creation, the domain of the *siṭra aḥra* (the "other side," the realm of evil). Only the highest emanation can descend to such depths, retain its identity, and eventually ascend again after having fulfilled its mission.[91]

Like most kabbalists, RSZ describes the siṭra aḥra in personalistic terms.[92] Although its personality varies, depending on the purpose of the discourse, its predominant traits are, not surprisingly, those of Tohu—pride, greed, selfishness.[93] In some discourses it nevertheless appears as a faithful servant completely subordinate to the holy side but endowed with the ability to simulate independence and thereby mislead man.[94] Elsewhere it is depicted as a vile, sinister creature with a voracious appetite for holy sustenance—the immanent source of all life—which it completely assimilates and which consequently loses its holy, vitalizing power. The creature must then be sustained through the encompassing light of maḳif (= Tohu), which it cannot assimilate. Since the immanent light has lost its identity and the encompassing light completely transcends it, the creature believes itself to be independent of the holy side.[95] Other discourses go further and depict it, in classical Zoharic-Lurianic style, as an insatiable beast that is not appeased by its allotted portion of ḳedushah (holiness) but gluttonously gobbles up more than it can digest. In "the future" it will therefore bring it all up and die.[96]

The general method for overcoming the siṭra aḥra naturally varies according to the way it is portrayed. If it is a reasonable, well-meaning harlot, it must be summarily rebuffed. If, however, it is a mindless, rapacious fiend, resistance is futile. It must be either appeased or allowed to gorge itself into self-destruction (this method, of course, is limited to the inner dynamics of the supernal realms and is never advocated as a strategy for man).[97] One discourse suggests, in effect, that both portraits are faithful. The first symbolizes the siṭra aḥra as it appears in Atsilut, the second as it appears below Atsilut, particularly in ʿAśiyah.[98] But this hardly mitigates the tension between Luria's mythological descriptions, which often seem to attribute independent reality to evil, and RSZ's own obvious tendency toward the opposite conclusion. Like Cordovero, he would have preferred an ontology in which the ḳelipot have no real existence; in which they are essentially forces of good in disguise. If they must be considered real, he would have preferred to limit the sustenance, and therefore the power, they draw from ḳedushah to the lower, emotive sefirot and, again, to only the "left side," the side of Gevurah. But apparently his Lurianic sources forced him to qualify if not contravene these preferred principles in various discourses.[99] Moreoever, the doctrines of tsimtsum and Shevirah actually pointed to the ontological primacy, and therefore supremacy, of the ḳelipot. The first divine act was after all, self-limitation—that is, Gevurah, the source of all subsequent concealments of divine light and thus the ultimate source of the ḳelipot, whose function is to conceal that light. Similarly, the first world was Tohu, the realm of isolated sefirot whose self-centeredness caused the Shevirah and the eventual appearance of the self-centered ḳelipot. These relations were undoubtedly among the kabbalistic considerations that suggested the higher-lower dictum, an idea perfectly suited to the paradoxical logic and complementary polarity that characterize RSZ's metaphysics.

Several variations of this useful principle appear in different contexts:

1. Its converse: what descends lower ascends higher.
2. What is higher naturally descends lower.
3. What is higher has the ability to descend lower (and elevate the lower).
4. What descends lower must be higher.
5. What is lower requires a higher emanation to elevate it.
6. What is lower provides a darker backdrop for the higher emanation, thereby revealing it more.
7. What is higher is more sensitive to what is lower.
8. What is higher can be revealed only in what is (commensurately) lower.[100]

As we shall see in subsequent chapters, the selective use or nonuse of one variation or another enabled RSZ ostensibly to resolve many other perplexing problems.

His approach to the problem of evil includes an explanation employing another fairly typical line of reasoning that deserves separate mention. As noted above, a basic Maggidic premise was that evil is the instrument of divine Pleasure, for God delights in its transformation into good. In one discourse, RSZ develops this idea further: Not only does God delight in this transformation but He has also obviously chosen to reveal this fact to us. Why? So that by remembering this delight we can withstand the suffering involved in this transformation. We must remember that, although good and evil are meaningless to Him, He nevertheless desires this transformation because He delights in it. But, we may ask, why does He not delight in something that does not cause suffering? Because, we are informed, pleasure is contingent on change, and God delights in the *novelty* of this transformation; however, this great transformation requires so great an effort that suffering is its necessary concomitant. The pleasure He derives from novelty is not, of course, innate, as it is in man, but is willed by Him for the purpose of benefiting creation. Ultimately, therefore, God derives pleasure from this transformation because He desires to derive pleasure from it; and He desires to derive pleasure from it because He is absolutely good and therefore desires to benefit others.[101]

The Universe and Its History

It is a commonplace that Maimonides, through his *Guide* and the philosophical parts of the *Mishneh Torah,* was the primary mentor of most of the philosophically oriented Jewish thinkers who followed him. He was, in other words, the father of the Jewish version of philosophical exegesis and metaphysics. Among kabbalists the same pioneering position was occupied by Naḥmanides, who, through his Torah commentary, became the father of kabbalistic exegesis and metaphysics. His stature as a religious and halakhic authority made him the preeminent kabbalist of his time. His disciples' pupils, through their supercommentaries, further disseminated his views and enhanced their authoritativeness. The final accolade was bestowed by R. Isaac Luria, who claimed supremacy for his own kabbalah and invalidated the works of all other "post"-Zoharic kabbalists—after Naḥmanides, whom Vital calls "the last of the true kabbalists." Since Naḥmanides' work was by far better known and more accessible than his predecessors', this was tantamount to naming him the supreme pre-Lurianic kabbalist.[102]

On issues over which Maimonides and Naḥmanides disagreed, kabbalists naturally and invariably followed Naḥmanides. On issues on which they agreed, it was, by the eighteenth century at least, heretical to demur. Creation ex nihilo was such an issue. A cornerstone of the *Guide,* it was unequivocally affirmed by Naḥmanides at the beginning of his Torah commentary. In both works it meant, as the words imply, bringing into being something from nothing by divine fiat.[103] But for Neoplatonists and kabbalists it also meant emanation of forms or sefirot out of God's essence. The crucial differences concerning divine will and the possibility of multiplicity implied by the two interpretations were already recognized by Isaac Israeli (ninth–tenth centuries), who originated a theory combining both. Wisdom, the first form, appears ex nihilo, and it then emanates the subsequent forms.[104]

RSZ's awareness of the problem was apparently limited to the semantic incongruity of referring to God as "nothing" and creation as "something." That is, in any case, all he chose to touch on in his discourses. Various discourses offer various solutions. One echoes Israeli: Ḥokhmah was created ex nihilo; the lower sefirot emanate from it. Thus Ḥokhmah, usually identified as Ayin (nothing), appears here as the first "*yesh*" (something).[105] Another discourse distinguishes between Atsilut, which is emanated, and the lower worlds, which receive the emanation only after it has broken through the concealing "curtain" (*parsa*) and has therefore become a new light.[106] This is, of course, essentially Israeli's solution in reverse. A third distinguishes between the spiritual worlds, which were emanated, and the physical world, which constitutes an entity of a completely different, infinitely lower order and therefore had to be created ex nihilo by the infinite power of sovev.[107] A fourth takes a purely emanationist position and solves the semantic problem by pointing out that the chief instrument of creation is Malkhut, a lowly ray of the Divine quite separate from His essence and thus aptly termed "Nothing."[108] A fifth reverses this approach and identifies the Ayin from which everything—including Ḥokhmah—comes into being as the creative ray (= potential) originally concealed and nullified in God's essence. When this ray reveals itself (i.e., when the potential is actualized), the yesh appears.[109] A sixth discourse, utilizing a standard kabbalistic definition, identifies Ayin with Ḥokhmah, yesh with Binah. Thus creation ex nihilo means the emanation of Binah from Ḥokhmah.[110]

But however the physical universe came into being, it is so far removed from the spiritual worlds that an intermediary is necessary to connect them. RSZ sometimes assigns this role to the angels, whose nature he discusses frequently and in considerable detail. Here, too, aggadic-Zoharic imagery apparently merged in his mind with Maimonidean philosophy to produce beings of contradictory qualities. On the one hand they appear as Maimonides' "natural and psychic forces," ranging from natural phenomena and human faculties and instincts to incorporeal "separate intellects."[111] Occasionally they are associated or identified with the spheres and stars, God's administrative assistants.[112] In any case they are impersonal powers, as fixed as the natural order they govern. Among their lower echelons are the "seventy princes" (Daniel 10:13, 20) who are responsible for sustaining the seventy nations;[113] but even the highest among them—the intellect of the sphere encompassing the universe—is a this-worldly being in the sense that its existence is predicated on the existence of the sensible world.

On the other hand they appear, to put it bluntly, as spiritualized humans. They are companions and servants of both God and man. Just as, according to the kabbalists, kabbalah transcends philosophy, these kabbalistic angels transcend the philosophical ones; their lowest stratum begins approximately where Maimonides' highest angelic stratum ends.[114] Like their philosophical counterparts, they are often compared with the holy, disembodied souls of Israel. Like these souls, they are to be found even in Atsilut.[115] Unlike them, they possess a five-hundred-mile-long body consisting of a subtle form of fire or air, or both. They therefore have the ability to materialize into visible forms.[116] Again, unlike the souls, it takes them time to flash from one part of the world to another.[117] Some are eternal; others live a week; still others, a day.[118] Among the eternal angels some are more, others are less eternal than the souls.[119] All possess distinctive personalities. They have names, and special interests and desires.[120] Some have achieved self-nullification, others have not and may therefore commit an angelic form of sin.[121] Since they originate in Tohu, they have strong, one-sided personalities (unlike the souls, which originate in Tiḳun and are pliant, multifaceted, and versatile). The angels known as the *Ḥayyot* (lit., beasts) of the Chariot are therefore directly responsible for the beasts of the earth, who share the same source and the same one-sidedness. For this reason the Ḥayyot used to derive intense pleasure from the sweet savor of the animal souls, their kindred spirits, that rose from the Temple altar.[122] Man's animal soul also descends from these Ḥayyot, and contemplating the fervent angelic Service during the blessings preceding *Ḳeri᾽at Shema* can therefore move this soul to similar ecstasy. The soul thus receives Love and Fear from the angels.[123] But while their place in the supernal hierarchy is immutable, man's soul can ascend ever higher, and his spiritual potential is unlimited.[124] Indeed, by studying Torah and fulfilling the other commandments, particularly when these acts are coupled with the proper kayanah, man actually creates and sustains certain angels, and they, in turn, purify and elevate his Service.[125]

This reciprocal relation is not, however, what RSZ underscores in most discourses. His clear axiological purpose in expatiating on the angelic hosts was to demonstrate that, for all their awesomeness, they were distinctly inferior to the divine soul residing in the body of every Jew. They are inferior in their mode of Service, and (according to one discourse) their lifespan is shorter because they are inferior in origin. Souls descend from divine Thought, the inner aspect of each world, while angels are created from divine Speech, the outer aspect.[126] Consequently, although angelic Love and Fear are noisier[127] and more conspicuous, the Love and Fear of a soul originating in Beri᾽ah, for example, are superior to that of the angels of that world. Only upon descending into a corporeal body does the soul lose this advantage.[128] Even then, however, its self-nullification before God transcends that of the archangels.[129] In the ideal world before the *ḥurban* (destruction of the Temple), therefore, souls were the benefactors and angels the recipients, and this will be the case "in the future."[130] Even today, great souls do not require angels to spiritualize their prayers.[131] Moreover, all angelic achievement is strictly limited in scope and contingent on Israel. The Service of angels is all ascent; they are unable to draw down the Or En Sof (through Torah and *mitsvot*) to illumine the lower worlds. Their Love and Fear are instinctive, not a product of struggle and free will. Their apprehension of Divinity extends only to their source in Malkhut. According to one discourse, even their power to administer the spheres and this world stems from the Service of Israel.[132]

Nevertheless, the fact remained that angels were pure spirits with spiritual bodies, while souls descended into corporeal bodies and were "imprisoned" there.[133] And despite all Hasidism had done for the body, it still retained its Platonic-Aristotelian image as something gross, impure, and corrupting. The soul's powers were consequently attenuated and, according to at least one discourse, the ever-crucial hierarchical advantage passed to the angels.[134] Other factors also contributed to the plausibility of this view. Angels were from Tohu, souls from Tiḳun, and, as noted above, this indicated ontological superiority. Also, there was in the background the Maimonidean legacy that placed the separate intellects far above human souls (which received the knowledge that rendered them immortal from the relatively lowly Active Intellect).[135] To complicate matters further, RSZ was faced with a plethora of conflicting statements in Lurianic works concerning the nature, function, and supernal origins of the angels. It was all but inevitable, therefore, that the discourses should exhibit the same phenomenon. Occasionally distinctions are or can be made by using the standard different-levels method, but the most accurate summation of RSZ's position is a generalized combination of two statements found in two discourses: Angels do, are, or originate from, sometimes one thing, sometimes its opposite, and sometimes both together.[136]

Once we descend below the level of the angels we arrive at our physical world, which turns out to be essentially the world of Maimonides. The ten spheres, separate intellects (including the Active Intellect), four elements, and the four levels of earthly existents, all make their appearance in the discourses. They are implicitly or explicitly associated with kabbalistic terms and concepts.[137] The underlying assumption here, too, is that no matter how sublime the philosopher's sphere or separate intellect may be, it barely touches the lowest rung of the kabbalistic hierarchy.[138] Since "the governance of this lower world is perfected by means of the forces overflowing to it from the spheres,"[139] and this overflow is, according to the kabbalists, ultimately derived from the refuse of the upper worlds, kabbalistic reasoning dictates that all the vitality of this world—even the highest form of vitality, *videlicet*, pleasure—derives from supernal refuse. This point is repeated and emphasized in many discourses.[140] Moreover, only certain lowly emanations flow from the spheres and their princes. The animal soul of both man and beast, the vegetative soul of flora, the mineral soul of inanimate creation, the religious inspiration of pious gentiles, the vitality of all gentiles, secular knowledge, and worldly success are among the examples given in various discourses.[141]

Similarly, whereas the Aristotelian philosopher knows only of the four elements that originate under the sphere of the moon,[142] the kabbalist's insight is much deeper, his mind's eye sees much higher.[143] He knows that there is a one-to-one correspondence between the four categories of earthly existents and the four elements; that the categories below descend from their spiritual counterparts above, and these, in turn, derive from the four letters of the Tetragrammaton; that the categories or elements also correspond to the four worlds, the four elements of the Scriptural word, and four categories of human faculties; that they are all found within each angel, each soul, each human body, each world; that each category contains the others; that the higher category nevertheless rules over the lower, although in their place of origin the hierarchy is reversed, for what is higher descends lower.[144]

In other words, for RSZ, as for most mystics, the individual phenomena of the natural order are largely irrelevant. What man must know and take to heart is that each phenomenon merely reflects its supernal source and that these sources are completely integrated, both with each other and with other emanations. Every component in the natural order is part of a cosmic jigsaw puzzle. Each piece is unimportant in itself and certainly not worth detailed study for its own sake. Its significance lies solely in the way it fits in with the other pieces. Once complete, the picture will exhibit the unity, symmetry, and harmony of the Creator, for RSZ never abandoned these criteria of divine perfection.

This approach, coupled with the scientific theories he considered authoritative, determined his treatment of natural phenomena in the discourses. The theories were those set forth in the only books on natural science accessible to him—those written in Hebrew. The most scientifically current of these in his possession was Joseph Delmedigo's

(1591–1657) *Elim*, in which Copernicus's heliocentric system is given favorable mention. But RSZ would have none of it. Through such works as Isaac ben Joseph Israeli's *Yesod ʿOlam* (1310), Gershom ben Shelomo's *Shaʿar ha-Shamayim* (thirteenth century), Raphael Hanover's *Tekhunat ha-Shamayim* (1756),[145] and, of course, Maimonides' *Guide* and Chapters 3–4 of *Hilkhot Yesode ha-Torah*, RSZ in effect made Aristotle and Ptolemy his mentors in astronomy, Galen his teacher of physiology, and Aristotle his instructor in physics. In these and other fields he accepted those theories that were mentioned in, or conformed with, the Zohar and Lurianic works. His natural science was thus essentially that of the Talmud, the *Guide*, and the Zohar—the supremely authoritative works of halakhah, philosophy, and kabbalah, respectively. It is therefore unlikely that the "scientific revolution" of the sixteenth and seventeenth centuries, had he known of its discoveries, would have appreciably affected his thought.[146]

As it was, he had no qualms about personifying natural phenomena and explaining them in supernatural (kabbalistic) terms, just as, for example, Maimonides explained the motion of the spheres in terms of their souls' desire for the separate intellects.[147] RSZ could therefore, with Maimonidean assurance, explain the fact that the inhabitants of the "bottom" of the earth do not fall off by pointing out that since the earth is circular, it partakes of ʿigulim, in which there is no bottom or top.[148] He could account for the seasonal changes in temperature by stating that these result from a given portion of the earth facing a given portion of the heavens during each season and receiving hot or cold emanations from their respective supernal source directly overhead.[149] He could explain the fact that fire burns only in the presence of air—that is, it *needs* air and is therefore, contrary to Maimonides, apparently inferior in the hierarchy of the four elements—by pointing out that though elemental fire is indeed higher than elemental air, physical air is more spiritual than physical fire and that, moreover, air has a higher sefirotic source than fire has.[150] He could, as noted above, account for the existence of time in terms of the interval between ratso and shov, and for the formation of dew in terms of a spiritual dew that moistens the earth overnight and enables it to produce the dew we see in the morning.[151] He could explain the existence of motion by observing that the elevation of sparks would be impossible without it.[152]

The purported presence, according to "works on nature," of oil in all things was explained by observing that oil descends from the sefirah of Ḥokhmah, the first and therefore most pervasive medium of creation. Various other properties of plants and foods were also explained in terms of the sparks or sefirot inhering in them. Thus, the intoxicating effect of wine could be either beneficial or detrimental because wine partakes of both Ḥesed and Gevurah.[153] Its power to gladden man's heart is the work of angels who create this effect ex nihilo.[154] The species of its parent plant, like the species of any plant, is determined by the species of intelligent spark hidden in its seed and responsible for its development. Once planted, the spark assembles compatible sparks and teaches them how this particular plant and its fruits are to be formed, and each spark produces its own fruit. Since fruit and produce require shells and husks for protection, the latter are rewarded for their service by acquiring some of the sparks' plant-producing wisdom: They are subsequently able to serve as fertilizer.[155] Once the fruit has grown, its position on the tree determines its quality; the higher the better, since it has had longer to be purified of any imperfections.[156] Sweet fruits derive their sweetness from an emanation from sovev, or divine Pleasure, or Ḥesed, according to various discourses; sour fruits, from Gevurah.[157] Every world has spiritual fruits corresponding to the fruits of the earth. Apples, for example, exist even in Atsilut, but they contain far more vitality and their sweetness is purely spiritual.[158] Physical sweetness in general, which RSZ often uses synonymously with "taste" (which in Hebrew is homonymous with "reason"), descends from spiritual sweetness, which for RSZ is synonymous with intellectual pleasure. Thus, it is the *taste* of the food that sustains man's brain, and his palate can actually taste the sweetness of an idea.[159]

Every "nation" and every animal, too, has individual traits emanating from its sefirotic source, and RSZ makes definitive statements about the respective character of Ishmael (Moslems), Edom (Christians), as well as lions, panthers, oxen, lambs, eagles, ravens, and others.[160] Similarly, night and day have different qualities because each has a different supernal source.[161]

The physical world as a whole is the result of three major and countless minor contractions of divine vitality. The residual emanation was hidden in many garments. Only then could a world of such gross physicality appear.[162] It "with all its contents is called the world of ḳelipot and siṭra aḥra. Therefore all mundane affairs are severe and evil, and wicked men prevail, as is explained in *'Ets Hayyim.*"[163] Yet its purpose is to benefit both God and man by bringing them, the infinite and the finite, together. God desired to establish His abode among men, and by preparing the world for His presence, man will, after the Resurrection, live to enjoy this presence forever.[164]

For RSZ, Resurrection means the highest possible revelation of the Or En Sof. "In the future all the souls of the righteous and of the Tannaim and the prophets that are now in the upper Garden of Eden, at the peak of levels, will become vested in their bodies, and they will arise at the time of the Resurrection to derive pleasure from the splendor of the Shekhinah."[165] This is because "the manifestation and the radiation [of the Or En Sof] as it is in the Garden of Eden is of the level of memale kol ʿalmin . . . a level of the evolution from one rung to another by means of intense contractions. . . . The manifestation of the radiation at the time of the Resurrection, however, will be from the level of sovev kol ʿalmin, which is not in a state of contraction, measure, and limit, but without limit and end."[166] This revelation transcends all opposites; it recognizes no distinction between body and soul or even between death and life (and therefore death can be transformed into life). It will provide a pleasure so intense that it alone will suffice to sustain life. It is—together with its precursor, the Messianic Era—the purpose and culmination of creation, and the soul's spiritual bliss after death is only a way station toward this supreme beneficence.[167]

Although this is Naḥmanides' position against Maimonides, RSZ apparently refrains from consistently adhering to Naḥmanides' terminology, occasionally equating ʿOlam ha-Ba with *Gan ʿEden*, and both or either with the rabbinic *le-ʿatid lavo*.[168] Similarly, the distinction between the Messianic and the Resurrection eras is often blurred, as it is in the Midrash, and occasionally the two are considered identical.[169]

Whatever the terminology, however, the soul's reward is a topic on which RSZ lavishes considerable attention. Following Maimonides, the Zohar, and Luria, RSZ identifies this reward as the intellectual delight of apprehending as much of God's nature as possible. Fulfilling the commandments, particularly with the proper kavanah, creates garments for the soul through which this delight must filter if the soul is to endure. "For the light [of the En Sof] is good and sweet . . . an infinitely immense delight. . . . It is not in [the soul's] power to absorb the pleasantness and agreeableness . . . without leaving its husk and becoming existentially nullified . . . were it not that from the aspect of this very light there will evolve and issue forth some minute radiation by way of an evolution of level after level, with many contractions, until a single garment [for each commandment] is created thereof . . . to garb the *Nefesh, Ruaḥ, Neshamah*. . . . It is analogous to someone looking at the sun through a fine and lucid speculum."[170]

Elsewhere the apprehension in Gan ʿEden is symbolized as the soul's sustenance there,[171] implying that this apprehension can be not merely appreciated from afar but totally assimilated. Different discourses give different sefirotic sources for it, different relations between it and terrestrial Torah-study, draw various distinctions between its manifestations in the upper and lower levels of Gan ʿEden, and provide many other minute (often conflicting)[172] details. RSZ's contribution to these standard kabbalistic discussions consists of his emphasis on man's infinite potential in this and the post-Resurrection world as opposed to his fixed place in the spiritual Gan ʿEden. This, he explains, is due to the influence and revelation of the unlimited sovev in the former as opposed to the differentiated specificity of memale in the latter. Consequently, while the soul's beatitude in Gan ʿEden strictly and eternally corresponds to its religious achievements in this world, as long as it still inhabits the lowly body—and again when it will reinhabit a body—its position is in constant flux, and it can attain ever-greater heights.[173] This is in keeping with the highest-lowest relation[174] discussed above, as well as with RSZ's inclination toward the (apparently) paradoxical.

The Messianic Era, when not submerged in a discussion of ʿOlam ha-Ba or le-ʿatid lavo, is generally described in purely mystical terms: It is the "revelation of the light of the blessed En Sof in this material world."[175] Physical men will still perform physical commandments but with a far deeper understanding,[176] for the Messiah, whose spiritual stature will surpass that of Moses, will teach them (and Moses)—or, as one discourse has it, they will teach themselves—the Torah's innermost secrets.[177] This revelation will thus surpass that of Sinai.[178] Gentile minds will also be elevated, so that they may apprehend God's unity.[179] Contradictory aggadic statements concerning the concrete conditions required for the Messiah's coming are dismissed with the observation that everything contains a mixture of good and evil and therefore no single condition can guarantee redemption.[180] Only the complete purging of evil through the elevation of all the fallen sparks can accomplish this. Consequently, teshuvah on a national scale is a sine qua non for redemption.[181]

Even the well-known dictum, quoted by Maimonides, that only political subjugation distinguishes our era from the Messiah's, is transformed into a statement concerning the degree of divine knowledge that will then be revealed.[182] In fact, although RSZ delivered an apparently prophetic discourse on *ḥevle Mashiaḥ* (pre-Messianic "birth pangs") shortly before Napoleon's invasion of Russia,[183] he never intimates, there or anywhere else, that there is some connection between the Messiah's coming and an actual physical return to the land of Israel and the rebirth of a Jewish state. For him, the *supernal* Land of Israel is the nation's true inheritance, and that land was never lost.[184] Indeed, fulfilling the commandments in exile draws down an even greater measure of sanctity than was present in the Holy of Holies.[185] The only earthly institution of the future Jewish state he mentions is the third Temple, and then only to assert that, unlike its predecessors, it will be eternal.[186] In one discourse, however, he asks: Since God normally dwells among the people of Israel anyway, why is a Temple necessary at all? (And answers: Pilgrimages to the Temple resulted in a greater degree of self-nullification and submission to God's will than would otherwise be possible).[187]

This does not mean, of course, that RSZ denied the Maimonidean conception of the Messianic Era. Indeed, a number of discourses echo it, while others identify Exile with economic (and, implicitly, with political) subjugation and the resultant preoccupation with one's livelihood; and redemption with freedom from such subjugation and preoccupation. However, the political, social, economic, and even religious consequences of this era were completely overshadowed by its far more eagerly anticipated mystical repercussions. RSZ can therefore state that he and his contemporaries awaited the Messiah more anxiously than did the sages of the Talmud, because only in these last generations will even the dregs of evil be purified, thereby assuring a far greater revelation than would have been possible earlier.[188] He even went so far as to predict the year of redemption: 1843.[189] But since every commandment connects with and activates one aspect of this future revelation,[190] and since the speculative kabbalist is acutely aware of this connection, his longing can be at least in part satisfied immediately. One will therefore not find in RSZ's discourses, just as one does not find in Cordovero's works, a note of eager expectancy. The more a kabbalist could internalize the identification of (the supernal effects of) the commandments with the (gradual triggering of the) Messianic revelation, the less the actualization of the Messianic Era excited him. Fulfilling the commandments was for him all but the equivalent of that actualization—it was the Messianic Era writ small.[191]

This is the clear and apparently original message of Chapters 36 and 37 of *Tanya* (Pt. 1). The crucial element in these chapters is RSZ's parallel between the Messianic-Resurrection Era(s) and the revelation at Sinai. He equates the Torah (i.e., its commandments, of which the Decalogue was the epitome) with this revelation. He cites the Talmud, which states that this revelation so overwhelmed the people that "at each [divine] utterance their soul took flight . . . but the Holy One, blessed be He, restored it to them with the dew with which He will revive the dead." He goes on to identify this dew with the Torah, and, in Chapter 37, essentially to equate the revelation accompanying Resurrection with that of the Messianic Era. He also identifies the fulfillment of a commandment with its effect: the emanation of one aspect of the Or En Sof. The equation implied by all these relations is quite striking: The (commandments of the) Torah equal the revelation of the En Sof equals the cause of their souls' expiration equals the cause of their souls' revival and sustenance (for the En Sof encompasses all opposites) equals the cause of the future Resurrection equals the cause of the Messianic Era equals the ultimate reward for fulfilling the commandments. Of course, RSZ, like all kabbalists, would insist on distinguishing between each element in this equation by linking it to a different supernal source, but the nonkabbalistic logic would remain the same.

If any doubt remains about the centrality of eschatology in RSZ's thought, it may be dispelled by referring to his statement in Chapter 36 that the Torah was given (not to perfect man or please God but) to enable Israel to enjoy the future revelation of the Or En Sof. Yet it seems that no area of his thought is complete without its paradox or tension, and in several discourses he completely negates the significance of reward and punishment. He compares man's struggle with evil to an animal fight arranged by noblemen for their amusement. The animals believe they are fighting in earnest and that their prowess will determine the true victor, but in fact they are being constantly manipulated by the noblemen, who want to prolong the fight to maximize their pleasure. In the same way, man believes that his struggle with evil is real and of cosmic importance; he is convinced that his freely chosen actions will determine the outcome. The truth is that it is all a game devised by God for His pleasure, and it is actually the struggle itself, not its outcome, that interests Him. When it appears that evil is getting the upper hand, He reins it in—not to suppress it but to prolong the struggle. It is only Malkhut, the sefirah furthest removed from His essential will, which has been programmed to mete out reward and punishment. These are merely a ruse to provide man with the incentive to engage in the struggle. Similarly, God has arranged for man continually to grope among opposing views in his search for the truth. Few things in this world are certain, hardly anything is what it appears to be, and evil triumphs over good with unsettling and misleading regularity. All this, RSZ explains, is contrived by God to maximize His pleasure, just as the noblemen derive additional pleasure from the confusion and ignorance of their fighting animals. To shift to a more familiar metaphor: the world is a stage, man an unwitting actor, God his playwright and audience, and the Torah his script.[192]

Occasionally RSZ uses a related metaphor to express a less novel concept: God plays hide-and-seek with man to test and stimulate his love and commitment.[193] But the animal-fight image is obviously the more striking and the more frequently discussed. One discourse explains it in more theocentric terms. Just as the animal fight creates an interesting diversion and thereby takes the nobleman's mind off his weighty preoccupations, so man's struggle with evil takes God's mind off His preoccupation with Himself—the only true reality—and induces Him to turn to and ultimately reveal Himself in this world. RSZ takes pains to point out that the animal fight succeeds in attracting the nobleman's attention precisely because it is an artificially contrived form of pleasure from an act that is in itself not pleasurable, unlike, for example, listening to music, which is intrinsically and naturally pleasurable. The nobleman requires a frivolous distraction that is utterly removed from his serious concerns rather than a true and sublime pleasure that he cannot enjoy in his present frame of mind. Similarly, the pleasure God takes in the battle below must be artificially contrived by Him, for otherwise nothing in creation would be capable of attracting His attention.[194]

Surprising as it may be, this view of reward and punishment is a logical extension of the acosmistic Hasidism of the Maggid. If this world is illusory,[195] man's actions in it and the reward or punishment for them cannot possibly have any intrinsic significance. And since God is ultimately all that really exists, these actions cannot be freely willed or performed by an independent agent; they must ultimately be willed and performed by God and for God.

RSZ's eschatology converges with his view of history. It, too, is related almost completely in metaphysical terms. RSZ's concern, like Luria's, is limited to exile and redemption, which correspond to the absence or existence of the Holy Temple. Expanding on aggadic implications to this effect,[196] RSZ portrays life during the Temple periods as idyllic and sublime. The divine emanations responsible for material and spiritual success were assimilated directly, without any intermediaries. The light of sovev, which transcends all distinctions, poured forth its bounty. Consequently, although the people of Israel enjoyed great material abundance, this did not impede them from achieving great spiritual stature as well. They were not tempted by sensual passions and could therefore direct all their desires toward God. Moreover, they were naturally drawn to serve God wholeheartedly and did not have to exert themselves to that end. Even their fulfillment of the commandments involving the lowly physical acts of eating and drinking was of a high spiritual order. Their prayers were characterized by all the fire, joy, and yearning of today's great *tsadiḳim*. Obvious miracles, which only the truly spiritual merit, were therefore commonplaces.[197]

Yet somehow the people sinned. The sins of commission—idolatry, immorality, murder—attributed to them by Scripture actually resulted from a sin of omission. They had been given dominion over the seven Canaanite nations for the purpose of elevating the sparks of the seven kings of Tohu, from whom these nations descended. Each of the seven contained, in potentia, all ten sefirot, and Israel therefore had to elevate seventy sefirotic elements. Because they failed, they were sentenced to the seventy years of Babylonian exile, during which they performed the necessary tiḳun and repented wholeheartedly.[198]

The second Temple, however, was destroyed for a far graver sin: groundless hatred of one's fellow Jew. This caused supernal discord, the exact opposite of the unity that is the hallmark of the "holy side." The souls of Israel, which had been harmoniously combined into a unified whole, were separated, fragmented into countless individual sparks, and scattered among the seventy nations. The interminable length of this exile is directly proportionate to the innumerable sparks that must be gathered and reintegrated. Moreover, because evil today is often hidden or camouflaged as good, it is much harder to eradicate. The people are unaware of the magnitude of their sins and therefore do not repent as they did during the Babylonian exile.[199]

The hardships and suffering that Israel must endure in exile are explained in similar terms. By sinning, they caused the vessels containing divine vitality to crack, thereby allowing the ḳelipot to feed off it. To prevent this situation from continuing indefinitely, the ḳelipot, as personified by the gentile nations, were shunted away from the supernal worlds, with their infinite measure of vitality, and given permission to derive vitality from Israel below. Eventually, therefore, they will have eaten their fill and, like a bloated leech, fall away and die.[200]

The disparity between the present exile and the Temple period is great indeed. The bodies of Israel no longer receive their vitality directly from the Shekhinah but through the mediation of the ten sefirot of *Nogah* (the neutral realm between good and evil). Their material attainments no longer emanate directly from the Shekhinah but from the seventy princes, who are no longer wholly subservient to Israel (as they were during Solomon's reign). The effects of Israel's holy acts and the influence of their holy souls are now concealed, and the world appears to function according to natural laws. The Shekhinah has departed from the land of Israel, and its spiritual level no longer exceeds that of other lands. Love and Fear are now great achievements that cannot be attained without angelic assistance. Every successive generation must take upon itself additional supererogatory acts and halakhic stringencies to counteract the progressive spiritual decline.[201]

But on a deeper level the picture is not so bleak. In fact, it is positively encouraging. Exile and redemption are described as offshoots of the ratso-shov cycle. Like shov, exile is merely a temporary ebb of divine vitality for the purpose of the renewed flow to follow. The greater the flow is to be, the longer the duration of the preparatory ebb must be. Thus, because the revelation of the final redemption will be far more resplendent than the revelation at Sinai, and because Israel will require concomitantly more purging and purification, this exile must last far longer than the Egyptian exile.[202] As for sin causing the exile, the truth is that the Temple was destroyed not only because of Israel's misdeeds but because the Temple had not received the highest emanations of the Or En Sof; these would have guaranteed its eternal existence, as, in fact, they will confer eternity upon the third Temple.[203] Again, exile among the seventy nations, which embody the three evil ḳelipot, serves not only as a punishment but also as an opportunity to purify these nations and prepare the world for the Messianic Era. Each nation possesses typical traits that must be purifed. The Poles, for example, are descendents of Esau, who lived by—and whose spiritual vitality was derived from—the sword. By killing Jews, the Poles' spiritual vitality spends itself on ḳedushah (the realm of the holy) and is purified. Thus, the more Jews they kill, the sooner their period of power will end and the Messianic Era begin. The descendents of Ishmael, however, who control the

Holy Land, have already used up their allotted portion of ḳedushah and are now sustained through the transcendent vitality of maḳif (see supra, p. 22 and pp. 75–76), which allows them to delay the redemption.[204]

In any event, the Temple's destruction and the resultant exile have only a low level of reality; they "reach" only as high as Malkhut, while for all the higher sefirot they and the concomitant lack of perfect yiḥudim are totally irrelevant.[205] It is true that Israel's prayers are not as effective as they were before the ḥurban, but this applies only to the visible spectrum of reality. Beyond that the prayers are as potent as ever.[206] If anything, in fact, Israel's love for God has *increased* during exile because of His inaccessibility, and He naturally reciprocates. The divine revelations on the first day of the holidays are not as conspicuous as they were during the Temple period, but the second day—*Yom Tov Sheni shel galuyot*—compensates for this.[207] Similarly, clear-cut miracles may have become rarities, but hidden miracles supplement them. Moreover, tsadiḳim, whose source is Ḥokhmah, know how to rearrange the letter combinations that vitalize every existent, and they are therefore still capable of performing palpable wonders.[208]

RSZ divides the generations of this exile into three periods: (1) from the Tannaim to the Amoraim; (2) from the Amoraim to the Geonim; and (3) from the Geonim until the Messiah, which he apparently identifies with the Talmud's *ʿiḳveta de-Meshiḥa*, the period immediately (!) preceding the Messiah.[209] Although the generations are in a steady spiritual decline,[210] and must therefore tailor their Service to their progressively grosser state,[211] the generations of exile have certain advantages. Distance, like absence, makes the heart grow fonder, and God actually loves the spiritually distant later generations more than He loved their predecessors.[212] Whereas the sefirah of Binah provided the wherewithal to elevate the sparks during the Temple period, resulting in fiery prayers from Gevurah, it is Ḥokhmah that provides the means and is the mode of Service in exile. Its keynotes are restraint, silence, and self-nullification; and just as Ḥokhmah transcends Binah, this Service transcends the externally impressive Service of the Temple period[213] (and of the more demonstrative worshippers of RSZ's own period).[214] Similarly, the emanations to the Holy Land during the Temple period originated in divine Speech—that is, the revealed aspect of Divinity—while today their source is divine Thought—the higher, hidden aspect. Consequently, the tsadiḳim residing in the land of Israel today may apprehend more than their counterparts before the exile did.[215] In fact, since history is circular, its beginning and end adjacent to each other, even the common man of ʿiḳveta de-Meshiḥa has a greater insight into theological truth than did his predecessors, for though he is further from the beginning, he is closer to the end.[216]

Man

Body, mind, soul, (vital) spirit, and their functions are inextricably interrelated in RSZ's thought. As noted above, RSZ's views on anatomy and physiology are essentially those of Galen, although occasionally he apparently accepts the incompatible theory of Harvey on circulation.[217] Following the Zohar, *ʿEts Ḥayyim*, and other kabbalistic works, RSZ superimposed on Galen's theories kabbalistic concepts and terminology, so that every part and function of the body corresponds to, or is activated by, or somehow associated with, one or more sefirot, and all are ultimately dedicated to *ʿavodat ha-berurim* ("the service of selection," or purification)—separating the kernel of good from the chaff of evil that constitutes the major part of the physical world. Often, in fact, anatomical and physiological assumptions seem to flow from the kabbalistic ideas RSZ wants to explain: If a certain relation exists among certain sefirot, it must also exist among the parts or functions of the body corresponding to those sefirot, and vice versa. In this, too, he was following kabbalistic precedent. If, for instance, the sefirah of Ḥokhmah is the first receptacle of divine vitality, then the human brain, where a reflection of Ḥokhmah resides, must be the receptacle containing the seed of human life. Ejaculation is preceded and accompanied by pleasure because the faculty of Pleasure—Keter—and Ḥokhmah, its first recipient, reside in the water of the brain. Since we know that semen is materialized Ḥokhmah, that Keter is the source and stimulus for Ḥokhmah's descent and accompanies it when it appears, and that "water propagates all forms of pleasure," this phenomenon is readily "explained."[218]

The relative position of parts of the body is determined by the symbolic position of their corresponding sefirot: The head corresponds to Ḥabad; arms, to Ḥesed and Gevurah; chest, to Tifʾeret, and so on. The head is physically highest because it contains and derives from the highest sefirot. It therefore also receives the highest form of vitality from the soul. The legs are the lowest because they correspond to Netsaḥ and Hod, the lowest peripheral sefirot, and they consequently receive the lowest form of vitality.[219]

The body as a whole has its source in the elemental Earth of Tohu.

Although this element is the lowest of the four in Tikun, it is the highest in Tohu, where the hierarchy is reversed. And since Tohu is ontologically prior to Tikun, the ignoble corporeal body actually descends from a source infinitely higher than the soul, whose source is, at most, Atsilut of Tikun. The body is brought into existence by the infinite light of sovev, while the soul derives its vitality from memale.[220]

But what is higher descends lower. The body's superiority becomes inferiority once it materializes as physical matter. Adam's body was originally spared this descent, being relatively spiritual (like the celestial spheres), but his sin resulted in a universal fall into physicality, and his body became coarse matter.[221] Two souls were "imprisoned" in it,[222] the vital, or animal, soul and the divine soul. For the great majority, the animal soul is the essential person. Clothed in the blood, it generates life-giving heat and is thus the source of all his vitality. It is also the determinant of his personality. Although it is spiritual, it is united with the body by vapors emitted by the blood. Although it is supraspatial, it is concentrated in the left side of the heart, whence it emits 613 emanations that permeate the 613 parts of the body. The higher emanations go to the higher, or "inner," organs—brain and heart; the lower go to the "outer," grosser organs—the limbs and viscera. Each emanation is uniquely suited to vitalize or activate its recipient vessel, which in turn is uniquely suited to accept just that emanation. The eye, for example, is uniquely suited to receive the emanation of sight, whose source is Ḥokhmah; the ear, the emanation of hearing, whose source is Binah; the brain, the emanation of intellect.[223]

These principles plus certain assumptions based on observation lead to interesting and, for us, rather surprising conclusions. The skull covers the brain—it must therefore derive from an overabundance of the highest form of cerebral matter, which the brain cannot contain.[224] It is thus associated with wisdom, and its extension, the beard, is therefore a sign of male intellectual superiority. The white beard of an older and presumably wiser man results from his partaking of Ḥokhmah to an even greater degree, for Ḥokhmah is the source of whiteness. Similarly, since the thirty-two white teeth derive from the thirty-two parts of Ḥokhmah, they, too, are associated with wisdom, which is why a child cannot speak intelligibly until its first teeth come in. Nor can it speak until it has tasted grain (Tal. B., *Berakhot*, 40a), for, as we have seen, "taste" embodies Ḥokhmah (and Keter). Nor can it walk until around the same age (two), when its mind receives an overabundance of the highest emanation from Keter, and the overflow then percolates down to its lowest limbs.[225]

Since the throat separates head from heart, it must be the mediating organ through which cold intellect is transformed into warm emotion. Also, since the voice it emits is generated by the warm rising vapors of the heart, it (the throat) must be the organ through which emotions become the articulate sounds of speech expressing these emotions. A similar role is played by the diaphragm, which acts as the intermediary between the upper and lower parts of the body, that is, the higher and lower forms of vitality emanating from the soul.[226]

Since, "according to medical science," there are indications that the brain (=mind, intellect, Ḥabad) controls the heart (=emotions, desire, the six emotive sefirot), and contrary indications that it is controlled by the heart, we must conclude that heart and brain are interdependent.[227] Various discourses therefore give precedence to one or the other as the supreme determinant of personality, depending, as always, on the point RSZ wanted to make on that occasion or during that period.

Because RSZ believed that spiritual forces are the causes of all phenomena, he also assumed that these causes, like their physical counterparts, must be contiguous with their effects. Thus, the hand that gives a charitable donation contains within it an emanation of Ḥesed emitted by the heart. Again, if the hand can write intelligible words—that is, words containing intellect—that intellect must actually reside in the hand. The original source of the intellect, to be sure, is the brain, but "veins" carry it to the hand, where it resides in potentia until it is actualized when the author writes. The writing fingers then transmit the intellect to the letters of the words they write, and this renders the words intelligible.[228] Similarly, since the mind or will can apparently cause instantaneous movement of the legs, they must contain mind or will. Although it probably occurred to RSZ that some time does in fact elapse, he was far more open to the alternate assumption that the cause of movement resides in the limbs themselves. One discourse goes so far as to state that the mind and legs have equal thinking ability, the only difference being that in the mind it is actualized while in the legs it is present only in potentia until triggered by the brain.[229]

The idea that every action or faculty has a specific sefirotic source blended naturally with the assumption that it must also have a *place* of origin, whether physical, spiritual, or some combination of the two. Acting, or exercising a faculty, meant drawing forth a power from its place—where it resides while in potentia—clothing it in, or projecting it to, another place, and then, when the goal is accomplished, allowing the power to return home. Thinking, for example, consists of drawing forth intellective power from the hylic intellect—the place of origin and generator of that power—clothing it in the subject at hand, and, when the issue has been sufficiently clarified, withdrawing the intellect and returning it, along with what it has apprehended, to its source.[230] If the conclusion is remembered, it takes up residence in that part of the brain that stores memory. If it is forgotten, it accompanies the intellect that gave birth to it back to the hylic intellect. Since the hylic intellect does not always produce sufficient intellective power to cope with every resolvable problem, and since (regular) production of this power is its only function, it is clear to RSZ that there must be a higher power responsible for these vicissitudes. And since it is higher than intellect, it must reside above the place of intellect, videlicet, in the membrane (and skull) covering the brain. When confronted with a difficult text, for example, this membrane can impede the flow of intellect from the brain and thus prevent it from coalescing with and eventually assimilating the intellect contained in the words of the text. If, however, the intellective flow is able to reach its object—whether it be the words of the text or the mind of a disciple—it, like all activated soul-powers, will leave a permanent imprint. There is a residue of friendship between estranged friends, of the teacher's soul in the pupil's, of the artisan's soul in his handiwork.[231]

When attempting to explain a Zoharic passage "from my flesh"—by elucidating the corresponding anatomical or physiological phenomena—RSZ combines all the sources at his command, no matter how disparate, to reach the required conclusion. For one passage, for example, he cites "medical works" that state that a child's skeletal system derives from his father's brain. He cites the Talmudic statement that a child's (white) bones derive from the father's (white) semen. By linking the word *ʿatsamot* (bones) to *ʿatsmut* (essence), and the word *moaḥ* (brain) to its homonym meaning marrow, RSZ explains why precisely the bones contain the nerves that transmit feeling from the brain throughout the body, how the bones thus constitute the essence of the body, and why Ezekiel was able to revive the dry bones in the valley of Kidron.[232]

Because eating is one of the body's most conspicuous functions, the one that literally unites it with the soul and the one that confronts it with its most common ethical challenge, RSZ lavishes much attention on its various facets. As always, to the physiology of Galen he adds his own characteristic ideas. Since food coarsens man, it must be inherently coarse. Since it awakens desires the hungry man lacks, it must actually contain these desires. In kabbalistic terms, although its source is Tohu—for which reason it can vitalize man, whose source is Tiḳun—its fall after Shevirat ha-Kelim invested it with these evil qualities.[233]

On the other hand, since food enhances one's ability to think, it must contain intellect, and different foods contain different forms of intellect.[234] Moreover, since food can be transformed into energy for Service, it must contain an element of good as well. By pronouncing the proper blessing before eating, and eating sparingly *le-shem Shamayim* (for the sake of Service), man separates this good from its evil shell and thereby elevates both himself and the food to its original transcendent source. This sifting—*birur*—of good from evil in the food he eats is reflected in his digestive process, which sifts the primary from the secondary vitality and waste products, and sends each to its proper destination in the body. Different discourses provide different and often contradictory details on just how the spiritual birur is accomplished.[235] What concerns us here is the statement that it is not the food itself but the divine vitality causing its existence that also keeps the body alive by vitalizing the soul.[236] In the same vein, one source implies that it is actually the divine, not the animal, soul that is responsible for vitalizing the body.[237] Thus, even the natural bodily functions of the Jew are ascribed to divine forces within him, forces that his forebears actually felt and perceived at Sinai.[238] In fact, even the corporeality of his body only resembles that of the gentiles but is really of a much higher order.[239] His pulse beats with the systole-diastole emanations of the Or En Sof, and the number of his days is determined not by physical factors but by the number of soul-powers he must elevate through his Service.[240]

Nevertheless, the soul remained pure spirit, the body gross matter, and time and again RSZ addresses the old philosophic-kabbalistic problem of why this spirit was forced to descend from its sublime place of beatitude to be imprisoned in ignoble flesh. Before summarizing his answers, we should note that in various discourses he attempts, indirectly perhaps, to take some of the sting out of this obviously painful question. We are told, for instance, that the higher aspects of the soul do not reside in the body at all, but hover over it or, according to some discourses, remain above in the supernal world and emit emanations that enter the body to assist the internal soul.[241] Even the internal soul, some discourses insist, does not itself vitalize the body, nor can it be called a vital force; this function and this description apply only to *its* emanations (which are, however, absolutely united with its nevertheless transcendent essence).[242] Although it is completely united with the body, the soul is not, according to most discourses, deeply affected by the body's vicissitudes but remains forever essentially perfect and unchanged. Even the complete loss of a faculty, such as blindness, does not indicate the impairment of the soul's ability to emanate sight but only absence of a suitable vessel for this emanation. Two proofs are adduced for this assertion: (1) A blind man can have normal offspring—therefore his soul must be whole; and (2) the soul of a man that has entered an animal through *gilgul* (metempsychosis) does not bestow upon the animal human faculties—therefore the impediment must lie not in the soul but in the animal's physical organs, which cannot assimilate human soul-powers.[243]

But these mitigating factors only blunt the question; they do not answer it. Nor does RSZ seem satisfied with any single answer. Obviously the soul must be able to achieve something greater by toiling in a body than it could by remaining above. But what can be greater than the bountiful revelation of the Shekhinah it originally enjoyed? RSZ's answers may be grouped under two headings: (1) Hasidic—the divine soul does not, in fact, descend to improve itself, but to purify and elevate the animal soul, the body, and, through them, the world with which it comes into contact;[244] and (2) kabbalistic—the soul descends in order to ascend to an even higher plane, an even greater level of bliss, an even greater degree of unity with God. Depending on the discourse, this is achieved in one of two ways: (1) By fulfilling the 613 commandments (during the course of its various *gilgulim*), the soul purifies the 613 garments through which, according to Luria, it must filter the Or En Sof in order to assimilate and fully benefit from it;[245] and (2) the soul's forced separation from its Source arouses in it a yearning for reunion far more intense than its original, natural desire for union. By struggling ceaselessly toward this end in an alien, hostile environment, it transcends its original limitations and reaches the level of a *ba'al teshuvah* (penitent), whose greater distance from God results in a proportionately greater longing for closeness, and this in turn results in a far greater revelation than can be achieved by the Tsadiḳ. The soul thus breaks through its original bounds of perception and passive enjoyment of a finite measure of Divinity to an infinitely expanding realm of ever-greater unity with, and revelation of, the Or En Sof.[246]

These two approaches illustrate the tension in RSZ's thought between the otherworldliness of Lurianic kabbalah and the relative humanism of Hasidism. Even when citing the Lurianic idea that the soul descends for its own sake, to achieve greater spiritual heights, RSZ complements it (in most discourses) with the Hasidic idea that it is precisely the struggle in and against a corporeal world that brings this about. Generally the emphasis is less on purifying the 613 soul-garments through the 613 commandments than on the obstacles physical man must overcome to fulfill them and the fact that these very obstacles, because of their transcendent source (Tohu), enable him to rise above his soul's limitations. Nevertheless, RSZ never abandoned the Lurianic doctrine, and, in a discourse delivered during the last year of his life, he characteristically insisted on the validity of both approaches.[247]

The previously mentioned doctrine of two souls, which RSZ adopted from Vital, is explained in a relatively straightforward manner in Part 1 of *Tanya*. Both the animal and the divine soul have all ten sefirah-faculties (=soul-powers). The animal soul resides in the blood-filled left side of the heart and is responsible for worldly desires; neutral and sinful speech and actions; and, through its emanations to the brain, neutral and sinful thoughts and the apprehension of secular knowledge. The divine soul resides in the brain, whence it emanates to the heart and other organs, and is responsible for the intellect and emotions directed toward serving God. In most men the two souls constantly compete for control of the three soul-garments—thought, speech, action.[248] Obviously the animal soul has a clear advantage, for besides being ontologically superior and therefore spiritually stronger, it is the soul directly responsible for speech, action, and, for most men, most of their thoughts. Counterbalancing this and tipping the scales in favor of the divine soul[249] is the divine spark illuminating its intellective sefirot, particularly Ḥokhmah, making contemplation of the Divine its most natural activity and infusing it with a suprarational devotion to God's will. RSZ couples this mystical concept of built-in divine assistance with the Stoic assertion that the intellect, by its very nature, rules the (worldly) passions[250]—if man only directs it toward God. This interweaving of nature with the supernatural is understandable in light of RSZ's identification of nature with the suprarational: "'Nature' is an applied term for anything that is not in the realm of reason and comprehension,"[251] a definition that may also help explain his approach to understanding natural phenomena.[252]

Since it is axiomatic in *Tanya* that the intellect gives birth to the emotions, the divine soul's innate tendency to contemplate the Divine must generate an innate love for God. This appears as RSZ's *Ahavah*

Mesuteret, the Love hidden in the soul of every Jew, which is Israel's inheritance from the Patriarchs.[253] The divine soul therefore possesses a natural desire and yearning "to separate itself and depart from the body in order to unite with its origin and source in God, the fountainhead of all life, blessed be He, although thereby it would become null and void, completely losing its entity therein, with nothing remaining of its former essence and being."[254] Except for Tsadiḳim, however, men are rarely conscious of this Love or desire. Only during prayer do they occasionally succeed in arousing it and thereby giving the divine soul complete dominion over the three soul-garments.[255]

During the rest of the day, the animal soul is constantly threatening to envelop its divine counterpart and cut off its emanations. While the divine spark in Ḥokhmah is never extinguished, its influence may be completely nullified, leaving man helpless before the physical desires that cause him to sin. For some, only the supreme test of devotion—the choice between forsaking God and martyrdom—can arouse this faculty of devotion from its dormant state.[256] For most, however, Ḥokhmah remains potent enough to exercise its influence whenever the animal soul threatens to conquer any one of their three garments; that is, whenever they are tempted to think a thought, utter a word, or perform an action not prescribed by the Torah. What they themselves must contribute is a continuous and powerful effort of will, which in turn requires, according to RSZ, frequent and intense intellectual contemplation of God's greatness and unity.[257] The main instrument in RSZ's ethics is therefore the intellect, and Ḥabad is indeed an appropriate name for his ethical approach. Still, intellect is really only the first rung on the ladder leading to *unio mystica,* and, as we shall see, its centrality should not be overemphasized. It is only the key that unlocks the door to will and desire.

The two-soul doctrine in *Tanya* obviously combines the basic elements of rabbinic and Platonic-Stoic psychology with the doctrine of Israel's genetic selection.[258] The animal soul corresponds approximately to the *yetser ha-ra* and the passions; the divine soul to the *yetser ṭov* and reason. Less obvious is its conformity with Maimonides' description in *Mishneh Torah.* The animal soul corresponds nicely to "ha-nefesh ha-metsuyah le-khol nefesh ḥayah," or "ha-neshamah"; the divine soul to "tsurat ha-nefesh."[259] By adding the sefirot as these souls' constituent elements, RSZ effectively, although no doubt unconsciously, combined the fundamentals of rabbinic, philosophic, and kabbalistic psychology into an original, cohesive doctrine.

As usual, however, the discourses add details that complicate matters considerably. Here a third soul makes its appearance—the rational soul, described as an intermediary between the two antagonists. The glimpses of this soul afforded us by various discourses seem to indicate that it is the permanent vitalizing spirit of the brain that can be appropriated by either soul for its use.[260] But, again as usual, there are contradictions. One discourse identifies it as the intellect of the divine soul, a second as the intellect of the animal soul, a third as the entire animal soul.[261] In *Tanya* the animal soul seems inseparably associated with the vital blood, so that it would naturally cease to exist when the body dies; in the discourses it is said to be eternal.[262] In *Tanya* this entire soul seems to correspond to the yetser ha-ra; in the discourses only its emotive faculties are so identified.[263] Its intellective faculties are not as evil, but because they are the means with which man understands secular and sense-related knowledge, they inevitably give birth to undesirable emotions. Chief among these is the love and desire for physical gratification in whatever form. In *Tanya* this desire is, in effect, also identified as the yetser ha-ra,[264] which the true Tsadiḳ has completely sublimated. In the discourses it is an immutable human trait resulting from Shevirat ha-Kelim and affecting even the Tsadik. What distinguishes him from lesser men is that he never succumbs to it: He never allows it to conquer, even temporarily, any of his three soul-garments.[265] This Tsadiḳ is therefore the equivalent of *Tanya*'s *Benoni*.[266]

In Part 1 of *Tanya* the supernal source of the divine soul is Ḥokhmah, but in the discourses RSZ linked it, at one time or another, with every other sefirah as well, including Keter.[267] The soul's degree of divinity ranges in the discourses from complete union with the Godhead to a completely separate, although still united, creation.[268] Ḥokhmah as the primary soul-power gives way to will (or pleasure, the two being very closely interrelated, as noted above). This encompassing power directs the other ten in an effort to achieve the supreme pleasure—union with God. In terms of Service, too, intellect—Ḥabad—plays a distinctly secondary role to the suprarational will, which is manifested as an intense love for God and desire for union.[269] This desire is variously referred to in Zoharic terms as *reʿuta de-liba* (desire of the heart) or *ʿumḳa de-liba* (depths of the heart); in Hasidic terms as *penimiut ha-lev* (the inwardness of the heart), *neḳudat ha-lev* (the point of the heart), or the *nitsots elohi* (the divine spark that, according to *Tanya*, resides in Ḥokhmah); or in Scriptural-Midrashic terms as *yeḥidah* (singular), which RSZ clearly considers a very appropriate name for that unique quality of the divine soul that moves it to devote itself single-mindedly and with singular zeal to achieving that union.[270]

Even in the discourses, however, this desire can be aroused only by intense contemplation and subsequent attachment to the object of contemplation through Daʿat, the faculty of concentration. Like supernal *Ratson* (Will), the faculty of Daʿat exists in two forms, transcendent and immanent. The transcendent form descends from Keter (=Ratson) to transform the pointlike flash of Ḥokhmah into the broad "river" of Binah. Like any power that unites opposites, it must transcend them so that it can overwhelm their respective sense of individual identity. It is this form that can bring about the suprarational reʿuta de-liba, the surging flame of desire for union with the transcendent Godhead. The immanent form unites and sustains the more containable Love and Fear born of contemplation. By keeping the intellect powerfully focused on its transcendent object, it integrates this Love and Fear and also prevents them from evaporating.[271]

The relation between intellect and emotion is discussed very frequently and in considerable detail. It, too, seems to change from *Tanya* to the discourses, although here it may be argued that the more speculative discourses simply illumine facets that were unnecessary to reveal in the more ethics-oriented *Tanya.* In any event it is clear that in *Tanya* (and in some discourses) the emotions are generally caused and completely controlled by the intellect. A mind engaged in contemplating sublime matters will eventually bring forth sublime emotions. Conversely, the powerful, untamed physical passions generated by the animal soul may always be tamed and sublimated by the intellect of its divine adversary. The greater a man's intellect, the greater his potential for arousing commensurately great emotions. A solid, powerful (i.e., intellectual) love of God, as opposed to a fleeting emotional rush, is invariably the product of a powerful mind's intense contemplation of God's greatness. A man of great compassion is the product of a great mind with a tendency toward Ḥesed, while a love for petty, materialistic things is the product of a weak or immature mind occupied with trivia.[272] In a different context RSZ supports this view of intellectual control by observing that the contemplating intellect not only gives birth to an appropriate emotion but, ideally, completely envelops it (in addition to sustaining it internally through Daʿat), so that it does not go astray.[273] In other words, like all good parents, the intellective faculties feed, clothe, educate, and discipline their emotive offspring; they are, according to *Tanya*, the primary molders of man's personality.

In the discourses this relation becomes far more complex. Other categories of emotion make their appearance. One is an instinctive variety having no original connection with intellect and reminiscent of Plato's "appetitive" faculty. It is described as a type of emotion man shares with beasts, such as his "love" for the sweet and dislike for the bitter. It may be controlled to some extent by the intellect, but it can never be completely sublimated. Although one would expect RSZ to locate its source in some lowly region of the animal soul, he points us in the opposite direction. The source of these most powerful emotions is will, the transcendent and most powerful faculty. From there these emotions may pass through the crucible of intellect to be purified (i.e., restrained by reason and thereby attenuated), but when this occurs they have actually lost their original character of emotion (*midot*) and become a form of intellect (*moḥin*). They are then replaced by successive waves of instinctive emotions.[274]

In most discourses, however, the emotions emanated by will—or pleasure—are not linked or identified with animal instincts but rather with the divine soul's instinct to reunite with its origin. These are the emotions responsible for reʿuta de-liba, the heart's will for union, and are generated and sustained by the transcendent form of Daʿat mentioned above. Both categories of emotions—which we may term the primordial and the intellectual, respectively—are often discussed in the same discourse, and contrasted.[275] Occasionally, however, particularly in the discourses of 5568, RSZ insists that intellect does not, in fact, give birth to emotions but merely elicits and channels them. He stresses that the emotions actually have deeper roots in the essence of the soul than does the intellect and are therefore innately more powerful. Consequently, only when it succeeds in drawing upon the divine soul's deepest resources can the intellect dominate the emotions. In general, though, intellect is characterized by weakness and submissiveness, emotion by power and assertiveness. They are not parent and offspring but innate adversaries who bow only to superior force. Yet in the same year (5568) RSZ delivered another discourse in which he states that the relation of intellect to emotion is that of concealment to revelation, and that only location and conspicuousness separate the love that is present in the mind that generates it from the love that is subsequently revealed in the heart.[276] Similarly, one discourse will identify the essence of man with intellect, another with emotion.[277]

The discourses tell us that the emotion that is purportedly felt in the heart consists of a rarefied form of warm vapor that can either ascend to the brain and cause it (further) to contemplate the object of the emotion; or to the organs of speech, via the throat, to produce the breath that activates them; or, if it is too deep a love to find utterance, the vapor is transformed into the breath of a kiss and thereby transferred to the object that originally gave rise to it.[278] The emotions are thus directly linked with the two "inner" soul-garments, thought and speech; and, since speech can elicit action, they are linked with the outer garment as well. Control over the emotions is therefore the key to controlling these garments.

But this does not mean that the garments are not also rooted in the soul itself,[279] which must, after all, be the source of all its manifestations. Of particular interest to RSZ (and to the Maggid) was the process whereby the soul produces letters, and this receives lavish and minute attention. What concerns us in this regard is that these letters—which are, of course, related to the letters of the written Torah, the utterances formed by God's "breath"—are said to originate in the very highest, most hidden recesses of the soul: Keter or Ḥokhmah or Binah, depending on the discourse. From there they descend to serve as vessels for the light of the intellect as revealed in thought and speech, much as the supernal kelim descend from Tohu both to limit and to reveal the orot of Tiḳun. Each letter of an intelligible word contains part of its intellective light (although the complete combination results in a light exceeding the sum of its components). Similarly, each letter of speech emanating from an emotion contains a small part of the emotion.[280]

The discourses differ on whether letters are an integral part of intellect or whether they first make their appearance in conscious thought.[281] They differ on whether uttering the letters (as words) adds to, or detracts from, the understanding of the concept as it appears in the intellect.[282] But they agree that the full profundity of an idea can never be verbally conveyed. While it is true that the greater a teacher's intellect, the greater his ability to elucidate, through analogies, the most abstruse concept, his disciple can never apprehend more than a fraction—one-tenth, according to one discourse—of all its implications.[283] On the other hand, because speech consists of warm, vital vapors rising from the heart, it can inspire far more enthusiasm than intellect in written form can do;[284] moreover, the spoken word is far more spiritual than the written—two ideas that help explain RSZ's general preference for the spoken over the written word.

Other details concerning the formation of letters and the psychological-physiological mechanism of speech are not significant enough for RSZ's religioethical thought to include here. It should be noted, however, that these details, along with those mentioned above, form an extremely complex network of interrelated connections among the soul, every soul-power, the intellect, the emotions, the three soul-garments, the body, and God's corresponding manifestations in both his roles of Creator and of King. For example: God's breath, the inner aspect of His speech (His voice being the outer aspect) is the immediate source of the divine soul, as Scripture states: "And He breathed into his [man's] nostrils the breath of life" (Genesis 2:7). The letters of God's speech are the building blocks of both the Ten Utterances that created the world and of the words of the Torah, which is the blueprint for creation and the constitution under which it is governed. The Ten Commandments, which encapsulate the entire Torah (= Ḥokhmah), therefore correspond to the Ten Utterances. God's breath and speech, through which He acts, are symbolized by the final he of the Tetragrammaton, the breathlike aspirate letter with which this world was created and which is also the source of the soul's vitality, as Scripture states: "For His people are part of God (lit., "For the portion of the Lord is His people [Deut. 32:19]); that is, part of the Tetragrammaton. This he corresponds to Malkhut, the actual instrument of creation and the sefirah that therefore symbolizes the Creator's relationship to it: that of King to subject(s). But since breath is produced by the heart—that is, the emotive sefirot—and these sefirot in turn are produced by the intellective sefirot, beginning with Ḥokhmah, the divine soul is ultimately rooted in Ḥokhmah (or in Keter, Ḥokhmah's source; or in divine Thought, Ḥokhmah's inner garment—depending on the discourse). The Jewish people are therefore fittingly called God's children, since a child, too, originates in its father's brain. And since what is true above is true below, human speech also originates in the Ḥokhmah of man's soul (or Binah, according to some discourses). The letters of speech—the letters of the Hebrew alphabet—are formed by the five organs of articulation, which correspond to the five supernal *Gevurot* that delimit the emanation of Ḥesed, the sefirah of revelation. Supernal Netsaḥ and Hod decide how the revelation may best be accomplished; that is, they prepare it for the recipient and are thus the source of the kidneys and testicles that prepare the semen (from Ḥokhmah and then Ḥesed) for ejaculation. Yesod enables the speaker to concentrate on, or *attach* his mind to, the listener-recipient and convey his message with pleasure and enthusiasm. Yesod therefore corresponds to the organ or act of *conjunctio*.[285]

The complexity of this labyrinthine network of associations is further increased by the homiletic license that allows RSZ to take a Scriptural word such as *hevel* (in Eccles., lit., vanity) and interpret it variously as connoting Ḥokhmah, midot, breath, voice, vapor, or emanations of any kind, including those responsible for movement of the body.[286] In such cases RSZ is not simply following the rabbinic tradition of multiple interpretations, or even the kabbalistic tradition that maintains that every Scriptural word has 70, or 600,000 or an infinite number of meanings.[287] More to the point, I believe, is that he is applying the Maggid's associative method to exegesis. This method, coupled with the Maggid's mystical point of departure, precluded any rigorous attempt to consider questions of context, grammar, and other clues to the *peshat* of the text. Consequently, in RSZ's discourses the distinction between peshat as medieval commentators understood it and other modes of interpretation is often blurred to the point of disappearing. What RSZ calls peshat is a far cry from what Rashi, let alone Rashbam, called peshat.[288]

RSZ's preoccupation with the phenomenon of speech, possibly the most intensely scrutinized subject in the discourses, is not hard to understand. For the kabbalist, letters and speech, either mental or oral, were, after all, the instruments for creating or revealing everything—the world, the Torah, man, and God. For the Beshtian Hasid they were the instruments through which he revealed or actualized his highest soul-powers—intellect, emotions, will, and desire. Indeed, in several discourses, RSZ defines Hebrew letters simply as (potential) emanations of vitality[289]—a definition encompassing everything.

We have already implied that despite their common origin, the divine souls of Israel are not all of a piece. Although every soul is irradiated by, and ultimately rooted in, Ḥokhmah of Atsilut, all souls are not created equal. An infinite number of soul-origin levels is possible as a result of Ḥokhmah's descent through the infinite number of sefirot and other levels of the four worlds. The immediate origin of most post-Biblical souls is actually traceable to one level or another within the three lower worlds, and even the protean soul of Maimonides is located no higher than Beriʾah.[290]

Here, too, one can discern the underlying tension between RSZ's Beshtian inclinations and his Lurianic axioms. On the one hand he makes a clear and conscious attempt to unify all the souls of Israel by ascribing to them a common supernal source and common religious and ethical instincts. Every divine soul smolders with intense love and yearning for union with God. Every Jew's animal soul is innately merciful and benevolent. But on the other hand, the myriad soul levels found in Lurianic works could not be ignored. Moreover, simple observation attested to the vast gulf separating the Service of the saintly and scholarly from that of the worldly and ignorant, and to personality differences even between men of similar spiritual stature. Since RSZ believed that every effect must have an innate, rather than an external, cause, it was obvious to him that real differences did exist between one soul and another. Differences in spiritual, intellectual, and vocational potential, as well as specific character traits, were traced to different levels of supernal soul levels, to varying degrees of predominance or revelation of one origin, soul-power, or another, or to some combination of these variables. These innate differences also determined, among other things, a man's potential for scholarship and leadership; the type of leadership he required; whether he would be more successful in the study of halakhah or kabbalah; whether his halakhic decisions would be generally lenient or stringent; the nature and constancy of his self-nullification; and the power of his emotions.[291]

It was, to be sure, remotely possible for the average man's embodied soul to become "impregnated" with the soul of a tsadiḳ, thereby allowing him to rise above his limitations; but RSZ mentions this possibility only once,[292] and only, it seems, because Lurianic doctrine requires it. The same reluctance is discernible in his mention of the Zoharic idea that a man's spiritual potential is predetermined by his father's thoughts during intercourse.[293] Both concepts vitiate one of *Tanya*'s basic theses: that every man is born with sufficient ability to realize the purpose of his particular soul's descent. In this respect, all souls are created equal, although virtually all require the inspiration and guidance of "the saints and sages, the heads of Israel in their generation," through whom even the most ignorant "are bound up and united with their original essence and root in the supernal Wisdom."[294] These leaders are the offshoots of Moses, the unifying intermediary between God and His people, and in each generation they alone have the ability to tailor that generation's Service to the *tiḳunim* required of its transmigrated souls (i.e., they alone know the sins and imperfections for which these souls have been sentenced to reoccupy a body rather than being allowed to reap their eternal reward). Each master and scholar commands a following of his own because each holds the key to the tiḳun of his followers (only). Indeed, his soul comprises all their souls, and by searching himself he can find their tiḳun.[295]

RSZ makes it very clear that this analysis applies only to the souls of

Israel. Gentile souls are of a completely different and inferior order. They are totally evil, with no redeeming qualities whatsoever.[296] Consequently, references to gentiles in RSZ's teachings are invariably invidious. In general terms, they were created only to test, to punish, to elevate, and ultimately to serve Israel (in the Messianic Era).[297] More specifically, even their wisdom is actually foolishness, because it leads to ego inflation and arrogance rather than to the self-nullification of Ḥokhmah. It pollutes the mind with the (potential) impurity of Ḳelipat Nogah; its highest achievements are descended from the most external aspect of the lowest supernal source.[298] All gentile endeavors, including acts of benevolence, are self-serving.[299] Their courts of justice are harsh and cruel.[300] Their charity does not meet the requirements of *tsedaḳah* because they lack the faith that makes tsedaḳah so valuable: the trust that God will provide for the donor and reimburse his donation.[301] Some discourses describe contemporary gentiles as star worshippers.[302] Those who believe in God are unwilling to cling to Him and incapable of Love or selfless devotion. In any case, they believe only in the immanent god of Aristotle, the First Cause of natural events.[303] They exalt spiritual worship because they deny that God's holiness can be revealed in the physical world.[304] They deny that the vitality of the cosmos is supernaturally renewed every instant and insist instead on its eternal nature to persist in existence.[305] Their philosophers' insight into God's unity does not approach the instinctive perception of a slightly mature Jewish child—or "even a woman."[306] Their thoughts and vile actions are all controlled by their respective supernal princes.[307] They deny individual providence and believe they are independent agents subject only to the control of these princes and the stars.[308] Their physical functions and the lands they inhabit are controlled by natural forces and the three evil ḳelipot.[309] Their material abundance derives from supernal refuse.[310] Indeed, they themselves derive from refuse, which is why they are more numerous than the Jews, as the pieces of chaff outnumber the kernels.[311] Their souls die with their bodies (while even the animal soul of a Jew is eternal).[312] Some gentiles manage to become proselytes because of the holy sparks that were scattered among Abraham's descendents before his circumcision,[313] and it is for these few proselytes that God bestows His abundance on all gentiles. In the future, however, they all will achieve the spiritual stature of Jewish women—and be capable of fulfilling commandments not contingent on a specific time—as well as their level of subordination to Jewish men.[314]

All this denigration of gentiles, particularly when contrasted with the many panegyrics to the souls of Israel, made the age-old problem of Jewish suffering even more distressing. All Jews were innately good, all gentiles innately evil. Jews were the pinnacle of creation and served the Creator, gentiles its nadir and worshipped the heavenly hosts. As servants provide physical sustenance for their masters, the gentile nations were intended to provide physical sustenance for Israel.[315] Yet in eighteenth-century Russia, as always during their exile, Jews were the oppressed and gentiles the oppressors. Upper-class gentiles were wealthy, politically powerful, and at ease in their native lands, while Jews were relatively poor, weak, and ever fearful of tomorrow's decrees. Worst of all, gentiles lived well precisely by exploiting their Jewish compatriots and causing them to live miserably.

For RSZ the kabbalist, however, this paradox was readily resolved, although he admitted that the solution was not readily explicable.[316] Since gentiles were simply the embodiment of the ḳelipot and siṭra aḥra,[317] their power and purpose could be explained in nearly identical terms. They exploit Israel because they must draw their sustenance from ḳedushah. They oppress them because they envy their spiritual superiority and resent their own subordinate role.[318] God permits them to indulge in their depravity because he knows it will lead to their downfall.[319] Their power and material success derive from the infinite lights of Tohu, their supernal source, which (as noted above) transcends Tiḳun, the source of Israel. Since Tohu also transcends all distinctions between good and evil, and its light of Ḥesed is not mitigated by Gevurah, it can bestow unlimited bounty even on the most depraved of men.

Israel, on the other hand, receives its portion of divine beneficence within the bounds of Tiḳun—the source of Torah—and consequently only according to its (Israel's) merits. By struggling and suffering among the gentiles, Jews not only can elevate everything influenced by the neutral Ḳelipat Nogah in their lands, but—particularly when their oppression by the forces of evil heightens their yearning for union with the source of good—they can break through the limitations of Tiḳun to the infinite goodness of Tohu. Their tribulations not only purge and purify them but arouse them to achieve a spirituality they could otherwise never have attained. Thus, the paradoxical purpose of their abject political and economic servitude is to merit that level of divine revelation that descends through Shevirat ha-Kelim to materialize as the undeserved worldly success of their gentile oppressors.[320]

3

Ethical Ways *and* Means

The tension between opposites that characterizes RSZ's metaphysics is fully reflected in his ethical thought. Obstacles to religious and ethical achievement exist in order to stimulate that achievement. The more and greater the opposition, the greater the potential achievement. Where opposition does not apparently exist or is not sufficiently felt, either God or man must reveal or create it.[1] For most men the way to religioethical perfection is the way of constant struggle and overcoming.[2] One discourse attributes this to the evil effects of exile,[3] but most imply that it is inherent in the nature and purpose of the aspiring Benoni. It is his destiny to strive but fail to "divest himself of corporeality," to transcend his limitations and the confines of his body and the physical world.[4] Moreover, the closer man comes to God, the farther he perceives himself to be, and this itself provides the stimulus to approach still closer in the quest for real nearness.[5]

Still, if the average man cannot *actually* achieve transcendence, he can achieve it mentally. He can nullify everything that appears to stand between him and God—ego, body, and world. This process is one aspect of *biṭul* (self-nullification), the most basic and preeminent value in RSZ's axiology (and in the teachings of the Maggid, R. Abraham, and R. Menaḥem Mendel of Vitebsk).[6] All other values, as well as all phenomena, are directly or indirectly related to it. The six workdays of the week, for example, exist only to enable man to renew his biṭul every Shabbat. Indeed, all of creation came into being for the purpose of acknowledging its essential nonbeing.[7] Although RSZ generally stops short of explicitly negating physical reality, he does go so far in some discourses. According to these, the world is merely a mirage, and man must constantly remind himself of this by meditating on its continuous (apparent) recreation from the nothingness that is its true state.[8] Only its Creator is real, and, as other discourses observe, for Him all phenomena, including human affairs, are no more "real" than a theatrical performance.[9] Elsewhere, however, RSZ states that creation, too, is real, but it must constantly nullify itself within the divine Ayin.[10] These two views apparently correspond to the two types of unity discussed in many discourses: *Yiḥuda Ilaʾah* (Upper Unity) and *Yiḥuda Tataʾah* (Lower Unity). Simply stated, the question of creation's reality depends on perspective. From the perspective of Atsilut and above, the world is already, and always has been, nullified. From the perspective of creation below Atsilut, a separate world exists and strives for nullification.[11]

The three rabbinic pillars of the world—Torah, Service (prayer), and acts of compassion—are all means for achieving this nullification.[12] Simply doing God's will in these areas is therefore insufficient; it must be done with the greatest possible biṭul.[13] One discourse boldly states that the biṭul accompanying the fulfillment of His will is axiologically superior to fulfilling that will.[14] Other discourses stress that the Torah was given only after a national act of biṭul. The highest form of Torah-wisdom is Ḥokhmah, the sefirotic exemplar of biṭul that corresponds to the most profound perception of God's absolute oneness and the concomitant nonexistence of anything else.[15] The highest form of prayer is the *ʿAmidah,* a silent, motionless act of devotion that is, or should be, the expression of biṭul par excellence.[16] The commandments and all other acts that accord with God's will are acts of ego-nullification, and their most perfect exponents, the Patriarchs, were therefore known as God's Chariot, a mere vehicle for His will.[17]

It follows, therefore, that doing anything contrary to one's natural instincts, urges, and desires—contrary, in other words, to one's ego (=animal soul)—is an act of biṭul. "Nullify your will before His will" is the key rabbinic dictum; "acceptance of the yoke" (*ḳabalat ʿol*), the key rabbinic value; and heteronomy, the primary ethical aspect of the commandments.[18] By suppressing his will in favor of God's will, man reveals the divine Will in this world, thereby realizing the purpose of its creation. Even the necessity for biṭul itself, usually explained in terms of God's unity, is occasionally grounded in His unfathomable will: Biṭul is essential to Service because He desires to derive pleasure from it.[19]

Because self-nullification includes nullification of one's intellect, the importance of simple and unquestioning obedience to God's decrees is repeatedly underscored. The central relationship between God and man is that of king to subject. This king is not a constitutional monarch but an absolute ruler who governs by fiat and whose every decree is its own justification. RSZ goes much further than Judah Halevi and even the Maharal of Prague in this respect, and, needless to say, he is completely at odds with such rationalists as Saadya or Maimonides on this issue.[20] The rationality or apparent irrationality of a commandment is totally irrelevant to Service. Nor is it desirable to build an edifice of rationality on a solid foundation of obedience.[21] Rather, one's entire religious posture must be permeated with absolute obedience, without concern for the function or purpose of the decree obeyed. Even an act that did not effect a vital supernal *yiḥud*—and therefore had, for RSZ, no "reason"—would, if commanded, be no less of a mitsvah. Were chopping wood a commandment, it would have to be obeyed with the same zeal and devotion as hearing the shofar on Rosh Hashanah.[22] This attitude is based on the assumptions that intellectual motivation is self-gratifying and that any admixture of personal desire or pleasure, whether emotional or intellectual, falls short of totally selfless Service.[23]

The importance of minimizing self-gratification in Service is also reflected in the fact that many discourses point to Fear, rather than Love, as the highest, or at least the most essential, religious emotion. Like the Maggid and several of the Maggid's other disciples, RSZ saw Fear, or awe, as the emotive concomitant of biṭul (= Ḥokhmah). Arising out of the subject's consciousness of his utter insignificance when confronting the King, it motivates him to serve selflessly, for he is painfully aware that only selfless Service can justify his existence by completely subordinating him to the King's self-justified existence. Love, however, can arise only in the heart of a man who feels he is an entity in his own right; he is less conscious of his insignificance than of his separateness from his beloved King. Love therefore motivates him to serve for the selfish, if lofty, purpose of drawing nearer to his beloved.[24]

Biṭul should thus encompass the entire man. His intellect must perceive that true knowledge consists of understanding how God is unknowable; how true goodness is identical with the infinite and therefore with the suprarational; how all existence is nullified within God and therefore cannot really be known;[25] and how secular knowledge—the knowledge of things other than God—is therefore false and, when pursued for its own sake, inimical to spiritual perfection.[26] Man's emotions must cringe before God's overwhelming presence. He is encouraged to meditate on his lowliness and distance from God in order to arouse feelings of spiritual self-pity and inadequacy.[27] He is reminded that even his natural concern for his physical health or for his family's well-being is reprehensible if it clashes, as it often does, with total self-abandonment to God's will.[28] Like preoccupation with one's livelihood, which will be discussed below, these concerns presuppose that physical life is innately desirable, when in fact the divine soul desires nothing more than to depart from the body and return to its Source. Only its obligation to create an "abode for Him below" keeps it involuntarily anchored in this corporeal world.[29]

Interpersonal relations and personal ambition should also be governed by the principle of biṭul. Modesty, self-effacement, and deference to one's betters—that is, everyone[30]—are the essential personality traits. Spiritual achievement must not lead to self-consciousness or self-esteem. Striving for deveḳut is, after all, the divine soul's natural tendency. It is the degree of effort that counts, and in this the simple cobbler may outshine the full-time scholar. Conversely, the scholar must remember that his minor misdeeds are spiritually more serious, both for his soul and for the supernal worlds, than the cobbler's relatively major sins.[31] This spiritual, self-effacing attitude will prevent him from casting a critical eye at any Jew, from insisting that only his mode of Service is proper, and from taking mundane matters seriously.[32] This last point is particularly important for the merchant, who must remember that all forms of worldly ambition—social, economic, or political—are to be suppressed or sublimated, for they derive from the ego and are not directed toward the only goal worthy of pursuit: union with God.[33]

All forms of self-concern are to be shunned. Even an act of Service tainted with self-interest, such as avoiding sin for fear of divine punishment, becomes partially evil and generates more serious evils.[34] Service must be motivated solely by a sense of duty to obey the King and reveal His Divinity on earth.[35] The less the subject enjoys it—indeed, the more he feels its coercive, heteronomous yoke—the purer and higher it is. The greatest single act of devotion is therefore the one that most strongly opposes man's strongest instinct, that of self-preservation. This is the act or attitude of *mesirat nefesh*—total self-abandonment. In most discourses, RSZ, translating mesirat nefesh as "delivering up one's will," identifies this with nullifying the ego-controlled will until it becomes wholly congruent with God's will.[36] In several discourses, however, RSZ discusses the supremacy of the highest form of mesirat nefesh, that of R. Eliezer ben Durdaya, the lifelong sinner whose brief burst of penitential self-nullification permeated even his physical being and caused him actually to expire. He thus managed, according to RSZ, to "reach" the supernal source of the commandments he had neglected all his life and attain an even higher level of spirituality than he could have attained by fulfilling them.[37] Although RSZ was realistic enough to realize that R. Eliezer could not serve as a model for others—in fact, it would generally run counter to God's will that man serve Him in *this* world[38]—he nevertheless uses this aggadah to illustrate the axiological primacy of total mesirat nefesh; that is, complete biṭul and freedom from corporeality through actively desired, but not actively sought, martyrdom. This form of mesirat nefesh encompasses both will and body, and therefore constitutes the highest level of Service possible.[39]

But while it is impossible and undesirable for most men to emulate R. Eliezer, it is possible and desirable to approximate his act of physical self-extinction through asceticism and occasional self-mortification. Denying the demands of one's body and animal soul nullifies these antispiritual forces at least partially by reducing their strength, influence, and significance. The divine soul's spiritual light can then manifest itself that much more easily.[40] While rejecting the extremes of Ḥaside Ashkenaz and R. Isaac Luria as too onerous for his generation, RSZ nevertheless advocates a significant degree of self-denial, particularly penitential fasting.[41] This, too, is a function of his emphasis on biṭul, for asceticism was considered (by most mystics) to be the only way in which the body could be negated, almost nullified, and thereby spiritualized.[42] Every act of self-denial, every suppression of instinct, habit, and physical desire is thus an act of mesirat nefesh writ small.[43] RSZ generally refers to such suppression by the Zoharic term *itkafya*, and in *Tanya* he makes a point of citing the Zohar's statement concerning "the great satisfaction before Him, blessed be He, when the siṭra aḥra is subdued [itkafya] here below, for then the glory of the Holy One, blessed be He, rises above all, more than by any praise, and this ascent is greater than all else."[44]

Most of RSZ's specific ethical ways are ramifications of the biṭul imperative. Their place in his hierarchy of ethical values is determined by their relation to this supreme value. The metaphysical ratso-shov cycle, for example, appears in this ethical context as Love (ratso)—a surge of yearning for union that threatens to tear the soul from its corporeal moorings—and Fear (shov)—a recoiling from this audacious movement motivated by the disciplined acceptance of the yoke of the commandments. Because Love involves desire and the aspiration to gratify that desire, it contains, as noted above, an egotistical element, whereas Fear and the concomitant devotion to the heteronomous commandments are the result of the suppression of all personal desire; that is, the posture of biṭul.[45] Accordingly, in one discourse ratso is linked with memale, since only memale has lower gradations that yearn to ascend; while shov corresponds to sovev, before which all levels are equally nullified.[46] In another discourse we are told that the ecstasy of ratso is not valuable per se but only because it is a necessary prelude to its counterpart: The greater the surge of ratso, the greater the self-restraint necessary to keep it in check, and it is precisely this self-restraint, which is a form of self-denial, that fulfils God's ultimate will.[47]

Much like Maimonides, who argued for God's "gracious ruse" in commanding certain beliefs and practices not for their intrinsic validity but because they were prerequisites for ultimately attaining the intellectual love of God,[48] RSZ urged his followers to cultivate certain attitudes and arouse certain emotions as prerequisites to what he believed were the Torah's ultimate religious goals. He advocated, for example, weekly or monthly periods of introspection and self-berating that, ideally, were to culminate in a tearful outpouring of the heart. This weeping was intended simultaneously to purge the soul of its spiritual guilt and of all its worldly worries; it would then be capable of serving God with unadulterated joy.[49] An important element in this introspective procedure is spiritual self-pity, the need for which RSZ discusses frequently. By arousing pity (raḥamim) for the divine spark imprisoned in his body and forced to participate in corporeal, secular, and even sinful actions, man arouses divine mercy (raḥamim) upon his lowly state and thereby enlists the divine assistance necessary for rising out of this mundane mire and returning to God through Love (*teshuvah me-ahavah*).[50] Although actually and pathetically insensitive to his soul's abject condition, man must stimulate, and even simulate, profound feelings of self-pity in order to attain this goal.[51] Similarly, although he may be incapable of actually feeling Love and Fear, he must at least arouse within himself the consciousness of his duty to feel these emotions, for without them wholehearted devotion to fulfilling the commandments is impossible. It is arguable, in fact, that RSZ employed a "gracious ruse" of his own; that he occasionally demanded of his followers attainments that were beyond them because he knew that their failure to live up to his expectations would result in self-abasement, a necessary steppingstone to self-nullification.[52]

The other key values frequently discussed in the discourses, such as incessant toil, striving, and spiritual fortitude, are also offshoots of the biṭul imperative. Service without unrelenting toil, both mental and physical, is not worthy of the name, for Service is synonymous with the struggle to nullify the ever-present impediments to union: the body and animal soul.[53] Complacency, the opposite of constant striving, is an egotistical state and therefore inimical to biṭul.[54] Fortitude enables man to retain his powerful, suprarational devotion to God's will in the face of the many obstacles he encounters daily. Having fortified himself during his morning prayers, he can ignore or overcome these obstacles by single-mindedly and steadfastly clinging to God; that is, by concentrating on the idea of unio and the selflessness (biṭul) necessary to achieve it.[55] He must be willing to abandon everything—health, wealth, family, and all personal pleasures and considerations—for this goal. Even the pleasure accompanying deveḳut should be shunned, and, since reason militates against such self-effacing zeal, reason, too, must be nullified.[56] In addition, all forms of Service must be performed without any feeling of personal achievement; to be aware of one's Service is a form of egoism.[57]

Although RSZ occasionally softens these demands,[58] they are characteristic of most of the ethical discourses, and they illustrate an interesting paradox of Hasidism in general. Much of Hasidic literature is based on the assumption that everything in the world and everything in the Torah speaks to each Jew *as an individual* and instructs him in the attainment of that level of perfection that his particular soul-powers allow him to attain. The Hasidic masters taught each man to be acutely aware of the value of *his* Service. They inculcated in him the belief that *his* Service, no matter how relatively humble, has cosmic significance; that it can move and sustain worlds, and hasten the Messianic Era, when all "will be able to apprehend the revealed divine light."[59] Yet even as he was assimilating this awareness and conviction, and acting accordingly, his motivation was to be absolutely selfless and his goal was to be self-nullification. In other words, although the Torah was given and everything was created for the purpose of elevating one's self (and, through it, one's surroundings), all attempts to achieve this must be selfless, and the ultimate elevation of the self consists of self-nullification.[60] This paradox resulted from the masters' need to join two divergent views of man. They retained the rabbinic affirmation of man's integrity and worth in a world separate from its Creator and married it to the mystical belief in a world essentially submerged in God, in which man is expected to reflect this submergence through self-nullification.

To be conscious of this paradox, as many of RSZ's followers undoubtedly were, is to live in a state of constant religious tension, which is exactly what RSZ wanted. These Hasidim alternated between periods of melancholy or even depression, when the awareness of their inability to achieve complete biṭul had the upper hand, and periods of elation, when the awareness of their supreme position in the hierarchy of creation came to the fore. RSZ encouraged this fluctuation[61] for several reasons. First, it mirrored the natural swings of mood most people regularly experience. These moods were to be transformed from feelings about oneself and one's worldly affairs into emotions fueling selfless Service. Several chapters in *Tanya* (to be discussed below) are devoted to detailed instructions on just how to achieve this transformation.[62] Second, like other Hasidic masters, RSZ believed that this fluctuation reflected the pulsating ratso-shov cycle, as well as the alternating ascendency of each member of the other pairs of ontological opposites that defined his universe.[63] It was therefore not only part of man's psychological makeup but a necessary element in the makeup of the universe as a whole. Finally, and perhaps most important, RSZ taught, as noted above, that God derives pleasure from tension, struggle, and novelty. Finite, corporeal man struggling to transcend his limitations, contending with internal religious tension, and succeeding, at least partially, at self-nullification—a novelty comparable to an exciting animal fight or a talking bird; this embattled, heroic creature combined all three pleasure-producing phenomena. Anything heightening the tension or increasing the intensity of the struggle was therefore valuable, even if it was contrived or created for that purpose only; for after all, by doing so man was only following God's precedent.[64]

In addition to toil, striving, and fortitude, which may be classified as ethical ways, three other general ethical values, which may be classified as ethical means, are central to RSZ's view of the good man, the Benoni—meditation, joy, and faith. These, too, have biṭul interwoven throughout their fabric, and, like every other aspect of RSZ's religioethical thought, they are interrelated.

Julius Guttman has described Maimonides' piety as being "of a markedly contemplative character,"[65] and we have already touched on the great power kabbalists attached to human thought.[66] Yet, over and above these influences, RSZ's emphasis on meditation as the key to religioethical perfection is extraordinary.[67] Meditation on one theme or another is for RSZ both a necessary accompaniment to every commandment and an overarching religioethical requirement in its own right. Although these themes are often couched in kabbalistic terminology, they are seldom merely series of technical Lurianic kavanot intended to effect certain sefirotic unions. They generally have intellectual content and are intended to elicit or stimulate certain emotions. Meditation may be on God, on man, on creation, or on one aspect or another of their interrelation. It may center on God's greatness: His creative ability, omnipotence, omnipresence, unity, or immutability;[68] on the meditator's own insignificance, frailty, sinfulness, and alienation from his Maker;[69] or on the continuous creation of every existent through the divine life force within it, on its actual nullification vis-à-vis this force, and on the nullification of this force vis-à-vis the Godhead.[70] The most detailed treatment of a meditation theme in *Tanya* and the discourses was reserved for introspective meditation, a fact that itself made the attainment of biṭul that much harder, since it is obviously impossible to nullify one's ego while frequently and assiduously contemplating its very real and very powerful presence. But this problem is only a facet of the general paradox of Hasidism mentioned above, and RSZ undoubtedly welcomed the religious tension it added.

The faith that RSZ promulgated in his teachings was not simply the belief in a creator ex nihilo who constantly sustains creation. This doctrine he considered to be self-evident and therefore not an object of belief but of knowledge.[71] Its essential details, however—that the act of creation does not change the Creator and that created existents have no independent reality—are occasionally termed objects of a belief inherited by all Israel from the Patriarchs, and occasionally objects of knowledge that, because of the soul's corporeal imprisonment and dimmed perception, require profound meditation to apprehend clearly. In any event, such facts belong to the realm of memale, which even gentiles can appreciate. The only true object of faith, says RSZ, is sovev, of which only Israel partakes and in which only Jews instinctively believe. This aspect of God infinitely transcends creation and His role as creator. It is this aspect, which resides even in the depths of the material world and vitalizes the ḳelipot, that gentiles—and Mitnagdim—do not accept. Gentiles insist on removing God from contact with the corporeal, while Mitnagdim, following the Vilna Gaon's "philosophical" theology, refuse to acknowledge His presence among the ḳelipot despite the fact that most Jews have always unquestioningly accepted this truth. In a long epistle to his followers RSZ tries to defend what he considers the traditional view. He finally concludes that no written argument can possibly resolve the issue; only an oral exposition to a select group of Mitnagdim could carry the day.[72] Needless to say, this group was in no mood to listen.

To his followers, however, RSZ could address epistles and discourses in which this belief is simply demanded. Accepting and remembering it will enable them to avoid anger and hatred and optimistically to weather all adversity, for they will realize that every painful experience, even though its immediate cause is a human agent, actually derives from the ḳelipot, the source of all evil, and that the ḳelipot, in turn, are vitalized by an omnipresent, absolutely good Creator. All evil, therefore, including all human suffering, is actually a hidden, incomprehensible, and therefore higher form of good.[73] "And this is the essence of the faith for which man was created: to believe that there is no place void of Him, and in the light of the King's countenance there is life, and therefore strength and gladness are in His place, because He is only good."[74] Since this belief is far from instinctive, RSZ felt that its acceptance and efficacy depended on inculcation and contemplation.[75]

The relation among the three major ethical means is thus apparent. Meditation is a prerequisite for attaining RSZ's form of faith, which in turn is a prerequisite for joyous acceptance of adversity and the positive, buoyant attitude that is a hallmark of Hasidism. Moreover, as RSZ explains frequently, meditation also directly gives rise to joy, because joy is actually "a revelation of the [pleasure] hidden" in the soul, and Binah, the faculty of meditation, is the instrument that reveals the hidden depths of Ḥokhmah, the repository of pleasure.[76] The ground is thus prepared for serving God with the pure joy that should accompany the fulfillment of His will (*śimḥah shel mitsṿah*). This joy is itself one of the highest levels of Service; indeed, only by attaining it was R. Isaac Luria able to scale the heights of spirituality.[77]

There remained, however, the problem of despondency that arises not from external but from internal, psychological causes. Periods of depression that everyone occasionally experiences, precisely because they are natural, universal, and recurrent, presented a major problem for RSZ's Benoni. Because RSZ posited a continuous state of war between the evil inclination and the good, and particularly because the combatants were about equally matched, speed, zeal, and energy were crucial to victory. "It is impossible to conquer [one's evil nature] with laziness and heaviness that originate in sadness and in a heart dulled like a stone, but rather with alacrity that derives from joy and from a heart that is free and cleansed from any trace of worry and sadness in the world."[78] RSZ therefore devotes much attention to psychological strategies for dealing with periodic depression. These episodes were to be examined and their nature determined. Those actually stemming from external vicissitudes were to be overcome with the faith described above.[79] Those stemming from feelings of dissatisfaction or guilt regarding one's past or present spiritual shortcomings must be postponed for regularly scheduled introspective sessions when such a negative self-image could be used to achieve positive results.[80] Those for which no specific cause could be found or for which faith proved insufficient were to be immediately transformed into such a session.[81]

But periodic depression was more than an occasional disadvantage for the divine soul. Since depression hindered Service, its source had to be the siṭra aḥra. If the depression was internally generated, its source had to be the siṭra aḥra within man, his evil inclination (yetser ha-ra).[82] The attempt to overcome such depression could itself therefore be seen as one of the major battles that the divine soul must regularly wage against its wily opponent. Consequently, sadness arising from one's apparent spiritual weakness—the inability to suppress profane thoughts, for example—could be overcome by simply accepting one's lot as an aspiring Benoni, as one of the vast majority of men whose purpose in life is constantly to struggle with profane thoughts, speech, and actions naturally arising from the animal soul and the yetser ha-ra. This should not only relieve the aspiring Benoni of his melancholy but actually lead him to rejoice in its cause; for by striving to overcome his nature he fulfils his mission in life, and by continually suppressing, but not overcoming, the siṭra aḥra, he is a source of constant pleasure to God.[83]

The two-soul doctrine that made this approach possible also permitted RSZ to advocate sublimating depression through self-abasement sessions without running the risk of deepening that depression. These sessions were to be appended to *Tiḳun Ḥatsot*, a period already devoted to lamentation. They were further tied to this ritual by a cause-effect relation and by the theme of spiritual pity: What better time to lament the divine spark's pathetic exile in (i.e., subordination to) the animal soul than during a session already set aside for lamenting its result—the Shekhinah's pathetic exile among the ḳelipot? In fact, since the divine spark (i.e., the divine soul) and the Shekhinah could be identified with Malkhut, and the animal soul derived from Ḳelipat Nogah, this simply amounted to taking a ritual originally centered on a metaphysical theme and centering it on its personalistic reflection, a common Hasidic phenomenon.[84]

But RSZ went further. Weaving rabbinic, kabbalistic, and Hasidic ideas into a cohesive doctrine, he insisted that such self-abasement sessions were often the only way to overcome the siṭra aḥra, whose entire power stemmed from delusory self-aggrandizement. Because a Benoni's "self" is actually his animal soul, and because this soul's poisonous influence derives from its arrogance and assertiveness, the antidote is clearly self-abasement and self-effacement.[85] Thus, like all obstacles to Service, periodic depression is actually an opportunity to enhance Service. Indeed, the perennially sanguine personality is at a disadvantage in not having a regular, natural stimulus for self-abasement. Similarly, the full-time scholar who is hard pressed to find fault with himself requires special attention. RSZ therefore took pains to provide him with the necessary meditation material and further urged him to consult musar works for additional assistance.[86]

Having achieved some measure of self-abasement during Tiḳun Ḥatsot, the meditator must then turn his attention to God's greatness and contemplate it in detail. The infinite contrast between his divine soul's present abject state of subordination to the animal soul and its original union with God should arouse self-pity and move him to tears. This weeping is a catharsis. It washes away his personal concerns, cleanses his heart of sadness, and permits joy to replace it.[87] The greater his self-pity and dejection, the greater the resultant joy.[88]

This joy is to be achieved by another meditative shift. He must now turn his thoughts from the depression-producing animal soul to the joy-producing divine soul. He must contemplate his invaluable ability to liberate this soul from its prison and exile, and the King's boundless joy when this long-lost prince is released and returns to Him.[89] He might also contemplate God's unity; that is, the fact that, in truth, nothing besides Him exists because all creation is nullified within Him. And "when one will deeply contemplate this, his heart will be gladdened and his soul will rejoice with [great] joy and singing, with all his heart and soul and might, in this faith that is great, for this is [the experience of] God's actual nearness, and this is the whole [purpose] of man and the goal of his creation, as well as the creation of all the worlds, both upper and lower, that He may have an abode below. . . . Behold how great is the joy of a common and lowly man when he is brought near to a king of flesh and blood who accepts his hospitality and lodges under his roof. How infinitely more so is the [joy in the] abiding nearness of the Supreme King of kings."[90]

The fact remained, however, that RSZ was advocating the conscious arousal of depression, if only as a means to attain unadulterated joy, and the question arose: How could he enlist the aid of a state of mind originating in the siṭra aḥra? Two answers with essentially the same rationale are provided. First, it is actually bitterness, not dejection, that he is advocating. Dejection is passive and inhibits Service, whereas bitterness arising from an active dissatisfaction with one's spiritual failings acts as a spur—an unpleasant but very effective stimulus to greater Service. Its source, to be sure, is Gevurah, but *holy* Gevurah, which must sometimes be aroused "in order to sweeten the stern judgments arising from the animal soul and evil nature . . . for the stern judgments [which give rise to the siṭra aḥra] can be sweetened only at their source [Gevurah]."[91] Second, even if a self-abasement session should result in real despondency, one must remember that this feeling is one of the tactics required to overcome the enemy, for "the method of subduing the siṭra aḥra is on the latter's own ground. . . . With regard to this it is written: 'In all sadness there is profit' (Prov. 14:23), the profit being the joy that follows the sadness."[92] It is noteworthy that this rationale runs counter to the reason RSZ gives for the need to achieve self-abasement in the first place: the arrogant, puffed-up siṭra aḥra must be degraded and deflated; that is, it must be fought by *opposing* its primary traits.[93]

Ideally, the transition from sadness to joy should be effected during a single meditation session. In Talmudic times, according to RSZ, men were sufficiently masters of their emotions to achieve this transition instantaneously, just prior to the morning prayers. They could then turn to God with a carefree, joyous spirit, without which Love, like prophecy, is impossible. "In this orphaned generation," however, a transition period of several hours is required: from Tiḳun Ḥatsot to the morning service.[94] Then, having finally attained a feeling of great joy, the worshipper must once again redirect his thoughts. Now he is obligated to recall his abject position in the spiritual hierarchy. He must not consider himself *completely* evil, as that would lead to defeatism; but he must remind himself of how far he still is from realizing his spiritual potential. The tension, in other words, must never slacken. If the meditator himself fails to maintain it, the siṭra aḥra is never remiss. The more successfully it is suppressed, the harder it fights; its reserves of profane thoughts and enticing distractions are limitless.[95]

Meditation giving rise to contemplative forms of faith and joy is thus the foundation of RSZ's religioethical system as presented in *Tanya* and the discourses. Hasidic practices, even practices that were major factors in the religious life of every Ḥabad Hasid, are relegated to the background. Inspirational song, fervent dancing, pilgrimages to the Rebbe, social gatherings for the purpose of mutual exhortation and inspiration (*farbrengen*)—all the external forms of a Hasid's religious life—are completely overshadowed by the emphasis on contemplative piety. Singing and dancing, in fact, are sometimes treated rather disparagingly as antiintellectual manifestations of emotionalism.[96] One discourse does emphasize the pleasure-producing quality of melody, and since, as we have seen, RSZ considered pleasure the highest of all powers, this is obviously a positive assessment.[97] A second discourse admits that some men require melody to arouse their Love and Fear.[98] A third claims superiority for wordless melody over songs with words because of its higher supernal origin.[99] Another adds that the highest and innermost yearnings of the heart, as well as its highest form of knowledge (Keter = pleasure) can be expressed only through wordless song.[100] Other discourses identify song with the biṭul of the angels and disembodied souls; its changes of tone and tempo with ratso and shov.[101] But, although RSZ himself composed a number of moving melodies, nowhere is song explicitly described as essential to proper Service.[102] Dancing is given even less axiological prominence, with one discourse stating that its effect on all except the greatest intellects tends to be detrimental: It excites the mind and deprives it of the tranquility required for contemplation.[103] The value of a farbrengen is only hinted at in several discourses that note the spiritual potency of a gathering of at least ten Jews.[104]

Yet we know from other sources that RSZ considered these practices to be invaluable, that he strongly encouraged them, and that he enthusiastically participated in them.[105] That this is not apparent from the discourses (or *Tanya,* Parts 1–3) reflects their circumscribed function and purpose. In them RSZ was addressing primarily the inner man, his ideas, thoughts, feelings, beliefs, drives, and values. Since the highest "inner" faculty of inner man was intellect, and the proper function of intellect was religious and theological contemplation, practices that impeded contemplation, even temporarily, could be considered problematic. The outer man and his institutions—his specific social, political, and economic activities; specific literary, scientific, and educational endeavors; and even external forms of religious endeavor—were generally not within the purview of the discourses. RSZ dealt with this man through personal contact, public and private letters, and halakhic monographs and responsa. Thus, he set forth detailed regulations governing his followers' pilgrimages to him in a series of *Taḳanot* (regulations) that reveal him as a strong, pragmatic, and efficient administrator.[106] These traits are even more evident in his many letters concerning the collection of funds for the new Hasidic community in the Holy Land.[107] Similarly, his basic views on the Zaddik's proper role in his followers' external lives appear not in the discourses but in several epistles and letters.[108]

Taken together with several references in the discourses,[109] these sources portray the Zaddik as a spiritual guide, a teacher of religious truths, and a source of inspiration. He has the ability to arouse Love and Fear in his followers, but only if they exert themselves unstintingly in study, contemplation, introspection, and self-improvement. True, their personal devotion to him must be boundless, and the spiritual beneficence of faith, Love, and Fear he bestows on them, both during and after his lifetime, is directly proportionate to this devotion. But every disciple "must prepare himself . . . with a great preparation and immense effort to receive these attributes."[110] Contrary to what many of RSZ's colleagues maintained, the Zaddik is not—to use an anachronistic metaphor—the locomotive to which one need only be attached in order to move forward. Every man possesses and must maintain and improve his own spiritual engine. The Zaddik is, rather, the master engineer who is called upon to assist in these tasks. But his expertise ends there. Questions about one's livelihood are outside his provenance. Only a full-fledged prophet such as Samuel could advise Saul on how to recover his father's property. Difficult times do not change this truth. In a long letter brimming with pathos and compassion, RSZ implores his impoverished followers to refrain from pouring out their hearts to him. Not only is he powerless to improve their lot, but by expatiating on their plight they make him unbearably miserable. Often, in fact, this problem caused him seriously to consider fleeing to the Holy Land.[111]

According to Schneersohn tradition, such appeals proved futile. Both RSZ and his successors continued to receive and attempted to resolve or ameliorate every kind of personal problem. But RSZ's insistence on independent religious effort bore fruit (although never as ripe and plentiful as he would have wished). He was absolutely convinced that in this, as in virtually all his teachings, he was only continuing the tradition of the Besht and Maggid. Indeed, the premises of this position appeared to him to be axiomatic: To arouse *true* Love and Fear without meditation is impossible; and to serve God properly without arousing Love and Fear is equally impossible.[112] His Zaddikist colleagues were distorting their masters' teaching. The Besht and Maggid would never agree that the essence of faith is faith in the Zaddik, in his ability unilaterally to elevate his followers. Such faith, no matter how strong, is too superficial a force materially to affect a man's behavior, let alone refine his character. "The thief at the tunnel's entrance calls upon God for assistance."[113] His faith in God does not prevent him from flouting God's will, nor can his faith in the Zaddik. Only by internalizing God's will through laborious study and meditation can one be assured of fulfilling it. This is the path that the Talmud describes as "long yet short"—long on effort and time, yet short in leading to the desired destination—while the path that glorifies simple, unintellectualized faith is actually interminable.[114]

The gulf between RSZ's approach to this issue and that of some of his colleagues can best be gauged from R. Abraham Kalisker's diatribes.[115] In letters beginning shortly after the publication of *Tanya* and spanning at least a decade, R. Abraham accuses RSZ of departing from the teachings of their masters. Inundating Hasidim with complex religioethical teachings, he claims, is simply counterproductive. It results in a sterile intellectualization of religion, the ethical and emotive elements of which are then either neglected or overshadowed by useless cognitive achievements. What is worse, the masses misinterpret and distort ethical teachings clothed in kabbalistic garb, and the teachings in *Tanya* are no exception. This work is merely the latest addition to an already overlong list of ethical guides that can, at best, only teach but not inspire, edify but not elevate. Most of the advice it contains is common knowledge, and all of it has proved futile in shaking the coarse masses of Poland-Russia out of their spiritual lethargy. Furthermore, it is possible to overdo a good thing. Torah is only the oil necessary to kindle the spark of fervent worship; too much of it extinguishes the flame. The Besht and the Maggid took great pains to avoid this possibility by pouring out Torah in small but potent doses. In this way they were able to inculcate lofty religious ethics and faith in the powers of the Zaddik. They thereby transformed their followers into truly God-fearing men, and "whoever has the fear of God in his heart has the entire Torah and perfect wisdom in his heart."[116] RSZ, however, publicly expatiates on esoteric aspects of the Torah from which only a handful of his followers can possibly benefit and which feed the delusions of spiritual grandeur harbored by many Hasidim. He would be far better advised to provide private guidance for the scholars and restrict his teachings for everyone else to "faith in the Zaddik and recognition of their [own] shortcomings."

According to R. Abraham, RSZ himself had repeatedly asserted that, unlike the ludicrous pretentions imbibed by Hasidim elsewhere, the Hasidim of White Russia must be taught honest introspection, meditation on their insignificance and their sins, true contriteness, and studied avoidance of unattainable, presumptuous religious aspirations.[117] But now even they are plagued by delusions and hypocrisy. Surely this is because RSZ's extreme modesty as a disciple prevented him from inquiring about and learning "the [proper] method of leadership from the mouths of the great."

In one of his early letters relating to this controversy, R. Abraham is so certain that RSZ will see the light that he urges him to support his efforts to discredit RSZ among RSZ's own followers. Every Hasid, he points out, must first refine his body and purify his soul through pure faith and the fear of God, particularly simple fear of punishment, which, contrary to RSZ, is absolutely essential for all and quite sufficient for most. Only then can he be very gradually exposed to the intellectual aspects of Hasidism, and even then, danger lurks, for "the source of ratiocination is the source of stern judgment," and "from reason flows immorality."[118] Indeed, a primary purpose of the Torah is to guard against the pitfalls of reason and speculation. The hazard, moreover, was particularly great in RSZ's environs, where, in R. Abraham's opinion, the masses were unusually crass[119] and therefore more prone to misconceptions.

Although RSZ was supported in this controversy by R. Levi Isaac of Berditchev,[120] neither the latter nor any other disciple of the Maggid shared RSZ's belief in the primacy of meditation for every Jew. Consequently, only RSZ poured forth torrents of kabbalistic teachings in order to provide his followers with ample and appropriate material on which to meditate (in addition to Zoharic discourses through which he discharged his obligation to teach the secrets of the Torah to anyone capable of understanding them). It is therefore surprising that he provided little guidance in specific meditation techniques.[121] Not until the appearance of his son's *Ḳunṭres ha-Hitpaʿalut* sometime in the 1830s[122] was this lacuna filled. Possibly RSZ felt that while the meditation themes he treated are universally valid, the ways in which one uses them must be personal; what works for one man will not work for another.

Equally puzzling, perhaps, is the discourses' relatively infrequent treatment of the need to refine one's character, a goal that RSZ is known to have emphasized no less than his mentors, R. Menaḥem Mendel of Vitebsk and R. Menaḥem Naḥum of Chernobyl, and for which he found ample precedent in Vital, who exhorted his readers to expend greater effort on avoiding undesirable character traits than on fulfilling the commandments.[123] Although the discourses point to certain qualities RSZ wanted his followers to cultivate—modesty, integrity, earnestness, compassion, generosity, patience, restraint, reticence, diligence, energy, self-discipline, sensitivity, judiciousness—he does not discuss these as independently valuable ethical traits[124] (although such an inference may possibly be drawn), but rather as prerequisites for, or adjuncts to, the proper fulfillment of certain religious obligations.[125] Thus, modesty is essential because it is the social counterpart of biṭul; compassion and generosity are necessary for the commandment of tsedaḳah; and diligence is required for the commandment of Torah-study.[126] RSZ's explicit ethical thought, in other words, is wholly theocentric; even when discussing man, it is God Who preoccupies him. Instead of the ramified ethical theory we might have expected, what emerges is a scattering of ethical insights that are completely subordinated to RSZ's foremost concern in the discourses—theology. (*Tanya*, of course, does deal primarily with ethics, but almost exclusively with religious ethics, the values relating to Service.)

Another salient general feature of the discourses is that whenever possible, RSZ concentrates on the positive and the desirable: "A little light dispels much darkness." In this he was following his Hasidic masters, who rejected the strident condemnation of sin found in musar works and emphasized instead man's ability to overcome his evil inclination and the character traits it generates.[127] It is true, RSZ admitted, that most people possess some undesirable qualities that are notoriously difficult to eradicate. Innate personality differences result in differences of ability to refine certain traits. However, one should not worry about these stubborn flaws but rather use them constructively wherever possible.[128] Although the traditional order of Service calls for man first to "turn from evil" and only then to "do good" (Ps. 34:15), and several discourses do indeed recommend this order, quite a few advocate avoiding confrontation or at least preoccupation with one's dark side and concentrating instead on God's greatness. Abundant meditation on the various facets of this theme and the concomitant fulfillment of the commandments will suffice to subdue this evil side by flooding it with light.[129]

But the average man could obviously not meditate constantly or be continuously engaged in spiritualizing endeavors. Despite the spiritual fortitude that RSZ's followers were exhorted to develop, sooner or later the exigencies of the *ḳelipah*-filled material world thrust themselves into the consciousness of every man unable to live the cloistered life of the scholar. Even the wings of thought did not permit the average Hasid to soar above his physical and temporal confines for long. Pain, poverty, persecution, daily dealing with a coarse peasantry—the usual quota of human and Jewish suffering augmented by an unusually harsh social and economic environment—combined to undermine even the most intense contemplative efforts. Informed as he was of every detail of his followers' hardships, RSZ apparently felt obligated to address himself to them even in the usually otherworldly discourses.

RSZ considered the need to seek one's livelihood a necessary evil,[130] and he approached it in much the same way he approached the problem of evil in general. Just as the ḳelipot had no power independent of the divine force vitalizing them, a man's vocation could not provide his livelihood unless it received an influx of Ḥesed, the sefirah of divine benevolence. All efforts at earning a living merely constitute the vessel required by Ḥesed to manifest itself in the material world.[131] Because of its lofty origin, the light of Ḥesed must be clothed in endeavors that mislead the masses into believing that material success is wholly contingent on, and commensurate with, man's vocational efforts: The more thought and planning he invests in his vocation, the more shrewdness, dedication, and energy he brings to it, the more successful he will be. The masses therefore become totally engrossed in mundane affairs that coarsen them spiritually and exhaust them physically and emotionally. Even during prayer, when their minds should be filled with God's unity and greatness, they remain immersed in their worldly concerns and thus unable to arouse Love and Fear. Forever worried about tomorrow, they are unable to serve God with joy today.[132]

RSZ's followers must avoid these pitfalls. Preoccupation with one's vocation means attributing real power to the vessel rather than to Ḥesed. It is a form of idolatry, cutting a Jew off from God and placing him in the camp of the gentiles, who are called dead even while alive.[133] It is as silly as the seriousness with which children play their trivial games.[134] It is utterly unreasonable, for if a man does not constantly worry about the tortures of Hell that may await him, why should he constantly worry that his livelihood may elude him? Why should he exert himself more to attain worldly pleasures that derive from supernal refuse than he exerts himself to rejoice in, and unite with, the Source of all true pleasure?[135] Although mundane vocational activities are necessary "to make an abode for Him below," they must be performed with a total lack of enthusiasm and an absolute minimum of mental effort. Only the body should be involved, not the intellect or emotions. In fact, overusing one's intellect in this direction is counterproductive, which is why the uneducated are often more successful businessmen than the intelligentsia: Having a weaker intellect to begin with, they are less likely to overuse it. Moreover, superfluous intellect is fair prey for the ḳelipot, who appropriate it for their own ends.[136] Only "a great man," according to one discourse, can prevent this,[137] which implies that such a man may be permitted to utilize his full intellectual capacity in business affairs. Another discourse, however, states that such great luminaries as R. Simeon bar Yoḥai could construct a vessel for Ḥesed without engaging in any mundane affairs at all.[138] (The typical resolution, of course, would be that there are different levels or types of great men.) In any event, worldly ambition in a world without independent reality is absurd. "The life of this world is not called life at all." Commercial zeal in the face of income that is predetermined on Rosh Hashanah is futile. Even if an astute merchant manages somehow to exceed his "salary," the surplus is not rightfully his, and he has accomplished nothing.[139]

Like other obstacles to Service, the need to earn a living really exists to goad man into achieving his full spiritual potential. Since he is unable to predict which path will lead to material success, his actions are not self-directed according to his own clear plan but rather depend on the vicissitudes God visits upon him. This leads him to acknowledge his total subservience to God's will and submit to it.[140] Forced to tear himself away from God's felt presence during the morning service and to do economic battle in a coarsening, hostile world, his innate yearning for eternal union is increased immeasurably. This intense yearning gives rise to the highest form of Service, the transcendent love *be-khol me'odekha* (with all your might; Deut. 6:5). The man of affairs thus has an advantage over the sheltered scholar, who lacks the daily contrast and conflict required to kindle this love. The prayer of the former should therefore be even more ecstatic, and in the fire of this ecstasy all the gentile words he uttered during his business transactions, all the physical benefits he derived from these secular words and affairs (i.e., everything purchased with the profits) are consumed, purified, and elevated. He thereby transforms the profane into the holy and contributes significantly to the preparation of God's "abode in the lower worlds."[141]

Nevertheless, the need to seek one's livelihood is only one of the means to this end and should not be overemphasized. Nor should it be underemphasized. Some kind of vocational vessel is indispensable; no one may sit back and rely on God's bounty. If he does not exert himself sufficiently he will not receive even his predetermined income.[142] But where does one draw the line? RSZ does not say, although it appears that he expected his followers to limit their efforts to achieving subsistence. Any greater zeal was both wrong in itself and could lead to material abundance, the forerunner of spiritual poverty. Those who did attain affluence were exhorted to treat their entire surplus as a charitable foundation devoted primarily to supporting the Hasidic community in the Holy Land and, when the need arose, to ransoming imprisoned Jews.[143]

Since a subsistence livelihood is only one step from poverty, and subsistence was the theoretical norm, even the poorest Hasidim could more readily accept RSZ's assertion that material poverty, like all forms of suffering, is a problem only for those who value physical above spiritual well-being.[144] Although "there is no suffering without sin,"[145] RSZ, like all kabbalists, saw sin less as an act of rebellion eliciting divine retribution than as a stain on the sinner's soul requiring cleansing, an impurity requiring purgation. A good God does not punish, He purifies. Suffering is therefore not an evil inflicted for an evil, but a great good bestowed with great love. Anyone who follows the sages' advice and scrutinizes his conduct will almost invariably find "sins that require purgation through afflictions." He must then contemplate God's great love for him, a love that "upsets the natural order of conduct," as in the metaphor of "the great and awesome king who, out of his great love, personally washes the filth from his only son." This awareness will arouse his love for God, Who will eventually reciprocate by transforming the hidden good of suffering into the revealed good that all can appreciate.[146]

The discourses also reiterate a number of other familiar approaches to the purpose of suffering. It humbles man and enables him to feel God's presence.[147] It removes the corporeal coarseness separating him from his Maker, elevates him above mundane limitations, and allows the divine light to permeate his being.[148] It purifies the otherwise corporeally tainted commandments he has fulfilled.[149] It weakens him physically, thereby strengthening him spiritually.[150] It is the supreme form of tension and pressure, which, as we have seen, are the indispensable generators of self-transcending Service.[151] And of course, as the Talmud teaches, it enables man to receive his full measure of reward in ʿOlam ha-Ba.[152]

As usual, however, RSZ goes beyond these approaches and demands biṭul. The most characteristic posture appears in an epistle on tsedaḳah. All desires for "the life of the flesh" must be uprooted.

"One's will must be nullified so that one has absolutely no will in any worldly matters, all of which may be subsumed under 'children, life, and sustenance'." Anyone who believes that an absolutely good Creator is constantly vitalizing all creation, including the sufferer himself; that no evil descends from above and everything is good, although it is not apprehended because of its immense goodness; anyone accepting these fundamental truths must conclude that his is the best of all possible situations, and he should rejoice accordingly. Conversely, any kind of melancholy or dissatisfaction with one's lot implies a lack of faith bordering on heresy.[153]

The ideal for RSZ, as for the Maggid (and other mystics), is complete indifference to all mundane vicissitudes. But RSZ goes still further. Not only is indifference desirable, it is obligatory. To harbor a feeling of displeasure over one's tribulations proves that "he is of the *ʿerev rav* (mixed multitude; Exodus 12:38) who act only for themselves." It means that he "loves himself to the extent of removing himself from under the hand of the Lord and living the life of heathens because of his self-love. That is why he desires the life of the flesh and children and sustenance. It would actually have been better for him had he not been created. For the purpose of man's creation in this world is to test him by these trials to ascertain what is in his heart: whether he will turn his heart toward other gods—namely the passions of the body that evolve from the siṭra aḥra—and desire these, or whether his desire and wish is to live the true life that evolves from the living God."[154]

The extent to which biṭul dominates RSZ's axiology is perhaps most apparent in his brief treatment of *biṭaḥon*—trust in God. Despite its deep Biblical roots and extensive development in aggadic and ethical literature,[155] biṭaḥon is not a prominent component of RSZ's ethical thought. Consisting as it does of a deeply felt emotion revolving around one's personal well-being, biṭaḥon is possible only where self-nullification is less than complete. A man who achieves true biṭul feels no emotion and is totally unconcerned for himself. It is for this reason, RSZ explains, that certain Biblical figures who were completely righteous acted in ways that indicated an apparent lack of biṭaḥon. They could not trust in God's protection because there was no "they" to do the trusting.[156]

While not explicitly denying the importance of biṭaḥon, by mentioning it so rarely, and even then only as inferior to biṭul, RSZ was in effect depreciating this traditional value. Such a result, however, was a rare exception, for, as we have observed, RSZ was anything but an iconoclast. When old values clashed with new, he instinctively sought to harmonize them. His attitude toward asceticism is a noteworthy case in point. Biṭul, as noted above, requires a significant degree of self-denial. Moreover, authorities that RSZ revered, such as Isaac Luria, Isaiah Horowitz, and Elijah de Vidas, embracing and augmenting the legacy of Ḥaside Ashkenaz, had made fasting and self-mortification a cornerstone of their religious ethics. They did not, in the main, distinguish between scholar and merchant, saint and sinner, strong and weak; everyone had to fast, because everyone required further spiritualization.[157] Sin, of course, remained the primary basis for fasting. A minor misdeed, even if unintentional, even if practically unavoidable, required dozens, sometimes hundreds, of penitential fasts. Losing one's temper required 151 consecutive fasts; a nocturnal emission, eighty-four; arrogance, fifty-one.[158] But fasting for no reason other than additional self-purification or purgation was also strongly encouraged. Vidas advocated weekly fasts of forty-eight hours. Any resultant weakness, he cautioned, was a sign of incomplete teshuvah.[159] If death should result, the ascetic will have died in the course of penance, a most desirable end.[160] The general rule was: The more fasts the better. Since *Sefer Roḳeaḥ* and Lurianic works differ on the number of fasts necessary for each transgression, Horowitz suggested following both.[161] Wearing sackcloth, wrote de Vidas, was also very beneficial, and Luria provided a kabbalistic basis for this practice. Other forms of penitential self-mortification described in *Sefer Roḳeaḥ* were also strongly recommended.[162]

Yet the Besht, who taught his followers to work with, rather than against, human nature, had denied not only the importance but even the validity of self-mortification.[163] God does not desire fasts, says RSZ flatly in a revealing letter to R. Isaac Yaffe of Kopys. Contriteness and humility are what fasts are supposed to accomplish, and, "according to my masters" (i.e., the Besht and Maggid), these can be achieved through meditation.[164] Nevertheless, RSZ could not bring himself entirely to reject voluntary penitential fasting, since it had, after all, been a common practice among the sages of the Talmud, had received extensive halakhic treatment, and particularly since it had received Luria's wholehearted approbation.[165] Consequently, he felt constrained to admit that "the mystery of the fast is remarkably effective for the revelation of the Supreme Will, similar to the offering, of which it is said: 'an aroma pleasing to God'." [166]

But the generations had declined. Luria's contemporaries were not only spiritual giants but physically robust as well. They were capable of following his regimen without any adverse effects. RSZ's contemporaries, however, were "forbidden to engage in many fasts";[167] for, contrary to Horowitz, Vidas, and Maharal,[168] RSZ held that frequent voluntary fasting was halakhically prohibited if it affected one's health or was unduly distressing. Scholars whose studies would suffer were also included in this prohibition. And while penitential fasting for known sins was still necessary to complete the purification process and to obviate the need for divine purgation,[169] it was possible to fulfill this requirement through the modified regimen RSZ recommended. The balance of fasts that would be required to satisfy pre-Beshtian demands should be redeemed through charity. "And though this might amount to a considerable sum, he need not worry about the injunction: 'One should not distribute more than one fifth [of one's possessions]' (*Ketuvot*, 50a), as this is not considered a [voluntary] 'distribution' for charity, since he does it to redeem his soul from fasts and affliction. This is no less necessary than medicine for his body or his other needs."[170] This redemption of fasts was not just a metaphor. The quota of Lurianic fasts was not abolished, nor was the value of fasting diminished. Anyone unable to redeem his fasts through charity should expect to be visited with tribulations and should rejoice in their purifying effect. Even without a known sin, in fact, and even in RSZ's weaker generation, every man would be well advised to spiritualize himself through weekly or monthly fasts.[171]

RSZ thus combined apparently divergent rabbinic, kabbalistic, and Hasidic teachings into a cohesive compromise position. Although he conceded that all these teachings were not universally and eternally applicable, this concession was based on the sources themselves and particularly on the universally accepted belief in the decline of the generations. Essentially, therefore, the ascetic teachings of all the authoritative sources[172] could be accepted as being equally and eternally valid. Only the extreme forms of self-mortification advocated in *Sefer Roḳeaḥ* for *Teshuvat ha-Mishḳal* were either tacitly ignored or transformed from physical suffering into mental anguish. Apparently RSZ considered this type of penance to be self-evidently beyond the ability of his weaker generation.[173]

This syncretistic approach to the ascetic practices required to complete the teshuvah process is also evident in RSZ's theory of the process itself. Rabbinic ethics, kabbalistic metaphysics, and Hasidic psychology are skilfully combined into a cohesive doctrine. Moreover, unlike other areas of his ethics, the discourses generally conform to or at most complement the positions set forth in *Tanya* (and *Igeret ha-Teshuvah*).

RSZ's theory of teshuvah revolves around the kabbalistic play on the word *teshuvah*, which divides it into a subject—the final he—and a predicate—*tashuv* (shall return). The purpose of teshuvah, in other words, is to restore the he of the Tetragrammaton to its original position, the position from which one's sin dislodged it.[174] Each letter of this divine name controls a series of divine emanations that create and sustain certain elements in the universe and in man's psychophysical makeup. The two hes are particularly significant for man, because the second, corresponding to Malkhut, Shekhinah, and divine Speech, is the source of every Jew's embodied soul, and the first, corresponding to Binah and contemplative thought, is the source of that component of his soul that remains above and inspires its embodied counterpart to break out of its physical prison and return to its supernal birthplace.[175] This return, which is accomplished through prayer (=the desire for deveḳut), Torah study (=the highest earthly realization of deveḳut), and the fulfillment of the (other) commandments, particularly tsedaḳah,[176] constitutes teshuvah par excellence and is, as we have seen, the very purpose of the soul's descent.[177] Continually incumbent upon all men, even the greatest Tsadiḳ,[178] this form of teshuvah is actually an overarching religioethical desideratum rather than a specific obligation; it incorporates all the ethical ways and means described above.

For most men, however, this mystical aspect of teshuvah is of less immediate concern than the basic aspect involving repentance for sin. Rooted as it is in the second he, the embodied divine soul that allows the animal soul to move man to sin causes one emanation of that letter—that is, of the Shekhinah or Malkhut—to go awry. Instead of illuminating the divine soul and sustaining the body of a Jew, this emanation is captured by the ḳelipot above, which use it to sustain themselves and the seventy princes that govern the gentile nations; and by the Ḳelipat Nogah below, which uses it to sustain the animal soul. Every sin, therefore, causes or perpetuates the individual soul's alienation from God (Malkhut), the exile of the Shekhinah among the ḳelipot, and the concomitant exile of Israel among the seventy nations.[179]

RSZ's ingenious literal interpretation of the Biblical words *ḥevel* (in Deut. 32:9) and *karet* (excission), coupled with a halakhic usage of the kabbalistic term *pegam* (defect), allows him to create a striking rope metaphor for the embodied soul's presin and postsin condition. An updated and actually more precise version of this metaphor would substitute electrical wire for rope. One end of this 613-strand wire is attached to the embodied divine soul, the other end to the soul's source in Malkhut, the second he of the Tetragrammaton. Each of the 613 strands transmits one part of the total divine current necessary to illuminate and sustain the soul. Transgressing a single commandment cuts (*pogem*) one strand. Transgressing a commandment punishable by karet, or even habitually transgressing a "minor" commandment, causes all the strands to be cut and leaves the soul with only a residue of divine sustenance. During the Temple Period, when the nation of Israel received its physical sustenance from the side of ḳedushah (holiness) only (and consequently was supposedly not subjugated by gentile nations), this residue was sufficient to sustain the sinner until age fifty or sixty, after which he invariably died. During the exile, however, he can be sustained indefinitely by the emanations that he allows the ḳelipot to capture. His life is then almost completely governed by the same impure forces that govern the lives of his gentile countrymen. All the emanations of the he that should have illuminated and sustained his soul are now coursing through the spiritual and physical veins of his oppressors and strengthening their hold on him and on the Shekhinah. It is still possible, however, for the divine residue to move him to teshuvah, that is, to restore the emanations of the he to ḳedushah.[180]

Corresponding to the two hes of the Tetragrammaton that inspire and sustain the soul are two levels of teshuvah: *Teshuvah Tata'ah* (Lower Teshuvah), which restores the second, or lower, he; and *Teshuvah Ila'ah* (Higher Teshuvah), which restores the first, or higher, he. These two levels also correspond to the injunctions "[1] turn from evil and [2] do good" (Ps. 34:15). Lower Teshuvah includes virtually all the traditional elements of repentance found in the Bible, Talmud, Midrash, and major ethical works, as well as the self-abasement and self-pity sessions described above. Profound contriteness and "bitterness of soul" (followed by fasting) shatter the ḳelipot "that form a dividing curtain" between man and God, as the Zohar explains for the verse: "The sacrifices of God are a broken spirit, a broken and contrite heart" (Ps. 51:18).[181] "Breaking one's heart"—specifically, the left side of one's heart, where the animal soul resides—breaks the spirit of the siṭra aḥra and its hold over the divine soul and (one part of) the Shekhinah.[182] This paves the way for Higher Teshuvah, which, according to several discourses,[183] is inspired by the soul's higher, disembodied element after all the barriers between it and its embodied counterpart have been removed. Lower and Higher Teshuvah can thus be combined into the general definition of teshuvah that appears in many discourses: uprooting one's will from sin and worldly desires and redirecting it toward God. This conforms with RSZ's view of will as the dominant soul-power. By turning one's will, and thus one's entire soul, away from sin, one deprives sin of the vitality it derived from the soul's divine spark; and by turning that will toward God, one arouses His goodwill in return. The sin disintegrates and the sinner is reunited with God.[184]

Before Lower Teshuvah the soul is comparable to an errant prince, the divine King's only son, who has strayed from his Father's palace and service. Lower Teshuvah reconciles Father and son, thereby enabling the prince to rededicate himelf to serving the King with wholehearted devotion. It enables him, in other words, to undertake Higher Teshuvah,[185] which consists essentially of the self-transcendent desire for deveḳut (=the Love be-khol me'odekha; Deut. 6:5) that is stimulated by contemplative prayer (Binah, the higher he). This desire "reaches" a level of Divinity that transcends the source of the commandments and that can therefore repair any supernal defect caused by their transgression or neglect.[186] The actual consummation of deveḳut is achieved by uniting, through Torah-study, the soul-garments of thought and speech with the thought and speech of God; and the soul-garment of action with the actions commanded by God, particularly acts of charity and compassion, which comprise the category of action most characteristic of God Himself.[187] Thus, in the final analysis, Higher Teshuvah is actually synonymous with the daily, dedicated Service that is every Jew's raison d'être. It is this Service that enables him to spend "all his days in teshuvah"[188] and to realize the mystical connotation of teshuvah—the return of his soul to God.[189]

KANSAS SCHOOL OF RELIGION
UNIVERSITY OF KANSAS
1300 OREAD AVENUE
LAWRENCE, KANSAS 66044

4

Torah *and* Commandments

The centrality of Torah-study in RSZ's Hasidism is reflected in the fact that this is the one religioethical area to which he devoted a halakhic monograph. *Hilkhot Talmud Torah* (Shklov, 1794) was his first published work; it was also the most comprehensive treatment of the subject in the six centuries since Maimonides originated the rubric. Like the other sections of RSZ's *Shulḥan ʿArukh*, it is a tour de force of halakhic synthesis, integrating not only a host of sources but also the exact formulations used in those sources. Unlike most of the other sections, however, *Hilkhot Talmud Torah* contains major decisions that are conspicuously original. Some of these are based on RSZ's analysis of the relevant texts, but others are apparently founded more on axiological than on purely halakhic considerations. Kabbalistic values and concepts in particular strongly influenced RSZ's halakhic approach to Torah-study.

Thus, he often cites the Lurianic belief that every Jewish soul must master and fulfil all 613 commandments in order to perfect itself and enjoy eternal beatitude.[1] This kabbalistic assumption apparently led him to emphasize those few rabbinic sources that seem to imply that every Jew is halakhically obligated to master the entire Torah.[2] RSZ was consequently the first to insist that it is a Biblical requirement for every father to teach, or ensure that his son learn, the entire Written and the Oral Torah:[3] the Bible, both Talmuds, all extant Midrashim and *midreshe halakhah*, and the (major) codes. The essential aspect of this curriculum, the essence of Torah, is the explication of the 613 commandments to a sufficient degree that one knows exactly how to fulfill them.[4] If the father is remiss or unsuccessful in discharging his obligation, it devolves upon the son himself.[5]

Studying and understanding the entire Torah, however, is still not enough; it is necessary to achieve total and immediate recall.[6] Obversely, it is a Biblical prohibition to forget a single detail of the Torah through lack of diligence. RSZ makes no allowance for the fact that the oral study and necessary memorization of the Talmudic period had long been supplemented or supplanted by book-learning and research. Just as the Torah is eternal, so must its method of study be eternally valid.[7]

Having mastered and perfectly memorized the entire Torah, one has fulfilled "mitsṿat yediʿat ha-Torah" (MYT), a phrase coined by RSZ and based on his striking distinction between this first part of the commandment to study Torah, and the second part, which is the obligation constantly to broaden and deepen one's understanding of the Torah.[8] Theoretically, MYT takes precedence over, and is axiologically equal to, all the other commandments.[9] In practice, however, since it requires unremitting diligence over the course of many years, short-term distractions, including the need to fulfill other commandments, do not really compete with it. Once the permissible or obligatory interruption ends, it is assumed that the student will immediately return to his studies. His obligation to raise and support a family, however, is clearly an exception to this rule, since it is patently impossible to devote most of one's waking hours to earning a living while simultaneously fulfilling MYT. RSZ resolves this dilemma by requiring the capable student—that is, one who has the capacity eventually to fulfill MYT as defined by RSZ—to postpone marrying until he has completed this part of the commandment. Moreover, this student is permitted, although not encouraged, to remain a bachelor indefinitely if he fears that the burden of a family will cause him to forget any part of what he has learned. Only if he feels unable to study "in purity" without a wife is he permitted to marry before fulfilling MYT. He must then resign himself, if necessary, to a life of deprivation in order to devote most of his time to Torah. In fact, RSZ intimates that the capable student is halakhically obligated to make Torah-study his main vocation even after he has fulfilled MYT.[10]

RSZ's tendency to elevate Torah-study, particularly MYT, above all competing claims on one's time and effort is discernible throughout *Hilkhot Talmud Torah*. He maintains, for example, that Torah-study in general is more valuable than any other commandment, and MYT is equal in value to all the other commandments combined.[11] The latter is true, however, only because "study leads to action"; that is, Torah-study is itself the fulfillment of a commandment, and MYT has the additional quality of being the first and necessary step toward the fulfillment of all the other commandments, since one cannot properly do unless one knows what to do and how to do it.[12] This should mean that a commandment may be superseded by MYT only if the subject studied relates to a commandment that the student is, or will be, obligated to fulfill. Yet RSZ insists that this is not the case. Even the study of laws relating exclusively to the Temple, the priests, and the kings of Israel takes precedence over the commandment to marry and procreate.[13]

Another example of RSZ's elevation of Torah-study is the reason he chooses for exempting a full-time scholar (*mi she-torato umanuto*) from reciting the ʿAmidah. Ignoring all three reasons given by the Talmud and cited by most authorities,[14] RSZ opts instead for the Talmudic formulation that Maimonides apparently transformed into his simple pronouncement of the ascendancy of Torah-study over prayer.[15] Prayer, says RSZ, is called "temporal life"—it is merely "pleading for compassion regarding worldly matters"—whereas Torah-study is "eternal life."[16] It is noteworthy that this is the opinion of a single Amora in the Talmud,[17] who uses it not as a rationale for exempting a scholar from the obligation to pray but as a basis for his criticism of a colleague who, he felt, spent too much time praying. Nevertheless, here, as throughout *Hilkhot Talmud Torah*,[18] RSZ follows Maimonides' intellectualistic approach to Torah-study. To put it more precisely, he generally tries to support his independent conclusions by attempting to show that a very close analysis of Maimonides' formulations will bear him out. When confronted with R. Asher's opposing view, RSZ reverses the general principle of Ashkenazic halakhah and follows Maimonides, particularly if the latter's opinion conforms with Lurianic doctrine. Thus, he comes down in favor of studying Torah even as a purely academic exercise, without any intention of fulfilling the commandments, because eventually, as the Midrash says, its light will redeem him, and because eventually, as the Kabbalah says, he will repent and redeem his Torah from the midst of the ḳelipot.[19]

But despite his general allegiance to Maimonides and Luria, RSZ's basic approach to Torah-study is drawn directly from his analysis of the relevant Talmudic passages. Apparently or actually conflicting statements in the Talmud are dialectically reconciled and incorporated into *Hilkhot Talmud Torah*, with all the inconsistency and ambivalence that this procedure entails. Thus, in two consecutive paragraphs, RSZ explains the practice of the "first Hasidim's" spending nine hours a day in prayer and meditation, in two different and apparently contradictory ways:

1. They were permitted to do this because they had already fulfilled MYT. Their remaining Torah-study obligation—constantly to enhance their knowledge—could be superseded by the deveḳut they achieved through meditation, because this deveḳut constitutes the highest form of Love and Fear, and Love and Fear transcend this part of the Torah-study commandment.
2. Although Love and Fear do not transcend this part of the commandment, they do equal it in importance, and the Hasidim were therefore exempt from studying Torah by virtue of the principle: "One who is engaged in fulfilling a commandment is exempt from fulfilling another commandment."[20]

Besides conflicting with each other, these two explanations are problematic for other reasons as well. Both are based not on halakhic texts but on RSZ's own judgment regarding the relative value of deveḳut and Torah-study; the first explanation fails to account for the halakhah that exempts a full-time scholar, including one who has fulfilled MYT, from prayer regardless of his ability to achieve deveḳut; and the second apparently overlooks the fact that the principle RSZ cites is applicable regardless of the relative value of the two commandments in question,[21] so that if the Hasidim relied on this principle, they could have justified their practice even if Love and Fear were less valuable than Torah-study.

To complicate matters further, RSZ states elsewhere that the commandment of teshuvah is equal in value to MYT and that therefore an inspiring preacher who moves the people to repent may ignore a conflicting Biblical commandment, just as one who is engaged in fulfilling MYT may ignore the Biblical commandment to marry and procreate.[22] The commandment hierarchy thus appears to be: (1) MYT and teshuvah, which are equally valuable; (2) Love and Fear (=deveḳut); and (3) the second aspect of the Torah-study commandment. Clearly Maimonides' statement, also cited in RSZ's *Hilkhot Talmud Torah*, that Torah-study counterbalances *all* the other commandments,[23] has been considerably modified.

This axiological ambivalence increases dramatically in *Tanya* and the discourses, in which RSZ is less limited in his choice of explanations and approaches. As in other religioethical areas, inconsistencies and contradictions abound. In fact, there is even more tension here, because though RSZ's view of the nature and purpose of Torah-study differs markedly from that of both his Lurianic predecessors and his Hasidic colleagues, he charactistically tries to incorporate many of their views into his.

According to R. Ḥayyim Vital, Luria saw the exoteric study of Torah primarily as a means to achieve the esoteric enlightenment necessary for the perfection of one's soul below and its reflection in the *macroanthropos* (*Adam ha-ʿElyon*) above.[24] Torah-study in Vital's version of Lurianic kabbalah is essentially a theurgic act consisting of the daily recitation of certain texts in a certain order with certain kavanot. These texts constitute the husk of the Torah, while the esoteric wisdom they contain constitutes its inner kernel. Similarly, the difficulties involved in understanding these texts, even on a literal level, are referred to as husks, or shells, that must be removed to get to the grain. Frequently the shell is too hard to remove and must be broken. This is the purpose of the intellectual effort involved in fathoming a difficult text and reconciling contradictions through *pilpul.* Luria was said to be very adept at this, generally interpreting each difficult passage six exoteric ways and one esoteric way (to correspond to the six weekdays and the Sabbath). It was also his custom to exert himself intellectually until he was perspiring and physically tired, in order to "smash the ḳelipah"—presumably a reference to the body, a shell that was always in need of breaking. Anyone similarly profficient at pilpul was urged by Vital, in Luria's name, to devote at most two hours daily to this war against the intellectual and physical ḳelipot. Anyone requiring much more time to deal satisfactorily with textual problems was advised not to bother trying to break the shells but to concentrate on simply reciting the required texts, as this recitation is the heart of Torah-study, while the intellectual effort required to understand the texts fully is merely an adjunct to it.[25] *Torah li-shemah,* according to Luria, does not mean study for the sake of understanding, or for the sake of fulfilling the commandments,[26] but for the sake of the first he of the Tetragrammaton, that is, to cause the Torah to descend from its source in Ḥokhmah to Binah.[27] Proper study, in other words, is an act of metaphysical manipulation. The source of Torah is the *lower* aspect of Ḥokhmah after it is clothed in *Zeʿir Anpin,* the six emotive sefirot. It is often referred to rather invidiously as "stern judgments."[28]

Vital's Introduction to *ʿEts Ḥayyim* reveals an extremely denigrating attitude toward the study of Talmud and, by implication, the study of halakhah. He clearly found the anti-Talmudic posture of many passages in the *R'aya Mehemna*[29] very congenial. The Talmud, says Vital, is the "maidservant" of the esoteric Torah, its "chaff" and "stubble." It is the troublesome Tree of Knowledge versus kabbalah's redeeming Tree of Life, the profane versus the sacred. Its study is slavery, and studying it exclusively prolongs the exile. Indeed, all the evil that has befallen the Jewish nation from the day they built the golden calf to the present is the result of the disproportionate attention given to Talmud over kabbalah. Moreover, quite a few of the commandments the Talmud explains, when not understood kabbalistically, are irrational and therefore the source of gentile ridicule. Although the Talmud must be studied and the commandments fulfilled, these activities are merely propadeutic measures to purify the body and prepare it to receive a soul enlightened by the Torah's secrets. Knowledge of these secrets through the study of kabbalah is the purpose of creation in general and man's existence in particular. Thus, regardless of how faithfully one fulfills all the other commandments, failure to study kabbalah means forfeiting one's share in the heavenly Gan 'Eden. This was Adam's real sin, and he was therefore punished by being expelled from the earthly Gan 'Eden.[30]

R. Moses Cordovero, RSZ's other main kabbalistic mentor, makes a more positive assessment of Talmud study, but he, too, describes it as merely a propadeutic discipline that provides the intellectual training necessary for understanding kabbalistic abstractions. The introduction to *Tiḳunim*, Cordovero observes, explicitly states that the study of kabbalah must be preceded by the study of Bible and Talmud.[31] These, however, are only the first two of the four stages of enlightenment, the third being mastery of the Zohar, and the highest the mystical ability to fathom the spiritual potency of the Torah's letters.[32] Nor does Cordovero set a minimum proficiency standard that one must attain before proceeding from Talmud to kabbalah. Anyone, it seems, who has reached the age of twenty with some Talmud under his belt may then concentrate primarily on kabbalah.[33] The kabbalah that he studies in this world, and *perhaps* the Talmud as well, will be what he studies in Gan 'Eden.[34] Although rigorous analysis of the kabbalistic texts is essential,[35] Cordovero also recommends closing the book to go out and roam the fields with a colleague in the hopes of attaining spontaneous mystical insights. He testifies that he and Solomon Alkabetz used to do this, with astounding results.[36] Thus, Cordovero, too, depreciated the relative value of halakhic scholarship and placed a premium on nonintellectual forms of Torah-study.

This tradition was continued and developed by the Besht, the Maggid, and the Maggid's disciples. The emphasis was not on diligence, comprehension, and mastery of the material, but on considerations extraneous to the material. Far less attention was focused on the value of study itself than on the proper mode of, and motive for, studying. The phrase *Torah li-shemah* became a catchall that was defined almost every way but literally. The word *li-shemah* (meaning, for its own sake) was turned on its head and was generally interpreted as referring to everything but Torah itself: for the sake of deveḳut, yiḥudim, Love, Fear, purification, mystical enlightenment, redemption of the Shekhinah, and even for the sake of spiritual power.[37]

Thus, the Maggid taught that one who studies with the proper kavanah acquires the wisdom necessary to change the established halakhah.[38] We may infer that this wisdom is spiritual rather than intellectual, for the Maggid also taught that to study properly one must first "kill" one's intellect.[39] The importance of innovation and change in halakhah also looms large in the teachings of R. Ze'ev Wolf of Zhitomir, who often concentrates on the utilitarian functions of proper Torah-study. Every generation, he taught, requires new forms of Service, and by purifying his body and elevating his soul through deveḳut, the Zaddik is able to rearrange the standard letter combinations in the Torah to reveal those forms suited to his generation. R. Ze'ev Wolf's references to Torah-study are almost exclusively to the study of Bible, which, as he defines it, is actually a matter of inspired letter manipulation rather than an intellectual act. Moreover, the source of the Zaddik's inspiration is not contemplation, and certainly not study in the usual sense; it is the perfection of his religious behavior, which transcends the Torah that originally gave rise to it. Consequently, the new tsirufim (letter combinations) he discovers need not be compatible with the masoretic reading. The primordial Torah, in fact, was given not as a comprehensible text but as a series of discrete letters. The Patriarchs arranged these letters into words according to the inspiration they derived from their righteous acts, and Zaddikim in subsequent generations must follow their precedent. The evil deeds of others, however, may result in invalid combinations, which in turn are used to justify those deeds.[40] Briefly put, it is not a valid halakhic conclusion that determines what is a righteous act; it is the righteous acts that determine what is a valid halakhic conclusion.

R. Levi Isaac of Berditchev differed with R. Ze'ev Wolf on the importance of intellectual effort but shared his utilitarian approach and his position on innovation in halakhah. The sages of the Talmud, he observes, interpreted the Torah as they saw fit, and contemporary

Zaddikim are only following in their footsteps. For example, the sages fixed the halakhah according to *Bet Hillel* because its lenient views derived from Ḥesed, and the sages perceived that the world of their time should be governed by Ḥesed. Contemporary Zaddikim may perceive that their world should be governed by a different sefirah and may change the halakhah accordingly. In other words, Zaddikim determine what is in the best spiritual interests of their generation and apply the Torah to serve those interests. Similarly, they can use the Torah to promote Israel's physical well-being. They can, for example, heal the sick through their Torah-study. Nevertheless, R. Levi Isaac categorizes Torah-study as a *mitsvah ḳalah*—a minor commandment—because, unlike *sukah*, it can be fulfilled at any time.[41]

R. Menaḥem Naḥum of Chernobyl disagreed with his colleagues on the issue of innovation. Like the Gaon of Vilna, he believed that all the valid interpretations of the Torah had already been advanced, and Torah-study therefore consists of reviewing and understanding those interpretations.[42] But he agreed that a Zaddik of perfect faith could and presumably should use the Torah to improve Israel's lot.[43] He also adopted a version of the Maggidic doctrine of inspirational Torah: A man who studies Torah li-shemah becomes a vessel for God's word and can effortlessly and ceaselessly pour forth the waters of His Torah without any preparation.[44] Echoing Vital and Cordovero, R. Menaḥem Naḥum identifies all difficulties of comprehension with the ḳelipot, and specifically with the ḳelipah created by the student's own sins; hence, the knottier the problem, the more heinous its source.[45]

R. Menaḥem Mendel of Vitebsk, RSZ's close colleague, adopted a compromise position. He insisted on the need first to exert oneself intellectually and then to go beyond comprehension, which he associates with man's evil inclination, to self-nullification and deveḳut. One of the greatest scholars among the Maggid's disciples, he nevertheless generally describes Torah-study as a gateway to the nonintellectual union of the soul with God.[46]

All of these approaches to Torah-study were offshoots of the Besht's or the Maggid's teachings, the essential elements of which have been outlined in Chapter 1. Several points should be added or restated here, however, in order better to assess the Beshtian-Maggidic heritage that RSZ tried to incorporate into his more traditional (=rabbinic) views.

Various statements of the Besht and the Maggid indicate that they saw Torah-study as both a means to achieve and an interruption of conscious deveḳut. To avoid an unconscionably long period without conscious deveḳut, they urged their disciples to pause regularly during study to revive it.[47] According to the Maggid, studying with the requisite Love and Fear enables the student to transform an intellectual act into a mystical experience in which he attaches himself to the sage whose words he utters.[48] Similarly, by meditatively attaching himself to the letters of the text, the student may merit prophetic powers.[49] According to a statement attributed to the Besht, Torah-study without the proper kayanah is devoid of sanctity.[50] To Luria's definition of li-shemah, which he cited,[51] the Besht added his own: "for the sake of the letter itself", that is, for the sake of adhering to the vitality of the Or En Sof that permeates it.[52] Like earlier Jewish mystics (and the Sufis before them), he maintained that the goal of knowledge was the absence of knowledge: to come face to face with an unknowable God. Nevertheless, this same Beshtian teaching stipulates that the first step must be intellectual apprehension.[53]

The subject of Torah-study appears relatively infrequently in Beshtian and Maggidic teachings, but it is one of the most prominent ethical topics in *Tanya* and the discourses. RSZ's discussions of the study, source, nature, function, purpose, and divisions of the Torah constitute a comprehensive and complex series of closely interrelated ideas. Ideally, these should be analyzed simultaneously, just as diverse components of one large mural should be viewed together to appreciate fully the artist's vision. But in practice, we can take only one concept at a time. We may begin by positing two broad rubrics that are validated by one of RSZ's own discourses: Torah-study and Torah itself.[54]

Torah-Study

The position of Torah-study in the hierarchy of the commandments was one of RSZ's primary ethical concerns. The easiest position to defend was that of absolute supremacy, since a number of universally known rabbinic dicta seemed to support this. The well-worn final clause of the first Mishnah in *Pe'ah*, "ve-talmud Torah ke-neged kulam"—"and Torah-study counterbalances all of them [the commandments]"—is a case point.[55] RSZ explains this in at least five ways (in addition to the functional explanation in *Hilkhot Talmud Torah*),[56] all of which, however, are predicated on the assumption that since Torah-study is the commandment performed with, and assimilated by, man's highest (=innermost) faculty, it must therefore be the highest commandment. Thus, in *Tanya* RSZ states that whereas fulfilling another commandment creates a garment for the soul in Gan ʿEden, Torah-study not only creates a garment but also constitutes the soul's nourishment, for the Torah studied in this world will sustain the soul in the next.[57] These standard Lurianic metaphors, however, are provided with an Aristotelian foundation. Like most medieval Jewish philosophers, with the notable exception of Crescas, RSZ in effect accepted Aristotle's dictum that "actual knowledge is identical with its object."[58] Man's intellect, in other words, not only contains the knowledge it acquires, it is identical with it, just as food becomes part of the body that assimilates it. Having acquired and retained knowledge of the Torah, thereby fulfilling MYT, means becoming one with the Torah, which is God's will and wisdom, which are identical with God Himself. This unique union is what makes MYT the greatest of all commandments, greater even than the second aspect of Torah-study: the commandment actually to study and articulate God's wisdom.

Elsewhere in *Tanya* RSZ adds that the study of halakhah in particular is greater than other commandments because it is performed with the inner soul-garments of thought and speech, which, together with the comprehending soul, unite with God's inner will as manifested in each halakhah. This will is identified with sovev, the revelation transcending the worlds; yet Torah-study draws it down upon the student and causes it to be revealed in him.[59] A variation of this idea is that the fate of all the worlds, and certainly of everything in this world, hinges on a single detail of a single halakhah. This, however, applies to "the outer aspect of the Torah," whereas its inner aspect, which is identified with the Godhead, completely transcends all the worlds.[60] Several discourses essentially sum it up as follows: Torah-study is the greatest of all commandments because it causes God's innermost vitality, Or En Sof clothed in Ḥokhmah, to be revealed in man's innermost organ, the brain, where *his* innermost vitality, Ḥokhmah, originates. And while it is true that man's soul per se transcends Ḥokhmah, as does the Or En Sof per se, the two levels of Ḥokhmah constitute vessels for their respective transcendent manifestations, so that by man's Ḥokhmah uniting with God's, man's soul unites with God.[61] Moreover, Torah-study is the commandment requiring and permitting the greatest degree of self-nullification,[62] which, as we have seen, is for RSZ the highest ethical achievement possible. And finally, the supernal Torah is the source, or "vitality," of all the other commandments, since it defines what the commandments are and explains how they are to be fulfilled.[63]

This last point, however, may be seen from another perspective. If Torah is essentially an instruction manual for the proper fulfillment of the commandments, surely they must occupy a higher position in the hierarchy of religioethical values, just as a house is more valuable than its blueprint. RSZ does, in fact, occasionally use this reasoning to reach this conclusion,[64] but his approach is far more complex than simply exalting Torah-study in one discourse and the other commandments in another. The axiological relation between Torah-study, mitsvot, and prayer, the three pillars of RSZ's religious thought, is one of the major ethical themes in *Tanya* and the discourses, and in the course of these teachings RSZ articulated or suggested virtually every possible variation of relation and interdependence: (1) Torah-study is greater than other commandments;[65] (2) other commandments are greater than Torah-study;[66] (3) Torah-study is of greater benefit to the student's soul; prayer and other commandments, to the world;[67] (4) Torah-study is more valuable for the scholar or Tsadik; the commandments for the layman or baᶜal teshuvah;[68] (5) Torah-study was or is greater in one era, mitsvot or prayer in another;[69] (6) Torah is greater only when studied with complete self-nullification, or when its depths are plumbed, as few but Rabbi Simeon bar Yoḥai managed to do;[70] (7) Torah and mitsvot are rooted in different supernal sources, each of which has an ascendent aspect that makes it superior to the other in that respect;[71] (8) Torah, mitsvot, and prayer are three different forms of Service and are not meaningfully comparable—they belong to entirely different spiritual hierarchies;[72] (9) Torah is greater than prayer;[73] (10) prayer (with deveḳut) is greater than Torah;[74] (11) Torah and prayer are opposite types of Service: Torah elicits the descent of the Or En Sof, prayer elevates man and the world to It;[75] (12) proper fulfillment of the Torah-study commandment requires the fulfillment of the other commandments;[76] (13) proper fulfillment of the Torah-study commandment requires fervent, selfless prayer;[77] (14) proper prayer requires Torah-study;[78] and (15) proper fulfillment of the other commandments requires Torah-study[79] and prayer.[80]

Similarly varied are the reasons given for Rabbi Simeon bar Yoḥai's—and any full-time scholar of equal caliber—being exempt from the obligation of prayer, that is, from reciting the ᶜAmidah. As in other questions regarding one commandment's superseding another, RSZ resorts to teleological explanations. The spiritual function or kabbalistic purpose of one commandment—to effect certain spiritual or sefirotic movements—is shown to be achievable, occasionally on an even higher level, by the superseding commandment.[81] The two commandments, in other words, have parallel purposes. Since each commandment may have a number of (interrelated) kabbalistic purposes, spiritual functions, or both, RSZ's explanations vary according to the purpose he chooses to emphasize. Prayer, for example, is variously described as providing the "wings" that enable other, more mundane forms of Service to reach the higher worlds; as an act of self-nullification; as the ethical offshoot of Malkhut; as ratso versus the shov of Torah-study (i.e., the ecstatic yearning for union with God vs. the obligation to remain imprisoned in the body in order to make this world fit for God's revealed presence [dirah be-taḥtonim]). This last characterization does not, of course, allow RSZ to assert that Torah-study can sometimes replace prayer. Instead, he suggests that Rabbi Simeon bar Yoḥai's spiritual powers allowed him to achieve the function of ratso through a single prayer and then devote the remainder of his life to shov, which is man's ultimate raison d'être. The other characterizations, however, allow RSZ to develop the parallel-purpose rationale[82] (despite the fact that in most discourses Torah and prayer are defined as completely different forms of Service competing for man's time).

RSZ's emphasis on the interdependence of Torah-study and other religious obligations was his response to the same problem addressed by the Ḥaside Ashkenaz in their day. Judaism had become over-intellectualized. It suffered from "hypertrophy of the intellect," a "psychic imbalance" between man's physical, moral, emotional, and imaginative faculties on the one hand, and his intellectual faculties on the other. "Repeatedly, the Pietists [of Ashkenaz] warned their generation that intellectual accomplishment [in Torah-study] was no substitute for spiritual growth, nor even a guarantee of religious integrity."[83] Repeatedly, RSZ warned his followers, in Talmudic words that in effect became a Ḥabad slogan: "He who says: 'I have only Torah', does not even have Torah."[84] The original meaning of this statement, as RSZ well knew, was that studying without fulfilling the commandments is worthless. But RSZ stretched it to cover all other ethical imperatives as well, particularly self-nullification.[85] Even study for the sake of understanding alone, often defined as Torah li-shemah, violated this implicit injunction, for it was not the Torah's wisdom but the Source of that wisdom that should be the object of man's desire,[86] and only through self-nullification could he attain it. The primary effort must be spiritual rather than intellectual, and proper Torah-study must be preceded and accompanied by biṭul.[87] The hubris of which

Mitnagdic scholars were often accused was therefore not only an indictment of their character but also of their scholarship. If their knowledge made them proud, then their knowledge itself was spiritually defective.

But the indictment did not end there. For self-nullification was more than a prerequisite for proper Torah-study; it was its essence and preeminent purpose. The student must see himself as merely a passive vessel for the revelation of the Torah's divine wisdom. He must shed his self-awareness through an intense desire for union with the Source of that wisdom. His personality then merges with that of the divine Lawgiver to the point where his own halakhic decisions are royal decrees originating in God's mind. In fact, by articulating the words of a halakhah with biṭul he causes God to utter the same words—originally uttered at Sinai—and thereby draws down upon his soul their sanctity. His words are literally God's words, and his authority is God's authority. RSZ took no notice of the paradox that, according to this view, supreme power can be achieved only through absolute self-nullification, because it was clearly the striving for biṭul, not for power, that he wanted to inculcate. Power was only a necessary, although apparently not an undesirable, consequence of proper Torah-study. By studying with biṭul one could eventually achieve the purpose of study: a still greater biṭul, both of man and of the world Torah governs. Occasionally RSZ makes contemplative prayer and Ḳeri'at Shema a precondition for studying with biṭul, but generally he indicates or implies that Torah-study, when properly performed, is itself both the precursor and the highest expression of biṭul.[88]

Although the desire for union with God—deveḳut—is necessary to attain biṭul, and (studying with) biṭul is necessary to achieve deveḳut, the two are not identical. Thus, while in *Tanya* and at least one discourse[89] Torah li-shemah is defined as studying to achieve deveḳut, in several other discourses this intention is referred to as a lower level of li-shemah or even as *lo li-shemah*.[90] According to these discourses, li-shemah means, quite literally, "for the Torah's sake"—to elicit an infusion of the Or En Sof into the Torah being studied and thereby into its source, the sefirah of Ḥokhmah. RSZ's various definitions of li-shemah will be discussed in more detail presently. Here, however, we are concerned only with the implication of this definition for the first category of his teachings regarding Torah-study: teachings relating to the student and the act of studying. By ruling out (studying with) biṭul for the sake of deveḳut as the highest goal of Torah-study, RSZ was addressing a conundrum inherent in his system. On the one hand, biṭul is presented as a state of absolute selflessness, while on the other it is the only path to the most intense and sublime form of self-gratification.[91] RSZ therefore points out that the biṭul he has in mind is to be pursued not for man's sake—to achieve deveḳut—but for the Torah's sake.

Related to the requirement of studying Torah with biṭul is RSZ's emphasis on studying orally, rather than in thought alone. Besides insisting that the halakhah requires oral study in order to fulfil the commandment,[92] RSZ, like most kabbalists, was fascinated by the power of speech, both human and divine. With respect to Torah-study, the fact that the Torah was revealed through the medium of divine speech suggested to him that speech, rather than thought, is the primary vehicle for the Torah's assimilation by man and the world. For this reason too, the ideal form of study is a kind of automatic speech, with man simply repeating God's speech in a state of complete biṭul.[93] By doing this he constantly reexperiences the Theophany at Sinai during which God alone spoke, and the people were passive recipients.[94] Subsequent Torah interpretations and developments were, as the well-known aggadah points out, potentially or actually included in the Sinaitic revelation,[95] so that the possibility of achieving apparently new insights is not ruled out. But just how to reconcile the intellectual activism necessary for achieving these highly desirable insights[96] with the passivism of biṭul is never explained.

In the course of many discourses RSZ concentrates on the various components of speech and their metaphysical functions in Torah-study. The breath that produces sound is associated with maḳif—a speaker's breath envelops him, as it were—and the breath of Torah utterances causes the light of the divine maḳif to descend and envelop the speaker's soul.[97] The sound itself, the human voice, reveals man's previously hidden thoughts and emotions; so, too, the voice of the student reveals the divine light of the Torah and causes it to be manifested in the commandments and in the world.[98] The assumption here, as in other areas discussed in the discourses, is that the Or En Sof, while latent everywhere, is essentially transcendent and must be "drawn down" into the physical world through strenuous physical effort. This effort also weakens the body and the animal soul, thereby making them more receptive to the spiritual influx engendered by Torah-study (or mitzvah-fulfillment). Consequently, the more forceful the Torah-utterance, the more spiritually effective it is.[99] In addition, by pronouncing a thing or act to be under the control of the ḳelipot—*ṭame* (impure), *pasul* (unfit), *asur* (forbidden)—one punctures their pride and deprives them of their only source of power. The divine maḳif aids in this process because it is aroused through the maḳif created by the student's speech, and, as noted above, "maḳif repels the *ḥitsonim*" (= ḳelipot).[100]

RSZ's emphasis on articulating the words of Torah,[101] in accordance with the halakhic view that makes this a sine qua non for fulfilling the Torah-study commandment, may have been intended to counteract the emphasis by other Hasidic leaders on contemplative Torah-study—study with and for deveḳut, rather than for the sake of fulfilling the commandment as defined by halakhah. This is not to say that these masters were uninterested in the latter purpose of Torah-study, but they did gloss over it in favor of this new formula and its various definitions. Moreover, they occasionally intimated that unarticulated study was halakhically valid and that contemplative deveḳut was incompatible with, and far superior to, Torah-study.[102] RSZ rejected such statements and suggestions by pointing out that, on the one hand, Torah-study must be oral to be valid, and, on the other hand, valid Torah-study was itself the highest form of deveḳut, for through it man was uniquely united with God through His will and wisdom.[103]

Had RSZ contented himself with these views, his position would have been clear and consistent. But he could not ignore the Besht's innovative doctrine of mystical deveḳut through the letters, as opposed to the cognitive content, of the Torah. This obviously clashed with the desideratum of understanding, as profoundly as possible, the meaning of the text being studied. On a more basic psychological level, this desideratum also clashed with the requirement that Torah-study be oral, since most people cannot simultaneously articulate the words and contemplate the meaning of a difficult passage. RSZ resolves this problem by assuring his followers that when properly performed, with joy and mesirat nefesh (self-sacrifice), oral Torah-study will not impede one's concentration.[104] But the Beshtian doctrine could not be so easily disposed of, since the Maggid, and presumably the Besht himself, considered letter-deveḳut and cognitive study to be inherently incompatible. RSZ was therefore forced to equivocate. In several discourses he implies that while letter-deveḳut without comprehension is valuable, coupled with (prior to or subsequent) comprehension it is even more valuable.[105] In one discourse he suggests that letter-deveḳut may be used (only?) at the beginning of a Torah-study session to arouse the Love and Fear that should accompany talmud Torah.[106] In several discourses he indicates or hints that it is precisely the letters, not their cognitive content, that elevate the student's soul,[107] and in several he attributed this power, as well as the power to draw down and reveal Divinity, even to the letters of halakhot.[108] Finally, in one discourse he clearly advocates studying Mishnah in two stages: first probing for the "peshat" and then binding oneself to the divine attributes permeating the words.[109]

Although the letter-deveḳut doctrine is based on the belief that the Or En Sof already permeates these letters, RSZ's general position is that it must be drawn down and revealed in them. Proper Torah-study causes an infusion of the Or En Sof into Ḥokhmah above, and into Ḥokhmah's reflection in the words being studied below. From the supernal Ḥokhmah, known as *Ḥokhmah Ila'ah* (Higher Ḥokhmah), the Or En Sof descends to the sefirah of Malkhut, known as *Ḥokhmah Tata'ah* (Lower Ḥokhmah), which is the source of that part of the divine soul that resides in the body. The soul of the Torah student is therefore also illumined by the Or En Sof, and he is thereby greatly spiritualized and edified. The criteria and prerequisites for proper Torah-study vary according to the discourse. They include Love, repentance, studying with biṭul, with an intense desire for God, praying with biṭul and mesirat nefesh, fulfilling the other commandments, studying orally, and, most basically, the constant awareness that one is studying the word of God.[110] Here as elsewhere RSZ underscored one or two aspects of his complex view per discourse, according to the need of the hour, the audience, and the flow of his thoughts.

RSZ's definition of Torah li-shemah is similarly multifaceted. It encompasses virtually all previous kabbalistic and Hasidic interpretations and generally ignores, as they did, the rabbinic interpretations of the medieval commentators (e.g., Rashi and R. Asher),[111] not because these were less valid, but because they lacked kabbalistic underpinnings. Except for one conspicuous passage in *Tanya* in which li-shemah is defined as "for the sake of binding one's soul to God by understanding the Torah,"[112] RSZ tends to follow his (other) kabbalistic sources in shifting the definition from the ethical to the metaphysical realm. Contrary to the general trend of Hasidic thought, he here takes an originally ethical concept and transforms it into a primarily theological one. Thus, at the beginning of the main analysis of this concept in *Tanya*, he subtly shifts from li-shemah—for her (Torah's) sake—to *li-shemo*—for His [God's] sake.[113] He explains that though the Or En Sof inheres in the letters of the Torah regardless of the intention man has when pronouncing them, their physicality impedes its revelation in full force. Uttering them with an ulterior, nonspiritual motive—for example, to attain wealth or honor—anchors them to the physical world until the student repents. Even peremptory Torah-study ("mitsvat anashim melumadah") remains unilluminated until the same passage is restudied li-shemah; that is, li-shemo—with the Love and Fear that include biṭul and mesirat nefesh and the desire for deveḳut. These are the wings that lift the words to the supernal worlds where they can be infused with a great stream of Or En Sof.[114]

It is God, therefore, and the Torah itself, who are the primary beneficiaries of Torah li-shemah. The Or En Sof is allowed, as it were, to illumine Ḥokhmah (=Torah) fully and constantly.[115] Halakhically, however, one completely fulfils the commandment to study Torah whether or not one studies li-shemah in this sense or in any other sense. Thus, by requiring repentance or repetition for not studying with Love and Fear, RSZ was transforming a kabbalistic-Hasidic imperative into a halakhic obligation (although he certainly would have denied that this was his intention). This metamorphosis, like similar ones in his teachings, was possible, if not inevitable, because of the blurring of the original conceptual boundaries between halakhah and kabbalah (and philosophy) that characterizes his religioethical thought.

In the discourses, where RSZ uses kabbalistic symbolism more freely than in *Sefer shel Benonim*, the word *li-shemah* can be and is applied to Ḥokhmah. One must study for the sake of drawing the Or En Sof into Ḥokhmah above and thereby into the letters or concepts of Torah below. This is accomplished by attaching oneself to the Or En Sof (=Keter, or Ayin, the source of Ḥokhmah) through teshuvah, prayer, biṭul, and mesirat nefesh. United with the Or En Sof, one can then bestow it upon the Torah being studied.[116] As noted above, the first step of attaching oneself to the Or En Sof is, in some discourses, identified with lo li-shemah. The Talmudic dictum requiring one to study even lo li-shemah, for through it one will eventually attain li-shemah, is accordingly reinterpreted as a necessary rather than contingent sequence of Service: Only after achieving lo li-shemah can one hope to achieve li-shemah.[117] Indeed, according to one discourse, only a fool would believe otherwise.[118]

Not surprisingly, although infusing Ḥokhmah with the Or En Sof is by far the most frequent definition of li-shemah in the discourses, a number of other definitions also appear. One discourse acknowledges this multiplicity and goes on to insist that the essential definition is: for the sake of deveḳut.[119] Other definitions include: Luria's "for the sake of the first he" of the Tetragrammaton;[120] with Love and Fear;[121] for the sake of drawing down an infusion of Ḥokhmah into Zeʿir Anpin;[122] and for the sole purpose of assimilating the divine knowledge rather than for any pleasure or benefit that knowledge can bring.[123]

Common to most of the definitions is the requirement that the intellectual act of Torah-study be coupled with a possibly incompatible emotive or contemplative act that heightens its spiritual significance. This incompatibility is distinct from, and less problematic than, the clash between letter-deveḳut and intellectual concentration, because the catalyst that transforms neutral Torah-study into Torah li-shemah is admittedly extraneous to the text itself. RSZ addresses the problem by intimating that the act that satisfies the li-shemah requirement should precede each Torah-study session.[124] An explicit directive to this effect is found in *Tanya*, in which, following the Maggid's teaching, RSZ recommends pausing every hour one studies to fulfill this requirement.[125] Several discourses, however, particularly those defining li-shemah as studying with biṭul and mesirat nefesh, as well as the implication in *Tanya* itself that, ideally, conscious Love and Fear should *permeate* one's Torah-study, indicate that RSZ never really succeeded in resolving this problem either.

Common to the most frequently mentioned definitions of Torah li-shemah is the kabbalistic idea that Torah-study, like every commandment, moves God by stimulating certain vital divine emanations. Proper Torah-study, as noted above, draws down the Or En Sof into Ḥokhmah, and from there into Malkhut. But it does not stop there. This lowest of the sefirot, through its reflection in man's soul, bestows that light upon this lowest of the worlds and transforms it into a potential "abode for Him below."[126] According to several discourses, the physical act of articulating the words of Torah, even if they are thoroughly familiar, draws the Or En Sof into those words and into the physical world, thereby spiritualizing them.[127] Other discourses mandate mesirat nefesh and biṭul during prayer as prerequisites for illuminating the world through Torah-study.[128] All agree, however, that by revealing God's wisdom—Ḥokhmah—in the world, one also reveals His Divinity in the world, since the Or En Sof resides primarily in Ḥokhmah. Indeed, according to one discourse, the true purpose of halakhah is to determine the precise manner in which the Or En Sof shall permeate every aspect of the corporeal world.[129] Moreover, because Ḥokhmah is the first creative principle, even a single detail of a single halakhah is instrumental in creating and vitalizing all the worlds, from the highest to the lowest.[130]

The powerful influence Torah-study has on God's "behavior" is often expressed by RSZ in the slogan: "Whoever reads and studies [Torah], God reads and studies with him"[131] (literally, opposite him). In the course of his teachings RSZ interpreted this Midrashic paraphrase as referring to all of the metaphysical effects that proper Torah-study can achieve. For less-sophisticated audiences he used it quite literally.[132] Regardless of the audience, he also used it to emphasize the eternal immediacy of Torah-study. The words and voice of the student were actually echoes of the words and voice of God at Sinai. God "gives the Torah" continuously, and man must reexperience the Sinaitic revelation every time he studies. Conversely, proper Torah-study causes God to "study" what man is studying, for when man consecrates the essence of his soul—his will—to Torah below, God consecrates the essence of His divine light—the Or En Sof—to Ḥokhmah above. Similarly, as God's Ḥokhmah is revealed in man's speech during Torah-study, so is that Ḥokhmah revealed in God's speech (=Malkhut) to sustain all the worlds.[133]

The power of Torah-study to move God in these ways flows in part from the Torah's supernal source and in part from the source and special abilities of the souls of Israel. Let us assume, as many discourses do, that the source of Torah is Ḥokhmah. For a created being to elicit an emanation of the Or En Sof into or from Ḥokhmah, that being must be able to "reach" that high. To draw down an emanation from the Or En Sof, one must have the ability to affect the Or En Sof, and likewise for Ḥokhmah. All Jewish souls have this ability in potentia because they are rooted in some aspect of the Or En Sof or Ḥokhmah. They can actualize it by binding themselves to the divine Ayin (=one aspect of the Or En Sof) through self-nullification during prayer. As we have seen, the precise supernal source of the souls of Israel varies according to the discourse. Inevitably, therefore, their hierarchial relationship to the source of Torah also varies. Some discourses place both on the same level, some place Torah above souls, and some place souls above Torah. All the discourses that touch on this relation, however, locate the source of Jewish souls in the inner aspect of Ḥokhmah or above.[134] The abstract kabbalistic symbolism is often brought home by citing the inspirational Lurianic notion that each (root-)soul originates in one of the 600,000 (thought-)letters of the Written Torah.[135] Apparently aware that many of his followers would still question the possibility of a body-bound soul affecting the infinitely lofty Or En Sof, RSZ occasionally points out that it is actually the portion of the soul remaining above, in its original supernal abode, that accomplishes this. This part of the soul alone is conscious of the spiritual gratification resulting from its achievement, although its embodied counterpart can occasionally be aroused to a feeling of overwhelming awe similar to that experienced by the nation at Sinai.[136]

As for the Torah's supernal source, the only valid generalization that can be made is that this source is most often identified as some aspect of Ḥokhmah. In kabbalistic terms, however, this means little, for even limiting the possibilities to Atsilut and above, they include: the entire sefirah of Ḥokhmah; its inner aspect; its outer aspect; Ḥokhmah of Malkhut; Ḥokhmah of Keter; Ḥokhmah of Arikh Anpin (in Keter); Ḥokhmah of ʿAtiḳ Yomin (also in Keter); and Ḥokhmah of Adam Ḳadmon. Such technicalities were highly significant for RSZ and his scholarly disciples, and it is therefore noteworthy that his teachings explicitly support all these possibilities. In fact, at one time or another he identified Torah with every sefirah, from Keter through Malkhut; with both or maḳif and or penimi; and with the Godhead Itself. Depending on the discourse, it is arguable that the Torah's source is above the chain of being or part of it; that it is the instrument of creation, its highest aspect, or completely transcends it.[137]

The supernal source of the Torah is one of the most frequently treated kabbalistic issues in the discourses. It was important to RSZ and his followers for both theosophical and axiological reasons. The Torah's position and consequent function in the divine hierarchy theoretically determined its position in RSZ's ethical thought.[138] If the source of Torah is higher than that of prayer, for example, then Torah-study is the higher activity and commensurately more time and effort must be devoted to it. The fact that the entire Torah is, according to most discourses, rooted in God's eternal Will and Wisdom—and not, for example, in ever-changing Malkhut—means that no part of it could ever fall into desuetude. Presently inapplicable laws, as well as laws that are theoretical by definition, must therefore be mastered as thoroughly as any others. Even repeating such a halakhah several times is an intrinsically valuable act, because the light of Ḥokhmah thereby drawn down spiritualizes the material entities discussed in the halakhah.

Torah

Like his metaphysics, RSZ's discussions of component parts and facets of the Torah revolve around pairs of complementary opposites: the Written Torah and the Oral Torah; the exoteric and esoteric; Torah in this world and in the next. A partial exception to the rule of complementarity is the relation of Torah to secular knowledge—the inner science to the "outer sciences" (*ḥokhmot ḥitsoniot*). Although we have seen that RSZ often speaks of the latter in sharply derogatory terms,[139] a fair number of discourses reveal a more ambivalent attitude. One discourse intimates that underneath many layers of sefirotic clothing, secular knowledge contains the same divine light that is the source of Torah.[140] Again, if Torah's source is, as other discourses state, the inner aspect of Ḥokhmah,[141] then secular knowledge still partakes of the level of Ḥokhmah that created and sustains the world[142]—hardly a negative assessment.

One discourse grants secular knowledge only a small amount of good commingled with a preponderance of evil. This element of good, however, can and must be salvaged by competent Torah scholars. Since they are forced to delve into the evil in order to do so, there is always the danger that they will remain there and forget the purpose of their intellectual descent. The extraordinary soul, however, is capable of redeeming the good in secular knowledge with only a cursory perusal of the subject matter and therefore runs no risk.[143] Another discourse supplements this idea by observing that by mastering the astronomy necessary for understanding the halakhot of intercalation, the student elevates this secular knowledge and transforms it into Torah. Here, too, however, RSZ adds the caveat that this can be achieved only by a select few.[144]

RSZ's opinion of the scientific advances made by "the nations" is similarly equivocal. While acknowledging their practical value, he minimizes their spiritual significance. The gentiles, he insists, may have progressed in material, technological knowledge, but they have regressed in spiritual, philosophical knowledge. Their achievements are in any case not due to their intellectual and creative ability but to the Jews' neglect of the esoteric aspect of the Torah, since the fortunes of Jews and gentiles fluctuate inversely, and when the inner wisdom of the Jews declines, the outer wisdom of the gentiles ascends.[145]

RSZ's frequent treatment of the Written-Oral Torah pair is, on the whole, less ambivalent but no less complex. The Zohar had linked them with Ḥesed and Gevurah respectively, and symbolized them as water and fire.[146] Luria, following other Zoharic passages, identified them with Zeʿir Anpin and Malkhut, bestower and recipient.[147] Cordovero cited both views, as well as a third, also found in the Zohar, identifying the Written Torah with Binah.[148] RSZ characteristically follows all these kabbalistic guides but often elevates the sefirotic level of discourse in general and the source and value of the Oral Torah in particular.

The Written Torah is generally identified with Ḥokhmah, the seed of God's wisdom, which is developed and brought to fruition in the Oral Torah—Binah, or Malkhut (="lower Ḥokhmah," the female counterpart of Ḥokhmah and also the organ of divine speech). The Oral Torah reveals what is hidden in the Written.[149] According to various discourses, the two are respectively symbolized in the Bible as, among other metaphors, father and mother; heaven and earth (i.e., bestower of rain and recipient); sun and moon; bridegroom and bride. They are also said to correspond to the hermeneutic principle of "generalization and detail" (*kelal u-perat*) and to the two hes of the Tetragrammaton.[150] Each has qualities the other lacks. The Written Torah comprises the actual words of God as dictated to Moses. The intellectual content of these words is largely unfathomable. Again and again, RSZ, following the Zohar,[151] alludes to the apparently trivial nature of Pentateuch narratives; surely, he implies, the Torah's significance and sanctity cannot be traced to such tales, no matter how astutely interpreted. Equally puzzling, in RSZ's view, is that even the legal sections of the Torah are written in the form of narratives—God told Moses to command the people thus and thus—rather than in the direct form of statutes. And reading these legal narratives without referring to the Oral Torah leaves one equally perplexed as to their true meaning.[152]

We must therefore conclude that the significance and underlying meaning of the words of the Written Torah are to be found not in their cognitive content but in their form. The configurations, "crowns," and specific combinations of the letters of the Written Torah are what reflect the supernal Ḥokhmah that is its source. The cognitive content of the words these letters comprise is very much secondary and may, when necessary, be completely ignored. This approach allowed RSZ readily to explain the halakhah's insistence on precision regarding the number and form of the letters in a Torah-scroll; the fact that even an ignoramus was permitted to recite the appropriate blessings over Torah-study every morning and when called up to the Torah reading in the synagogue; and, perhaps most important, it provided a solid foundation for the Besht's doctrine of letter-deveḳut. It also accounted for the apparently trivial content and often incongruous narrative style of the Pentateuch, because the content and style of the Written Torah were intended to conceal, not reveal, its true significance. The purpose of the Written Torah is not to set forth intelligible concepts and laws but to reveal the suprarational manner in which the Or En Sof can be drawn down into the lower worlds; to *narrate*, by means of certain combinations of certain letters, God's primordial plan for revealing His Divinity in the world.[153]

This approach also dovetailed nicely with Naḥmanides' well-known description of the Pentateuch as a series of divine names, and with the rabbinic term *miḳra*, which could connote both "reading" and "calling" (to someone). By simply reading the Pentateuch, man was calling to God by name and thus assuring that He would "turn toward him", that is, reveal Himself in the world and in the reader's soul. Since calling to someone is a vocal act, RSZ saw this as an additional reason to articulate the words of the Written Torah rather than reading them silently. And since reading, not comprehending, is the essential requirement, anyone literate enough to read Hebrew can fulfill the commandment to study Torah by reciting the Pentateuch.[154]

Study of the Oral Torah, on the other hand, is essentially an intellectual act. In kabbalistic terms, it is an act of birur—sifting, separating, and selecting the good from the evil, the permissible and desirable from the prohibited and undesirable. And, according to the Zohar, the faculty that performs birur is the intellect: "be-ḥokhmah itberiru."[155] This is the primary vehicle for revealing God's will and determining how He wants the world ordered. Such a determination requires concentrated intellectual effort because ever since Shevirat ha-Kelim and Adam's sin, good and evil have been commingled in all things. Everything must therefore be scrutinized, using the divine ratiocination of the Oral Law to discern (halakhically) whether or not the entity, emotion, or act in question contains a redeemable element of goodness, a spark of the Or En Sof that was imprisoned and hidden among the ḳelipot. As Luria observed, these malevolent metaphysical "shells" attempt to obscure the captive sparks by surrounding the true halakhic decision with intellectual barriers of difficulties and doubts. It is the Torah-student's mission to break through these impediments by concerted mental effort, intellectual acuity, and a degree of asceticism sufficient to weaken the Ḳelipat Nogah that influences his body and animal soul (thereby allowing the light of his divine soul to illumine the halakhah). The more closely intertwined good and evil are in a given issue, the finer the distinctions that must be made to distinguish between them, the more fully he accomplishes the birur mission. This is because birur in the true sense consists less of distinguishing between the clearly good and the clearly evil than of distinguishing between the actually good and the apparently good. Its main sphere of operation is therefore in the grey realm of Ḳelipat Nogah. Every Jew has property in this realm that he alone can purify and elevate by diligently applying himself to his personal portion in the Torah. Since he cannot know which portion is his, he must apply himself equally to the entire Torah. Those areas in which he finds himself to be most creative are "his" areas and cumulatively comprise his portion in the Torah, the portion that sustains his soul because his soul is rooted in it.[156]

The Lurianic idea of concentrated study for the sake of weakening or breaking the ḳelipot and achieving birur is related to Luria's division of Torah-study into two independent acts: recitation and ratiocination.[157] RSZ adopts this division in a number of discourses, adding that ratiocination corresponds to ratso, the elevation of man's soul to the Divine, and recitation corresponds to shov, the drawing down of Divinity into this world.[158] This would suggest that letter-deveḳut is possible even when studying the Oral Torah, and, as we have seen, several discourses apparently point in this direction. Most discourses, however, as well as *Tanya* and *Hilkhot Talmud Torah*, clearly reject this possibility. According to these sources, study of the Oral Torah fulfills the Torah-study commandment only if it combines articulation with comprehension.[159]

Nor is this the only major inconsistency in RSZ's approach to the study of the Oral Torah. The need for assiduous application, for example, is explained both in strictly Lurianic terms—to shatter the ḳelipot; to "sweeten the judgments of Leah"—and in terms that vitiate Luria's assumptions. Quite a few discourses emphasize the positive aspects of halakhic debate, the stimulating effect of apparently inconsistent or otherwise difficult halakhic discussions. Several discourses transform the *Raʿaya Mehemna*'s derogatory reference to Talmudic dialectics as "libun hilkheta" into a laudatory phrase. Contradictions between sources and scholarly disagreement are seen not as unfortunate obstacles but as necessary ingredients for halakhic creativity. This creativity is described, in glowing terms, as drawing forth the hidden wisdom from the depths of Ḥokhmah, thereby revealing the highest reaches of the Or En Sof. Although the apparently casuistical Babylonian Talmud refers to itself as "darkness" in comparison to its relatively straightforward Palestinian counterpart,[160] it is precisely from this darkness of intensive halakhic scrutiny and debate that the light of God's true will emerges. Halakhic dialectics are actually a joy to both man and God; to man because of the pleasure involved in intellectual probing and discovery; and to God because, like every king, He is pleased when His subjects exert themselves to discover all the latent implications of His edicts. Thus, He finds particularly gratifying those halakhot uncovered only in the generations of the *aḥaronim*, since these halakhot were revealed by scrutinizing the implications of a given commandment even more carefully than had been done by previous generations.[161]

Man's ability to innovate in halakhah indicates that he is very much an active participant in its development. But, as we have seen, several discourses describe the ideal Torah scholar, the Talmudic sage, as a purely passive vessel for the revelation of the words God spoke to Moses on Sinai.[162] Other discourses, however, ascribe to the sages of the Talmud the power arbitrarily to decide the halakhah in accordance with their respective perceptions of the proper channeling for the supernal flow of the Or En Sof. Their decisions are not, it seems, determined either by tradition or by reasoning from first principles, but by the supernal source of their souls. The soul of Hillel, for example, derived from Ḥesed and led him to decide that the proper channeling for the Or En Sof should generally be toward Ḥesed, or leniency. His debates with Shammai—Gevurah—were thus actually only the mundane manifestations of their souls' respective sources and perceptions.[163] Similarly, the authority of these and other Talmudic sages to decide the halakhah stemmed less from anything they did on earth than from the lofty origins of their souls.[164]

Nor do the contradictions end there. We have seen that RSZ often places Torah at the top of his axiological hierarchy. Yet there are discourses that describe the essential function of the Oral Torah as an attempt continually to discover more and more prohibitions;[165] that speak of it as a limiting, restrictive force, spiritually weighing and measuring the desirability of all phenomena and thereby depriving man of the expansiveness and freedom that he enjoyed before the Torah was given and will enjoy again "in the future";[166] that cite the Lurianic observation that the beneficial sefirotic unions in Atsilut are incestuous and are prohibited in this world only for fear of benefiting the ḳelipot;[167] that associate the Oral Torah with Fear, rather than Love of the King, as a result of which His subjects are constantly seeking new ways to avoid even the remotest possibility of transgressing

His will.[168] It is true that one discourse mitigates its description of the Oral Torah as deriving from the restrictive realm of Gevurah by observing that this offspring of Gevurah is actually the essence of Ḥesed, for it causes Divinity to descend and be revealed in a finite world.[169] But the other discourses cited clearly indicate that the Torah's restrictions really are restrictions: The untrammeled freedom of the pre-Torah world of Tohu has been severely limited by the Torah-world of Tiḳun.[170]

The Written-Oral Torah pair also contains its share of the paradoxical. The Written Torah originates in God's Reason—Ḥokhmah or Binah—yet one may validly study it by using not human reason but human speech only. The Oral Torah originates, according to many discourses, in God's Speech—Malkhut—yet one may validly study it, according to most discourses, only by combining human speech with human reason, memory, or both. In fact, reason and memory are the primary instruments for its study, speech being required only to reveal the Or En Sof they elicit. Again, according to some discourses, the Written Torah originates in Ḥokhmah; the Oral, in Binah (or Malkhut); according to others these sources are reversed;[171] but according to most, the Oral Torah is higher because it is the vehicle for revealing God's will.[172] (Indeed, one discourse considers the Written Torah as merely the catalyst that permits the development of the Oral).[173] Those discourses that link the Oral Torah with Ḥokhmah have no trouble accounting for its supremacy, for Ḥokhmah is, after all, higher than Binah. Those that link it with Binah or Malkhut point out that Binah is lower in manifestation but higher in origin, for what is higher descends lower, and "their beginning is wedged into their end" (Keter inheres in Malkhut).

Other discourses, however, place the Written Torah higher, since the Oral Torah is merely an explication of the Written.[174] In fact, all the halakhot of the Oral Torah are latent in the Written.[175] Moreover, the Written Torah is God's word, the Oral is man's.[176] Because the Written Torah is higher, it descends lower, into inanimate written letters produced by the outermost soul-garment (action); whereas the Oral Torah, being lower in origin, only descends to the level of the intermediate soul-garment (speech, the product of an animate being).[177] Since the Written Torah descends to the level of action, one might expect that it would permeate the higher level of reason as well, but this is not the case. The halakhah prohibits reciting the Pentateuch by heart because, RSZ implies, one may be tempted to elaborate on the text according to the dictates of human reason, and the Written Torah transcends reason.[178]

More inconsistencies appear in RSZ's references to the component parts of the Written and Oral Torah. One discourse states that, unlike the Pentateuch, the value of the Prophets and Writings will be nullified in the future,[179] while another suggests that *all* the narrative portions of the Bible, including the Pentateuch, are on the same level and must be forgotten so that the soul may assimilate the spiritual Torah of Gan ʿEden.[180] Some discourses consider the Mishnah more comprehensible than the Gemara, and its study more gratifying, while others reverse these judgments.[181] Most discourses place Gemara above Mishnah in the axiological hierarchy, but here, too, one finds exceptions.[182]

Nevertheless, it is possible to isolate certain trends from this maze of contradictions. The Mishnah contains the entire Gemara in condensed form. Its function is to articulate God's will and wisdom in the form of halakhot—statutes without apparent or sufficient reason. Halakhah is the essence of the Torah and will survive, in one form or another, in both Gan ʿEden and ʿOlam ha-Ba. The Gemara's function is to provide explication and ratiocination for the statutes of the Mishnah. The Beraita is an inferior and less lucid form of legislation. In sefirotic terms, the Gemara derives from the intellective sefirot, the Mishnah from the emotive sefirot, the Beraita (extraneous) from the external sefirot, Netsaḥ, Hod, Yesod. The Six Orders of the Mishnah are said to correspond to the six emotive sefirot; by studying *Zeraʿim*, for example, one causes the Or En Sof to illumine the sefirah of Ḥesed. The sixty-odd tractates of the Talmud correspond to these six sefirot in their expanded form; that is, in the form each assumes when revealing its complete array of ten component sefirot. The four study areas of kabbalah, Gemara, Mishnah, and Pentateuch are related to the four supernal worlds, although exactly how depends on the kabbalistic source a given discourse employs.[183]

The exoteric Torah is superior to the esoteric because it contains the halakhah. By apprehending it one apprehends the essence of God's wisdom. Kabbalah, on the other hand, is a suprarational discipline and therefore can only point the mind to the existence of certain aspects of that wisdom. In addition, the exoteric Torah, while not as inspirational as the esoteric, is nevertheless more spiritually nourishing, just as bread is more nourishing than sweets. It also provides the garment that allows the soul to assimilate the revelation of Gan ʿEden and actually permits us to catch a glimpse of that revelation in this world as well.[184] One discourse goes even further and flatly states that Talmud study in this world is higher than the apprehension of souls in Gan ʿEden.[185]

This is one side of the ledger. On the other side we are faced with the mundane subject matter of the halakhot, which disturbed RSZ as much as the narrative portions of the Pentateuch. An example he cites several times is the beginning of the tractate *Bava Metsia*. Two men come to court holding a garment each claims to have found. According to the Gemara's analysis, one is obviously lying. Is it possible, asks RSZ, that the study of a trivial case such as this, involving a physical garment and a liar, has more than trivial value? Is it possible, moreover, that God's wisdom consists of nothing loftier than such basic moral and religious imperatives as the Ten Commandments, some of which could have been arrived at by human reason alone? We could not, of course, expect RSZ's answer to involve concepts of social utility and benefit, since for a mystic the very existence of society is relatively inconsequential. The answer, then, could only be that these halakhot are only a façade for the masses, who are unable to appreciate their esoteric interior. Indeed, according to many discourses, the halakhot themselves contain the deepest secrets of the Torah, *Ṭaʿame Torah*, which are usually defined as the (kabbalistic) reasons for the halakhot. Taʿame Torah are glimpsed in Gan ʿEden, and by the greatest tsadiḳim even in this world, but will be fully revealed only "in the future." The study of halakhah is so vital because it enables us to receive these glimpses and revelations. The exoteric Torah appears trivial because "what is higher descends lower"; in fact, its trivial subject matter *proves* its lofty origin. Fundamentally, therefore, the entire Torah is esoteric, with different aspects of it clothed in different garments. This essential core of the Torah derives from the inner aspect of Ḥokhmah (= the essence of divine Pleasure) and is limitless. When clothed in the esoteric garment of kabbalah, it completely transcends the ḳelipot, thereby rendering birur through dialectics—pilpul—unnecessary.[186]

The kabbalistic garment itself is, according to one discourse, separable into Ṭaʿame Torah (the reasons of the Torah), the surface of which was skimmed by Luria in *Peri ʿEts Ḥayyim*, and *Razin deʾOraita* (the secrets of the Torah), which are to be found in the *Idra Raba* and *Idra Zuṭa* of the Zohar.[187] RSZ is primarily concerned with Ṭaʿame Torah, which he associates or uses synonymously with the esoteric reasons for the commandments—*Ṭaʿame Mitsvot*—and for individual halakhot, as well as with the cantillation notes of the Written Torah (*ṭaʿam* here connoting the pleasure elicited by the musical rendition of the words). Taʿame Mitsẓot, in turn, is sometimes used to denote the explanation in the Oral Torah of how the mitsẓot are to be fulfilled. The thread running through these definitions is RSZ's association of reason with pleasure. The *true* reason for a halakhah or commandment is not grounded in God's Intellect but in His Pleasure (to the extent that the two are separable). That Pleasure is the core of the Intellect that formulates the halakhah, and that Intellect, in turn, constitutes the core of divine Pleasure. Thus, according to some discourses, the true reason for any given halakhah is hidden in the relevant exoteric reasoning of the Talmud and is associated with the pleasure produced by the cantillation of the Torah. This reason can be fully revealed only in the future, when all the divine sparks have been extracted from the ḳelipot through the fulfillment of the commandments, thereby removing the obstacles to the revelation of the highest aspect of Divinity—Pleasure—in this world. This revelation of divine Pleasure is, as we have seen, identical with the revelation of the highest aspect of Ḥokhmah, which is the source for the birur process that makes this revelation possible. Nevertheless, RSZ makes it quite clear that the Torah of the "future," which, according to some discourses, the Messiah will receive, will completely transcend reason; it will be *revealed*, not understood; spiritually appreciated, not intellectually apprehended. The Torah of the future, in other words, will consist of God's revealed presence.[188]

But we need not wait until then to acknowledge that even the ostensibly rational Oral Torah is actually suprarational. Unaided human reason could never have formulated the legal principles and drawn the halakhic conclusions found in the Talmud. On the contrary, human reason rejects many if not most of these conclusions, and this is equally true of civil as of ritual law. Clearly, then, the validity of halakhah stems not from its rationality or reasonableness but from its being God's will (which is motivated by His pleasure). This will happens to be articulated in intellectual form, but it is God's intellect, not man's. To be certain of the compelling rationality of any aspect of the Torah is to labor under a delusion, for if even worldly matters are often not what they seem, how much more must this apply to the Torah. It is consequently understandable why, although intellectual apprehension is the highest form of pleasure, Talmud study is not, according to some discourses, a pleasurable experience: Both the trivial subject matter and its essential irrationality militate against it. Thus, when RSZ speaks of the value of intellectually apprehending the Torah, he speaks only of the Torah's form, which happens to be intellectual, not of its substance, which is divine Pleasure and can only be experienced, not understood.[189]

Since RSZ consistently reserved this experience for the Messianic or post-Messianic era, it was important that he explain to his followers what they could expect in the interim. How did their Torah-study in this world relate to the intellectual pleasure they would enjoy in Gan ʿEden? What possible contribution could knowing the disposition of the disputed garment case make to the knowledge of God they would bask in above? As always, the discourses yield several answers. One approach describes the Torah of this world as a parable (*mashal*) through which the Or En Sof, which is the parable's "meaning," may be assimilated (to some extent) by the disembodied soul. This supreme pleasure is actually hidden in the Torah's words and concepts, and is revealed in Gan ʿEden by removing their terrestrial garb and uncovering their spiritual essence. Nevertheless, the Torah studied above retains its intellectual form. Its subject matter may be described as an introduction to the Ṭaʿame Torah, comprising concepts similar to the kabbalistic reasons for the halakhot in the Zohar and Lurianic works. Presumably, those halakhot that are already explained in *Peri ʿEts Ḥayyim* and elsewhere will be studied in greater depth and understood more clearly. Thus, like kabbalists before him, RSZ assumes, at least in some discourses, that the souls in Gan ʿEden spend their time studying Advanced Kabbalah. The trivial, terrestrial issues of the halakhah are jettisoned—must, in fact, be forgotten—and their inner, spiritual meaning delights the soul. But just how the kabbalah of this world differs from that of the next is never explained. On the contrary, RSZ provides several examples of the study matter of Gan ʿEden that indicate that they are identical.[190]

Some discourses maintain that the subject matter of Gan ʿEden is not kabbalah per se, but Talmud with kabbalistic interpretations.[191] Others insist that the Talmud is studied above exactly as it is studied below, word for word, concept for concept. The difference is not in subject matter or interpretation but in the degree of Or En Sof that can be revealed to disembodied souls.[192] Both of these views agree on one point: The soul above studies what it studied below. Talmud-study does not simply provide the garment that enables the soul to assimilate the revelations of Gan ʿEden; it provides the subject matter that elicits that revelation. One need not worry about exhausting all the possible valid interpretations of the Talmud during the centuries or millennia spent in Gan ʿEden because every statement of the Mishnah has 600,000 valid interpretations for each of the four supernal worlds.[193]

RSZ's ambivalence regarding the relative importance of halakhah and kabbalah is reflected in his various statements on what and how one should study. Maimonides, following the Talmud, had laid down a rather puzzling principle of dividing one's study time into equal thirds and allocating one part to Scripture, one part to Mishnah, and one part to Gemara.[194] Since these subjects are obviously far from equal in scope and difficulty, various solutions had been offered to justify such a curriculum. As long as one assumed, as Maimonides and RSZ did, that the Talmud's statement was to be taken literally, the subjects one subsumed under each category determined the amount of time available to study them. If kabbalah, like metaphysics, is part of "Gemara," the amount of time one could devote to it is far less than if it were included under Scripture. Since the practical halakhot of the Talmud had to be mastered first,[195] and since such mastery requires a good many years, it would be necessary to postpone studying kabbalah for at least that period. Moreover, according to the requirements of RSZ's *Hilkhot Talmud Torah*, a man unable to memorize perfectly all the practical halakhot was obligated to spend his entire life reviewing those that he could remember with review, in order to avoid transgressing a Biblical prohibition. Such a man would therefore be permitted to study only halakhah (during the period allotted to Mishnah and Gemara) and occasionally aggadah or ethical literature, as these latter are also considered "practical" in that they inspire the reader to fulfill the commandments properly. Even one who had mastered all the practical halakhot was permitted to study other areas only for the amount of time each day that he did not need to review these halakhot. He was advised, however, to use this period to gradually plow through the entire Torah at least once, even without remembering anything, for, according to the kabbalists, "in the future" his memory will be refreshed. Thus, although the (kabbalistic) "Midrashim of Rabbi Simeon bar Yoḥai" are included in this curriculum, clearly the time even such a respectable scholar can allot to them is negligible.[196]

A scholar whose memory permits him to set aside a greater portion of the day for studying other areas is obligated gradually to memorize all the other halakhot as they are formulated in the Mishnah, and this obligation takes precedence over the one-time completion of the entire Torah.[197] Such a person, too, would presumably have no time at all to study kabbalah. Consequently, only a member of the intellectual elite who had actually mastered the entire Torah, according to the definition of that mastery in *Hilkhot Talmud Torah*, could ever have the halakhic opportunity (and obligation) of studying kabbalah systematically.

On the other hand, if, as the discourses indicate, kabbalah is subsumed under Scripture[198] (since the Zohar is based on Scripture and since, for the kabbalist, Scripture has no real nonkabbalistic significance), the amount of time one can allot to it increased dramatically, and even an ignoramus in halakhah may devote sufficient time to kabbalah to become a proficient kabbalist. The same applies to aggadah, which *Hilkhot Talmud Torah* categorizes as "Mishnah," and the discourses as "Scripture."[199]

These contradictions cannot be resolved by positing that in *Hilkhot Talmud Torah* RSZ was writing primarily as a halakhist while in the discourses he appears primarily as a kabbalist, since the categorization in *Hilkhot Talmud Torah* combines the halakhic opinion of Maimonides with the kabbalistic view of Vital.[200] It is arguable, however, that RSZ's approach to Torah-study in *Hilkhot Talmud Torah* was purely theoretical. Ideally, men were to proceed with their studies according to the laws set forth there. But in this less-than-ideal world, the curriculum set forth by R. Dov Baer in RSZ's name,[201] which corresponds essentially to what we find in two of RSZ's discourses,[202] was the one RSZ expected his disciples to follow.

The central subject was to be the halakhah included in R. Joseph Karo's *Shulḥan ʿArukh*, including as much of its basis in earlier sources as time permitted. Full-time scholars who were supported by parents or in-laws were first to study the relevant tractate of the Talmud with the Tosafot pertaining to actual halakhic decisions, and R. Asher's juridical commentary. They were to concentrate on the latter's final rulings, review the corresponding sections of R. Jacob ben Asher's code (*Ṭur Shulḥan ʿArukh*) several times, study R. Joseph Karo's commentary (*Bet Yosef*), and review each section of the code and commentary two or three times. They were then to proceed to Karo's *Shulḥan ʿArukh* and R. Moses Isserles' glosses, review each section several times, and finally to do the same with each section of RSZ's edition of the *Shulḥan ʿArukh*, making sure that they could trace every decision in it to its source. Hasidim who had to spend part of the day earning a living were in effect advised to substitute R. Isaac Alfasi's Talmudic compendium for the Talmud and proceed as above. Those who were "extremely preoccupied [with their business affairs] and had no more than two or three hours a day to set aside for Torah-study" were to go from the Mishnah and Alfasi directly to RSZ's *Shulḥan ʿArukh*, so that even they could master the halakhah in its original language and context. In addition, all of RSZ's followers were expected to set aside periods for the study of Bible, Midrash, the ethical material in the Zohar, kabbalistic ethical works such as *Shene Luḥot ha-Berit* and *Reshit Ḥokhmah*, and to devote Sabbath entirely to the study of Zohar and Hasidism.[203]

There is no mention here of dividing one's study time into thirds. Nor is there any mention of the requirement to memorize perfectly everything of the Oral Torah that one has learned, before proceeding to something new. Indeed, there is no reference at all to RSZ's *Hilkhot Talmud Torah*, which suggests that R. Dov Baer did not consider it a practical guide to Torah-study; and since the guidelines he lays down represent RSZ's own pedagogical approach, neither, apparently, did RSZ himself.

Commandments

The commandments—mitsṿot—comprise a category that RSZ usually treats in juxtaposition with Torah and hence clearly excludes Torah-study. Occasionally he does discuss this category separately, and occasionally he refers to it as *mitsṿot maʿaśiot*; that is, commandments fulfilled essentially through physical action, as opposed to those, like Torah-study and prayer, whose essence consists of an intellective or emotive act. However, since one aspect of the Torah-study commandment requires pronouncing the words being studied, Torah-study may justifiably be subsumed under this category. Consequently, when speaking of the "mitsṿot" in general, or even of mitsṿot maʿaśiot, RSZ may or may not be referring to this aspect of Torah-study as well. This ambiguity applies also to the Zoharic formula that RSZ regularly cites or alludes to when discussing mitsṿot separately: "The 248 [positive] commandments are the 248 members of the King."[204] Although Torah-study is one of the 248, RSZ often applies this metaphor to the commandments *as opposed* to Torah-study. In any case, it is used with such regularity as almost to constitute a slogan,[205] possibly because it allows RSZ to integrate religious, metaphysical, physiological, and eschatological motifs within a single striking image.

The basis for the original Zoharic statement is R. Simlai's assertion in the Talmud that the 248 positive commandments correspond to the 248 members—*evarim*—of the human body enumerated by the Mishnah.[206] Although the Mishnah refers only to the number of bones in the human skeleton, it does not use the word *ʿatsamot* (bones), but the more general term *evarim*, which can also mean limbs or organs. Kabbalists therefore concluded that each positive commandment corresponds to and affects one part of the body.[207] If this is true of the positive commandments, it should also be true of the 365 negative commandments, and these were said to correspond to the 365 "veins" (*gidin*).[208] Since what is true below must be true, and in fact originates, above, and since man is created in God's image, the commandments must originate in God's "body," the configuration of divine emanations that create and sustain everything that exists. Conversely, since man's divine soul is a spark of Divinity, it, too, comprises 613 emanations, which are clothed by 613 powers of the animal soul, which vitalize the 613 parts of the body. Just as each part of the body constitutes the appropriate physical vessel for the particular soul-power that vitalizes it, so does each commandment constitute the appropriate supernal vessel for a specific divine emanation. These vessels, as we have seen, limit and channel the divine light, thereby allowing it to descend and be revealed in the lower worlds.[209]

The supernal source of the commandments is, according to most discourses, the outer aspect of Keter,[210] that is, God's suprarational Will. Occasionally RSZ emphasizes that this Will is, in fact, permeated by the inner aspect of Keter—divine Pleasure—and that fulfilling a commandment causes this highest of all divine faculties to be revealed below.[211] Occasionally he stresses that the commandments are simply pure expressions of divine Will, with no rationale whatsoever.[212] And occasionally he insists that all the commandments have reasons, albeit reasons that are beyond human reason. Those commandments that appear to have a humanly discernible rationale or purpose are actually a more blurred reflection of the divine Will than are commandments that clearly transcend human reason.[213] These three approaches are quite compatible, since, as we have seen, the ultimate "reason" for God's Will is divine Pleasure, and this Pleasure transcends divine Reason on one level (Atsilut), and is identical with it on another (ʿAtiḳ).

Since Keter is an encompassing light—sovev, or maḳif—its emanation creates encompassing vessels for the permeating lights of the four worlds, as well as encompassing garments for the divine soul to wear in Gan ʿEden. Each commandment creates a vessel for one of the 613 emanations that sustain these worlds and a soul-garment for one of the 613 soul-emanations. The discourses vary regarding the exact metaphysical process by which the commandments accomplish these functions. Whether the commandments elevate the worlds and the soul to sovev or draw its light down; whether they create the vessels, draw the light into them, or both, depends on the discourse one consults.[214] In fact, a number of discourses appear to maintain that the main function of the commandments is not to illumine the lower worlds but to enhance the (permeating) lights of Atsilut.[215] This would resolve the problem, implicit in RSZ's general approach, of how the light of maḳif, which by definition transcends the vessels, can be drawn down *into* the vessels.

Such variations and inconsistencies are notably lacking in Part 1 of *Tanya*, which concentrates almost exclusively on the religioethical functions of the commandments and yields a systematic, cohesive exposition of the subject. Instead of simply indicating the *correspondence* of the commandments with the 248 "members of King"—that is, the correspondence between the commandments and the supernal vessels required to draw down the divine light—RSZ examines the nature of the relation between light and vessel as translated into the relation between soul and body. This relation could, of course, be portrayed in a number of ways, but for RSZ its essence was biṭul: Each of the 613 parts of the body is completely nullified with respect to the soul-power that vitalizes it. Thus, the hand moves instantly and automatically when activated by its corresponding soul-power. The soul involved here is, of course, the animal soul, which inheres in the blood and enables the outer "garment" of the divine soul—action—to function. The "vitality," or energy, that enables the animal soul to act derives from Ḳelipat Nogah, which sustains all permissible sources of nourishment. This neutral vitality may either be elevated to the realm of the holy by moving (part of) the body to fulfill a commandment, or lowered to the realm of evil by moving the body to commit a prohibited act. Either way, this vitality is subordinated to, and nullified within, the religioethical value that permeates the act. The word *permeates* applies here because RSZ characteristically reifies the concept of religioethical value: An act with a positive value is said to be permeated and vitalized by God's Will (= Keter = sovev = the Or En Sof), just as the body is permeated and vitalized by the soul. This, it should be noted, is the crucial element in RSZ's theory of mitsyot. Every human action is *alive*, it has a soul, and that soul is its religioethical value. Just as the human soul can achieve biṭul, so can the soul of every action it performs. The act of stretching out one's hand to give tsedaḳah, for example, is completely nullified within the Or En Sof that permeates it. That part of the animal soul that vitalizes the arm is equally nullified, as is the physical arm itself (since, as noted, the arm is constantly nullified within the soul-power that vitalizes it), as is the outer "garment" of the divine soul, which motivates the animal soul to fulfill the commandment. Moreover, since the commandments draw down the encompassing light of sovev, the rest of the body and animal soul are also enveloped in the divine light of this commandment.[216] Actually dedicating one's entire body to fulfilling God's will, using every member solely for that purpose, is the highest degree of biṭul the body can attain, and this was the level attained by the Patriarchs.[217]

Because the light of sovev transcends perception, we are unaware of these consequences of the mitsyot.[218] Nevertheless, fulfilling a commandment generates a specific reward that the soul will experience both in Gan ʿEden and "in the future." The soul-garment created by fulfilling a given commandment enables the part of the soul corresponding to that commandment to enjoy the Or En Sof of Gan ʿEden. For, as noted above,[219] this overwhelming infinite light must be filtered through these garments if it is to be tolerated by the finite soul. Furthermore, since all the matter-energy with which a commandment may be performed is sustained by the Ḳelipat Nogah, fulfilling a given commandment also elevates one or more elements of this ḳelipah. Every Jewish soul has its share of Ḳelipat Nogah to elevate through the performance of all 613 commandments, and it must return in successive gilgulim (metempsychoses) until it has carried out its mission. When every soul has completed its work, the entire Ḳelipat Nogah will be transformed into the realm of the holy, all the fallen sparks will be restored,[220] the three impure ḳelipot will no longer be able to derive their sustenance through Ḳelipat Nogah, and all evil will vanish like so much smoke. This will open the door to the era of the Messiah and the Resurrection, that is, to the revelation of God's glory (= Keter = sovev = Or En Sof).[221] on earth. Having achieved their purpose, the commandments will then, according to some discourses, fall into desuetude. Others insist that the commandments are eternal; only their form and function will change, although exactly how is unclear.[222] Part 1 of *Tanya* is silent on this issue, presumably because it is not relevant to one's religious and ethical conduct.

The power of the commandments, specifically the mitsyot maʿaśiot, to draw down the revelation of Keter into the physical world derives not only from their being rooted in Keter, but also from their utilization of the physical world and physical action to fulfill God's will

(=Keter). Each commanded act is a manifestation of that will, and therefore of the Source that emanates it, in this world. Only physical action performed with physical matter can "reach" Keter and reveal it below, for what is higher descends lower, and the lowest manifestation of Divinity—physical matter—is thus the vehicle for revealing the highest.[223] Only physical man can take a mundane act or object and make it transcendent—a mitsvah—by using it to perform God's will; it is a mitsvah only after, not before, man has fulfilled it.[224]

We would therefore expect the kavanah with which a commanded act is performed to play a relatively minor role in this process, and, judging from *Tanya* alone, our expectation would be confirmed. RSZ is at pains to point out that while a commandment without kavanah is like a body without a soul, this particular body is nevertheless viable and valuable in its own right.[225] In fact, the implication in *Tanya* is that the Messianic Era and the Resurrection are contingent solely on the physical fulfillment of the commandments.[226] What kavanah adds is an influx of the Or En Sof that benefits the soul in Gan ʿEden,[227] just as Torah li-shemah benefits the student's soul but does not change the objective value of Torah-study or its spiritual effect on this world. The kavanah of a mitsvah is defined in *Tanya* as the desire for deveḳut through the fulfillment of that mitsvah,[228] and its reward is, very fittingly, the attainment of that desire in Gan ʿEden. The greater the intellectual content of one's kavanah, the greater the intellectual beatitude in Gan ʿEden. Thus, kavanah born of intellectual love (and fear) of God elevates a commanded act to the intellective world of Beriʾah, where the act unites with the Or En Sof carried by the sefirot of that world and irradiates the soul after it leaves the body and ascends to the Higher Gan ʿEden (=Beriʾah). Kavanah born of the natural, hidden love (Ahavah Mesuteret) of the Jewish soul elevates the act only to the (emotive) world of Yetsirah, the Lower Gan ʿEden, where the intellectual beatitude enjoyed by the soul is commensurately less. In either case, "the reward of a mitsvah is the mitsvah itself," and that reward is created to a large extent by the kavanah with which it is fulfilled.[229]

As always, however, the skein that RSZ coils so tightly in *Tanya* comes partly unraveled in the discourses. Here the definition of kavanah varies, with some discourses defining it as in *Tanya*, others as the simple intention to obey the King, and still others in Lurianic terms: to achieve yiḥudim, to draw down the Or En Sof in a specific way through specific sefirot.[230] A number of discourses maintain that the latter two definitions constitute successive stages of Service, obedience (ḳabalat ʿol) being the basic, essential motive for fulfilling the commandments, while contemplating their metaphysical effects is a second and clearly secondary level of kaṿanah.[231] If this appears to be a confusing description—a second and implicitly higher stage that is reached only after having passed the first, and yet is less important than the first—it is because here again RSZ tried to combine two essentially contradictory approaches, in this case that of Lurianic kabbalah, which requires that each mitsṿah be accompanied by a complex set of kaṿanot, and that of the Talmud, which at most requires only that a commandment be performed with the intention of fulfilling God's will (and which may not require even that). RSZ was clearly inclined to embrace the Talmud's position. Indeed, in several discourses he describes fulfilling a commandment with only Lurianic kaṿanot as a kind of business transaction in which certain beneficial sefirotic movements are acquired in exchange for certain kaṿanot.[232] But because of his ideological allegiance to Luria, he could not ignore these kaṿanot completely. His solution was to promote them to a higher position, thus putting them beyond the reach, and beyond the concern, of most of his followers. His Hasidim were then left with the obligation to fulfill the commandments out of heteronomous obedience, Love, and Fear—a triad of "kaṿanot" with a solid foundation in the Bible, Talmud, and Maimonidean philosophy.[233]

The discourses also vary on the function of kaṿanah, some indicating that it is the kaṿanah, not the act, that draws down the light of memale into the vessels created by the commanded acts.[234] Some discourses distinguish between the proper kaṿanah of the Tsadiḳ and that of the Benoni;[235] others distinguish between commandments whose main purpose is to serve as reminders of certain religious truths, and whose kaṿanot serve just that purpose, and commandments whose main purpose is achieved through the physical act of performing them.[236] One discourse asserts that all kaṿanot are supererogatory (presumably because the halakhah is that mitsṿot require no kaṿanah), and the only thoughts required prior to performing a commandment are introspective: to contemplate one's alienation from God due to one's pathetic immersion in mundane activities; and to resolve to rise out of the terrestrial quagmire and approach Him through His commandments.[237] This variation of the function of kaṿanah as set forth in *Tanya* is apparently a popularized version that RSZ delivered for the general public. The functions outlined in other discourses, however, differ both from what is found in *Tanya* and from each other.

The discourses also reveal several noteworthy facets of RSZ's theory of mitsyot. The function of the blessings preceding many mitsyot—*birkhat ha-mitsyot*—is described in the same terms as the function of kayanah: to draw down the light of sovev.[238] Consequently, the ideal time for kayanah is while reciting the blessing.[239] Negative commandments, although naturally devoid of both berakhah and kayanah,[240] are nevertheless superior to the positive, just as the negative attributes of God are more valid than the positive.[241] As God transcends description in positive terms, so does the divine light of these commandments transcend the vessels of positive action. The restrictions they impose involve salutary self-denial and result in a higher level of biṭul. Their sefirotic source is Gevurah, which is ultimately superior to Ḥesed (the source of the positive commandments); their corresponding source in the divine soul is Fear, which is superior to Love; their targets are the three impure ḳelipot, whose source transcends that of ḳedushah; and the emanation they generate is the light of sovev, which is superior to memale.[242]

Rabbinic enactments—the seven rabbinic "commandments" that together with the 613 Biblical commandments constitute the 620 (= Keter in numerical value) hollow pillars of light that encompass the soul that has fulfilled them[243]—derive from an even higher source than the negative commandments. Thus, although, like the latter, their purpose is to separate the soul from evil, their light is containable in vessels of positive action, for what is higher descends lower.[244] At the same time, however, RSZ maintains that because of their lofty source, rabbinic commandments cannot be clothed in the physical letters of the Written Torah but could only be revealed in the Oral Torah[245]—this despite his previously cited statement that precisely because the source of the Written Torah is higher than that of the Oral can its light descend to the level of physical letters, for what is higher descends lower. Consistent with his explanation of the superiority of rabbinic enactments, however, is his attribution of transcendent value to consuetudinary practices, which reflect a supernal source so lofty that it cannot even be contained in the Oral Torah.[246] Similarly, commandments requiring no berakhah are said to be superior to those requiring a berakhah because their sefirotic source cannot be reached through a berakhah; one can therefore only perform the prescribed action, thereby creating a vessel for the light of that source, and trust that the light will descend of its own accord.[247]

Such a hierarchy of values is evidently made possible by RSZ's selective use of the higher-lower principle. Another noteworthy example of this selectivity is his explanation of the halakhic principle *ʿaśeh doḥeh lo taʿaśeh* (a positive commandment takes precedence over a negative commandment). The unstated problem, of course, is that according to RSZ's hierarchy, negative commandments should take precedence. One discourse sidesteps the issue by simply stating that "light repels darkness"[249]—the light drawn down by a positive commandment supersedes the negation of darkness accomplished by its negative opposition. Another discourse, however, employs the higher-lower principle: Positive commandments take precedence because they reveal their supernal source in physical action and gross matter. Because it descends lower, this source must be higher than that of the negative commandments.[250]

With the exception of Sabbath and the holidays, the individual commandments most frequently discussed or cited in the discourses are ritual commandments involving physical objects and things; for example, *tefilin*, *mezuzah*, *tsitsit*, *etrog*, sukah, *milah*, the sacrifices. The most important exceptions to this rule are commandments involving personal religious development—for example, Torah-study, prayer, teshuvah—and one interpersonal commandment with which RSZ was very much preoccupied: tsedaḳah (charity). This preoccupation was no doubt partially due to his role as the major fund-raiser for the Hasidic community in the Holy Land, a cause to which he devoted himself unstintingly. His many pastoral letters on the importance of tsedaḳah, written for the purpose of raising funds for this community,[251] may therefore reveal more about his personal compassion and suasive ability than about his axiological posture. However, Part 1 of *Tanya*, numerous discourses, and the mystical message he penned hours before his death[252] attest to the supreme value he attached to this commandment. In fact, he frequently observes that tsedaḳah is the epitome of all the commandments, for it consists of precisely what they are intended to accomplish: the bestowal and "descent" of benefit from giver to recipient. Although every commandment causes a descent of the Or En Sof from higher sefirah to lower and eventually to this world, a charitable act mirrors this flow exactly and may thus be literally called "God's work." Although every commandment elevates one power of the animal soul—the power vitalizing that part or those parts of the body performing the commandment—a charitable donation elevates the entire soul at once, since all its powers were exerted to earn the money donated. Even a man who did not, in fact, have to labor for the money is nevertheless elevating his entire animal soul by donating funds that he could have used to sustain it. A single charitable donation therefore elevates more of the Ḳelipat Nogah than do several other commandments combined and hence is rightfully said to "hasten the Redemption" more than any other commandment.[253]

5

Love *and* Fear

Judging from *Tanya* alone, Love, Fear, and the apprehension of God's unity from which, ideally, they were to flow, are the foundations of RSZ's conception of Service. Thus, in the introduction to Part 2, which itself was originally intended to serve as an introduction to Part 1,[1] we read: "It is well known that Fear and Love are the roots and foundations of the service of God. . . . And the first thing that arouses Love and Fear, and their foundation, is the pure and faithful belief in His Unity."[2] RSZ apparently reasoned that after contemplating his acosmic doctrine of unity in *Sha'ar ha-Yiḥud*, one could then proceed to arouse the requisite emotions with the aid of *Sefer shel Benonim*, most of which is actually a systematic exposition of the various types of Love and Fear that one can experience.[3] The terms and concepts of this exposition are taken from *Ḥovot ha-Levavot*, *Sefer Ḥasidim*, *Sefer Roḳeaḥ*, *Zohar*, *Sefer ha-Iḳarim*, and *Reshit Ḥokhmah*.[4] Certain theoretical refinements derive from the Maggid and possibly the Besht. The basic framework, however, is clearly Maimonidean.[5] Yet despite all this indebtedness, RSZ's approach contains original organizing elements that transform his eclectic borrowings into a distinctive, cohesive system.

One such element is his insistence that the only Service worthy of the term *'avodah*—which not only denotes a specific commandment or set of commandments but also connotes the proper fulfillment of all the commandments—is Service motivated by (both) Love and Fear. For RSZ these emotions are not only "a stimulus to zealous and properly motivated performance of the commandments,"[6] they themselves constitute that motivation. Love and Fear not only enhance Service, they are the sine qua non of Service, for without them man cannot truly desire to do God's will; and without that conscious desire, fulfilling a commandment, which should be a holy, transcendent act, becomes merely a habitual, pedestrian act. Although halakhically one has discharged one's obligation, spiritually one has accomplished nothing. "Without Love and Fear [the commandment] cannot take wing"; it remains a mundane act performed by mundane man.[7] Consequently, when RSZ writes at the beginning of *Tanya* that Love is the "root" of the positive commandments and Fear the root of the negative commandments,[8] it may be taken quite literally: Without Love and Fear to provide the motivational nourishment, the commandments cannot survive, let alone flourish.

But the metaphor can be carried even further. Just as the sole purpose of a plant's roots is to provide it with the nourishment necessary for growth, so the sole purpose of the commandments to love and fear God is to provide the motivation and dedication necessary for the fulfillment of the other commandments: "The [only] purpose of Love is the Service [arising] from Love."[9] Although formulations resembling this idea may be found in the works and words of his predecessors,[10] RSZ's fusion of Love with Service is unusual, if not unique. The Love he wanted to inculcate in all his followers is synonymous with a desire for deveḳut,[11] and the consummation of deveḳut, as he repeatedly stresses, is the fulfillment of the commandments.[12] More specifically, the thirst for God that Love arouses can be quenched only through Torah-study, and the desire to embrace Him can be satisfied only through the practical commandments.[13] The union with God for which every man must strive is not the mystical union of his soul with its source but rather the union of all of his faculties with God's will as expressed in the Torah. Once this is achieved, the unio mystica follows automatically.

RSZ's emphasis on Love for the sake of Service is reflected in the two basic categories of Love identified in *Tanya*: *Ahavat ʿOlam* and *Ahavah Rabah*. Ahavat ʿOlam is the Love arising from contemplation of God's greatness and the concomitant realization that He is the Source of all pleasure. Since man naturally desires the pleasurable, he will naturally desire the Cause of all pleasure with an intensity that will eclipse all other desires.[14] Ahavat ʿOlam is accordingly described as a love "that shall flare up like a glowing fire in his heart, like flaming coals, so that his soul shall yearn and long, with passion and desire, to cleave to the blessed En Sof with his whole heart, soul, and might."[15] Originating in the divine soul and the right side of the heart, it inexorably spreads to the left side and the animal soul, replacing this soul's desire for physical and egotistical pleasures with the desire for the Source of all pleasure. Eventually, with God's help, the animal soul is purged of all temporal temptation. It becomes as holy as its divine counterpart, and the only pleasure it enjoys is the pleasure of contemplating God's greatness. At this stage one has achieved a measure of the beatitude of Gan ʿEden, where this same pleasure is enjoyed. To desire and enjoy only the pleasure of contemplation—and, obversely, to despise all that separates the soul from God, thereby inhibiting that contemplation—is to attain Ahavah Rabah, or *Ahavah be-Taʿanugim*, which is the highest earthly reward God can confer.[16]

Ahavat ʿOlam is thus the Love that is generated by man's intellectual efforts and gives rise to perfect Service, while Ahavah Rabah is the Love that is beyond his efforts and is bestowed by God as reward for that Service. Because Ahavat ʿOlam is commensurate with the knowledge of God one attains, it varies according to the power and application of one's intellect. Ahavah Rabah, on the other hand, is akin to the Innate Love (Ahavah Mesuteret) hidden in every Jewish soul in that both are divine gifts that transcend the abilities of any individual. Anyone lacking the intellectual capacity to arouse Ahavat ʿOlam may nevertheless achieve perfect Service by arousing his Innate Love. At least one passage in *Tanya* implies that this Love and Ahavat ʿOlam are distinct species born of different contemplative paths.[17] Other passages, however, suggest that Innate Love is a genus of which Ahavat ʿOlam is one species.[18]

In any case, Ahavat ʿOlam is unique because the contemplation that gives rise to it is wholly theocentric. Innate Love, however, like the other types of Love discussed in *Tanya*, is aroused through a combination of anthropocentric and theocentric themes; that is, by meditating upon one aspect of man's relationship to God. The causal nexus between arousing Innate Love and achieving perfect Service is systematically set forth in Chapters 18–25 of *Tanya*. This exposition may be summarized as follows.

The positive commandments are the "members of the King." By fulfilling them we affirm and reveal God's unity in the world. Similarly, by fulfilling the negative commandments we negate the denial of that unity; that is, we negate the validity of idolatry. To affirm and refuse to deny God's unity are the respective purposes of the first two of the Ten Commandments. These two commandments—the only ones the nation distinctly heard from God—therefore embody the entire Torah. Because of the divine spark inhering in the faculty of Ḥokhmah of the divine soul, every Jew would choose martyrdom over even *appearing* to deny God's unity. History attests to the willingness of even the simplest Jewish peasant to lay down his or her life rather than deny this unity through apostasy. But the truth is that *every* act contrary to God's will, no matter how apparently insignificant, is a negation of His unity. By constantly remembering that he would literally die for God's unity, every Jew can readily and consistently overcome the temptations of the siṭra aḥra,[19] since this self-restraint is far less painful than actual martyrdom. Similarly, the effort required to reveal that unity through the fulfillment of the positive commandments is far less than the supreme effort he would surely muster when faced with the ultimate choice. Thus, Innate Love is a combination of the soul's natural desire to reveal God's unity and its natural fear of negating that unity.

Three other types of Love are also discussed in *Tanya*: Love of life; filial Love, arising from the contemplation of the son-father relationship between the soul and its Source; and reciprocal Love, arising from the contemplation of God's infinite beneficence.[20] The first two are described as being "greater" than Ahavat ʿOlam[21]—although why this is so is not explained—but because their supernal source is Ḥesed, they cannot match the intense, fiery desire of Ahavat ʿOlam, which derives from Gevurah. Moreover, Ahavat ʿOlam is a consequence of apprehending God, which is supremely valuable in itself. Therefore, although the other types of Love are easier to achieve, one must also strive to attain the intensity of Ahavat ʿOlam, so that the Torah-study that must follow it, as shov must follow ratso, will be motivated by a desire as powerful as that of a parched desert wanderer pining for an oasis.[22]

Nor must the arousal of Fear be neglected. Although Fear is included in the Innate Love that can be aroused through the contemplation outlined above, it also requires a separate and intense contemplative effort in its own right. Because the most basic and essential element of the commandments is their heteronomous character, and because the crucial relation between God and man with respect to the commandments is the relation of decreeing King to submissive subject, the rabbinic "fear of Heaven," which results in the self-effacing acceptance of the "yoke of Heaven's kingship," is the most basic and essential requirement for the fulfillment of the commandments. This Fear, which RSZ calls "Lower Fear" (*Yirʾah Tataʾah*), is itself divisible into a higher and lower category, depending on the contemplative theme that gives rise to it. Similarly, Higher Fear (*Yirʾah ʿIlaʾah*), a concept originated by Bahya ibn Pakuda, is differentiated from Lower Fear by, although not only by, the contemplative theme that gives rise to it. The more theocentric the theme, the less concerned with how God relates to creation and the more concerned with how He completely transcends creation, the higher the Fear that is aroused. Like Ahavah Rabah, however, Yiraʾah ʿIlaʾah cannot be achieved without first achieving the perfect Service that is made possible through the lower types of Love and Fear. Indeed, RSZ intimates that the higher Love and Fear constitute a contemplative *via passiva* attainable only by Tsadiḳim. These categories of Love and Fear therefore receive very little attention in *Tanya* (or, for that matter, in the discourses). RSZ makes it quite clear that the aspiring Benoni should concern himself almost exclusively with the *via activa*—the proper fulfillment of the commandments. The natural order of Service according to *Tanya* is therefore: (1) the contemplation that arouses Lower Fear, which enables man to serve God (particularly with respect to the negative commandments) as a servant serves his master and a subject his King; (2) the contemplation that arouses Ahavat ʿOlam, or one of the other types of Love, which enables man to minister to God (particularly with respect to the positive commandments) as a son ministers to his father; (3) fulfillment of the commandments in spite of all internal and external obstacles—which constitutes perfect Service; (4) the contemplation that, with God's assistance, arouses Higher Fear; and (5) Ahavah Rabah—the foretaste of Gan ʿEden that perfect Tsadiḳim enjoy on earth.[23]

Although Love and Fear are latent in every divine soul, the ability to arouse them to consciousness depends on the supernal level from which one's soul derives. The higher this is, the higher the degree of consciousness to which one can arouse them, and the greater their behavioral impact will be. Even the possessor of the lowest soul of Israel, however, can and therefore must arouse his latent Love and Fear at least to a level of consciousness that will enable them to motivate his Service and allow him to become a Benoni.[24]

RSZ's insistence in *Tanya* that contemplative Love and Fear are the indispensible foundations for Service is a significant departure from the teachings of his masters. The Besht and the Maggid saw Love and Fear primarily as important adjuncts to, or as the culmination of, prayer and the other commandments. The Love and Fear they discuss—usually referred to by the Zoharic catchphrase *deḥilu u-reḥimu*—are often merely synonymous with religious fervor rather than with the two psychologically distinct emotions of the Bible and rabbinic literature. Contrary to RSZ's view, they are, even at their inception, affective rather than reflective, mystical rather than motivational. They are, in fact, rarely analyzed at all, and on those rare occasions the definitions and categories obviously differ from what we find in *Tanya*.[25]

In RSZ's discourses, however, the masters' teachings are readily discernible. As we have repeatedly seen, the kaleidoscopic discourses are often incompatible with *Tanya*'s systematic exposition of a given theme, and this is particularly true of the nature and categorization of Love and Fear. Except for the basic definition of Ahavat ʿOlam, the nature and definition of every category of Love and Fear discussed in *Tanya*, as well as the interrelations of these categories, undergo many metamorphoses in the discourses. Indeed, virtually no specific statement about these themes can be made that is not contradicted somewhere in RSZ's teachings. Ahavah Rabah, for example, is variously described as the highest form of Love attainable through contemplation; as attainable only through Torah-study; and as a divine gift unattainable through human endeavor; as arising from one theme of contemplation or from another; as attainable only by the elite or, because its root is Innate Love, as attainable by all; as fiery ecstasy that flickers sporadically and as a steady, tranquil love comparable to the flow of water; as comparable to the love between son and father and as comparable to the love between man and wife; as a love whose essential characteristic is surging emotion and desire for deveḳut, and as a love whose essential characteristic is the desire for the revelation of Divinity on earth.[26]

The contemplation that arouses Ahavat ʿOlam also varies from discourse to discourse. At least six major themes are mentioned: (1) God the immanent Creator; (2) God as the source of all pleasure; (3) His transcendence; (4) His beneficence; (5) man's alienation from Him; and (6) acosmism.[27] One early discourse neatly disposes of the issue by observing that the content of one's contemplation is irrelevant so long as it produces the requisite Love,[28] but this position is anomalous with respect to most discourses and particularly with respect to *Tanya*, where RSZ prescribes specific contemplative themes for arousing specific types of Love and clearly implies that other themes would be ineffective.

The hierarchical positions of Love and Fear and of Ahavat ʿOlam, Ahavah Rabah, and the other types of Love discussed in *Tanya* also vary in the discourses, a fact which led RSZ's editors to posit additional categories to accommodate the conflicting statements.[29] This standard expedient, however, falls far short of reconciling all the contradictions and is in any case inapplicable to the statements that define the same categories, judging by the terms used to denote them, in contradictory ways. To complicate matters further, RSZ himself introduces new or hybrid categories of Love in the discourses and occasionally changes their definitions as well.[30] A detailed account of RSZ's discourse teachings on Love and Fear would therefore simply constitute a series of inconsistent statements and definitions. It is, however, possible to uncover several conceptual threads running through all these teachings that allow us to make a few essential generalizations.

Although Fear is the more basic emotion, it is, paradoxically, more difficult to attain, for in exile, fear of the ḳelipot—the gentile powers controlling Jewish lives and livelihoods—overshadows fear of Heaven.[31] Fear of divine retribution, a motive that is disparaged in the Zohar and elsewhere,[32] is mentioned favorably as a useful steppingstone to higher motivations, but it is mentioned very rarely.[33] Lower Fear born of regular, intense contemplation is the type of Fear most frequently demanded. Higher Fear, which is related to, or identical with, self-nullification, is presented in the discourses as a desideratum that most men can attain at least periodically.[34] These two types of Fear appear to correspond to the via activa and via passiva, as do Ahavat ʿOlam and Ahavah Rabah respectively. They also correspond respectively to the Talmud's ethical conception of Love-Fear and to the Maggid's mystical conception. RSZ characteristically insists that the two are quite compatible. Their relation, like that of other opposing principles of Service, is actually the dialectical relation of ratso and shov, each movement stimulating and complementing its opposite, each necessary both for its own sake and for the sake of creating the tension necessary for spiritual progress.

The ultimate source of this tension, as we have seen, is the existential polarity between God and man. Man is commanded to strain all his faculties to bridge this infinite gap, yet to remain within the confines of a finite physical body residing in a physical world. Every act and desire, while motivated by the egotism that is an inescapable part of being human, must nevertheless be as selfless and as God-directed as humanly possible. RSZ was acutely aware that a religioethical system emphasizing the causal relation between individual effort and spiritual achievement gives greater play to one's egotistical instincts than a system that sees all human achievement as divinely bestowed. Nevertheless, because these two approaches mirror the existential God-man polarity, both are valid. Thus, in *Tanya*, which is comparatively anthropocentric, RSZ emphasizes the importance of individual effort in achieving Love and Fear, while in the discourses, which are more theocentric, the stress is on the Love and Fear that only God can bestow.[35]

A related issue is the question of induced ecstasy; that is, an emotionalistic state that is consciously elicited, as opposed to an emotion that flows naturally from contemplation. Because ecstasy is by definition a thrilling, intensely pleasurable experience, self-stimulated ecstasy involves a far greater degree of egotism than the ecstatic Love (Ahavat ʿOlam) that arises spontaneously from intellectual apprehension. For though apprehension itself is also pleasurable—indeed, it is the highest form of pleasure—it is considered relatively selfless because the pleasure it produces is (initially) confined to those soul faculties in which God is primarily revealed and which can therefore lose their identity in Divinity. These intellectual faculties of the divine soul are thus far more resistant to the blandishments of the egotistical animal soul than are the emotive faculties.[36] This difference is due not only to the different ontological properties of these faculties but also to the nature of their different functions. Unlike intellectual apprehension, in which the knower and the known merge, Love requires a subject who loves and a separate object that is beloved. This is because Love, for RSZ, means the *desire* to unite with God; once union is achieved, Love vanishes and is replaced by pleasure.[37] Indeed, the intensity of Love is directly proportional to the perceived spiritual distance between man and God (just as the intensity of Fear is inversely proportional to that distance).[38] Thus, to achieve Love man must see himself as a separate entity, which is precisely the error of the siṭra aḥra. Yet this egotistical perception must give rise to a selfless desire for God, a desire motivated not by pleasure but by obedience. Man must love God, or arouse his Innate Love, only because he is commanded to love, because it is his duty to do God's will and thereby cause *Him* pleasure.[39]

The tension and paradox of this position naturally resulted in different views among RSZ's disciples regarding the degree of ego involvement and emotionalism that RSZ would countenance.[40] Although in *Tanya* he is clearly concerned about the intellectual integrity of the Love that one arouses,[41] it is possible to argue, as did R. Aaron of Starosielce, that while this is desirable, it is not absolutely necessary. Because it is the emotive element in Love that most directly motivates man to fulfil the commandments, this element must be aroused even at the expense of intellectual integrity and selflessness—induced ecstasy is better than nothing. The discourses, however, make this view quite untenable. Time and again RSZ insists on an absolutely honest and selfless Love. The commandment to love God obligates man to immerse his mind in contemplative themes that should evoke a desire for the Divine. What happens after he has fulfilled this obligation is not his concern. If he merits it, God will bestow upon him the requisite Love; if not, he has nevertheless done his duty and fulfilled the commandment. Similarly, Love can be regularly aroused only after one has merited the Fear that is a divine gift. The basic assumption in *Tanya* regarding Ahavat ʿOlam—that it is a natural result of apprehension—is often repudiated. Apprehension does not automatically give rise to Love because true apprehension is impossible: Man cannot really know and therefore cannot really appreciate God's greatness. Love is not the effect of apprehension but its reward. It is commensurate with one's contemplative effort because God's rewards are commensurate with man's efforts. It must be grounded in apprehension not because apprehension is its cause but because only intellectual Love is selfless and lasting. Although this Love is a conscious desideratum, it must not be actively, let alone aggressively, pursued. Having achieved it, one should, ideally, remain unconscious of the achievement. The highest form of Love is not acquisitive but passive. One begins by desiring to possess God and progresses to the desire for the spiritual proximity that allows the soul to "behold the King's majesty." Ultimately one may achieve an asymptotic relationship with Him in which Love (which requires a subject who loves), biṭul (the extinction of that subject's identity), and Fear (which is Love's complementary opposite) can coexist. Again, while this may be the goal, one's conscious will must be directed not toward achieving it but only toward the heteronomous Service through which one may—or may not—achieve it. Consciously pursued ecstasy does not motivate man to fulfill the commandments, often degenerates into profane love, and inflates one's ego. The only Love that is valid—in the sense of being honest, true, selfless, and lasting—is Love that is not consciously sought but is bestowed by God as a reward for selfless Service, particularly for the contemplation of God to the point of abstraction, or at least to the best of one's ability.[42]

The most propitious time for this contemplation is during prayer. Indeed, the primary purpose of prayer, according to RSZ, is to arouse Love and Fear,[43] and in this, too, he differs from his masters and colleagues for whom prayer was primarily a mystical experience that freed the soul from its mundane moorings and enabled it to "stroll in the upper worlds." Briefly put, it was, in their view, a deliberately orchestrated attempt to achieve deveḳut. The worshipper was to begin his ascent slowly and proceed gradually until ecstasy overwhelmed him. The words and letters of the liturgy were to be used as visual stimuli to induce this state, much like the letters and words in the treatises of Abraham Abulafia.[44] The worshipper was to contemplate not their meaning but their forms; sufficient concentration on these holy configurations and combinations would produce the trance that is the precursor of deveḳut. Love and Fear—generally synonymous, as mentioned above, with religious fervor, or hitlahavut—were not the goals of prayer but were rather to be used as emotional stimuli to achieve deveḳut. Halakhically questionable activities that ostensibly contributed to this enthusiasm, including carousing before prayer, were accordingly tolerated or even encouraged. Anything impeding emotional arousal during prayer, including Lurianic kaẏanot, was accordingly discouraged. Neither cognitive contemplation nor intellectual apprehension was to compete with the intense desire for deveḳut that alone can spiritualize the letters of prayer and the worshipper. Contemplation of God's greatness was not the essence of prayer, as RSZ maintained, but merely the lowest rung on the ladder to deveḳut. All of the worshipper's thoughts and efforts were to be directed toward achieving this goal. Although this process involves continually monitoring his emotional state and a heightened self-awareness, he was expected somehow to rise above self-concern and to pursue deveḳut selflessly. For the Maggid, of course, the acme of deveḳut was self-nullification in the divine Ayin. The worshipper becomes merely a receptacle for divine Speech and is totally unaware of his ecstasy, which, ideally, is a quietistic rather than an emotionalistic phenomenon. Nevertheless, the Maggid, like the Besht, also emphasized the pneumatic power of fiery prayer and the need for the worshipper consciously to utilize that power to ascend to God in a flame of desire.[45]

RSZ, on the other hand, taught that the highest goal of prayer is to reveal Divinity in the world. Rarely is otherworldly deveḳut the focus of a discourse on prayer. Instead, the emphasis is generally on intense contemplation of God's greatness, which inspires and purifies the animal soul and gives rise to the Love and Fear that are the roots of the commandments. Their fulfillment, in turn, creates an "abode for Him below," allowing Him to reveal His Divinity in the material world. Moreover, the act of contemplation itself reveals the latent presence of God in man. Consequently, whether or not it is formally one of the 613 commandments, prayer must be considered the very foundation of Service. Obversely, lack of devotion to contemplative prayer—to the daily intellectual effort required to arouse Love and Fear—is a fundamental flaw in one's Service, and it was to this misdeed among his followers that RSZ attributed the Mitnagdic persecution they and he suffered.[46]

Although he often follows the Maggid in identifying biṭul as the ultimate purpose of prayer, RSZ's biṭul, unlike the Maggid's, is generally described as an effect of conceptual contemplation. It is rooted less in desire than in intellect, and its function is less to allow the worshipper's soul to rise to God than to empty it of everything that is not directed toward Him, thereby allowing His latent presence to reveal itself.[47] (The actual revelation is effected by studying Torah and fulfilling the [other] commandments.) Since this presence is responsible for the worshipper's innate capacity to devote himself totally and unstintingly to God's will, it is equally accurate to state, as RSZ often does, that the purpose of prayer is the arousal of mesirat nefesh.[48] Similarly, because mesirat nefesh is usually defined as the subjugation of man's will to God's will, RSZ can state that the essence of prayer is the arousal of the Fear that constitutes the basis of ḳabalat ʿol—the acceptance of the heteronomous yoke of the commandments.[49] Discourses that identify the purpose of prayer as the arousal of an intense desire for God counterbalance this by emphasizing that only Torah-study—not rapture—can satisfy this desire, and that this is the reason why Torah-study should immediately follow prayer.[50]

As always, however, RSZ's approach was syncretistic. A number of discourses diverge from the mainstream and apparently support the view of his teachers that the primary purpose of prayer is spiritual ascent.[51] Other discourses emphasize the importance of kabbalistic yiḥudim,[52] while still others redefine in psychological terms Zoharic theosophical statements regarding the function of prayer.[53] Similarly, like all Hasidic masters, RSZ often shifts the emphasis of Lurianic concepts from God to man. Luria, for example, saw the four halakhic divisions of the daily liturgy as corresponding to an ascending progression of sefirotic unions in each of the four supernal worlds, beginning with ʿAśiyah and culminating in Atsilut.[54] RSZ cites this scheme but adapts it to his purpose. The prayer progression that concerns him most is the worshipper's movement from contemplation, to Love-Fear, and finally to complete biṭul in the ʿAmidah. The four sections of the liturgy are seen as a graduated series of contemplative themes that were intended to arouse a carefully planned succession of emotions and spiritual attitudes.[55] The Zoharic metaphor denoting prayer as the ladder to God is expanded to include not only the soul's ascent but also, and primarily, the drawing down of Divinity into the world.[56]

Thus, in addition to requiring the soul's progressive ascent through the four sections of the liturgy, RSZ insists that each stage—or at least each of the first three—must combine both ratso and shov.[57] His approach can perhaps be best characterized as elevation (=spiritualization) for the sake of revelation,[58] or elevation of the worshipper, the world, and the commandments for the sake of permitting the revelation of Divinity in them. The worshipper and the world that sustains him are elevated through the fiery Love that counteracts the "foreign fire" of the animal soul's desires,[59] while the commandments that were not provided with the "wings" of kaṿanah (=Love and Fear) when they were performed[60] are elevated through the contemplative prayer that is kaṿanah par excellence.[61] Although the letters of prayer themselves should certainly be no more difficult to elevate than the letters of the Torah-study and the physical acts of the commandments, RSZ nevertheless cites the Zoharic motif of angels elevating Jewish prayers and occasionally maintains, like the Zohar, that without such intercession the letters of prayer could not ascend.[62] On the other hand, he virtually negates the Besht's doctrine of elevating profane throughts by limiting it to perfect Tsadiḳim who have no such thoughts of their own and are therefore capable of elevating those of their lesser contemporaries. A mind preoccupied with the contemplative themes RSZ provides would in any case be far less susceptible to these thoughts, but if they should attack, the defense RSZ advocates is not elevation but vigorous repulsion coupled with the arousal of spiritual self-pity.[63]

RSZ also differs from his masters and colleagues on the issue of petitionary prayer. One of the most influential and pervasive doctrines of Meir Ibn Gabbai's *ʿAvodat ha-Ḳodesh* was that all Service, including prayer, must be "for the sake of the Supernal", that is, for the sake of the supernal yiḥudim. Even Service for its own sake, as advocated by Maimonides,[64] is decried as a reprehensible Aristotelian concept, but Service for personal benefit is presented as totally unacceptable, even sinful. Despite the Bible's indications to the contrary, the Talmud's description of the ʿAmidah as "[a request for divine] compassion,"[65] and the obvious rabbinic understanding of the Middle Benedictions of this prayer as supplications for personal and national benefits,[66] Ibn Gabbai virtually rules out the propriety of petitionary prayer.[67] This view—albeit with dispensations for certain situations and for the common man[68]—was promulgated by RSZ's masters and colleagues as prayer "for the sake of the Shekhinah."[69] Various ingenious interpretations were offered to reconcile this principle with the Biblical-Talmudic conception of petitionary prayer,[70] but none could really get around the clear contradiction.

RSZ, on the other hand, touches on the doctrine of prayer for the sake of the Shekhinah just once in *Tanya* and rarely, if ever, in the discourses. Moreover, in his metaphysical formulation of this concept he follows the Zohar and Luria, rather than the Besht and Maggid.[71] His own doctrine of prayer for the sake of revealing Divinity enabled him smoothly to integrate the rabbinic view of petitionary prayer with the general principle of prayer for the sake of the Supernal, although not as Ibn Gabbai understood it. Since all worldly benefits are the direct result of specific combinations of divine sefirotic emanations, the ʿAmidah could be seen as a series of petitions for these emanations. Alternately, the petitionary benedictions can be seen as the vessels required to draw down the light of the Or En Sof. In either case, RSZ was able to make a seamless transition from simple petitionary prayer to prayer for the sake of the Supernal, that is, for the sake of revealing the supernal emanations of Divinity on earth. Lurianic kayanot also had a place in this approach, since each specific emanation or series of emanations can be effectuated only by contemplating the Divine name that controls it. These names comprise the supernal bureaucracy through which the petitioner must make his way to have his petitions granted. Just as the minister of agriculture is powerless to grant a petition that should be addressed to the minister of health, so the ailing worshipper cannot expect to have his prayers for recovery answered unless he addresses them, by the proper name, to the sefirot responsible for health and not, say, to the sefirot responsible for abundant harvests.[72]

Of course, as a faithful disciple of the Maggid, RSZ could not stop there. Lurianic kayanot were necessary, but not, or no longer, sufficient. Since God's will, and not the "minister's," is ultimately responsible for the supplicant's illness, it is this will that must somehow be changed. To do this the supplicant must transcend this will, reach its Author, and persuade Him to change it. This can be achieved only through total biṭul during the ʿAmidah preceded by mesirat nefesh during Ḳeriʾat Shema. By nullifying and transcending his own will the supplicant can transcend God's original will and persuade Him to nullify it.[73]

But despite the elaborate mystical garb in which he feels constrained to clothe it, RSZ's conception of petitionary prayer remains essentially that of the Bible and Talmud: a request for a benefit that physical man can appreciate. Thus, contrary to his mentors who insist that only through purely spiritual prayer can one's material needs be satisfied,[74] RSZ maintains that these needs should indeed be the focus of the ʿAmidah.[75] Contrary to his mentors who taught that all the worshipper's efforts were invariably to be directed toward achieving deveḳut, after which all his material needs would automatically be satisfied, RSZ taught that, occasionally at least, it is precisely fervent petitionary prayer that generates deveḳut.[76] Prayer, in other words, is not only worship but also—and sometimes primarily—supplication.

RSZ's approach to the soul of prayer—its functions and purposes—is reflected in his teachings regarding its body—the halakhic and Hasidic practices surrounding it. One is obligated to pray daily because the world is renewed daily and because "a man's evil inclination overpowers him daily."[77] This inclination is the essence of the animal soul, which regularly renews its strength through the nourishment man provides it. In addition, every Jew's animal soul consists of a fixed number of Ḳelipat Nogah–elements that must be elevated to ḳedushah. The number of days allocated for his life on earth corresponds to the number of elements he is born to elevate. Contemplative prayer, as mentioned above, purifies his materialistic animal soul; daily contemplative prayer is therefore necessary in order regularly to weaken this soul's regularly reinforced concupiscence and to elevate the Ḳelipat Nogah–element that gives purpose to his existence that day. During the night, his divine soul, which must effect this elevation, is dormant, and when he wakes in the morning his animal soul completely dominates his faculties. Since will is the key to all the faculties, this imbalance can be corrected by rededicating the divine soul's will to God, that is, by arousing its innate mesirat nefesh and desire for God through contemplative prayer. This galvanizes the entire divine soul, enabling it to oppose its counterpart for hegemony of the faculties and eventually to elevate that day's Ḳelipat Nogah–element.[78] It follows, therefore, that eating before the morning prayer should be prohibited, for the additional infusion of Ḳelipat Nogah–forces into the animal soul would provide it with an insurmountable advantage over the still-dormant forces of ḳedushah.[79]

On the other hand, it is precisely the challenge of Ḳelipat Nogah–forces that stimulates the divine soul to its greatest efforts. The sheltered life of full-time scholars actually puts them at a disadvantage in this respect, and RSZ often uses this point to encourage the "men of affairs" (*baʿale ʿeseḳ*) among his followers to redouble their efforts in the area of contemplative prayer. Although he insists, as we have seen, that this must be a daily undertaking without a single day's respite, and that merely sporadic devotion to this obligation can have grave consequences, he realizes that many may be too preoccupied with their quest for livelihood to engage in this difficult, daily quest for Love and Fear. On Shabbat, however, when even the ʿAmidah shifts from man's needs to God's praise, they are obligated to apply themselves to contemplative prayer with even greater fervor than the scholars. All the intense spiritual yearning that was frustrated during the week can and should now come gushing forth in a mighty torrent of desire. The unique, memorable pleasure accompanying this emotional release can be most easily realized on Shabbat because, as we have noted, this day is characterized by the revelation of divine Pleasure. Even the scholar's Shabbat prayers are therefore more pleasurable than his weekday prayers. The contrast for the man of affairs, however, is that much greater. If he cannot adequately devote himself to contemplative prayer on a daily basis, although a concerted effort is absolutely necessary to personalize the Shabbat revelation, his Shabbat Service, at least, should be an experience that will carry him through the entire week. It should provide him with a resevoir of Love and Fear large enough to overcome all obstacles to the fulfillment of the commandments in a spiritually hostile world.[80]

This perceived hostility, coupled with the mystical goal of all Hasidic prayer, gave rise to the practices and mannerisms that Mitnagdim found so objectionable.[81] We have already observed that the political and economic subjugation of Jews to gentiles during the exile was seen as a reflection of the supernal subjugation of ḳedushah to ḳelipah.[82] While the material and spiritual impediments to perfect Service were becoming progressively greater as the Messianic Era approached, the spiritual resources necessary to overcome them were being progressively depleted. The generations were declining even as their obstacles to Service were increasing. The contemporary worshipper's attempt to arouse Love and Fear was comparable to a man trying to reach the stars while drowning in a sea of physical desires, profane thoughts, and incessant worries about his livelihood. His soul was vastly inferior to the souls of previous generations, and his body was coarser and less responsive to spiritual stimuli. Consequently, he had to pray with a much greater degree of contemplative effort and at much greater length in order to achieve the requisite Love and Fear. RSZ maintained that each major level of descent in the spiritual stature of the generations required additions to the liturgy and a commensurate increase in the time and effort demanded of the worshipper. Thus, the liturgy of the First Temple period was very brief, while that of the Second Temple period was somewhat longer; the sages of the Talmud generally devoted only a few minutes to the Morning Prayer, but RSZ's followers could not possibly discharge their obligation in less than an hour. The sages were also generally capable of arousing the requisite Love and Fear without any visible or audible signs of inner conflict, simply because whatever conflict they had to engage in was minimal. For RSZ's contemporaries, however, "the time of prayer is a time of war," and they were obligated to tap all their intellectual, emotional, and physical resources to emerge victorious.[83] Just as an army waging a desperate struggle is fully justified in adopting new strategies to ensure victory, so were his contemporaries fully justified in adopting the Lurianic liturgy.[84] Just as soldiers in wartime will sing to improve morale, shout to encourage each other and frighten the enemy, and move against their foe with vigor and alacrity, so must the contemporary worshipper often conduct himself during prayer. The ideal prayer, of course, as even the Besht had taught, was one in which all these adjuvant actions were sublimated in motionless, silent, mystical rapture. But this ideal could be achieved in RSZ's generation only by the very greatest Tsadiḳim.[85] Because their souls were in constant communion with God, they were capable of achieving ecstasy (or Love-Fear and biṭul) quickly and effortlessly. They could therefore confine their prayers within the halakhic time limits. Lesser Tsadiḳim, however, had to wait for the initial supernal breakthrough of their superiors and were forced to exceed these limits; whereas the common man, insensitive as he was to these spiritual-supernal vicissitudes, had no justification for tardiness.[86]

Although RSZ saw contemplative prayer as the heart of Hasidism, there were no authoritative ethical works in this area (as in the area of Torah-study, for example) to which he could refer his followers for specific instructions and guidelines. This was uncharted territory for which only he could provide the map. He drew it in epistles and ordinances spanning most of his years as Hasidic master. Their tone is not just hortatory but demanding and imperative, and they include specific penalties for Hasidim who fail to comply.

He took it for granted that his followers, like other Hasidim, would congregate to pray not in their local synagogues but in separate quarters. This was necessary both because of their distinctive manner of praying and because of the Lurianic liturgy they adopted.[87] The leader of the Morning Service was to gather about him a quorum of Hasidim who could be counted on to pray together, audibly, word by word, and deliberately enough so that the service would take about ninety minutes (as opposed to the half-hour that was the usual length of the synagogue service). This was to be a prayer battalion, and the leader was its commanding officer. It was to commence action no later than the beginning of the service in the local synagogue. Contrary to common Hasidic practice, it was to engage in no banter or frivolousness of any kind before (let alone during) the service. RSZ, following the Talmud, unequivocally condemned this custom, which other Hasidic groups rationalized as a necessary preparation for serving God joyously and ultimately achieving deveḳut. He insisted that the only verbal preparation necessary or permissible for the battalion was what the sages included in the liturgy. Each soldier, however, was expected to prepare himself privately before entering action. Hasidim unable to join this elite, stationary task force were exhorted at least to avoid the common Hasidic practice of flitting to and fro in the room while praying, and they, too, were expected to prepare themselves for prayer to the best of their abilities.[88]

Preparation consisted of study and meditation. Its purpose was to put the worshipper into a contemplative, reverent, supplicant frame of mind and to make him emotionally receptive to Love and Fear. He was to meditate at length on the vast contrast between his pitiful insignificance and God's infinite greatness. During this preparatory period he was to concentrate primarily on the former, whereas when reciting the *Pesuḳe de-Zimrah* he was to concentrate on the latter. Specific preparatory themes included his sinfulness, his immersion in mundane affairs, and the oppressive exile that his behavior helps perpetuate. The ideal opportunities for this meditation were when reciting Tiḳun Ḥatsot and when studying kabbalistic musar works, particularly *Reshit Ḥokhmah*. These practices triggered the necessary self-abasement sessions described in Chapter 3[89] and were therefore strongly recommended. Having thus fulfilled the Mishnaic dictum of preparing for prayer by arousing "a reverent frame of mind,"[90] the worshipper must then fulfil a second—and, according to RSZ, contradictory—rabbinic dictum[91] by turning his thoughts to the joy-producing meditation outlined in Chapter 3.[92] One discourse, following a third rabbinic dictum,[93] recommended the study of halakhah, which itself gladdens the heart and purifies the mind of all mundane concerns.[94] Finally, the worshipper was urged to purify his body by immersion in a *mikṿah* and to arouse divine assistance in spiritualizing his faculties by giving tsedaḳah. Having thus mobilized all his personal resources, he was now ready to join his fellow combatants in the daily battle that is prayer.[95]

6

Conclusions

The teachings of the Besht, the Maggid, and Rabbi Shneur Zalman continue to evoke heated controversy, both among adherents and opponents of Hasidism and among scholars trying to analyze the movement and its significance. Because it remains a major force in Jewish life, it is not readily amenable to objective examination. Even outstanding scholars have allowed personal bias to cloud their approach and tendentious judgments to vitiate their conclusions. Standard critical and philological criteria have been ignored in favor of superficial study, plausible assumptions, and an essentially visceral theory relating early Hasidism to late Sabbatianism.

The past two decades or so have seen some improvement in this situation. Israeli scholars such as M. Piekarz, Z. Gries, and A. Rubenstein have begun to lay the foundation for a sound analytical approach. Long-accepted assumptions and conclusions advanced by Dubnow, Scholem, Tishby, Weiss, and Schatz have finally been questioned or repudiated. One can no longer confidently maintain, with Dubnow, that the Hasidic movement resulted from a widening of the gap between the intelligentsia and the masses; that eighteenth-century Polish Jewry felt unusually oppressed by its communal leaders; that it suffered from an unusually benighted cultural milieu and longed to break out of its constricting halakhic and cultural confines. One can no longer maintain, with Tishby, Scholem, and Weiss, that Hasidism was an offshoot of Sabbatianism. One can no longer affirm, with Weiss, the existence of non-Beshtian Hasidic groups on the periphery of early Hasidism; of a marked tendency in the Besht's teachings toward pantheism, religious anarchy, and antirabbinic values; or of an obsession with ecstatic deveḳut (communion with God). Nor can one continue to maintain, with Schatz, that early Hasidism repudiated remorse for sin.

The present study argues that it is impossible to determine the specific historical factors and religious trends that gave rise to eighteenth-century Hasidism. Nor is a purely phenomenological analysis of its teachings particularly illuminating. It is, however, possible to examine its innovative ideas or new emphases and relate them to the contemporaneous ideational revolution known as romanticism. Both emphasized God's immanence rather than transcendence; the positive aspects of diversity and change; the importance of sensation, emotion, optimism, and confident action. Both were oriented toward subjectivity, organicism, and individualism. Both pointed to intuition and the unconscious as supreme sources of knowledge. Both were particularly conscious of the contrast between man's potential greatness and his actual weakness, and particularly fascinated with genius, energy, and power. Both represented a shift of values and concerns; from metaphysics to psychology, from the world to man; from being to becoming, actuality to potentiality; from achieving—or, in the case of God, comprising—a state of serene uniform perfection, to an ever-restless striving for a dynamic, ever-increasing perfection encompassing real contradictions in constant dialectical tension.

These ideas and values, introduced or emphasized by the Besht and Maggid, were adopted or adapted by RSZ, who saw himself as the third in a single line of succession of Hasidic masters. His Hasidic thought was articulated primarily in a series of discourses spanning about two decades (to 1813) and varying greatly in length, style, and content, depending on the period, the audience, and the need of the hour. His purpose was to inspire, not to fashion a system of religioethical thought. It is unlikely that he ever intended all the discourses to be compared for the purpose of analyzing his view on any given theme. Trying to pour his teachings into conceptual molds—trying, in other words, to solidify what was intended to remain fluid—as I have done here, yields the conclusion that the outstanding features of RSZ's Hasidic thought are syncretism, tension, and paradox. Nevertheless, only by making this attempt can one arrive at some basic, valid generalizations that emerge from the apparent discord.

RSZ the man combined great intellect, diligence, and discipline with a smoldering religious emotionalism, sincere humility, profound compassion, and a gift for organization. His Hasidism naturally reflects these traits. It was axiomatic to him that every Jew was created for the sole purpose of serving God. This much was clear from the Bible and rabbinic teachings. It was equally clear from these and later sources that wholehearted devotion to Service could be motivated only by Love and Fear. It was an almost imperceptible step from these universally accepted beliefs to the principle that constitutes the foundation of RSZ's Hasidic philosophy: Service without Love and Fear is not really Service at all. Although perfunctory or habitual fulfillment of the commandments generally satisfied one's halakhic obligation, it does not satisfy one's existential obligation. One could be devoted to halakhah without being devoted to God; indeed, this was precisely what most Mitnagdim had achieved.

The key issue was therefore not how to fulfill the commandments, for which the Talmud and *Shulḥan ʿArukh* provided adequate guidance, but how to attain Love and Fear, for which no written guide existed. Maimonides had advanced the view that Love must be intellectual and contemplative, from which it apparently followed that only an intellectual elite could attain it. RSZ fully accepted Maimonides' premise but rejected this conclusion. Service was every man's duty; Service without intellectual Love was impossible; God would never oblige man to do anything beyond his capacity: Therefore, intellectual Love must be within every Jew's grasp. All that was needed was the training in how to reach for it, and this was the function of Jewish leaders from the time of Moses. Under RSZ's leadership this training consisted primarily of diligently studying the Hasidism he taught and meditating on it, especially before and during the prayer.

The potential ability of every Jew to attain Love and Fear collided with the obvious fact that most did not actually attain them, at least not to the extent that true Service demanded. This for RSZ merely reflected the necessary struggle between the average Jew's divine soul, which constantly strives to spiritualize and bring him close to God, and his animal soul, which joins with the body it animates to coarsen his character and thereby alienate him from God. Consequently, although intended ultimately to elicit Love and Fear, the immediate purpose of studying and contemplating Hasidism was to refine—which for RSZ meant to spiritualize—one's character.

The first and most important character trait to strive for was absolute humility before God. The animal soul, which closely approximates the ego, operates by setting itself up as a real entity opposed to its divine counterpart. Accepting it as such is man's first step toward allowing it to entice him away from God, since this acceptance is tantamount to recognizing the existence of a reality other than God.

Whereas the divine soul is actually a spark of Divinity and not a separate entity, man's "self"—his ability to refer to himself as "I"—stems from this animal soul, and the key to resisting its blandishments is humility to the point of self-nullification. This religioethical imperative is for RSZ a corollary of those seminal commandments that require affirmation of God's absolute unity. Full and continuous perception of this unity, of the truth that nothing but God exists, is granted only to disembodied souls, but one is obligated to approach it on earth by continuously uniting the three "garments" of the animal soul—thought, speech, and action—with the thought, speech, and action of God as revealed in the Torah and its commandments. Although the animal soul itself generally retains its secular character, it nevertheless becomes an indispensable vehicle for serving God and acknowledging His unity.

While the basic theory that Love and Fear are attainable through meditation is Maimonidean, RSZ took this rarified intellectual approach and transformed it into a way of life for every Jew. His teachings provided Hasidim with abundant meditation material, as well as high-minded topics for discussion whenever they met. His personal guidance illumined the path for individual Hasidim who consulted him on spiritual problems. He taught them to love each other as brothers, share their joys and sorrows, meet periodically for local gatherings (farbrengen), during which a little food, a few drinks, and many moving melodies smoothed the way for mutual encouragement and exhortation. The goal was selfless Service, but along the way one also attained faith in God's absolute goodness and the joy of dedicating one's life to Him amid the fellowship of a like-minded brotherhood of votaries. This rare fusion of the intellectual, emotional, social, and spiritual facets of Judaism provided Ḥabad Hasidim with the fortitude to withstand the perennial persecution to which Russian Jewry was subject.

RSZ's Hasidism is based on a worldview taken primarily from the Talmud and Midrash, the works of Maimonides, the Zohar, and Lurianic kabbalah. Maimonides' nonhalakhic works were validated by his unsurpassed stature as a halakhist, while the rabbinic and kabbalistic works were for RSZ divinely inspired sources that revealed different but complementary truths about God, man, and the world. Since RSZ did not subscribe to the "double truth" theory, this meant that all the teachings about all the fields discussed in these works—whether religion, science, metaphysics, or psychology—had to be consistent. It also meant that one could legitimately take a concept treated in the *Guide* and reinterpret it in terms of Zoharic or Lurianic kabbalah. The chain of being, which for Maimonides started with the physical world and ascended to the celestial spheres and Active Intellect, was extended to include the Zohar's sefirot and the many other divine manifestations that constitute Lurianic metaphysics. Maimonides' creation ex nihilo was reinterpreted to mean creation through or from the first sefirah. This approach predated Beshtian Hasidism, and RSZ accepted it as a given.

From his Hasidic mentors RSZ adopted the method of explaining theosophical concepts in psychological terms. This was justified by the belief that man was God's corporealized reflection, and particularly by the fact that the moving force behind a Jew's desire and ability to serve God was his divine soul. Since the soul's workings were considered far more accessible than its Source, they were the ideal medium for achieving some understanding of God's nature and unity. Meditating upon that understanding would eventually lead to the Love and Fear of God that were the basis of selfless Service.

RSZ's Hasidic thought underwent considerable development between the year *Likuṭe Amarim* (*Tanya*) was published in 1796 and his death in 1813. It is therefore not surprising that the discourses delivered during these years depart frequently from the teachings embodied in this work. Similarly, as he matured and acquired more confidence in his own religioethical conclusions, RSZ parted ways with the Besht and the Maggid on a number of their key doctrines, such as Zaddikism, the elevation of profane thoughts, and the nature and purpose of Torah-study. These differences, which appear even in *Tanya*, were never acknowledged as such, for RSZ apparently remained convinced that he was merely continuing and elaborating the teachings of his Hasidic masters.

So, too, despite his professed allegiance to the teachings of R. Isaac Luria, RSZ in fact differed with Luria in several fundamental areas of religious thought and conduct. The key to the nature of these differences, as well as to the differences between RSZ and his Hasidic masters and colleagues, lies in RSZ's more faithful adherence to classical rabbinic attitudes and values. Thus, contrary to Luria as mediated by R. Ḥayyim Vital, RSZ retained the supremacy of Talmud-study, particularly as it relates to halakhic decisions, in his hierarchy of studies; and he retained the positive assessment of Talmudic dialectics. Contrary to his Hasidic masters and colleagues, RSZ reaffirmed the validity of petitionary prayer, and, as previously noted, he taught that for most men emotionalistic deveḳut, or Love-Fear, was the basis, not the consummation, of proper Service; indeed, the emotionalistic aspect of Love-Fear, although desirable, was not really necessary, for only intellectual conviction and volitive commitment were indispensable. Contrary to both Luria and his Hasidic masters, RSZ emphasized Service for the sake of revealing Divinity in the world, rather than for the sake of elevating, perfecting, or purifying one's soul. Although very much a mystic, he was, uniquely perhaps, a *this*-worldly mystic. In theory, at least, he democratized kabbalistic Judaism, opening it to every man who would personally strive to achieve its goals. And more than any of his mentors, he succeeded in fusing these goals with those of classical rabbinic Judaism.

Nevertheless—and here the paradoxical in RSZ's thought is seen in sharp relief—in a number of discourses he went beyond the most radical teachings of his mentors by portraying God as, in effect, the Supreme Manipulator, Who arranges for either good or evil to triumph in accordance with what amuses Him at the moment, and for Whom man's actions and efforts are otherwise inconsequential. Such religioethical nihilism is utterly at odds with RSZ's other teachings and, indeed, with all of traditional Jewish thought, which generally posits, at least implicitly, that God desires the good to triumph because He is the essence of goodness. Similarly, RSZ ignored in practice his own halakhic decisions regarding the curriculum and method of Torah-study in favor of a less demanding and more practical program; and, while occasionally echoing the invidious descriptions of both the exoteric Written and the Oral Torah found in his kabbalistic sources, he nevertheless repudiated their practical conclusions.

Ultimately, each of the main traditional components of Service underwent a significant shift of emphasis in RSZ's thought, so that there were clear differences between the way Ḥabad Hasidim performed a mitzvah and the way contemporary Mitnagdim or even other Hasidim performed that mitzvah. Torah-study remained for RSZ the supreme commandment, but proper study now required far more than diligence and intellect; it required spiritual preparation through contemplative prayer and refinement of character. Understanding the text was no longer the end of study but the means for uniting man's intellect with the intellect of God. Moreover, it enabled man to determine God's will in every contingency. Since pleasure generally motivates will, determining God's will is tantamount to determining what gives Him pleasure. With the proper preparation, this determination is accompanied by the conformity of man's will and pleasure to God's, so that one desires and enjoys only what God desires and enjoys.

Fulfilling His will through a commandment as dictated by halakhah then becomes both an act of selfless devotion and a supremely joyous and pleasurable step toward self-fulfillment. Hence, RSZ's emphasis on studying with an eye toward the halakhic decision, since this revealed God's will, whereas the discussions leading up to the decision were reflections of His wisdom, and "the purpose of wisdom is teshuvah and good deeds" (*Berakhot*, 17a)—returning to God through the commandments.

The commandments that received RSZ's closest attention were Torah-study, prayer, and tsedaḳah. Torah-study was for RSZ the vehicle for revealing, or "drawing down," God's will and uniting with His wisdom; prayer, the vehicle for ascending to Him through the Love and Fear born of intense meditation; and tsedaḳah—sustaining the needy—was the act that most closely approximated God's own primary activity: sustaining all creation. It also dovetailed with the Besht's emphasis on compassion for, and brotherly love among, all Jews and was indispensable in maintaining the impoverished Hasidic community in the Holy Land. Indeed, most of RSZ's pastoral letters consisted of impassioned appeals for tsedaḳah for this community, buttressed by erudite kabbalistic explanations of the supernal significance of such support. These letters formed part of a well-organized system of fund-raising that occupied a good part of RSZ's time and spared few, if any, of his followers. Whatever a family did not require for bare subsistence could not legitimately be withheld from those who had even less.

Although these commandments, like all the commandments, were to be heteronomously fulfilled simply because they were God's will, the joy and vitality that should accompany Service were of paramount importance. The traditional supremacy of Torah-study in the hierarchy of religious values had made Judaism intellectually top-heavy. Emotional development, both religious and personal, was largely overshadowed by the quest for intellectual achievement. Great scholars and rabbinic leaders were too often cold and condescending. Relations with family, friends, community, and even communion with God during prayer were frequently neglected for the sake of single-minded devotion to Torah. Feelings of elation or depression, as well as spontaneous or extreme emotional outbursts of any kind, were considered to be contrary to the basic rabbinic values of sobriety, self-discipline, and moderation.

Following the Besht and Maggid, RSZ taught that every natural emotion could be channeled toward Service, and that, indeed, perfect

Service required full emotional, as well as intellectual development. His goal was to educate truly spiritual men who were nevertheless not aloof or otherworldly, but warm, concerned, vital, and sensitive. The Ḥabad Hasid, like the Mitnagdic scholar, was expected to be highly disciplined, diligent and persevering in his studies. He was expected to master and strictly adhere to every halakhah in the *Shulḥan ʿArukh* that pertained to his daily life. If sufficiently capable, he was expected to master the entire Biblical and rabbinic corpus—the entire Torah.

But in addition, the Ḥabad Hasid had other demands made of him. He would not be admired for living a cloistered life, regardless of how great the resulting scholarly attainment. He would, however, be admired, as one wealthy Hasid was, for contemplating a discourse dealing with God's unity while engaged in a large-scale business transaction. Ideally he developed an open, well-rounded personality. The study of Hasidism coupled with contemplative prayer refined his character, while RSZ taught him how to manage such emotions as depression, which could not be refined. Scholarly yet sociable; reticent yet a capable singer of Hasidic melodies and relater of Hasidic tales and traditions; austere and somewhat ascetic, yet possessing a refined appreciation of this world's pleasures; earnest but not humorless or somber; deeply religious but not unctuous or pietistic; modest but self-confident; devoted to RSZ but fully capable of thinking for himself: this Hasid personified the profound and paradoxical system that came to be known as Ḥabad Hasidism.

Excursuses

Excursus A

These three are representative of the major trends in the study of Hasidism, particularly before Dubnow. Graetz's proclivities are well known. S. H. Horodetsky's desire for a romantic, "spiritual," nonhalakhic type of Judaism grounded in aggadah and supposedly characterized by Beshtian Hasidism is most evident in "Ha-Gra ve-ha-Besht," *Ha-Shiloaḥ* 17 (1907): 348–56, and is the keynote in the introductions to his doctored edition of *Shivḥe ha-Besht* and to *Ha-Ḥasidim veha-Ḥasidut* (both Berlin, 1922). E. Zweifel's *Shalom al Yiśra'el* (1864–1872) contains theoretically useful material from various valuable sources, but inexact quoting, passages combined to better illustrate a point, and haphazard attribution make this material, as it stands, practically worthless. To make Hasidism more palatable to its detractors, Zweifel characterizes it as emphasizing traits that he knows will appeal to them (and that, not surprisingly, happen to appeal to him, too). If only they could see it as he does, peace would reign over Israel. He consequently manages seriously to suggest that the movement's essential goals were the elimination of pilpul and certain minor "details and customs"; the avoidance of mundane affairs, controversy, and strife; the encouragement of frugal living, of a negative attitude toward money, a positive attitude toward all men, and a modest, self-effacing attitude toward oneself (*Shalom al Yiśra'el,* ed. A. Rubenstein [Jerusalem, 1972, p. 121]). Needless to say—at least to anyone familiar with Hasidic thought in its historical context—this picture, like Martin Buber's, is nothing but a self-portrait. (On Buber, see G. Scholem, "Martin Buber's Interpretation of Hasidism," in *The Messianic Idea in Judaism* [New York, 1974], pp. 227–51; G. Scholem, "Martin Buber's Conception of Judaism," in *On Jews and Judaism in Crisis,* ed. W. J. Dannhauser [New York, 1976], p. 165ff.: "Upon closer inspection, Hasidism's love affair with the world turns out to be Buber's love affair with the world" [p. 169]; R. Schatz, "Martin Buber, Master of Hasidic Literature," *Judaism* 9 [Summer 1960]: 277–82; S. Katz, "Martin Buber's Misuse of Hasidic Sources," in Katz's *Post-Holocaust*

Dialogues: Critical Studies in Modern Jewish Thought [New York, 1985], pp. 52–94).

Separate mention must also be made of A. Z. Aescoly, *Le Hasidisme* (Paris, 1927), and Torsten Ysander, *Studien zum Bestschen Hasidismus* (Uppsala, 1933), which exemplify the irresponsible scholarship that has plagued this field. In one slim volume Aescoly purports to take us from Hasidism's roots in kabbalah, as outlined in unreliable secondary works, through several generations of its developments. His method consists primarily of taking a sampling of quotes from some Hasidic works and subjecting them to a combination of speculation and skepticism. Ysander takes a sampling from works he uncritically attributes in toto to the Besht and proposes to separate the purely Beshtian ideas from their kabbalistic antecedents. One will search in vain through this voluminous work for a single footnote directly citing the Talmud, Midrash, or those kabbalistic works from which the author claims to have distilled pure Beshtianism. Instead one finds (again) an almost total reliance on dubious secondary works plus a handful of quotes—largely from *Keter Shem Tov* and *Tsava'at ha-Ribash*—subordinated to Ysander's own verbose meditations.

A fairly comprehensive bibliography of secondary literature on Hasidism to ca. 1815 may be obtained by combining relevant works in the (partially overlapping) bibliographies of the *Hebrew Encyclopaedia,* vol. 17, col. 768–69, 820–21; the *Encyclopaedia Judaicia,* vol. 7, col. 1426–27; the works cited by Louis Jacobs in his edition of *Tract on Ecstasy* (London, 1963), p. 33 n. 5; his *Hasidic Prayer* (New York, 1973), pp. 184–86; and the following list, in chronological order, of works or parts of works of scholarly interest: *Sefer ha-Ḳan* (Jerusalem, 1969); *Ḥasidim u-Mitnagdim,* ed. M. Wilensky (Jerusalem, 1970); A. Rubenstein, "Igeret ha-Beshṭ le-R. Gershon mi-Ḳutov," *Sinai* 67 (1970): 120–39; S. Baumbinger, "Le-Igeret ha-Beshṭ," *Sinai* 68 (1971): 170–98; I. Etkes, "Shiṭato u-Fa'alo shel Rabi Ḥayyim mi-Volozhin ke-Teguvat ha-Ḥevrah ha-Mitnagdit le-Ḥasidut," PAAJR 38–39 (1970–1971), Heb. section 1–47; A. I. Kahn's introduction to his edition of *Magid Devarav le-Ya'aḳov* (Jerusalem, 1971); Nissan Mindel, *Rabbi Schneur Zalman of Liadi* (New York, 1971); Norman Lamm, *Torah li-Shemah* (Jerusalem, 1972); G. Nigal, "Moro ve-Rabo shel R. Yiśra'el Ba'al Shem Ṭov," *Sinai* 71 (1972): 150–59; A. Chitrik's note to Nigal's article, *Sinai* 73 (1973): 190; A. Rubenstein, "'Od le-'Inyan Igerot ha-Beshṭ," *Sinai* 73 (1973): 175–80; M. Zucker, "Ketav Yad me-Reshit ha-Ḥasidut," *Ḳiryat Sefer* 49 (1973): 223–35; G. Nigal's note, in ibid., 451–52; B. D. Weinryb, *The Jews of Poland* (Philadelphia, 1973), ch. 12 and Appendix 4; appendix and addenda to the Kehot Publication Society edition of *Magid Devarav le-Ya'ḳov* and *Or Torah* (New York, 1973); G. Nigal, "Maḳor Bilti Noda be-Sifrut Hanhagot ha-Ḥasidit", *Ḳiryat Sefer* 48 (1973): 154–84; introduction and notes to the Soncino Press edition of *Tanya* (London, 1973); I. J. Schochet, *The Great Maggid* (New York, 1974), ch. 15; J. Weiss, *Meḥḳarim be-Ḥasidut Breslav,* ed. M. Piekarz (Jerusalem, 1974); N. Lamm, "The Letter of the Besht to R. Gershon of Kutov," *Tradition* 14 (1974): 110–25; A. Rubinstein, "Ḥasidim ve-Ḥasidut be-Ṿarsha," *Sinai* 75 (1974): 61–84; I. Etkes's review of Lamm's *Torah li-Shemah, Ḳiryat Sefer* 50 (1975): 638–48; I. Tishby, "Ḳudsha Berikh Hu, Oraita, ve-Yiśra'el Kula Ḥad: Maḳor ha-Imrah be-Perush Idra Raba le-Ramḥal," *Ḳiryat Sefer* 50 (1975): 480–92; I. J. Schochet's introduction to his edition of *Keter Shem Tov* (New York, 1975); M. Piekarz, "Ha-Teʿudah ha-Rishonah bi-Defus le-Torat ha-Ḥasidut," *Molad* 35–36 (Winter 1975): 183–87; I. Tishby, "Ḳitrugo shel R. Yiśra'el mi-Shḳlov ʿal ha-Ḥasidim," *Ḳiryat Sefer* 51 (1976): 300–303; G. Nigal, "Ḥeṭ, Tokhaḥah, u-Teshuvah be-Mishnat R. Elimelekh mi-Lizensk," *Bar Ilan* 13 (1976): 234–49; G. Nigal, "ʿAl R. Aharon Shemuel ha-Kohen-mi-Talmide ha-Magid mi-Mesritch," *Sinai* 78 (1976): 255–62; G. Nigal, "Maḳor Rishoni le-Sifrut ha-Sipurim ha-Ḥasidit ʿal Sefer Keter Shem Ṭov u-Meḳorotaṿ, *Sinai* 79 (1976): 132–46; G. Nigal, *ʿIyunim bi-Ketav-Yad Ḥasidi Ḳadum* (Haifa, 1976), pp. 177–92; Y. Rafael, "Genizat Ḥerson," *Sinai* 81 (1977): 129–50; Z. Gries, "ʿArikhat Tsava'at ha-Ribash," *Ḳiryat Sefer* 52 (1977): 187–211; A. Ben Ezra, "Le-Toldot Hitnagdut ha-Gra le-Ḥasidut," *Tarbiz* 46 (1977): 133–40; M. Piekarz, *Bi-Yeme Tsemiḥat ha-Ḥasidut* (Jerusalem, 1978); L. Jacobs, "The Doctrine of the Zaddik in the Thought of Elimelekh of Lizensk," (University of Cincinnati, 1978); E. Kupfer, "Teʿudot Ḥadashot bi-Devar ha-Maḥloḳet ben Rashaz mi-Liadi u-ven R. Avraham ha-Kohen mi-Ḳalisk," *Daʿat* 1 (1978): 121–41; Z. M. Rabinowitz, "Meḳorot u-Teʿudot le-Toldot ha-Ḥasidut be-Polin" *Sinai* 82 (1978): 82–86; *Peraḳim be-Torat ha-Ḥasidut,* ed. A. Rubinstein (Jerusalem, 1978); A. Rubenstein, "ʿAl Rabo shel ha-Beshṭ ṿe-ʿal ha-Ketavim she-Mehem Lamad ha-Beshṭ," *Tarbiz* 48 (1978–1979): 146–58; Rachel Elior, "Ḳuntres ha-Hitpaʿalut le-R. Dov Baer Schneerson," *Ḳiryat Sefer* 54 (1979): 384–92, and S. D. Levin's note in ibid., pp. 829–30; Z. Gries, "Sifrut ha-Hanhagot ha-Ḥasidit ke-Biṭui le Hanhagah ve-Etos," thesis, Hebrew University, 1979, and bibliography, pp. 285–90; *Migdal ʿOz,* ed. Y. Mondshein (Kfar Habad, 1980); Hayyim Lieberman, *Ohel Raḥel* (New York, 1980), 2 vols.; Y. Liebes, "Ha-Tiḳun ha-Kelali shel R. Naḥman mi-Breslav ve-Yaḥaso le-Shabta'ut," *Zion* 45 (1980): 201–45; critique of Liebes by Y. Mondshein, *Zion* 47 (1982): 198–223; and Liebes's reply, ibid., 224–31; Z. Gries, "Sifrut ha-Hanhagot ha-Ḥasidit meha-Meḥtsah ha-Sheniyah le-Me'ah ha-18 ve-ʿad li-Shenot ha-Sheloshim le-Me'ah ha-19," *Zion* 46 (1981): 198–236 (references infra to "Sifrut ha-Hanhagot" are to Gries's thesis, not this article), and appendices to this article, ibid., 278–305; Y. Hisdai, "ʿEved Hashem be-Doram shel Avot ha-Ḥasidut," *Zion* 47 (1982): 253–92; and the works discussed infra.

Excursus B

She'elat Yabets (Lemberg, 1884), Pt. 1, no. 41, p. 38a–b. This section of the responsum has been incorrectly summarized in Herman Pollack's *Jewish Folkways in Germanic Lands* (1648–1806) (M.I.T. Press, 1971), p. 79. Emden does not advise his medical-student questioner "to desist from his secular studies as it can only bring confusion." Nor does he write that "no man is entitled to have two tables" (sacred and secular), Pollack's mistranslation of אין כל אדם זוכה לשתי שולחנות—"not every man merits two tables." Emden is, in fact, opposed only to the study of philosophy (*higayon*) and to attending a university where gentile (i.e., Christian) customs and values hold sway. He tries to make the student aware of the religious dangers involved in studying in such an institution in general, and of the halakhic problems involved in the study of medicine in particular. But he does not press him to discontinue his studies. What is more, he asks the student to kindly bring him up to date on the latest advances in alchemy, a "science" that particularly fascinated him (as it did Jonathan Eybeschutz; see *Yaʿarot Devash* [Lemberg, 1863], pp. 8d–9a). And he ends by describing himself as a man who is no less a lover of the sciences than his correspondent, but who has unfortunately not succeeded in mastering them.

On Emden's wide-ranging secular interests and reading, see *Megilat Sefer,* pp. 96–98; Abraham Bick (Shauli), *R. Yaʿaḳov ʿEmden: ha-Ish u-Mishnato* (Jerusalem, 1974), pp. 92–98; see also Emden's *Miṭpaḥat Sefarim* (Jerusalem, 1970), Pt. 2, ch. 8, par. 21, p. 36 (on the *Guide*) and ch. 9, par. 42, pp. 71–75 on Abraham Ibn Ezra and astrology; Saadia Gaon; alchemy and practical vs. theoretical sciences; and the study of languages and the humanities. Despite his clearly voracious reading habits, he invariably insisted that secular works may be perused only occasionally, unsystematically, and only when Torah-study is prohibited. See *She'elot Yabets,* Pt. 1, no. 10; *Miṭpaḥat Sefarim,* pp. 72–73 (p. 72 is continued in column two of p. 73), and par. 54, p. 80; *Megilat Sefer,* p. 98. On his relations with Mendelssohn, see the references under "Emden" in the index of Alexander Altmann's *Moses Mendelssohn* (University of Alabama Press, 1973).

Excursus C

Manuscript work has, however, been initiated in the past two decades by Z. Gries (see Excursus A), S. Zucker (ibid.), and R. Schatz(-Uffenheimer.

Hereinafter: Schatz). See Schatz's "Perusho shel ha-Besht le-Mizmor 107," *Tarbiz* 42 [1972–1973]: 154–84, and the introduction to her edition of *Magid Devarav le-Ya'akov* (Jerusalem, 1976).

It should be noted, however, that Schatz has not, in fact, established that the commentary to Psalm 107 is attributable to the Besht. The following considerations lead me to this conclusion:

1. None of the Besht's disciples or colleagues attributed such a commentary to him.

2. R. Menaḥem Naḥum of Chernobyl is our clearest, most authoritative source for the fact that the Besht initiated the custom to recite this Psalm Friday afternoons (Schatz, p. 155). Yet he does not mention the "Besht's commentary" that explains the significance of this practice in detail. Is it possible that he knew of the custom but not of the commentary? There is nothing more "radical" in this commentary than in the teachings concerning the Zaddik's descent that are found in the works of R. Jacob Joseph of Polonnoye. Consequently, there is no reason why the Besht's disciples would (all!) have refrained from mentioning it and attributing it to him.

3. The well-attested commentary of the Besht to one verse of Ps. 107 differs significantly from the rest of this commentary in both style and content (as Schatz herself observes [p. 171]). It was clearly inserted by the author or compiler from another source (as Schatz surmises).

4. To my knowledge, none of the extant, attested Beshtian teachings or writings contain the kind of detailed, technical kabbalistic explication that characterizes this commentary. Its complex style is conspicuously different from the Beshtian insert and from most, if not all, authentic Beshtian teachings.

5. The emphasis on the Zaddik's descent is a hallmark of the teachings of R. Menaḥem Mendel of Bar (see Excursus D). This, along with the external evidence cited by Schatz (p. 161), makes him a far more likely candidate for attribution. G. Scholem shares this view (*The Messianic Idea,* p. 189; *Devarim be-Go* [Tel Aviv, 1976], p. 344, n. 3).

Excursus D

The conclusions of Weiss's pioneering article, "Reshit Tsemiḥatah shel ha-Derekh ha-Ḥasidit," *Zion* 16 (1951): 46–105, which are based on related assumptions, have also been shown to be untenable. See Piekarz, *Bi-Yeme Tsemiḥat ha-Ḥasidut,* pp. 22–25, 96f., 207, 276–78.

Among the points that should be noted regarding R. Menaḥem Mendel's "radicalism":

1. According to Weiss, R. Menaḥem Mendel repudiated the Besht's

innovative synthesis of Torah study and deveḳut, insisting, like earlier kabbalists, that separate times must be set aside for each and, unlike earlier kabbalists, that the time for deveḳut should be increased at the expense of the time previously allocated for Torah. The editor of *Tsava'at ha-Ribash,* Weiss maintains, pointedly omits any reference to such a radical doctrine in order to render his other non-Beshtian doctrines more acceptable.

In fact, this doctrine does appear there (no. 29; see also the alternate reading in Schochet's edition, pp. 8–9), but even if it were missing it would prove nothing, because the same directive to maximize deveḳut time at the expense of Torah-study is twice quoted in the Besht's name by R. Jacob Joseph (*Keter Shem Tov,* no. 374, 379).

2. Weiss identifies R. Pinḥas of Korets as another representative of the more radical, peripheral Hasidism that appealed to the simple masses by promulgating unrestrained enthusiasm, emotionalism, and ecstasy as its highest values.

In fact, R. Pinḥas is representative of a more conservative trend in early Hasidism that criticized the Maggid's preoccupation with deveḳut and instead emphasized the supreme importance of fulfilling the mitsyot simply because they are God's will. (See the quotations in R. Schatz, *Ha-Ḥasidut ke-Misṭiḳah* [Jerusalem, 1968], p. 139ff.) He repeatedly denigrated strenuous, conscious attempts to achieve ecstasy in prayer, maintaining that the act of prayer is itself divine, and man is powerless to elevate it any further (Heschel, *ʿAle ʿAyin,* p. 227). He also criticized the religious pretentiousness, presumptuousness, and flamboyance of the uninspired imitators among the Maggid's disciples (a critique that, incidentally, was a common refrain among contemporary Mitnagdim, several of the Maggid's disciples themselves, and the Besht himself; see *Keter Shem Ṭov,* no. 4, 395; *Liḳuṭim Yeḳarim,* no. 243; *Or Torah* [Kehot], p. 44a).

The parallels Weiss finds between the works of R. Pinḥas and R. Menaḥem Mendel are nugatory and may in any case be found implicitly in (other collections of) the Maggid's teachings and explicitly in the works of R. Menaḥem Mendel of Vitebsk; see *Or Torah,* p. 96b; *Peri ha-Arets* (Lublin, 1928), p. 68: יראת ה׳ היא הדביקות היותר גבוה מכל אהבות.

3. Weiss's identification of R. Meshullam Feivush of Zbaraz as the disciple of Rabbi Menaḥem Mendel who carried on his non-Beshtian traditions is equally untenable. R. Meshullam himself tells us that he heard R. Menaḥem Mendel speak only several times and that his main master was the Maggid R. Michel of Zloczow (beginning of *Yosher Divre Emet,* p. 110a in A. Kahn's ed. of *Liḳuṭim Yeḳarim* (Jerusalem, 1974). R. Meshullam's *Yosher Divre Emet* is a plea to the uninspired imitators mentioned above to abandon their pretentions and return to the simple religious integrity that had

always been the hallmark of the truly devout. Its negative position on deveḳut for the masses and its traditional approach to Torah-study (see no. 38) are actually antithetical to the views expressed and implied in *Darke Yesharim*. (Z. Gries's suggestion that R. Meshullam had a split personality [*Ḳiryat Sefer* 52, pp. 200–201] is thoroughly unconvincing). The only apparent resemblance between them is their negative attitude to the Besht's doctrine of elevating profane thoughts; however, the similarity is only superficial. The omission of the doctrine from *Darke Yesharim* may or may not imply opposition; even if it does, the reason remains a mystery. If R. Menaḥem Mendel could jettison Torah-study in favor of deveḳut, he was hardly the man to reject the elevation doctrine because of its radicalism. R. Meshullam, on the other hand, does not reject the doctrine but only limits its applicability to the spiritual elite. Although this qualification was apparently widely ignored in the great enthusiasm generated by early Hasidism, there is evidence, Weiss to the contrary, that it had been included in earlier formulations of the doctrine; see *Or Torah,* 44a; M. Piekarz, *Bi-Yeme Tsemiḥat ha-Ḥasidut,* p. 276; G. Nigal, "ʿAl Meḳorot ha-Deveḳut be-Sifrut Reshit ha-Ḥasidut," *Ḳiryat Sefer* 46 (1971): 344.

4. Weiss's statement that *Liḳuṭim Yeḳarim* does not contain any reference to this doctrine is simply untrue; see nos. 118 (pp. 25b–26a), 129 (p. 35b), 194, 212, and esp. 155, which expatiates on the subject in greater detail than any other passage I have seen.

To sum up: there is no evidence either for the existence of a radical, non-Beshtian periphery in early Hasidism or for a conscious literary effort to "reform" the Beshtian doctrine on elevating profane thoughts, let alone for any conscious literary efforts to propagate such a hybrid strain of Hasidism.

Excursus E

I am referring to the school of Scholem, Tishby, Weiss, and Schatz.

A telling example of this procedure is I. Tishby's attempt to link early Hasidism with Sabbatianism through the kabbalistic works of R. Jacob Koppel Lifschitz, *Shaʿare Gan ʿEden* and *Sidur Ḳol Yaʿaḳov* (in *Netive Emunah u-Minut* [Ramat Gan, 1964], pp. 204–27). Acquaintances or admirers of Lifschitz brought these works to the Besht for his approval, and, after perusing several sections of each ("shenayim ṿe-shalosh delatot"; ibid., p. 205), he enthusiastically gave it. This is one fact. A second fact is that Lifschitz and the ascetically inclined Maggid flourished in Mezhirech contemporaneously. A third fact is that Lifschitz was influenced by R. Ḥayyim Lifschitz, who was apparently his older brother and mentor, and who quotes Nathan of Gaza in his works (pp. 206–208). This apparently moved Tishby painstakingly to scrutinize these two works of R. Jacob Koppel for Sabbatian influences (p. 208), a process that yielded the fourth and final fact: They do indeed contain Sabbatian kabbalah (which, however, is not necessarily identical with Sabbatian messianic and antinomistic beliefs, as Tishby realizes) (p. 215). Moreover, if interpreted as Tishby chooses to interpret them, certain passages may yield indications that Lifschitz secretly harbored Sabbatian messianic and antimonistic beliefs (p. 215). Let us grant, for the sake of argument, that this purely speculative point has been established as another fact.

Here the facts end, and the tendentious guesswork begins. Surely, argues Tishby, the Besht knew, as some of his contemporaries allegedly knew, that Lifschitz was a Sabbatian. True, the works the Besht saw contain anti-Sabbatian diatribes, but why would he be fooled by such transparent ruses if certain unnamed and unknown contemporaries allegedly knew better (p. 225)? True, Lifschitz managed to fool two centuries of scholars as well, and not until Tishby trained an Emden-like Sabbatian searchlight on his works was he finally "exposed" (p. 215); but after all, the Besht was a *contemporary* who passed through Mezhirech from time to time; surely *he* knew. And yet he literally embraced Lifschitz's works. True, he had given them only a brief, cursory perusal and obviously could not possibly have detected what apparently required weeks of careful, single-minded study on Tishby's part. But he *did* embrace them and he *must* have known; ergo, the Besht was ideologically a Sabbatian (of sorts; see p. 226).

Tishby sees striking parallels between Lifschitz and R. Jonathan Eybeschutz (pp. 220–23) but fails to take his line of reasoning to its logical conclusion. If the Besht was a kind of Sabbatian because he was Lifschitz's contemporary, lived nearby, and esteemed his works, then so were the hundreds or thousands who heard and admired Eybeschutz's sermons and teachings, both before and after R. Jacob Emden's campaign (see G. Scholem, *Kabbalah* [New York, 1974], pp. 405–407). We may therefore conclude that large parts of the Jewish communities of Prague, Altona, Hamburg, and Wandsbek were crypto-Sabbatians, as were all the rabbis of Poland and Moravia who supported Eybeschutz against Emden. Indeed, if appreciating the teachings or works of an alleged—or later-to-be-exposed—Sabbatian makes one a Sabbatian, who knows how many Sabbatians continue to lurk among us today?

But Tishby is not satisfied with Sabbatianizing the Besht only. Surely, he reasons, the men who brought Lifschitz's works to the Besht were ideologically aligned with both Sabbatianism, through Lifschitz, and the new Hasidism, through the Besht. Therefore, the early Hasidim of Mezhirech included Sabbatians (pp. 225–26). That Lifschitz's alleged Sabbatianism was known to his friends or admirers and that they were therefore also Sabbatians is simply taken for granted.

And then there is the Maggid, who not only shared certain ascetic practices with certain Sabbatian groups (as well as with non-Sabbatian pietists; see Dinur, cited by Tishby, n. 178) but actually lived in Mezhirech while Lifschitz was active there (ibid., p. 226). Is it not probable, asks Tishby, that he was a member of Lifschitz's crypto-Sabbatian circle (i.e., the circle Tishby claims existed on the basis of his interpretation of certain passages in Lifschitz's works)?

This assumption is in marked contrast to Scholem's asseveration that "by no stretch of the imagination can the Maggid be considered a partisan of Sabbatianism" (*The Messianic Idea,* p. 197). Using Tishby's reasoning, future historians may someday conclude that all the adult orthodox Jews of Jerusalem in the year 1980 were members of Neturei Karta. Indeed, this theory would have the distinct advantage of referring to a sect definitely known to have existed in Jerusalem that year. Clearly the evidence and logic of this article can be considered compelling only after one has determined a priori that an ideological link existed between Sabbatianism and early Hasidism.

The Besht's positive appraisal of *Sefer ha-Tsoref* (Scholem, *Major Trends,* pp. 331–33) is even less significant than his approval of Lifschitz's works. Its author, R. Heschel, flourished in distant Vilna and Krakow, and the Besht need not have come into contact with anyone who knew him personally. See also A. Rubinstein in *Tarbiz* 48 (1978–1979): 156–58, who refutes Scholem's attempt to link R. Heschel with R. Adam Baʿal Shem; and infra, Excursus F.

A broader, more balanced, and more reasonable approach to the question of early Hasidism's relation to Sabbatianism has also been advocated (and demonstrated) by Abraham Rubinstein, "Ben Ḥasidut le-Shabtaʾut" in *Peraḳim be-Torat ha-Ḥasidut,* ed. A. Rubinstein (Jerusalem, 1978), pp. 182–97. This article, which I came across after I had written this note, makes some of the same points in a different way; see pp. 182–88. See also M. Piekarz, *Bi-Yeme Tsemiḥat ha-Ḥasidut,* pp. 299–302.

Excursus F

Scholem considers it "a fact of great importance that, between the new Hasidim and the old to whom Rabbi Heschel Zoref belonged, there was a link, if only an unconscious one" (*Major Trends,* p. 333). This may be important for psychohistorians, but it is hardly important for an understanding of what the Besht's teachings meant to the conscious minds of his disciples and followers.

Elsewhere Scholem writes: "The comparison current in Sabbatian literature between the Messiah and the red heifer that 'purifies the defiled and defiles the pure' is transferred by the Rabbi of Polnoye and his pupil Gedalya of Linietz to the Hasidic Zaddik. It is quite unthinkable that such a statement could have been made by any Jewish moralist and it clearly shows the impact of Sabbatian thinking" (*The Messianic Idea,* pp. 197–98). The homily Scholem cites from *Toldot Yaʿaḳov Yosef* to support his assertion does not, in fact, contain such a comparison. It deals with the ethical problem of establishing a balance between self-importance and humility, and is explicitly applied not only to the Zaddik but to all men (145b). Only the elite, however, can understand the solution, just as only Moses was able to fathom the reason for the commandment of the red heifer (145c).

This is not to say that Sabbatian-like teachings are completely absent from *Toldot* (see the discussion on pp. 33–35 on the fall of the Zaddik), but I doubt whether this is one of them. In any case, we must remember that the teachings of R. Jacob Joseph are not always identical with the teachings of the Besht. On the general question of Sabbatian influence, see now M. Piekarz's very plausible analysis in *Bi-Yeme,* pp. 299–302, and A. Rubinstein, "Ben Ḥasidut le-Shabtaʾut," pp. 188–97.

Excursus G

See Schatz's quotations, pp. 45–46, which she misinterprets to mean that the Maggid advocated "indifference to the result of the religious act" (p. 45). In fact, "she-lo ye-ʿayen be-ʿavodato" (ibid., n. 12) means: Avoid extreme religious self-consciousness, a state of mind fostered by many ethical works. And **שאין מתחשב אם המלך אוהב אותו כדי שיאהבנו, אלא מתחשב גדולתו כדי שיבוש ממנו** (ibid., n. 13) actually urges a form of selfless worship. The results of one's religious acts remain as important as ever; what is depreciated is contemplating these results for self-serving (although spiritual) purposes. Similarly, the quotation from *Tsavaʾat ha-Ribash* (p. 46, n. 17), particularly when compared with its variants (see Schochet's edition, no. 75, p. 24), clearly urges not indifference to the result of one's prayers but a total contemplative immersion in the words to the exclusion of any conscious thought concerning their supernal effects.

This misinterpretation leads to the more serious error of concluding that the Maggid (and/or his disciples) completely opposed remorse for sin and actually considered remorse to be a major sin itself (p. 49)—an astounding claim for which no evidence is adduced. Vague references to the teachings of R. Isaac of Radvil (p. 49, n. 32) prove nothing about the Maggid or about the meaning of these teachings themselves. The citation from a manuscript of R. Ḥayyim Haykil of Amdur (p. 50, n. 34) again proves nothing about the Maggid and in any case simply exhorts us not to *overdo* the depression that accompanies remorse (and this was undoubtedly R. Isaac's intention as well). The citation from *Tsava'at ha-Ribash,* Schatz's major proof-text (p. 49), is seriously misinterpreted. The clause **וגם אם הוא באמת קצת חטא** refers not to remorse but to the minor infraction in question. The Maggid here warns against exaggerated preoccupation with one's remorse and guilt over a minor sin. This depressed, negative state of mind, he explains, is counterproductive, as it impedes further spiritual progress and growth: **ומכח זה יבוטל בעצבותו מעבודת הבורא.**

No other proof-texts are presented—and with good reason. For neither the Maggid nor his disciples tried to negate the entire weight of Jewish ethical tradition, beginning with the Bible itself and stretching through the Talmud, Midrash, codes, and ethical works of every variety, that sees remorse as an integral and indispensible part of teshuvah.

Excursus H

ההבחנה היסודית של הקורא במקורות אלה בהכרח שתיעשה גם על ידי שיקול דעת סטאטיסטי, ובעיקר על פי האינטואיציה הנרכשת עם קריאה במקורות אלה. דרך זו עומדת במבחן האוביקטיביות באותה מידה שעומדת כל דרך בעלת קריטיריונים לתיאור תופעות דתיות ומגמותיהן.

I fail to see how the intuition acquired by reading one of a thinker's many works—Schatz's presentation is based almost exclusively on *Tanya*—can be considered a valid criterion for assessing his religious posture; or what statistics has to do with understanding his thought; or how intuition can be termed objective.

Following is a summary of the major errors in Schatz's article. All of these points will be dealt with (in more detail) in the course of this study. References in parentheses following a point are to passages in *Tanya* to the contrary. Only Part 1 or 2 of *Tanya* will be cited, since these are the only parts Professor Schatz uses. Schatz avers that

1. (Pp. 517–18) RSZ denied the ontological reality of the sefirot and transformed them into Maimonidean attributes (51b–52b, 73a–74a).

2. (Pp. 520, 527) RSZ does not mention such Lurianic motifs as Shevirat ha-Kelim and the raising of the sparks. Even if this refers to Part 1 of *Tanya* only, the claim is false (11a–12b, 13b [end of ch. 8], 30a, 48b).

3. (P. 520) According to RSZ's pantheistic views, man need not contend with the physical world in order to redeem it (10b, 39b–42b, 46b–49a).

4. (Pp. 520, 528) The transcendent world of the kabbalists and the Maggid has no religious significance for RSZ. Man must concentrate only on drawing nearer to God's immanent presence in *this* world (p. 55a, note; chs. 47, 50).

5. (P. 522) RSZ transferred the concept of evil from the metaphysical to the psychological realm. He completely removed its demonic aspect (11a [end of ch. 6]; 27b, 47b, and esp. 29b–30a where RSZ contrasts the psychological siṭra aḥra with its metaphysical source).

6. (P. 522) RSZ does not see thought as spiritualizing action but only as a separate sphere of religious endeavor (53a–56a).

7. (P. 523) The context of *Tanya,* 33b–34a, concerning undesirable thoughts is: "during Service."

8. (P. 525) A man who is by nature less susceptible to sinful behavior has a simpler and less strenuous form of Service demanded of him (ch. 30).

9. (P. 525) It is unnecessary to exert oneself in search of a spiritual meaning in the Torah, to go beyond the peshat (see this volume, Chapter 4).

10. (P. 526) The Benoni need not strive for a level of spirituality or deveḳut beyond that which he attains through the fulfillment of the commandments without ulterior motives. Schatz cites 53b to prove her point. In fact, 8a, 53a–b, and 56a prove the opposite. The conscious arousal of Love (the desire for deveḳut [8a]) and Fear are prerequisites for even the lowest level of acceptable fulfillment of the commandments.

11. (P. 526, n. 63) RSZ's ideology is completely congruent with that of R. Ḥayyim Volozhin. In fact, there is a crucial difference between them regarding the axiological hierarchy of Torah-study and other commandments (see this volume, Chapter 4).

12. (P. 527) The passage Schatz cites to prove that RSZ is opposed to the striving for deveḳut (57a) actually only indicates that for RSZ, Fear is a more basic requirement for Service than Love. This is clear from both its wording and its context.

See also Moshe Hallamish's critique in his unpublished thesis, "Mishnato ha-ʿIyunit shel R. Shneur Zalman mi-Liadi" (Hebrew University, 1975), p. 253f, 371f (this work is discussed below). Rachel Paloge-Elior, in a thesis written under Professor Schatz, not surprisingly accepts and repeats Schatz's conclusions: see "Torat ha-Elohut ve-ʿAvodat Ha-Shem be-Dor he-Sheni shel Ḥasidut Ḥabad" (Hebrew University, 1976), pp. 132–33, 144, 195, 217, 267, 316, 320, 333. It should also be noted that in addition to many individual misinterpretations of Hasidic texts in Schatz's *Ha-Ḥasidut ke-Misṭiḳah* (see, e.g., Excursus G), all of her Chapter 9 ignores the interrelationship between the metaphysical and psychological realms traditionally based on the verse: "And from my flesh shall I behold God" (Job 19:26); see this volume, Chapter 1, n. 377. This connection was so well known that it did not have to be repeated every time one realm was treated without reference to the other. There is thus no validity to inferences (echoing R. David of Makov; see Wilensky, II, 164, 244) that certain key kabbalistic concepts originally located in the metaphysical realm (e.g., tsimtsum) were completely removed from this realm and transferred to the other (*Ha-Ḥasidut,* pp. 123–25; *Molad,* p. 518). Statements such as **אלהים שבוי בחוקיות של המחשבה האונטית במובן זה, שאם האדם אינו חושב — אין לחשיבה האלהית כל משמעות ... האלהות אינה „חושבת" כדמות פרסונאלית בעלת מחשבות משלה** (*Ha-Ḥasidut,* p. 123) illustrate the extremes to which this misconception may be carried. To teach, as the Maggid did, that God's thought is affected by man's (ibid., p. 124) is a far cry from denying that God's thought has a supremely significant independent reality completely transcending human thought.

That man's thoughts and actions affect God is an aggadic and kabbalistic commonplace (see A. J. Heschel, *Torah min ha-Shamayim* [London and New York, 1962], vol. 1, pp. 65–90, 232–36; I. Tishby, *Mishnat ha-Zohar* [Jerusalem, 1961], vol. 2, p. 10), which the Besht and Maggid emphasized and expanded. Together with the *homo imago Dei* motif and the idea that God dwells in every Jew (see Chapter 1, n. 377), it provides the necessary backdrop for a proper understanding and accurate assessment of the Maggidic teachings that Schatz finds so radical because she misinterprets them so radically.

An equally untenable summary of RSZ's philosophy is presented by Jacob Agus in "Torat Ḥabad," *Sefer ha-Shanah li-Yehude Amerikah* 10–11 (1959): 352–410. The overall quality of this article may be gauged by comparing Agus's following statement with two relevant passages from *Tanya* (out of many which could be cited): **מושג הצמצום [של ר' שניאור זלמן] כולל את הרעיון שאין חוקי התורה כמו שהם רצונו של הקב"ה, שכן רצונו וחכמתו של הקב"ה קבועים במקום ש„אין מחשבה תפיסא ביה" כלל ... אלא שיש איזה יחס של הקבלה בין מצוות התורה ורצונו האמיתי של הקב"ה** (Agus, p. 380).

רצון העליון הוא הוא הדבר הלכה שמהרהר ומדבר בה, שכל ההלכות הן פרטי המשכות פנימיות רצון עליון עצמו (*Tanya,* 28b).

אף דהקב"ה נקרא אין סוף ולגדולתו אין חקר ולית מחשבה תפיסא ביה כלל, וכן ברצונו וחכמתו כדכתיב אין חקר לתבונתו ... הנה על זה אמרו במקום שאתה מוצא גדולתו שם אתה מוצא ענותנותו, וצמצם הקב"ה רצונו וחכמתו בתרי"ג מצוות התורה ובהלכותיהן ובצירופי אותיות תנ"ך ודרשותיהן שבאגדות ומדרשי חכמינו ז"ל בכדי שכל הנשמה או רוח ונפש שבגוף תוכל להשיגן בדעתן ולקיימן ... וכדי שתהא כל מחשבה תפיסא בהן. ואפילו בחינת דבור ומעשה שלמטה ממדריגת מחשבה תפיסא בהן (*Tanya,* 8b).

Excursus I

Several examples:

1. On p. 860, Cordovero's well-known colored-glass simile is reproduced, although RSZ, in his many references to the orot-kelim problem, rarely uses it (v. *Likuṭe Torah,* II, 28c; *M* 5562, II, 441) and certainly does not emphasize it.

2. The essential elements of Schochet's explanation of Shevirat ha-Kelim (pp. 867–69) are either never mentioned or never emphasized by RSZ.

3. The imagery Schochet quotes (p. 855) from Cordovero to distinguish the four supernal worlds is controverted by RSZ (*Likuṭe Torah,* II, 46b–d).

4. In the chapter on tsimtsum, Schochet (and similarly Hallamish, p. 96) confuses RSZ's discussions of the original tsimtsum with discussions of the subsequent concealments; so that, although RSZ's works are quoted with rare frequency, his teachings on the subject are misstated.

5. The reason for creation cited on p. 827—God's need to actualize His creative potencies—is rarely or never mentioned, let alone emphasized, by RSZ.

Excursus J

The existing ones—by Heilman, Teitelbaum, Glitzenstein, and Mindel—are neither, and the first two contain quite a few inaccuracies. H. M. Heilman's *Bet Rebi* (Berditchev, 1903) also contains much valuable material in the form of traditions orally transmitted by "one of his [RSZ's] grandsons" but generally falls somewhere between biography and hagiography (see infra). Teitelbaum in Volume 1 of *Ha-Rav mi-Liadi* makes up for paucity of sources by relying on hearsay and speculation. A. H. Glitzenstein's *Sefer ha-Toldot: Rabi Shneur Zalman mi-Liadi* (New York, 1975) is an unsynthesized, incomplete, and incompletely documented anthology of various Ḥabad sources, including *Bet Rebi.* N. Mindel's *Rabbi Schneur Zalman of Liadi* (New York, 1969), is clearly written, contains useful translations of important sources, and a few items from unpublished manuscripts and sources not used by his predecessors; but it leaves this desideratum unfulfilled.

Besides dating discrepancies and factual lacunae, a major gap in all the biographies is the period in Lyady—1801–1812. Glitzenstein, for example, in his four-hundred page volume devotes to it a three-page chapter; two pages consist of a letter by RSZ. The impression given is that, except for a fund-raising trip in 1810, RSZ spent the entire decade ministering to his disciples in Lyady. Yet the datelines of discourses transcribed by R. Pinḥas Reizes of Shklov and others indicate that he traveled extensively. For example, we find him in Shklov in the winter of 1804 (Rabbi Aharon Chitrik, editor of the recently published volumes of RSZ's discourses [see infra], has informed me that other manuscripts indicate that this should be emended to 1807); in Mogilev in the spring of 1807; traveling to an undisclosed destination (possibly Vitebsk; see J. I. Schneersohn, *Sefer he-Śiḥot 5701* [New York, 1964], p. 112) in 1809; in Vitebsk in the summer of 1811; in Dubrovna in the winter of 1812; in Shklov in the summer of that year; and in Minsk, apparently some time during this decade (*Ma'amre Admor ha-Zaḳen: Hanaḥot ha-Rap* [New York, 1958], pp. 1, 8, 13, 40, 55, 82, 121, 127, 135, 154, 160). What was the purpose of these trips? How long did they last? With whom did RSZ come into contact? What do they reveal about Mitnagdic opposition during this period? These and other questions await the attention of a competent historian.

The events of 1810 are the subject of a study by Yehoshua Mondshein, *Biṭa'on Ḥabad* 13 (Kislev, 1971): 10–20. The presently inaccessible private library of R. Joseph Isaac Schneersohn apparently contains, among other invaluable manuscripts, a journal of RSZ's communal activities and travels (J. I. Schneersohn, *Sefer ha-Śiḥot* [New York, 1967], p. 29).

Excursus K

A lengthy book review would be required to treat these in detail. Some examples follow. Points not immediately refuted, and some that are, are explicitly or implicitly dealt with in the course of this study.

Ch. 1, passim: Here, as throughout the thesis, Hallamish relies almost exclusively on *Bet Rebi* for his historical information. He completely ignores R. Joseph Isaac's traditions, yet cites R. Samuel Zalmanoff, one of the latter's devoted Hasidim, as a historical authority (p. 4).

P. 27: Hallamish tries to date all the discourses of the *Sidur* between 1799 and 1803. His method is untenable and his conclusion invalid. For example, the discourses printed in the *Sidur,* pp. 3c, 5a, 23c, 26c, 88c, 137c, 235c, 250d, 268a, 281a, 286c, 287b, 301a, 307c, 309a, were delivered in 1804 (see *M* 5564, pp. 347–54 and notes); *Sidur,* pp. 39c, 75d, 77b, 102a, 104a, 217a, 219d, 220b, 236c, 257a, 303a, 304c, were delivered in 1806 (see *M* 5566, pp. viii–xi). *Sidur,* pp. 128c, 173a, were delivered in 1807 (see *M* 5567, pp. ix–xi and notes).

P. 60: Hallamish maintains that for RSZ, there is no ethically neutral realm in the world. In fact, the realm of Ḳelipat Nogah, in which and with which all commandments are fulfilled, is ethically neutral.

P. 104: Hallamish claims that according to RSZ, man's actions do not cause supernal revelations but only remove the impediments to these revelations. See this volume, pp. 146, 154–55, 170–75.

P. 117, n. 70: Hallamish echoes Tishby in maintaining that RSZ practiced self-censorship to avoid mentioning Lurianic concepts in his written works.

P. 122: Hallamish reaches the conclusion that for RSZ, creation is voluntary—as if this were ever in question.

Pp. 136–38: Hallamish follows Schatz in claiming that for RSZ, evil has no metaphysical reality. See this volume, pp. 75–76.

P. 145: Hallamish mentions a central concept in RSZ's ontology—"What is higher descends lower"—without appreciating its significance and ramifications. See also p. 279. See this volume, pp. 74–77.

P. 191: Hallamish apparently attributes the Maggid's talking-bird metaphor to RSZ.

P. 193, n. 54: Hallamish concludes that the faculty of pleasure is "higher" for RSZ than for the Maggid. See supra, pp. 36, 41.

P. 198: Hallamish reasons that for RSZ, divine Will (*Ratson ʿElyon*) is not suprarational because in one passage, Will (*Ratson Taḥton*) is identified with knowledge (Daʿat), and in another passage Ratson Taḥton is said to be a manifestation of Ratson ʿElyon; therefore Ratson ʿElyon must also be identified with the rational faculty of Daʿat. Using such Euclidean logic on the discourses, one can "prove" that every divine faculty is identical with every other divine faculty, a conclusion that, while ultimately valid, undermines the entire enterprise of kabbalistic dialectics. Moreover, a number of discourses clearly suggest that divine Will transcends divine Reason. See this volume, p. 170.

For a similar oversimplification of sefirotic relations, see p. 213 on the relation of sight, Ḥokhmah, to hearing, Binah.

P. 205: Hallamish incorrectly maintains that Chapter 33 of *Tanya* vitiates RSZ's original typology of Tsadiḳ-Benoni-Rasha.

P. 210: Hallamish maintains that RSZ's sefirotic investigations are intended only to lay the groundwork for his psychological teachings. In fact, many discourses, particularly those explaining Zoharic passages, contain little or no psychological material. Like all kabbalists, RSZ considered these investigations intrinsically valuable and part of the mitzvah of talmud Torah. See this volume, pp. 163–68.

P. 216: Hallamish discusses the introduction to *Tanya* without mentioning RSZ's crucial statement that it was written as a book of "responsa to many questions that all our faithful in our country have constantly asked, seeking advice, each according to his station, so as to receive moral guidance in the service of God; for time no longer permits replying to everyone individually and in detail on his particular problem. I have therefore recorded all the replies to all the questions, to be preserved as a sign ["le-mishmeret le-ʾot" (Numbers, 17:25)] and to serve as a visual reminder for each and every person, so that he will no longer press for admission to speak with me in private. For in these [responsa] he will find peace for his soul and true counsel on every matter that he finds difficult in the Service of God."

In other words, *Tanya* is essentially a book of practical religio-ethical advice and therefore contains only enough kabbalistic metaphysics to explain the basis for RSZ's approach to each problem. Thus, regarding the doctrine of tsimtsum, for example, RSZ quite properly observes: "As for the intricate details of the tsimtsumim—this is not the place for their explanation. But in general they are . . ." (*Tanya,* 67b). Yet in chapter after chapter of Parts 2 and 3 of his thesis (e.g., p. 179), Hallamish reiterates what he clearly considers to be a highly significant finding: Technical kabbalistic explanations and refinements of RSZ's ideology do not appear in *Tanya*.

P. 219: Hallamish interprets "*ʿiyun Torah*" in *Tanya* (98a) as referring to the study of kabbalah. This is unfounded.

P. 222: Hallamish generalizes about the role of intellect according to "the discourses of the *Sidur,*" as if this were a monolithic category.

P. 224: Hallamish distinguishes between man's "social traits," which he says derive from the animal soul, and religious traits, which derive from the divine soul. RSZ makes no such distinction.

Pp. 247–48: Hallamish claims that RSZ departed from the Maggid in valuing self-imposed *ḥumrot* (stringencies). The proof-text he cites, *LT,* III, 85a, actually refers to ḥumrot imposed by halakhic and aggadic texts, which the Maggid, no less than RSZ, accepted as authoritative. See now *MK,* 87–88, 93.

P. 250: Hallamish incorrectly claims that RSZ does not see deveḳut as a separate spiritual state but only as a concomitant of talmud Torah. See this volume, pp. 140 and 147, and Ch. 5.

Pp. 257–58: Hallamish speculates on the ideological basis for RSZ's emphasis on Torah-study sessions immediately following the morning prayers. In fact, this emphasis is based wholly on explicit statements to that effect in the Talmud (*Berakhot,* 64a), *Ṭur,* and *Shulḥan ʿArukh* (*Oraḥ Ḥayyim,* 155; see also RSZ's *Shulḥan ʿArukh*).

P. 263: Hallamish incorrectly claims that RSZ considered the positive commandments more important than the negative. See this volume, p. 175.

P. 284: Hallamish is given to such egregious understatements as: **התפלה נתפסת כאחת נקודות השיא בעבודת ה׳.**

P. 299: Hallamish incorrectly maintains that RSZ transformed Lurianic kavanah into meditation on the inner meaning of the words. See this volume, pp. 188–91.

P. 302: Hallamish engages in untenable speculations regarding the differences between *Tanya* and the discourses.

P. 307: Hallamish maintains that RSZ mentions biṭaḥon rarely because trust is a passive quality and RSZ is an "activist." In fact, as we shall see, RSZ does not stress biṭaḥon because it is not completely compatible with the still more passive quality of self-nullification. See this volume, p. 131.

P. 311: Hallamish incorrectly maintains that RSZ does not demand greater devotion to the Zaddik-scholar than was demanded by the rabbis of the Talmud; cf. *Tanya,* 146a–147a.

P. 395: Hallamish cites the list of RSZ's books in Hilman, *Igerot,* p. 148, as proof that RSZ had only second-hand knowledge of early kabbalists. However, this list represents only a fraction of the works RSZ studied.

Another methodological flaw worth mentioning is Hallamish's principle of organization. His several dozen chapter headings serve to separate ideas that RSZ saw as organically interconnected.

Notes

Primary sources for the Hasidism of R. Shneur Zalman are as follows (With two exceptions, all of these volumes were published by Kehot Publication Society. Subsequent editions of some of these, and of some of the Kehot publications cited in the notes, have appeared since this study was completed):

Beʾure ha-Zohar. New York, 1955.
Boneh Yerushalayim. Jerusalem, 1926.
Likuṭe Torah. New York, 1965.
Maʾamre Admor ha-Zaken:

Hanahot ha-Rap. New York, 1958.
Ethalekh-Lyozna. New York, 1958.
5562. New York, 1964.
5568. New York, 1964.
5566. New York, 1979.
5567. New York, 1979.
5564. New York, 1980.
5565, I and II. New York, 1981.
5569. New York, 1981.
5563, I. New York, 1981.
5570. New York, 1981.
ha-Ketsarim. New York, 1981.
5562, II. New York, 1981.
5563, II. New York, 1982.
5568, II. New York, 1982.
ʿal Parshiot ha-Torah veha-Moʿadim, I. New York, 1982.
ʿal Parshiot ha-Torah veha-Moʿadim, II. New York, 1983.
ʿInyanim. New York, 1983.
ʿal Maʾamre Razal—Shas, Zohar, Tefilah. New York, 1984.
Neviʾim. New York, 1984.

Ketuvim, I and II. New York, 1985.
Seder Tefilot mi-kal ha-Shanah ʿal pi Nusaḥ ha-Arizal. New York, 1965.
Shene ha-Meʾorot. Lvov, 1846.
Shulḥan ʿArukh [of RSZ]. New York, 1960.
Tanya, comprising: (1) *Sefer Liḳuṭe Amarim,* Part 1: *Sefer shel Benonim;* (2) *Sefer Liḳuṭe Amarim,* Part 2: *Shaʿar ha-Yiḥud veha-Emunah;* (3) *Igeret ha-Teshuvah;* (4) *Igerot ha-Ḳodesh;* (5) *Ḳunṭres Aḥaron.* Soncino Press edition, London, 1973.
Torah Or. New York, 1975.

Abbreviations used in the notes for these and other works are:

AJS Review.	*Association for Jewish Studies Review*
BY.	*Boneh Yerushalayim*
BZ.	*Beʾure ha-Zohar*
EJ.	*Encyclopaedia Judaica*
EL.	*Ethalekh-Lyozna*
HTT.	*Shulḥan ʿArukh, Hilkhot Talmud Torah*
JJS.	*Journal of Jewish Studies*
LD.	*Liḳuṭe Diburim*
LT.	*Liḳuṭe Torah*
M.	*Sefer ha-Maʾamarim* (followed by the year)
M Iny.	*Sefer ha-Maʾamarim—ʿInyanim*
M Ket.	*Sefer ha-Maʾamarim—Ketuvim*
M Nev.	*Sefer ha-Maʾamarim—Neviʾim*
M. Par.	*Sefer ha-Maʾamarim ʿal Parshiot . . .*
M Raz.	*Sefer ha-Maʾamarim ʿal Maʾamre Razal*
MK.	*Maʾamre Admor ha-Zaḳen ha-Ḳetsarim*
RP.	*Hanaḥot ha-Rap*
PAAJR.	*Proceedings of the American Academy for Jewish Research*
S.	*Sefer ha-Śiḥot* (followed by the year)
Sidur	*Seder Tefilot mi-kal ha-Shanah . . .*
Tal. B.	*Talmud Bavli* (Babylonian Talmud)
Tal. Y.	*Talmud Yerushalmi* (Palestinian Talmud)
TO.	*Torah Or*

A brief remark on pagination may help the reader: *BZ, LT,* the *Sidur,* and *TO* have four columns on each folio, denoted a–d. *LT* is divided into five parts, each with its own pagination: I, Exodus; II, Leviticus; III, Numbers; IV, Deuteronomy; V, Song of Songs. Thus, the notation below of *LT,* II, 24b guides the reader to *Liḳuṭe Torah,* Part II (Leviticus), p. 24 (Hebrew folio numbers), col. b (i.e., the second column on p. 24).

Chapter 1. Teachers and Teachings

1. See RSZ's letters in *Igerot Ḳodesh,* ed. S. D. Levin (New York, 1980), pp. 48, 66, 89, 99, 113–14, 124, 141; *Igerot Baʿal ha-Tanya u-Bene Doro,* ed. D. Z. Hilman (Jeru-

salem, 1953), pp. 76, 114–15, 174; Kehot edition of *Keter Shem Ṭov* (New York, 1982), Appendix, nos. 29, 97, 138 n. 145, 140, 169, 177, 225, 231, 253; Rabbi M. Schneerson, *Ha-Yom Yom,* 4th ed. (New York, 1961), pp. 57, 113; Nissan Mindel, *R. Schneur Zalman of Liadi* (New York, 1971), pp. 39, 70, 98–101; Kehot edition of *Magid Devarav le-Yaʿaḳov,* and *Or Torah* (New York, 1972), Appendix, nos. 76, 90, 92, 93b, 97.

2. See, e.g., his assessment of the ideological conflict between the Gaon of Vilna and the Besht. The former, says Dubnow, emphasized action; the latter, kavanah. Both were religious extremists. S. Dubnow, *Toldot ha-Ḥasidut* (Tel Aviv, 1944), p. 109. See also Z. Gries's apt comment, "Sifrut ha-Hanhagot ha-Ḥasidit me-ha-Meḥtsah ha-Sheniyah le-Meʾah ha-18 ve-ad li-Shenot ha-Sheloshim le-Meʾah ha-19," *Zion* 46 (1981): 233 n. 164.

3. See Robert M. Seltzer, "Coming Home: The Personal Basis of Simon Dubnow's Ideology," *AJS Review* 1 (1976): 285, 294–301.

4. Dubnow, *Toldot,* p. 21.

5. B. Z. Dinur, *Be-Mifneh ha-Dorot* (Jerusalem, 1955), pp. 83–227. Dinur's study, in turn, formed the basis for Joseph Weiss's approach to the subject. See infra, p. 12 and notes, 43.

6. Dubnow, *Toldot,* pp. 22–36. Dubnow's explanation continues to influence the study of Hasidism. See, e.g., Samuel Dresner, "Hasidism and Its Opponents," in *Great Schisms in Jewish History,* ed. Raphael Joseph and Stanley M. Wagner (University of Denver, 1981), pp. 124–30, where it is faithfully repeated.

7. Particularly in Spain; see Y. Baer, *A History of the Jews in Christian Spain* (Philadelphia, 1971), I, pp. 263–66, II, pp. 40–71. On sixteenth–seventeenth-century Poland, see H. H. Ben Sasson, *Hagut ve-Hanhagah* (Jerusalem, 1959), ch. 7, ch. 12, pp. 202–17, and ch. 13, esp. pp. 239–40, on the Lvov incident of 1576.

8. See Ben Sasson, *Hagut,* p. 3.

9. Jacob Katz, *Masoret u-Mashber* (Jerusalem, 1958); published in English translation as *Tradition and Crisis* (New York, 1961), p. 229. Katz also observes that Polish communal organization was more similar to Sephardi than to Ashkenazi prototypes (*Masoret,* p. 100); hence my selection of Spain as analogue supra, n. 7.

10. Katz, pp. 267, 105–106 n. 27, 110 n. 43.

11. See Ben Sasson, *Hagut,* pp. 158–59, 229–31.

12. Jacob Emden, *Megilat Sefer,* ed. D. Cahana (Warsaw, 1896), p. 125.

13. See M. Piekarz, *Bi-Yeme Tsemiḥat ha-Ḥasidut* (Jerusalem, 1978), pp. 98–104; J. Dan, *Sifrut ha-Musar veha-Derush* (Jerusalem, 1975), p. 230; Ḥayyim Dov Friedberg, *Toldot ha-Defus be-Polanyah,* 2d ed. (Tel Aviv, 1950); Z. Gries, "Sifrut ha-Hanhagot ha-Ḥasidit ke-Bitui le-Hanhagah ve-Etos" (thesis, Hebrew University, 1979), p. 109; Elijah ha-Kohen, *Shevet Musar* (Jerusalem, 1962 or 1963), ch. 29; R. Alexander Süsskind, *Yesod ve-Shoresh ha-ʿAvodah* (Makhon Hari Fishel, Jerusalem, 1958 or 1959), Introduction.

14. See Dan, *Sifrut ha-Musar,* p. 230; and J. Dan, "Goralah ha-Hisṭori shel Torat ha-Sod shel Ḥaside Ashkenaz," in *Studies in Mysticism and Religion Presented to G. G. Scholem,* ed. E. E. Urbach (Jerusalem, 1967), p. 99.

15. *Sefer Ḥasidim,* passim; *Sefer Roḳeʾaḥ Hilkhoth Ḥasidut;* J. Dan, *Torat ha-Sod shel Ḥasidut Ashkenaz* (Jerusalem, 1968), p. 232f.; Dan, *Sifrut ha-Musar,* pp. 98–99; H.

Soloveitchik, "Three Themes in the *Sefer Ḥasidim*," *AJS Review* 1 (1976): 311–25. Soloveitchik's masterful analysis of the postures and values of Ḥaside Ashkenaz in this article (pp. 311–57) completely supersedes previous studies by Y. Baer and G. Scholem.

16. On which see G. Scholem, "Ha-Tenuah ha-Shabta'it be-Polin," in *Bet Yiśra'el be-Polin,* ed. I. Heilperin (Jerusalem, 1954), II, pp. 36–76.

17. As Katz has shown in *Masoret u-Mashber* (Tradition and Crisis). S. Ettinger's critique of this point in his review, in *Ḳiryat Sefer* 35 (1959): 13–18, is unfounded.

18. J. Sarachek, *Faith and Reason* (New York, 1935); D. J. Silver, *Maimonidean Criticism and the Maimonidean Controversy: 1180–1240* (Leiden, 1965); A. S. Halkin, "Yediah Bedersi's Apology," in *Jewish Medieval and Renaissance Studies,* ed. A. Altmann (Cambridge, Mass., 1967), p. 175f.; *Encyclopaedia Judaica* (hereafter *EJ*), vol. 11 (1972), col. 753; *EJ Yearbook,* 1973, col. 125; Herbert A. Davidson, "The Study of Philosophy as a Religious Obligation," in *Religion in a Religious Age,* ed. S. D. Goitein (Cambridge, Mass., 1974), pp. 53–69; *Encyclopedia Talmudit,* vol. 15, col. 55–80. For the pre-Maimonidean period, cf. particularly the versions of R. Hai's responsum in *Teshuvat Ribash* (Isaac b. Sheshet), no. 45, and *Kitve ha-Ramban,* ed. H. D. Chavel (Jerusalem, 1963), I, p. 350.

19. Baer, *Jews in Christian Spain,* II, pp. 253–59.

20. See the letters published by A. Marx, *Studies in Jewish History and Booklore* (New York, 1944), p. 87f.

21. Isaiah Horowitz, *Shene Luḥot ha-Berit* (Jerusalem, 1960), II, p. 92ff.; Joel Sirkes, *She'elot u-Teshuvot ha-Baḥ ha-Yeshanot* (New York, 1966), no. 4.

22. Ben Sasson, *Hagut,* pp. 13–16, 35–37; on Maharal, see A. F. Kleinberger, *Ha-Maḥshavah ha-Pedagogit shel ha-Maharal mi-Prague* (Jerusalem, 1962), p. 80f.; on Yaffe, see Lawrence Kaplan's unpublished dissertation (Harvard, 1975), "Rationalism and Rabbinic Culture in Sixteenth-Century Eastern Europe: Rabbi Mordecai Jaffe's *Levush Pinat Yikrat*"; on Gans, see M. Breuer, "Ḳayim li-Demuto shel Tsemaḥ David le-R. David Gans," *Bar Ilan* II (1973): 97–118; see also ibid., pp. 97–98 on Isserles, and p. 103 on the close ties between Prague and Cracow (and Venice). On Delmedigo, see Isaac Barzilay, *Yosef Shlomo Delmedigo (Yashar of Candia)* (Leiden, 1974).

On the flow of culture from Prague to Poland and Lithuania in the previous century, see Ephraim Kupfer, "Li-Demutah ha-Tarbutit shel Yahadut Ashkenaz ve-Ḥakhamehah be-Me'ot ha-14 ve-ha-15," *Tarbiz* 42 (1973): 130–32. On the social and economic ties between the Jews of Poland and the Jews of Germany, Austria, Bohemia, and the Netherlands, see Gershon Hundert, "An Advantage to Peculiarity? The Case of the Polish Commonwealth," *AJS Review* 6 (1981): 27–31.

23. *EJ,* XIII, col. 730; reprinted in H. H. Ben Sasson, *Trial and Achievement: Currents in Jewish History* (Jerusalem, 1974), p. 163. On Hasidism in Pinsk, see *EJ,* XIII, col. 541. On social and economic conditions in Lvov and Poland in general in 1718, see Emden, *Megilat Sefer,* pp. 63, 70. Note that Emden, who had lived in Germany, Holland, and Moravia, would have preferred to settle in Poland and did not do so only because his wife refused to leave her family in Moravia.

24. See his introduction to *Ma'aśeh Ṭuvyah* (Venice, 1707); *EJ,* V, col. 692.

25. See Barzilay, *Delmedigo,* p. 35 n. 2, David B. Ruderman, *Science, Medicine, and Jewish Culture in Early Modern Europe,* Spiegel Lectures in European Jewish History, no. 7, ed. Lloyd P. Gartner (Tel Aviv University, 1987), pp. 22–25.

26. Yeḥiel Heilprin, *Seder ha-Dorot* (Warsaw, 1878), p. 252; Barzilay, *Delmedigo,* pp. 84–85.

27. See his responsa, *Ḥavot Yaʾir* (Lvov, 1893), nos. 1, 9, 109, 124, 172, 210, 219.

28. *Pinḳas Vaʿad Arba Aratsot,* ed. I. Heilprin (Jerusalem, 1945), p. 466.

29. See Oppenheim, *Ḳehilat David* (Hamburg, 1786), pp. 140, 152, 170–72, 378–406 passim, 438–60, 496–512 passim, 562–72, 590–610, 646–62, 686–88.

30. Ibid., p. 390, no. 1119.

31. See his responsa, *Ḥakham Tsevi* (Amsterdam, 1712).

32. Emden, *Megilat Sefer,* pp. 11, 16–17. They apparently pursued their secular studies after yeshiva hours.

33. See *Yaʿarot Devash* (Lemberg, 1863), e.g., pp. 8d–9a, 16b, 22d–23a, 33c (from which it is evident that he knew the *Guide* well), 35b, 36a–37a, 47c; *Shem ʿOlam,* ed. A. S. Weismann (Vienna, 1891), esp. p. 41f. On his assessment of Mendelssohn, see his letter of 1761 in *Kerem Ḥemed,* III (1838), p. 224, praising him as an accomplished scholar of all the sciences, philosophy, logic, and rhetoric. According to G. Scholem, *Kabbalah* (New York, 1974), this letter provides "incontrovertible testimony to Eybeschutz's awareness of Mendelssohn's ideological approach" (p. 406).

34. S. Fuenn, *Ḳiryah Neʾemanah* (Vilna, 1915), p. 108f., p. 117, no. 55.

35. *EJ,* X, col. 187–88.

36. Fuenn, *Ḳiryah,* p. 124, no. 60.

37. *EJ,* XII, col. 1420.

38. See his *haskamah* to *Ḥavot Yaʾir.*

39. Emden, *Megilat Sefer,* p. 125. On other ties between Jewish communities in Europe, see ibid., pp. 107–109, 112–13.

40. Printed at the beginning and end of *Ḥavot Yaʾir.*

41. *EJ,* V, col. 692.

42. Ibid., VI, col. 1155–56, 1074 (reprinted in Scholem, *Kabbalah,* p. 405). See also Jacob Katz, *Out of the Ghetto* (New York, 1978), p. 22.

43. See Barzilay, *Delmedigo,* pp. 67, 309. The Italian scholar was R. Simone Luzatto of Venice. Delmedigo's observations regarding his correligionists' intellectual attainments, however, were far from objective. His general antipathy to Talmudists, his depreciation of the Talmud and Talmud-study (the focus of scholarship in Poland), and his admiration of Karaite scholars and scholarship render his assessments questionable. See ibid., pp. 305–13.

44. See Jacob Horowitz, *Yesh Noḥalin* (Jerusalem, 1965), p. 68. This work, completed in 1616, comprises the Testament of Jacob's father, R. Abraham, and the son's notes to it. Note that many, if not most, of R. Jacob's disagreements with his father regarding religious conduct are based on the kabbalistic values of Luria's school, which R. Jacob adopted.

45. See Scholem, *Kabbalah,* pp. 74–79, 425, 445–46; G. Scholem, *Sabbatai Ṣevi* (Princeton, 1973), pp. 68–80.

46. See R. Ḥayyim Vital's introduction to *Shaʿar ha-Haḳdamot* of *ʿEts Ḥayyim* (Warsaw, 1891), pp. 4c, 5b; Jacob Hayyim Tsemaḥ, *Nagid u-Metsaṿeh* (Jerusalem, 1965), "Introduction."

47. Levin, *Igerot Ḳodesh,* p. 89. *Igerot Ḳodesh* contains several letters and parts of letters from manuscripts that were not available to D. Z. Hilman when he compiled *Igerot Baʿal ha-Tanya,* as well as all of RSZ's letters found there, with useful notes by R. Shalom Dov Baer Levin. See also Hilman, ibid., p. 98 n. 10, citing R. Hayyim Volozhin's introduction to R. Elijah's commentary to *Sifra di-Tseniʿuta,* which bears out RSZ's understanding of R. Elijah's view.

48. See Emden's introduction to *Miṭpaḥat Sefarim.* According to Scholem, *Sabbatai Ṣevi,* "It was precisely the 'Lurianic' kabbalah stemming from (Israel) Sarug that fathered the kabbalistic doctrines of Sabbatian theology" (p. 210). I have dealt with these doctrines in an unpublished paper, "Nathan of Gaza as Sabbatian Ideologue."

49. Altmann, *Moses Mendelssohn* (University of Alabama Press, 1973), p. 11.

50. A. J. Heschel, "Le-Toldot R. Pinḥas mi-Ḳorets," in *ʿAle ʿAyin,* Schocken Jubilee Volume (Jerusalem, 1951), p. 215; Menaḥem Naḥum, *Meʾor ʿEnayim* (Jerusalem, 1968), p. 291: **כל שבע החכמות, חכמת הרפואה, ושארי חכמות . . . גם המה תורה, והתורה היא החיות שלהם**; *Ḥesed le-Avraham* (Warsaw, 1883), p. 34a: **בכל אומה יש מדריגות, כל אומה קרוב יותר לקדושה, ומי שקרוב יותר מכל אומה לקדושה מעלה כל המדות שלו לקדושה ומעלה כל האומה לקדושה, רק שאעפ״כ אינם משיגים רק נפש של הקדושה שיונקים ממנו**; Menaḥem Mendel, *Peri ha-Arets* (Lublin, 1928), p. 7: **והאמת היא כי הוא [הרמב״ם במורה נבוכים] הוציא מפיו קדוש דברים אמתיים ברומו של עולם אע״פ שלא כיון בהם**; *Or Torah,* 62b: **שלמה נתחכם מחמת שלמד מתחילה חכמות בני קדם והכיר יתרון אור החכמה עילאה מן החשך**. On R. Elijah of Vilna, see R. Israel of Shklov, *Peʾat ha-Shulḥan* (Safed, 1836), "Introduction"; B. Landau, *Ha-Gaʾon he-Ḥasid mi-Ṿilna* (Jerusalem, 1967), ch. 17; Y. Dienstag, "Ha-ʾim Hitnaged ha-Gra le-Mishnato ha-Filosofit shel ha-Rambam," *Talpiot* 4 (1949): 253–69; on RSZ, see H. Y. Bornstein's appendix to M. Teitelbaum, *Ha-Rav mi-Liadi u-Mifleget Ḥabad* (Warsaw, 1913), II.

I do not, of course, mean to suggest that these or any Hasidic masters encouraged their followers to study philosophy or the sciences. The "positive value" of these subjects was strictly limited to the spiritual elite, who could extract the benefits without endangering their faith and commitment. Membership in this elite was limited to the masters themselves and a few select disciples. Even great scholars were not necessarily safe from the potentially pernicious effects of these studies. RSZ, for example, felt that R. Elijah's theological objections to Hasidic teachings flowed from his rationalistic, philosophic approach to theology; Levin, *Igerot Ḳodesh,* p. 88 (all subsequent references are to this edition).

51. See Gries, "Sifrut ha-Hanhagot" (thesis), pp. 47 n. 8, 72, 75, on the understandable confusion in this area.

52. See infra regarding Joseph Weiss.

53. S. Dresner, *The Zaddik* (New York, 1960), p. 245.

54. See, e.g., *Toldot Yaʿaḳov Yosef* (Lvov, 1863), p. 194c, quoted by Dresner, *Zaddik,* p. 246: "I have written only 'headings of chapters' because I am afraid of revealing secrets and because of forgetfulness."

55. Joseph Weiss, for example, comments on the problem in "A Circle of Pneumatics in Pre-Hasidism," *JJS* 8 (1957): 208, but never allows it to influence his method. G. Scholem, *Major Trends in Jewish Mysticism* (New York, 1972), speaks misleadingly of "the writings of the Maggid" (p. 339). RSZ's observation is in *Igeret ha-Kodesh* (Part 4 of *Tanya*), XXV, p. 138b: **ולא ידעו לכוין הלשון על מתכונתו**; and 141a: **לא ידע המלקט לכוון הלשון בדקדוק כי הבעש״ט ז״ל היה אומר ד״ת בל״א ולא בלה״ק**. See also the introduction of R. Solomon ben Abraham of Lutzk to *Magid Devaraṿ le-Yaʿaḳov*, ed. R. Schatz (Jerusalem, 1976), p. 3: **פעם אחד שאל אדומ״ר זלה״ה [המגיד] למה אני כותב מה שאני שומע [ממנו], והשבתי לו כי ראיתי כותבי כתבים מקצרים מאד מכוונת אדומ״ר ולפעמים אינם מבינים וכותבים לפי הבנתם. ואמר לי אף על פי כן איך שיהיה נכתב הכל טוב, למען היות למזכרת לעבודת הבורא ב״ה**.

56. See J. Weiss, "Via Passiva in Early Hasidism," *JJS* II (1960): 149–53.

57. *Liḳuṭim Yeḳarim*, ed. A. I. Kahn (Jerusalem, 1974), no. 50: **כשאני מדבק מחשבתי בבורא יתברך אני מניח הפה לדבר מה שירצה**.

58. *Magid Devaraṿ le-Yaʿaḳov* (New York, 1972), appendix, p. 74: **מורי זלה״ה היה נוהג כשנפלה לו איזה השגה היה אומרה בפה, אף שלא יבינו השומעים כ״כ, שהיה מדברה כמו בפ״ע כו׳**. See also appendix to Kehot edition of *Keter Shem Ṭov*, p. 99, no. 219: **אז דער רבי פלעגט זאגען תורה איז דאס געווען א חידה**.

59. Cf. Gries, "Sifrut ha-Hanhagot" (thesis), pp. 79–81.

60. The homilies of the Besht's grandson, R. Moses Ḥayyim Ephraim of Sudylkow (*Degel Maḥneh Efrayim [1803]*) contain relatively few teachings he heard directly from the Besht. These are generally distinguished from secondhand teachings and may therefore be considered fairly reliable. They reveal little, however, that is not already revealed in R. Jacob Joseph's works. Moreover, according to the widely accepted dates, Ephraim was only about twelve years old when the Besht died.

61. See I. Schochet's edition of *Tsaṿaʾat ha-Ribash* (New York, 1975), "Introduction," p. x n. 19; G. Nigal, "Maḳor Rishoni le-Sifrut . . ." *Sinai* 79 (1976): 132–46.

62. See A. Kahn's introduction to his edition.

63. Cf. Piekarz, *Bi-Yeme*, p. 372; Z. Gries, "ʿArikhat Tsaṿaʾat ha-Ribash," *Ḳiryat Sefer* 52 (1976–1977): 188, 210.

64. See Schatz's edition of *Magid*, "Introduction," p. 18; Gries, "ʿArikhat," pp. 193, 210.

65. Joseph Weiss, "The Kavvanoth of Prayer in Early Hasidism," *JJS* 9 (1958): 186–87 n. 47; and his "Talmud Torah be-Reshit ha-Ḥasidut," in *Sefer ha-Yovel Tifʾeret Yiśraʾel* (Rabbi Israel Brodie Festschrift) (London, 1967), p. 158f.

66. Gries, "ʿArikhat," p. 210.

67. Other anthologies containing mostly or exclusively Maggidic teachings have been analyzed by Gries, "Sifrut ha-Hanhagot" (thesis); for a brief description, see pp. 49–50.

68. See Schatz's introduction to her edition of *Magid;* Kahn's introduction to his edition of *Liḳuṭim Yeḳarim;* Gries, "ʿArikhat," pp. 187–210.

69. Gries, "Sifrut ha-Hanhagot" (thesis), p. 73f.

70. M. Piekarz's *Bi-Yeme Tsemiḥat ha-Ḥasidut* breaks with this tradition. Although he does not deal with the philological questions relating to Beshtian-Maggidic teachings (see, however, pp. 21–22 on the Besht), Piekarz does show that

"radical" doctrines attributed to the Besht were rooted in earlier non-Sabbatian ethical works, and that key "Hasidic" concepts appear in contemporary non-Sabbatian works of authors who were not associated with the movement or were even clearly opposed to it. On the whole, this is one of the best works in the field to date.

71. Discussed in Dan's *Sifrut ha-Musar*.

72. See e.g., G. Nigal, "ʿAl R. Aharon Shemuel ha-Kohen . . . ," *Sinai* 78 (1976): 256 n. 12, concerning R. Aaron Samuel ha-Kohen; Nigal, "Maḳor Rishoni le-Sifrut . . . ," p. 134 n. 9, concerning R. Aaron of Apta, editor of *Keter Shem Ṭov*.

73. See, e.g., *Tsaṿa'at ha-Rav ha-Tsadiḳ mi-Talmide ha-Ribash* (Jerusalem, 1948), p. 46: **ללמוד בכל יום ספרי הקדמונים כגון חובות הלבבות, ראשית חכמה, של"ה חלק א', ושער הקדושה, ושארי ספרי מוסר הקדמונים דווקא, כי לא תבינו מספרי הצדיקים שהיו בזמנינו כלל וכלל אם לא קבלתם דברי מוסר הקדמונים בלבבכם באמת. וכך קבלתי מאדוני מורי ורבי, ומאד מאד אני מזהיר אתכם על זה.**

The anonymous author was not, in fact, the Besht's disciple, but he was apparently affiliated with the movement (see p. 53) and may have been associated with R. Ze'ev Wolf of Zhitomir (p. 55).

74. See also Z. Gries, "Sifrut ha-Hanhagot" (*Zion*), p. 231; and his thesis, p. 134. Gries's interpretation of the texts adumbrating Maggidic teachings, however, is questionable. I detect no tendency to antinomism in the passages he cites from *Sefer Ḥasidim* and *Shene Luḥot ha-Berit* (see p. 148 of the thesis), but rather an attempt by Horowitz to heighten the spiritual tension involved in obeying God's commands and a poignant but otherwise unremarkable elaboration by Azkari of well-known rabbinic and kabbalistic ethical ideas. See, e.g., Zohar, II, 184a. Nor can the Maggid's teachings be characterized as antimonistic (p. 152 of the thesis).

75. These are the salient characteristics of R. Schatz's work in the field, a detailed critique of which requires separate treatment. See, however, Excursuses G and H.

76. Dinur's admirable achievement of collecting much relevant material is unfortunately marred by his tendentious interpretation of it. This is particularly true for the great Messianic tension he imposes on this period—an issue that has received considerable scholarly attention. See G. Scholem, *The Messianic Idea in Judaism* (New York, 1974), pp. 178–96. Scholem's view is, I believe, the closest to what a balanced study of the texts actually supports.

77. See Gries, "Sifrut ha-Hanhagot" (thesis), ch. 3.

78. See Scholem, *Major Trends,* p. 347; Scholem, *On the Kabbalah and Its Symbolism,* pp. 11–15.

79. See also Gries, "Sifrut ha-Hanhagot," p. 209; A. Rubinstein, "ʿAl Rabo shel ha-Beshṭ . . . ," *Tarbiz* 48 (1978–1979): 155.

80. Cf. *Or Torah,* 27a.

81. Cf. *Toldot,* 129b, 141a, 194a; Dresner, *Zaddik,* pp. 216–18.

82. Cf. Schatz's edition of *Magid,* p. 24 et passim. Future references to *Magid* are to this edition except when noted otherwise.

83. Cf. R. Schatz, *Ha-Ḥasidut ke-Misṭiḳah* (Jerusalem, 1968), p. 55f; R. Eli-

melekh of Lyzhansk, *No'am Elimelekh,* ed. G. Nigal (Jerusalem, 1978), *Vayeshev,* 19b: **אם היה מסתכל ברוממותו תמיד בלי הפסק היה בטל מהמציאות . . . לכן ה׳ ברחמיו נתן לנו תרי״ג מצוות שנעסוק בהם בגופינו לעבודתו. והם תועלת לאדם שיהיה אפשר לו לקיים בדביקותו ית׳.**

84. Cf. *Tanya,* Pt. 1, chs. 21 and 22, Pt. 2, introduction, chs. 3 and 6; *Boneh Yerushalayim* (Jerusalem, 1926), p. 176; Schatz, *Ha-Ḥasidut ke-Misṭiḳah,* pp. 26–30.

85. Cf. Weiss, "Via Passiva"; Schatz, *Ha-Ḥasidut ke-Misṭiḳah,* pp. 99–100; *Or Torah,* 85a; R. Ze'ev Wolf of Zhitomir, *Or ha-Me'ir* (New York, 1954), p. 161a.

86. Cf. *Tsava'at . . . mi-Talmide ha-Ribash* (Jerusalem, 1948), p. 10; Schatz, *Ha-Ḥasidut ke-Misṭiḳah,* p. 34.

87. Cf. Schatz, *Ha-Ḥasidut ke-Misṭiḳah,* p. 155.

88. Cf. Dresner, *Zaddik,* 5.

89. Cf. M. Wilensky, *Ḥasidim u-Mitnagdim* (Jerusalem, 1970), vol. 1, pp. 18, 66, 224, and passim.

90. See *Sufis of Andalusia,* ed. and trans. R. W. J. Austen (London, 1971), pp. 24, 48, 52–57, 63, 78, 81–82, 85–86, 94–96, 105, 112, 119, 131 n. 3, 155; A. J. Arberry, *Sufism* (London, 1969), pp. 40, 62, 75–80, 90, 101; W. M. Watt, *The Faith and Practice of Al-Ghazzali* (London, 1953), pp. 60–61, 76; S. H. Nasr, *Islamic Studies* (Beirut, 1967), pp. 14–15, 19, 45, 49, 59; S. H. Nasr, *Three Muslim Sages* (Cambridge, Mass., 1964), pp. 104–18; 168 n. 7.

91. E.g., Scholem, *Messianic Idea,* pp. 197, 362 n. 37; G. Scholem, "Shete 'Eduyot ha-Rishonot 'al Ḥaburot ha-Ḥasidim veha-Beshṭ," *Tarbiz* 20 (1949): 236–40.

92. Scholem, *On the Kabbalah,* p. 15.

93. Weiss, "Kavvanoth of Prayer," p. 178.

94. G. Scholem, "Devekut," in his *Messianic Idea,* p. 208.

95. See Piekarz, *Bi-Yeme,* pp. 348–56, on the various connotations of this term in contemporary non-Hasidic ethical works and in the works of R. Jacob Joseph of Polonnoye.

96. *Likuṭim Yekarim,* 21; *Keter Shem Ṭov* (Kehot Publication Society, New York, 1982), 44.

97. *Keter Shem Ṭov,* 94, 164. Cf. Horowitz, *Shene Luḥot,* p. 107b (new pagination): **אשרי המדבק עצמו בהבל פיו וראיית עיניו באותיות התורה.**

98. *Keter Shem Ṭov,* 96, 127, 279, 284; *Magid,* pp. 94–95, 148. Cf. Cordovero's *Shi'ur Ḳomah* (Warsaw, 1883), p. 188: **צריך המכוין להמשיך רוחניות ממדריגות העליונות עד המדריגה העליונה ההיא למהר שאלתו, והכוונה כי הבל פיו של אדם לא ריק היא . . . אמנם רוחניות מתהווה מהבל פיו של אדם וצריך אל הרוחניות ההיא כח להפריח שאלותיו ולהעלות אותיות עד המדריגות הנרצות לו, וזה עיקר הכוונה, להמשיך כח, כדי שבכח ההיא יעלו האותיות למעלה ויתהוו במקום רומו של עולם, וימהרו בקשתו**. Although the context is prayer rather than Torah-study, and the word *deveḳut* is missing, the idea of holy letters ascending through thought-power is identical. That such letters can or must actually ascend may have been suggested by the well-known passage in Tal. B. *Pesaḥim* 87b: **לוחות נשברו ואותיות פורחות**. Cf. also R. Ze'ev Wolf's *Or ha-Me'ir,* pp. 117a (in the Besht's name) and 118b.

99. *Keter Shem Ṭov,* 399.

100. Scholem, *Messianic Idea,* p. 215. The other formulations: *Keter Shem Ṭov,* 289, 399.

101. See Excursus D, 1.

102. On deveḳut as the *ultimate* purpose of Torah-study, see Piekarz, *Bi-Yeme,* pp. 359–60.

103. Weiss, "Kavvanoth of Prayer," p. 169 n. 11. I. Etkes adopts Weiss's view in "Shiṭato u-Faʿalo shel Rabi Ḥayyim mi-Volozhin," *PAAJR,* 38–39 (1970–71): 5 (Heb. section).

104. *Keter Shem Ṭov,* 423; *Liḳuṭim Yeḳarim,* 74.

105. See Scholem, *On the Kabbalah,* pp. 37–44, 65, 167; Zohar II, 179a–b, III, 73a, 204a; *Zohar Hadash, Shir,* end; Ruth, 92a; *M. Nev.,* p. 186.

106. Moses Cordovero, *Pardes Rimonim* (Cracow, 1592), *Shaʿar* XXVII, ch. 1. Cordovero mentions the work *Berit Menuḥah* as providing a glimpse of this wisdom. It is perhaps no coincidence that this is one of the relatively few books mentioned by name in Beshtian teachings. See e.g., Moses Ḥayyim Ephraim, *Degel Maḥneh Efrayim* (Jerusalem, 1963), pp. 4, 103, 223.

It is also noteworthy that the author of *Degel* surmises that the Besht's interpretation of "Torah li-shemah"—for the sake of the word and letter itself—is actually identical with Luria's interpretation of the phrase—for the sake of the final *he* of the Tetragrammaton (p. 108; cf. p. 112). See infra, Chapter 4, pp. 152–54. Faced, in other words, with an apparently novel Beshtian interpretation, the Besht's grandson, and presumably many of his other disciples, tended to identify it with a more traditional one. This is hardly the attitude one would expect from religious radicals.

107. Talmud B., *Giṭin* 60a and Rashi 60b, s.vv. **ודברים שבעל פה**.

108. RSZ occasionally advocates using its letters as vehicles for attaining Love and Fear but never implies that this procedure suffices to fulfill the commandment of Torah-study. See Chapter 4, pp. 151–52.

109. Cordovero, *Pardes, Shaʿar* XXVII, ch. 1; RSZ's *Hilkhot Talmud Torah* (included in Parts 5–6 of his *Shulḥan ʿArukh*), II, 12–13. Cordovero's view found its way into many ethical works; see Piekarz, *Bi-Yeme,* pp. 356–59. See also *Bet Yosef, Oraḥ Ḥayyim,* 47, end (concerning the obligation for women); *Ṭur* and B.Y., *Oraḥ Ḥayyim,* 46, end (*Shulḥan ʿArukh,* 46, 9); *Magen Avraham,* 2: *Oraḥ Ḥayyim,* 50.

Cordovero also attached value to the uncomprehending recitation of the Bible of kabbalah, the Zohar, but with the caveat that the student must persevere until he is able to understand and ultimately to analyze the text in depth. Such recitation, in fact, seems to be, in Cordovero's view, a necessary prerequisite for every beginner. It constitutes his introduction into the strange, mystical world of the Zohar, and only after a lengthy orientation can he be expected to begin to make sense of his new surroundings. What is more, even accomplished kabbalists such as Cordovero himself often had to resort to this approach when confronting unfamiliar material, for "God grants understanding to the student of this wisdom only very gradually" (*Or Neʿerav,* Pt. 3, ch. 3. On the need for in-depth analysis of kabbalistic texts, see also Pt. 1, ch. 6 and Pt. 3, ch. 4, end).

In one passage, however, Cordovero suggests that uncomprehending recitation of the Zohar has independent religious value as well: It arouses in the reader's soul the joy and awe of one who is studying the secrets of the Torah with the righteous in Gan ʿEden, and "although he does not see [i.e., is not conscious of this effect], his *mazal* sees" (*Or Ne'erav,* Pt. 5, ch. 2. Cf. Tal. B., *Megilah,* 3a). Not surprisingly, it is this facet of Cordovero's view that was propagated in such popular works as *Ḳitsur Shaloh* (Jerusalem, 1960), p. 242.

110. See Scholem, *Major Trends,* pp. 131–35, and Abulafia's works cited there.

111. See G. Scholem, *Reshit ha-Ḳabalah* (Tel Aviv, 1948), p. 113.

112. Ibid., p. 136ff. Pp. 139–44 also reveal a striking similarity between the mysticism of the Maggid and that of R. Azriel. See also ibid., p. 119.

113. Baḥya, *Ḥovot ha-Levavot* (Warsaw, 1875), X, 4 and 7; *Guide,* III, 51, p. 623 (S. Pines's translation, University of Chicago Press, 1974).

114. See I. Tishby, *Mishnat ha-Zohar* (Jerusalem, 1961), vol. 2, 286–87.

115. This particular metaphor of light is not found in Hasidic works. I have used it because it enables me to encompass the various forms of contemplative deveḳut through which Hasidism urged the implementation of: "In all thy ways acknowledge Him." See also *Keter Shem Tov,* 39, 163.

116. Ibid., 99, 222 (for the concept, not the metaphor).

117. Ibid., 112, 409, 171. See Piekarz, *Bi-Yeme,* pp. 238–40.

For the doctrine of the sefirot (sing. sefirah) and the other kabbalistic concepts alluded to in the following discussion, see Chapter 2, pp. 58–63.

118. *Keter Shem Ṭov,* 366.

119. *Magid,* p. 130. This contrasts strikingly with the Vilna Gaon's wholly negative approach: **אני מזהירך שתרגיל עצמך לישיב יחידי, כי חטא הלשון שקול ככל העונות . . . ועל כל דבור הבל צריך להתקלע מסוף העולם עד סופו. וכל זה בדברים יתרים. אבל בדברים האסורים . . . אי אפשר לשער גודל היסורים וצרות שסובל בשביל דבור אחד**; *Hebrew Ethical Wills,* ed. I. Abrahams (Philadelphia, 1976), pp. 314–15. See also p. 320: **אדם הזוכה לחסום פיו זוכה לאור הגנוז בשפע בלתי שיעור . . . ובזה יכופר לו כל עון ונצול משאול תחתית . . . והגדר העיקרי הוא התבודדות, שלא תצא מפתח הבית חוצה כי אם לצורך גדול מאד או לעשות מצוה רבה . . .** Such an attitude was partly responsible for the Mitnagdic condemnation of the convivial social gatherings that characterized Hasidism (see Wilensky, *Ḥasidim u-Mitnagdim,* I, 38, 46, 57, 59, 62, II, 60, 230, 235, 334–35). Indeed, some Hasidim themselves criticized these gatherings. See *Tsava'at . . . mi-Talmide ha-Ribash,* p. 49, no. 33, which echoes the Gaon's advice, and p. 48.

120. For examples of pre-Hasidic works dealing with this problem, see Piekarz, *Bi-Yeme,* pp. 271–72.

121. See Scholem, *Reshit ha-Ḳabalah,* pp. 107–108.

122. Scholem, *Major Trends,* p. 341. Cf. *Keter Shem Ṭov,* Appendix, no. 241.

123. *Keter Shem Ṭov,* 56.

124. See ibid., 53; cf. 253.

125. See ibid., 39.

126. See *Degel Maḥneh Efrayim,* p. 76.

127. *Keter Shem Ṭov,* 287.

128. See Weiss, "Reshit Tsemiḥatah shel ha-Derekh ha-Ḥasidit," *Zion* 16 (1951): 68, 101. Cf. Piekarz, *Bi-Yeme,* pp. 273–79.

129. Piekarz, *Bi-Yeme,* pp. 273–79, Rubenstein, "Ben Ḥasidut le-Shabta'ut," in *Peraḳim be-Torat ha-Ḥasidut,* ed. A. Rubenstein (Jerusalem, 1978), pp. 182–97.

130. *Keter Shem Ṭov,* 399; *Magid,* p. 27; Zohar I, 264b.

131. *Liḳuṭim Yeḳarim*, 48, 50; *Keter Shem Ṭov*, 195.

132. *Keter Shem Ṭov*, 25–26, 32, 34.

133. Weiss, "Kavvanoth of Prayer," pp. 167, 177f.

134. *Liḳuṭim Yeḳarim*, 12, 17, 54.

135. Ibid., 119.

136. Ibid., 33.

137. Ibid., 118.

138. Ibid., 29, 38; cf. *Or Torah*, p. 84b–85a.

139. *Or Torah*, p. 97b.

140. See Schatz, *Ha-Ḥasidut ke-Misṭiḳah*, pp. 28–30, 95–111.

141. *Keter Shem Ṭov*, 395.

142. *Or Torah*, p. 44a; *Keter Shem Ṭov*, 244.

143. *Tsaṿaʾat ha-Ribash*, ed. Schochet, p. 18. (Subsequent references to *Tsaṿaʾat ha-Ribash* are to this edition.)

144. Zohar II, 69a–b.

145. Scholem, *Major Trends*, pp. 267–68; Scholem, *Sabbatai Ṣevi*, pp. 33–44. See Chapter 2, p. 62, and the Glossary, s.vv. Shevirat ha-Kelim.

146. Ḥayyim Vital, *ʿEts Ḥayyim, Shaʿar* XLII, chs. 4, 6, 7; RSZ, *Tanya*, Pt. 1, chs. 1, 24, 37, Pt. 4 (*Igeret ha-Ḳodesh*), pp. 144–45; RSZ, *TO*, p. 27d.

147. *Tanya*, Pt. 2 (*Shaʿar ha-Yiḥud ṿeha-Emunah*), ch. 1; Vital, *Liḳuṭe Torah* (Tel Aviv, 1963), p. 96a.

148. *Tanya*, ch. 22.

149. Introduction to *Tiḳune Zohar*. This section—s.vv. *Pataḥ Eliyahu*—was (and is) recited by users of kabbalistic prayerbooks every Friday afternoon.

150. This was RSZ's belief. See, e.g., *Keter Shem Ṭov*, Appendix, no. 136 and n. 143, nos. 220, 225, 262 (R. Pinḥas b. Ḥanokh Henekh of Shklov, also known as R. Pinḥas Peizes, was one of RSZ's prominent disciples). See also *Degel Maḥneh Efrayim*, pp. 34, 48.

151. See Dresner, *Zaddik*, p. 177; *Keter Shem Ṭov*, 51.

152. *Keter Shem Ṭov*, 26–27; cf. S. Horodetsky, *Torat ha-Ḳabalah shel ha-Ramaḳ* (Berlin, 1924), p. 221, nos. 12 and 15.

153. *Keter Shem Ṭov*, 70.

154. Ibid., 89.

155. Ibid., 63–64.

156. Ibid., 406.

157. Ibid., 134, 254.

158. *Magid*, p. 152.

159. Ibid., p. 131; see Vital, *Ets Ḥayyim*, beg.

160. *Tsaṿaʾat ha-Ribash*, p. 29. This clearly (and perhaps intentionally) contradicts Maimonides' view in his Mishnah Commentary, *Sanhedrin*, ch. 10: התענוגים הנפשיים הם תמידיים, בלתי נפסקים . . . המלאכים והכוכבים והגלגלים . . . יש להם תענוג גדול מאד במה שהשכילו מן הבורא יתהדר ויתרומם, והם על ידי כך בתענוג תמידי בלתי פוסק (J. Kafiḥ's trans. [Jerusalem, 1965], p. 204).

161. *Or Torah*, p. 27a.

162. See Piekarz, *Bi-Yeme*, pp. 200–202, regarding R. Jacob Joseph's vehement opposition to the idea of sinning for the sake of repenting.

163. Schatz, *Ha-Ḥasidut ke-Misṭiḳah,* pp. 48, 72 et passim. Cf. M. Piekarz, *Bi-Yeme,* p. 205; R. Ze'ev Wolf, *Or ha-Me'ir,* 66a.

164. See *Tanya,* Pt. 1, ch. 1, p. 5a, ch. 26, ch. 31.

165. *Guide,* III, 8–11. Cf. R. Ḥayyim ben Bezalel, *Sefer ha-Ḥayyim* (Lemberg, 1865), Pt. 4, ch. 3.

166. Baḥya, *Ḥovot ha-Levavot, Shaʿar ha-Perishut,* I; Roḳeaḥ, *Hilkhot Ḥasidut;* Dan, *Sifrut ha-Musar,* pp. 62–64.

167. Cf. Gries, "Sifrut ha-Hanhagot" (*Zion*), pp. 234–35.

168. See Piekarz, *Bi-Yeme,* pp. 74–78.

169. Mordecai ben Samuel, *Shaʿar ha-Melekh.* Pagination according to Grodno, 1805, edition: *Seliḥot,* ch. 2; Pt. 5, ch. 4, p. 40a; Pt. 2, ch. 6, pp. 88a, 98a–b, 112a–b.

170. Ibid., p. 104a; cf. *Ṭur, Shulḥan ʿArukh,* and commentaries, *Oraḥ Ḥayyim,* 288. This was not, in other words, the rabbinic "establishment" view, as Dubnow suggests (see supra, n. 6).

171. *Elul,* ch. 8.

172. P. 102b.

173. Ibid.

174. Ibid., p. 113b.

175. Ibid., pp. 93b–94a, 110b.

176. Ibid., p. 94a.

177. Ibid., p. 114a.

178. Ibid., p. 111a.

179. Ibid., p. 116b; Pt. 5, ch. 4, pp. 39b–40a.

180. *Igerot Ḳodesh,* p. 40.

181. Dubnow, Weiss, and Schatz, among others, have stated or implied as much. See, e.g., Schatz, *Ha-Ḥasidut ke-Misṭiḳah,* p. 136, on the "anarchic mentality" of Hasidism; Weiss, "Via Passiva," p. 143, n. 18 on pantheism; Dubnow, *Toldot ha-Ḥasidut,* pp. 35–36, 58.

182. See *Degel Maḥneh Efrayim,* pp. 55, 135.

183. Appendix to Kehot edition of *Magid-Or Torah,* no. 97. On the reliability of Schneersohn tradition in general, see infra in text, pp. 41–44.

184. See, e.g., *Degel Maḥneh Efrayim,* p. 18.

185. For the following, see *Magid,* pp. 21, 39, 128, 154, 169, 186, 221, 235, 266, 1990 ed., p. 398; *Or Torah,* pp. 21b, 27a, 38a–b, 41a, 53b, 55b, 66b, 86b, 98b. Cf. also Schatz's index under *taʿanug.* Opponents of Hasidism, such as Avigdor b. Ḥayyim (RSZ's nemesis in the year 1800), were strongly opposed to the confident, optimistic outlook taught by the Hasidic masters even without understanding its ideological underpinnings. See Wilensky, *Hasidim u-Mitnagdim,* I, pp. 244, 263.

186. Cf. RSZ's *Liḳuṭe Torah,* II, 29a–b.

187. F. M. Cornford, *Before and After Socrates* (Cambridge University Press, 1972), p. 60.

188. *Nicomachean Ethics,* trans. Martin Ostwald (Liberal Arts Press, 1962), Bk. 1, ch. 10, 1100b15–20. And true happiness is contingent on self-sufficiency; ibid., Bk. 1, ch. 7, 1097b5–15. See also H. A. Wolfson, *Philo* (Cambridge, Mass., 1947), II, pp. 173–77.

189. *Nicomachean Ethics,* Bk. 10, chs. 7, 8.

190. Ibid., Bk. 10, ch. 4, 1174b5–10.

191. Ibid., 1175a2–5.

192. *Guide,* III, 51.

193. *Mishneh Torah, Hil. Teshuvah,* VIII, 3.

194. See Werner Jaeger, *Paideia: The Ideals of Greek Culture,* trans. Gilbert Highet (Oxford, 1939–1947), I, pp. 45, 66, 101–102, 163, vol. 3, p. 45.

195. *The Republic,* trans. F. M. Cornford (Oxford University Press, 1971–1972 reprint), pp. 139, 142, 314, 345; Jaeger, *Paideia,* I, pp. 44, 160.

196. Aristotle, *Nicomachean Ethics,* 1106a–1109b.

197. Quoted from *Timaeus* by Thomas S. Kuhn, *The Copernican Revolution* (Cambridge, Mass., 1974), p. 28. As for the Aristotelian-Platonic universe being self-contained and self-sufficient, see ibid., pp. 28, 78.

198. Kuhn, *Copernican Revolution,* pp. 90–93, 51, 146–47. See also Aristotle, *Nicomachean Ethics,* p. 157 n. 26 of Liberal Arts Press, 1962 ed.

199. Kuhn, *Copernican Revolution,* pp. 227–28.

200. *Mishneh Torah, Hil. Yesode ha-Torah,* I, II; *Guide,* trans. S. Pines (University of Chicago Press, 1974), I, 54, pp. 124–25.

201. *Guide,* III, 8–11.

202. Ibid., II, 28, p. 335.

203. Ibid., III, 8, pp. 431–32.

204. Cf. ch. 6 of Maimonides' "Eight Chapters" (introduction to his commentary on *Avot*). Maimonides can distinguish there between rational and incomprehensible commandments because in the latter case it is not matter tempting, but God testing.

205. *Guide,* III, 34, p. 534.

206. Ibid., II, 39.

207. Ibid., III, 17, p. 474. This doctrine was, as is well known, widely disputed. What concerns us here is not the doctrine itself but the assumption behind its assertion of the supremacy of intellect.

208. See ibid., I, 68; Maimonides' Mishnah Commentary, *Sanhedrin,* ch. 10; Aristotle's *De Anima,* Bk. 3, ch. 5, and *Nicomachean Ethics,* p. 172 n. 64.

209. See Abraham Maimonides, *The High Ways to Perfection,* trans. and ed. S. Rosenblatt (New York, 1927); and *Mivḥar Sifrut ha-Musar,* ed. I. Tishby and J. Dan (Jerusalem, 1971), pp. 109, 114, 120–21; Dan, *Sifrut ha-Musar,* pp. 14, 55.

210. See, e.g., Vital's *Sha'are Ḳedushah* (Warsaw, 1876), pp. 32–35; Eleazar Azkari, *Sefer Ḥaredim* (Jerusalem, 1966), "Introduction."

211. See, e.g., R. Ezekiel Landau's responsa, *Noda bi-Yehudah,* II, 107.

212. See Ben Sasson, *Hagut ve-Hanhagah,* pp. 100, 239–42.

213. Although the two were interrelated; see Katz, *Tradition and Crisis,* p. 205.

214. Cf. Gries, "Sifrut ha-Hanhagot" (thesis), p. 208.

215. *Ḥovot ha-Levavot* remained enormously popular. See, e.g., *Migdal 'Oz,* ed. Y. Mondshein (Kefar Ḥabad, 1980), p. 422; *Tsava'at . . . mi-Talmide ha-Ribash,* p. 46.

216. Wilensky, *Ḥasidim u-Mitnagdim,* I, 188.

217. *Kuzari,* IV, 16.

218. See *Magid,* pp. 58–59, 68, 185; *Or Torah,* pp. 19b, 21a, 83b, s.v. *Rani,* and

esp. 46a: **אלף [= הקב״ה] לבד כביכול אינו צורה שלמה, אמנם כשיתדבקו יחד נעשה צורה שלמה**; *Keter,* 19.

219. See Schatz's index under *mishle av*; 1990 ed. of *Magid,* p. 407; cf. *Or Torah,* pp. 52a, 80b, 84a, 85b, 88b, 100b, s.v. *Gadol.*

220. In this and other respects, the God of the Maggid resembles the God of Charles Hartshorne. See Hartshorne's *Creative Synthesis and Philosophic Method* (London, 1970), pp. 12–17, 263. More to the point, if Abraham Heschel is right, and the evidence he presents is compelling, the God of the Maggid is none other than the God of the prophets and the God of R. Akiva; see *The Prophets* (New York, 1962), p. 233; *Torah min ha-Shamayim* (London and New York, 1962), I, 44–51, 65–90, and Heschel's analysis of R. Akiva vs. R. Ishmael on deveḳut and Love, pp. 153–68, and on God's need for man's Service, pp. 232–36. Cf. Horowitz, *Shene Luḥot ha-Berit,* I, 46b–55a.

See also Steven Katz, "Eliezer Berkovits and Modern Jewish Philosophy," *Tradition* 16 (Fall 1977): 124–31.

221. See *Magid,* p. 112: **וכן מוכרח תמיד להיות שהעולמות יהיו מקבלין אהבת הבורא, דהיינו השפע, בבחינת מטי ולא מטי, כנשר יעיר קנו, נוגע ואינו נוגע**. For parallel passages, see Schatz's index under *maṭi ṿe-lo maṭi.*

222. *Keter Shem Ṭov,* 4; Appendix to Kehot edition, p. 36. This theme receives particular emphasis in R. Ze'ev Wolf's *Or ha-Me'ir,* pp. 45b, 62b–63, 100b–102b, 264a, et passim.

223. *Or ha-Me'ir,* p. 263.

224. *Keter Shem Ṭov,* 286; Appendix, p. 21: *Tsaṿa'at ha-Ribash,* p. 31; *Or Torah,* p. 37b.

225. See *Keter Shem Ṭov,* 42.

226. See Schatz's index in *Magid* under *ayin; hishtanut.*

227. *Keter Shem Ṭov,* 114, 141, 159.

228. Ibid., 366; *Degel Maḥneh Efrayim,* pp. 109–10.

229. See *Tanya,* introduction to Pt. 2, p. 76a; R. Menaḥem Mendel of Vitebsk, *Peri ha-Arets,* p. 11. On the incessant struggle for continued spiritual progress, cf. Tal. B., *Berakhot,* 64a: R. Ḥiyya b. Ashi said in the name of Rav: The disciples of the wise have no rest either in this world or in the world to come, as it says, "They go from strength to strength, every one of them appears before God in Zion" (Ps. 84:8).

230. See R. Jacob Joseph, *Toldot,* pp. 130d–131a.

231. See *Degel Maḥneh Efrayim,* p. 151.

232. Isaiah Horowitz devotes a large section at the beginning of *Shene Luḥot ha-Berit* to an explication of this interrelationship; see pp. 5a–29a.

233. See Zohar, III, 73a, 93b, I, 60a; Scholem, *On the Kabbalah,* pp. 44–47; Scholem, *Major Trends,* p. 233. This was a popular theme in contemporary ethical works; see Piekarz, *Bi-Yeme,* pp. 105–109.

234. *Toldot,* p. 95c; Dresner, *Zaddik,* p. 200f; *Keter Shem Ṭov,* 363; *Degel Maḥneh Efrayim,* p. 169.

235. Cf. Piekarz, *Bi-Yeme,* pp. 108–109.

236. *Toldot,* p. 131a.

237. *Keter Shem Ṭov,* 133; cf. Dresner, *Zaddik,* p. 132f.

238. *Toldot,* p. 65d; cf. *Degel Maḥneh Efrayim,* p. 196.

239. See Dresner, *Zaddik,* pp. 125, 275, n. 18.

240. Ibid., pp. 170–219 and notes. See also Piekarz, *Bi-Yeme,* pp. 288–91.

241. This is clearly implied in the homily that is the major source of the Besht's doctrine (see Dresner, *Zaddik,* p. 207) and is explicitly asserted by one of his important disciples, R. Menaḥem Naḥum of Chernobyl: "Every man, even those in the category of Intermediate—with the exception of the [truly] wicked—must occasionally fall from his level in order to elevate those that are beneath him; that is, that are below his level"; *Me'or 'Enayim,* p. 83.

Scholem (*Messianic Idea,* p. 198) claims that the Sabbatian-like version of the teaching concerning the "unavoidable and necessary" fall of the Zaddik originated with the Besht. He does not, however, document this statement, and I doubt whether it can be documented.

242. J. Weiss, *Meḥḳarim be-Ḥasidut Braslav,* ed. M. Piekarz (Jerusalem, 1974), pp. 99–102. Even if Weiss were correct, however, the disseminators of such a doctrine could find solid support in the Zohar. See now Elliot Wolfson, "Left Contained in the Right: A Study in Zoharic Hermeneutics," *AJS Review* 12 (Spring 1986): 27–52, esp. notes 35 and 45.

243. Moreover, it was a doctrine comprising ideas and motifs that were emphasized in ethical works of contemporaries who were apparently unaffiliated with the Besht and unfamiliar with his teachings; see Piekarz, *Bi-Yeme,* pp. 105–12.

244. See, e.g., Talmud B., *Sanhedrin,* 65b: אלמלא בקשו צדיקים היו בוראים עולם; *Mo'ed Ḳatan, 16b:* אני מושל באדם, מי מושל בי — צדיק, שאני גוזר גזירה והוא מבטלה; *Bereshit Rabah,* LXVII, 1.

245. *Keter Shem Ṭov,* 230, 272, 273.

246. See Ch. 2, n. 213; G. Scholem, "Ha-Bilti Muda u-Muśag—Ḳadmut ha-Śekhel be-Sifrut ha-Ḥasidit," in *Hagut* (Hugo Bergmann Festschrift) (Jerusalem, 1944).

247. See A. Lovejoy, *The Great Chain of Being* (Cambridge, Mass., 1936), p. 292f.; A. Lovejoy, "The Meaning of Romanticism for the Historian of Ideas," *Journal of the History of Ideas* 2 (1941): 237–78; Jacques Barzun, *Classic, Romantic and Modern* (Boston, 1961), pp. xxi, 6, 10, 13, 16, 80, 87, 93, 175, 192; M. Peckham, *The Triumph of Romanticism* (Columbia, S.C., 1970), pp. 8f., 33–35, et passim.

248. "The Hassidic Movement—Reality and Ideals," *Journal of World History* 11 (1968): 261–62; repeated by Piekarz, *Bi-Yeme,* p. 383. Cf. Max Weber's distinction between three types of authority—rational-legal, traditional, and charismatic—in *The Theory of Social and Economic Organization,* trans. A. M. Henderson and T. Parsons (Oxford University Press, 1947), Pt. 3.

249. Cf. Gries, "Sifrut ha-Hanhagot" (*Zion*), pp. 228–32. Gries rightly sees Hasidism's appealing socio-religious innovations as the major contributors to the movement's rapid growth.

250. See ibid., p. 229 nn. 148–50; Wilensky, *Ḥasidim u-Mitnagdim,* II, 285–87; Hilman, *Igerot Ba'al ha-Tanya,* e.g., nos. 6, 13–16 by R. Menaḥem Mendel of Vitebsk; and many letters of RSZ, passim.

251. N. Lamm, "The Letter of the Besht to R. Gershon of Kutov," *Tradition* 14 (1974): 114.

252. *Toldot,* pp. 99a, 107d, 127c, 132a, 184b–c; Dresner, *Zaddik,* p. 284 n. 26. See also G. Nigal, "ʿAl Meḳorot ha-Deveḳut be-Sifrut Reshit ha-Ḥasidut," *Ḳiryat Sefer* 46 (1971): 344.

253. Hilman, *Igerot Baʿal ha-Tanya,* pp. 105–10, 113.

254. *Noʿam Elimelekh,* passim.

255. *Ḳedushat Levi* (Jerusalem, 1946), pp. 80–81, 102, 131, 167–68, 186–87.

256. See Mindel, *R. Schneur Zalman,* pp. 70–74; Hilman, *Igerot Baʿal ha-Tanya,* p. 33; *Tanya,* ch. 13, p. 18b.

257. Like Service (*ʿavodah*), Love and Fear are capitalized throughout this study whenever their exclusively religious connotations are intended.

258. *Tanya,* chs. 17, 41, 42. "Practical commandments" are *mitsvot maʿasiot,* commandments requiring physical action.

259. Ibid., ch. 2, p. 6a–b, ch. 19, 32.

260. See appendix to the Kehot edition of *Keter Shem Ṭov,* pp. 39–40, 71–74, 78, 84, 103, 111.

261. Teitelbaum, *Ha-Rav mi-Liadi,* pp. 12, 15, 28, 32, and passim.

262. See, e.g., ibid., p. 13 n. 1.

263. Ibid., pp. 29, 72, n. 1, 160f., et passim.

264. See, e.g., ibid., p. 72 n. 1.

265. See ibid., ch. 1.

266. "Contemplative Mysticism and Faith in Hasidic Piety," *JJS* 4 (1953): 19–29. E.g., see p. 22: "The mystical theology of the Great Maggid and of Habad can be formulated in a series of terms such as: immanence, pantheism (panentheism), impersonal G-d, emanation"; p. 24: "The crucial problem in the Habad school is the certainty of the mystical experience"; p. 27: "In Hasidic mysticism [i.e. Habad], sin has lost its depth from the moment that it is admitted that religious enthusiasm is but the transformation of the 'will to evil'."

Except for a single reference to R. Dov Baer's *Ḳunṭres ha-Hitpaʿalut,* which proves nothing about the existence of a single "crucial problem" for the entire "Habad school," no evidence is offered to support these statements.

267. *Hebrew Encyclopaedia* (1969), XVII, col. 775f.

268. "ʿIyunim be-Torat Shneur Zalman mi-Liadi," *Molad* 171–72 (November, 1962): 513–29.

269. "The Basis of Habad Philosophy," *Judaism* 16 (1967): 324–40.

270. Such as his conclusion on pp. 329–30 that Maimonides was a Spinozistic pantheist: "The implication of the Maimonidean identification of the sekhel, maskhil, and muskhal is that the Deity, as rightly understood by Spinoza, is identical with the totality of existence. All existence is simply the thought of G-d and has no reality outside of Him." This would make RSZ, who essentially accepted this Maimonidean formulation, and Aristotle, who originated the concept, Spinozistic pantheists as well. But cf. Pines's introduction to his translation of the *Guide,* pp. xcvii–xcviii. Pines's conclusion, however, is not at all identical with Schapiro's and is based on textual analysis, not loose speculation.

271. Schochet, *Mystical Concepts,* p. 805.

272. Ibid., p. 804.

273. Ibid., ch. 5, for example, purports to discuss the controversial subject of *orot ve-kelim* "as it appears in Chassidism" (p. 862 n. 1) but contains only two references to RSZ's teachings; and those are found in *Tanya,* wherein the subject is barely touched.

274. See, e.g., ibid., pp. 842 n. 3, 826. On RSZ's use of this method, see infra, p. 56.

275. On the tendency of Idealists to explain by multiplying, see Aristotle, *Metaphysics,* 1078b30–35.

See, e.g., RSZ's *Sidur,* p. 217c, on the relationship between Lurianic kabbalah and that of Cordovero.

I have singled out for critique only those studies that I believe, for one reason or another, to be worthy of separate comment. A more complete bibliography is provided by Hallamish as an appendix to his thesis (see Selected Bibliography).

276. RSZ's eldest son, R. Dov Baer (1773–1827); RSZ's grandson and R. Dov Baer's son-in-law, R. Menaḥem Mendel (1789–1866); R. Menaḥem Mendel's seventh and youngest son, R. Samuel (1834–1882); R. Samuel's second son, R. Shalom Dov Baer (1860–1920); R. Shalom Dov Baer's only son, R. Joseph Isaac (1880–1950); R. Joseph Isaac's son-in-law and agnatic descendent of R. Menaḥem Mendel, R. Menaḥem Mendel Schneerson (b. 1902).

277. Although sizable excerpts were originally copied directly from the journals and then published.

278. All published in New York by Kehot: *Ḳunṭres 18 Elul 5703* (1955); *U-Ma'ayan mi-Bet Hashem* (1958); *Biḳur Chicago* (1957); *Limud ha-Ḥasidut* (1947); *Torat ha-Ḥasidut* (1946). Also very valuable is Rabbi M. Schneerson's anthology *Ha-Yom Yom . . . ,* 4th ed.; and *Torat Shalom* (New York, 1946), transcriptions of discourses and talks of R. Shalom Dov Baer.

279. On RSZ's journals, see *Ha-Tamim,* 2d ed. (Kefar Ḥabad, 1971), p. 140 (new pagination); on R. Moses's (RSZ's youngest son, b. 1779 [*S* 5704 (New York, 1967), p. 150]), *S* Summer 5700 (New York, 1961), p. 40, *S* 5704, p. 59; on R. Menaḥem Mendel's, *S* Summer 5700, pp. 96–98, 127, 173, *Ha-Tamim,* p. 150, *LD,* I, 146, IV, 1167; on R. Samuel's, *M* 5709 (3rd edition, Kefar Ḥabad, 1971), p. 91 (second pagination); *LD,* I, 41–42, 195; on R. Zalman Aharon's (R. Shalom Dov Baer's older brother), *LD,* I, 30–32, 36–37, II, 466–69, IV, 1167; on R. Joseph Isaac's, *S* Summer 5700, pp. 95, 171–74, introduction to *U-Ma'ayan, S* 5703 (New York, 1965), pp. 182–85, *S* 5701, pp. 92, 150.

280. The dating, detail, and precision were part of a traditional policy; see *LD,* I, 62, 195, *S,* 5703, p. 147. See also *M* 5710, 3d ed. (New York, 1970), p. 262. Some examples of the conscientiousness with which R. Joseph Isaac adhered to this policy: *Ha-Tamim,* pp. 168–78, 252–68, 460–76, 757–63; *S* 5703, pp. 182–85; *U-Ma'ayan,* "Introduction," passim; *S* 5704, pp. 5–9, 11, 19–20, 66, 81, 95, 100–101; *LD,* I, 25, 59, 83, 134 et passim; *M* 5709, pp. 83–89; *S* 5701, pp. 123, 126; Schneerson, *Ha-Yom Yom,* pp. 58, 86, 92, 111; see also J. I. Schneersohn, *Igerot Ḳodesh me'et . . . Rabenu Yosef Yitsḥaḳ* (New York, 1982), vol. 1, p. 58, and the references infra, n. 281.

281. See, e.g., *LD,* III, 967–68; Schneerson, *Ha-Yom Yom,* p. 52; *S* 5704, p. 16; *S* 5701, pp. 64, 94; *Ḳovets Mikhtavim,* appended to *Sidur Tehilat Hashem,* 14th ed. (New York, 1966), pp. 683–84.

282. On R. Samuel Bezalel, see *S* 5701, p. 96 and the index to *Ha-Tamim;* on R. Menaḥem Naḥum's dates, see *LD,* I, 31, 37; on R. Zalman Aharon's journals, see supra, n. 279. For examples of traditions transmitted by other Ḥabad Hasidim, see *Ha-Tamim,* p. 463f.; *S* 5704, pp. 95–96; see also *S* Summer 5700, pp. 29, 54f., 171.

283. *LD,* I, 62; *M* 5709, p. 43; *Ha-Tamim,* p. 158.

284. See Excursus K.

285. See his introduction in B. Mintz's edition (Tel Aviv, 1961), pp. 13–14, 23–25, Heb. pagination.

286. Dinur, *Be-Mifneh,* pp. 91–92; G. Scholem, "Demuto ha-Hisṭorit shel R. Yiśra'el Baᶜal Shem Ṭov," *Molad* 18 (1960): 347 (reprinted in *Devarim be-Go*); H. Szmeruk, "Mashmeᶜutah ha-Ḥevratit shel ha-Sheḥitah ha-Ḥasidit," *Zion* 20 (1955): 59. See also Scholem's critique of Dinur in *Molad* 18 (1960): 336. For Weiss, see infra, n. 291.

287. Dinur, *Be-Mifneh,* p. 91.

288. *Shivḥe ha-Beshṭ,* "Introduction," p. 24.

289. Dinur, *Be-Mifneh,* p. 91 n. 32.

290. See Peckham, *Triumph of Romanticism,* essay 4, and p. 424f.

291. "A Circle of Pre-Hasidic Pneumatics," *JJS* 8 (1957): 199–213.

292. G. Nigal, "Moro ẏe-Rabo shel R. Yiśra'el Baᶜal Shem Ṭov," *Sinai* 71 (1972): 150–59.

293. There are, of course, exceptions. See Wilensky, *Ḥasidim u-Mitnagdim,* II, 290, on the Besht's reply concerning one who has forgotten to say "Yaᶜaleh ve-yavo."

294. Quoted by Nigal, "R. Aharon Shemuel ha-Kohen," p. 257 n. 27 from *Ḳore me-Rosh* (Berditchev, 1811), pp. 73–74: **הנני מעיד בעדות נאמנה בפני המעיין מה ששמעתי מפי חותני הרב המאור הגדול המפורסם מוהר״ר יואל ולה״ה אב בית דין דק״ק סטאפאן, אשר הרב המפורסם אור ישראל וקדושו מוהר״ר ישראל בעש׳ט נתאכסן בביתו, ונסע עמו ללוותו לכבודו על עגלה אחת לכפר אחד רחוק שני פרסאות מהעיר, ושם הדרך היא דרך יער, והיו האילנות מקשקשין וצפרים מצפצפים, וצוה הבעש״ט זלה׳ה שיעמוד העגלה רגעים, ושמע הצפצוף והקשקוש, ואמר לחותנו הרב ז״ל שאומרים לו ששכחו דבר נחוץ בתוך העיר, חפץ הצריך להם. ואמר לי חותני הרב שכמעט חרה לו על דבריו מחמת שהיה הדבר רחוק בעיניו שבדורות הללו ימצא מי שיודע זה. אבל בסוף נמצא שכן הדבר ששכחו חפץ נחוץ והוצרכו לשלוח אחריו. כ״ז אני מעיד ששמעתי מפי חותני.**

295. See ibid., p. 259.

296. See, e.g., *Ha-Tamim,* p. 159; *LD,* II, 461–67.

297. "Introduction, p. 6.

298. The unpublished MSS are presently inaccessible.

299. Introduction to Vol. 1 of his *Shulkḥan ᶜArukh, Oraḥ Ḥayyim.*

300. Mindel, *R. Schneur Zalman,* p. 29, citing an unpublished portion of Rabbi J. I. Schneersohn's *Memoirs* (not to be confused with his journals and diary); Schneerson, *Ha-Yom Yom,* 17.

301. *M* 5709, p. 90 (second pagination). The philosophical works mentioned there by name are *Guide, Kuzari, ᶜIḳarim,* and the works of Joseph Solomon Delmedigo. RSZ considered the first three important enough to merit special study

sessions during which he taught them to R. Menaḥem Mendel (after he turned thirteen) and presumably also to R. Dov Baer (*S* Summer 5700, pp. 40–41; *S* 5702 [New York, 1964], pp. 4–5). R. Menaḥem Mendel, in turn, taught them, together with RSZ's "Hasidic" interpretations, to R. Samuel (*S* Summer 5700, p. 41).

In addition, RSZ used these private sessions with R. Menaḥem Mendel to teach him ibn Gabbai's *ʿAvodat ha-Ḳodesh* and Vital's *ʿEts Ḥayyim,* the latter "according to the method of philosophy" (ibid.).

It may be worth noting that Delmedigo's *Elim* was one of the books in RSZ's library in 1800 (Hilman, *Igerot Baʿal ha-Tanya,* p. 149).

302. *S* 5704, p. 16.

303. Presumably, "aggadah" means Talmudic aggadah, and "Midrash" means aggadah found in *Midrash Rabah* and similar works.

304. Probably Lurianic; see *M* 5708, p. 178, and Mindel, *R. Shneur Zalman,* p. 29.

305. See *Ha-Tamim,* p. 145.

306. *M* 5708, pp. 176, 190; *S* 5704, p. 131; *LD,* III, 964–65. This group must apparently be distinguished from a minyan of simple devotees whom RSZ managed to enlist after his conversion to Hasidism. The scholars of Vitebsk began to shun him (see *Ha-Tamim,* p. 625), and he was forced to content himself with anyone who would help provide him with a socially supportive circle and an organizational base of operations; see *S* 5701, p. 66; *S* 5704, pp. 131–32, 137.

307. By this time the dictum in *Avot,* IV, 14, had been transformed from pragmatic, contingent advice to an ascetic practice necessary for religious perfection. See Zohar, III, 247a: בזמן שאתה מכתת רגליך ממדינה למדינה תזכה לראות פני השכינה.

308. *M* 5708, p. 176; *LD* III, 966; *S* Summer 5700, p. 174, par. 2.

309. Schneerson, *Ha-Yom Yom,* pp. 78, 106. Mindel's dating *R. Schneur Zalman,* p. 36), based on *Bet Rebi,* should be amended.

310. *M* 5708, p. 176.

311. Schneerson, *Ha-Yom Yom,* p. 78.

312. *M* 5708, p. 176; *"Torat ha-Ḥasidut,"* pp. 10–12.

313. Even Solomon Maimon grudgingly granted him "a certain [i.e., a type of] knowledge of men"; *Solomon Maimon, An Autobiography,* trans. J. Clark Murray (Boston, 1888), p. 169.

314. *Bet Rebi,* Pt. 1, ch. 2, in the name of "one of his [RSZ's] grandsons."

315. See Mindel, *R. Schneur Zalman,* p. 280 n. 14.

316. *Ha-Tamim,* pp. 142–43. Cf. *S* 5704, pp. 99–100.

317. Appendix to the Kehot edition of *Or Torah,* nos. 93b, 97, 104.

318. This was noticed as early as 1770 by his teacher-colleague, R. Menaḥem Mendel of Vitebsk (author of *Peri ha-Arets,* also known as Rabbi M. M. of Gorodok; see *Ha-Tamim,* notes, pp. 141–42); *S* 5704, p. 100.

This difference of form must be added to the natural tendency (mentioned supra) for students to remember, emphasize and elaborate those aspects of their teachers' thought that they find most congenial.

319. See Gries, "Sifrut ha-Hanhagot" (thesis), p. 70 n. 61. On the kinds of issues discussed during RSZ's sessions with the Maggid, see Kehot edition of *Magid,* appendix, no. 63.

320. *S* 5701, p. 115.

321. Statements in the Talmud, Midrash, and *Kuzari* about the spiritual greatness of all Israel rarely single out the simple Jew for special consideration; one example (Tal. B., *Berakhot,* 57a): אפילו ריקנין שבך מלאים מצוות כרמון. See also *Shir ha-Shirim Rabah,* 2:4.

322. Noted and admired even by the generally cynical Aescoly, *Le Hasidisme* (Paris, 1927), p. 93. For a good example see Hilman, *Igerot Baʿal ha-Tanya,* p. 30; cf. *S* Summer 5700, p. 142.

323. Schneerson, *Ha-Yom Yom,* p. 106.

324. *M* 5708, p. 190.

325. *Ha-Tamim,* p. 144. See also *LD,* II, 413–14. Common occupations (apparently both in Lyozna and Lyady) included laborer, miller, farmer, traveling peddler; *S* 5703 (New York, 1965), p. 8.

The date of RSZ's move to Lyozna is unclear. Schneerson, *Ha-Yom Yom,* "Introduction," p. 4 (reprinted in *LD,* III, 1013), gives 1767. *S* 5701, p. 26, indicates that he was already established in Lyozna by 1768, but the context clearly suggests a later date and a possible copyist's error. Similarly, *Ha-Tamim,* p. 145, implies that no move occurred between 1768–1769 and 1773–1774. But according to *S* 5704, pp. 131–32, in 1771 RSZ was still living with his father-in-law in Vitebsk. And according to *Ha-Tamim,* p. 794, he came to Lyozna ca. 1772–1773. This is the only inexplicable, significant discrepancy concerning RSZ that I have found in R. Joseph Isaac's dating.

326. See Hilman, *Igerot Baʿal ha-Tanya,* pp. 16–26, 52. The private library of Rabbi M. Schneerson contains a 1792 MS copy of the letters written from Tiberias by R. Menaḥem Mendel and R. Abraham between 1788 and 1791 (MS no. 684). See also *Degel Maḥneh Efrayim,* p. 234.

327. *LD,* I, 59. R. Menaḥem Mendel of Vitebsk had settled in Gorodok.

328. See, e.g., *LD,* III, 1126.

329. *Ha-Tamim,* p. 142.

330. And was recognized by his colleagues. R. Menaḥem Mendel, for example, writes in 1788, concerning RSZ: שהשליך נפשו אחר גוו לכתת רגליו לדרוש ה׳, ונעשה עפר תחת רגלי הצדיקים; Hilman, *Igerot Baʿal,* p. 36.

On RSZ's devotion to the Maggid, see *M* 5708, p. 170; Schneersohn, *Ḳunṭres 18 Elul,* p. 22. On his estimation of the Maggid's spiritual powers, see appendix to Kehot edition of *Or Torah,* p. 73, no. 93a.

331. *Ha-Tamim,* pp. 138–42.

332. Cf. Gries, "Sifrut ha-Hanhagot" (thesis), pp. 46, 49.

333. Ibid., pp. 156–57; Hilman, *Igerot Baʿal ha-Tanya,* pp. 175–76.

334. Hilman, *Igerot Baʿal ha-Tanya,* p. 153.

335. See Gries, "Sifrut ha-Hanhagot" (thesis), pp. 107–108.

336. *Ha-Tamim,* pp. 144–46; *LD,* II, 471–78; *S* 5704, pp. 110–14, 163; Schneersohn, *Ḳunṭres Biḳur Chicago,* p. 13.

337. *M* 5708, pp. 232–33; Schneerson, *Ha-Yom Yom,* p. 62. Understandably, only a few of these very early (before 1780) teachings have survived; see *LD,* III, 912, 1011; *Ha-Yom Yom,* pp. 30, 40, 53, 69, 89, 98, 103; *S* 5703, p. 118; *S* 5701, pp. 26, 66, 100, 126, 144; *M* 5709, p. 206; *Torat ha-Ḥasidut,* p. 23.

338. E.g., *S* 5704, pp. 143–44; Schneerson, *Ha-Yom Yom,* p. 29 (from the Lyady period); *S* Summer 5700, p. 154. See also Schneersohn, *Torat Shalom,* p. 33.

339. *Ha-Tamim,* pp. 146–50; *LD,* I, 58, II, 243, 483, 492, 551; *S* 5702, p. 4. A number of Ḥeder One disciples, including R. Pinḥas Reizes and R. Aaron of Staroselye, studied with RSZ for over twenty years; *LD,* II, 413; *S* 5704, pp. 110–11; *S* 5703, p. 123; introduction to R. Aaron's *Shaʿar ha-Yiḥud veha-Emunah.* They and his other outstanding disciples were (and obviously had to be) proficient in Lurianic kabbalah as well; *S* 5704, p. 103. The regular course of study in Ḥeder Two and Three was three years; *LD,* I, 58.

340. *LD,* I, 207; *Ha-Yom Yom,* p. 34; Schneersohn, *Ḳunṭres 18 Elul,* p. 21; *S* 5704, p. 16; *S* 5701, pp. 146–48, 112. Interestingly it was R. Pinḥas Reizes, not RSZ, who brought Dov Baer up to date on the discourses he had missed; *S* 5704, pp. 111–12.

The teachings R. Menaḥem Mendel heard from RSZ are embodied in his voluminous works, particularly in the several dozen volumes of *Or Torah.* In these volumes it is generally impossible to determine where RSZ's teaching ends and R. Menaḥem Mendel's explication begins; however, there are many discourses, particularly in his *Beʾure ha-Zohar* (vol. 1, New York, 1968; vol. 2, New York, 1978), in which he explicitly or graphically (by means of parentheses) makes the distinction. (Note that the abbreviation BZ refers, in these notes, to the work edited by R. Dov Baer and published New York, 1955.)

341. *S* 5704, p. 111; *LD,* II, 41–42, IV, 1477. Cf. also *S* 5701, p. 55.

342. Mindel's account, *R. Schneur Zalman,* chs. 10 and 11, is useful for obtaining a general outline of these incidents.

343. Schneersohn, *Torat Shalom,* pp. 33, 60, 78, 100–101; *LD,* I, 42f; *M* 5709, pp. 91–92 (second pagination); *Limud ha-Ḥasidut,* pp. 9, 13 (= *Ha-Tamim,* pp. 36, 39); Schneerson, *Ha-Yom Yom,* p. 49; *Sidur,* 361b.

344. *MK,* ed. S. D. Levin.

345. Schneerson, *Ha-Yom Yom,* pp. 29, 76.

346. A representative sampling of these was published in *Torah Or* and *Liḳuṭe Torah.*

347. Most of the extant transcripts are in their hand. See *MK,* p. 607.

348. MS no. 1012 in Rabbi M. Schneerson's library indicates that this was the practice in R. Samuel's day, and I see no reason to assume that it was an innovation.

349. *Ha-Tamim,* p. 39.

350. Hilman, *Igerot Baʿal ha-Tanya,* pp. 58–59.

351. See, e.g., MSS nos. 820 and 821.

352. Sometimes, however, RSZ instructed him to incorporate these within the discourse; Schneerson, *Ha-Yom Yom,* p. 49.

353. Appendix to *Torah Or,* 8th ed. (New York, 1976), pp. 19a (143)–20a (144). The second title page, attributing its transcription to R. Judah Leib and not mentioning R. Menaḥem Mendel at all, is simply due to the latter's modesty.

354. Ibid., p. 18b (284). The long interval between the two publication dates was due to the closing of most Jewish presses in the interim. See also Schneerson *Ha-Yom Yom,* p. 28.

355. *LD,* I, 207; cf. Schneerson, *Ha-Yom Yom,* p. 70, and *M* 5562 (New York, 1964), pp. 293–94. A second edition of the *Sidur* with additional discourses was published in Berditchev, 1818.

356. The term *hanaḥah* (pl. *hanaḥot*) is Ḥabad jargon for a transcription. It probably refers either to the act of "placing" the oral discourse on paper or to the fact that the transcription was unedited by the Rebbe and therefore merely an assumption—hanaḥah—of what he actually said. "Rap" is the acronym for Rabbi Pinḥas (Reizes).

357. The latter part of the MS, however, contains discourses delivered in Lyady. Cf. *EL,* p. 229f., and *M* 5562, pp. 56–94. See *MK,* pp. 590–93, for Levin's hypothesis.

358. R. Aharon Chitrik has informed me that there exist, for example, five other variations of the discourse published in *Torah Or, Yitro,* p. 66f. In studying R. Dov Baer's transcriptions, even R. Menaḥem Mendel occasionally had difficulty distinguishing between the original discourse and his father-in-law's explanatory interpolations. See R. Menaḥem Mendel's *Beʾure ha-Zohar,* II, 794: **איני יודע אם כ"ז מאדומ"ו נ"ע או ביאור מו"ח נ"ע.**

Two published collections preceded *EL* and *MK: Shene ha-Meʾorot* (Lvov, 1846) and *Boneh Yerushalayim* (Jerusalem, 1927). *MK* incorporates both, along with variants from other MSS. I cite them in this study because *MK* was published after I had completed most of my research. See also Y. Mondshein, "Shene ha-Meʾorot," in *Ḳovets Yagdil Torah,* XXVIII (Shevat-Adar, 5739 [1979]): 182–84.

359. See *MK,* pp. 589–608.

360. Schneerson, *Ha-Yom Yom,* pp. 16, 74; *M* 5709, p. 91 (second pagination); cf. Schneerson, *Ha-Yom Yom,* p. 38; *M,* pp. 29 note, 60 note; *M* 5563, II, 861; *M* 5568, II, 926 n. 6, 927 nn. 8, 9; *M Nev.,* pp. 126–38.

361. Schneerson, *Ha-Yom Yom,* pp. 20, 21, 74, 96; *Sidur,* 360b, 361b; *M* 5568, II, 928 nn. 9, 10; *M Iny.,* pp. 471, 528 (n. to p. 357); *M Nev.,* pp. 166, 266 (notes).

362. Three of the works are not used at all: (1) R. Dov Baer's *Beʾure ha-Zohar,* because, for some unfathomable reason, Hallamish feels it is more attributable to R. Dov Baer than *M* 5568, a transcription by the latter that he does use; (2) *Boneh Yerushalayim;* and (3) *Shene ha-Meʾorot,* which are not even mentioned.

363. See, e.g., p. 139 of Hallamish's dissertation.

364. See, e.g., pp. 35, 61, 64–65, 127–32, 253f., 307, 396–400.

365. E.g., Friedberg, *Toldot,* pp. 34, 74, 86, 93; Scholem, *Kabbalah,* pp. 77–79; Scholem, *Sabbatai Ṣevi,* pp. 68–93; M. Benayahu, *Haskamah u-Reshut bi-Defuse Venetsiah* (Jerusalem, 1971), pp. 105–13.

366. Cf. *LD,* I, 25.

367. See introduction to *Tanya.*

368. See H. Lieberman, *Ohel Raḥel* (New York, 1980), II, 24–36.

369. Ibid.; Schneerson, *Ha-Yom Yom,* p. 34. The standard edition of *Tanya,* reprinted many times, is Vilna, 1900. *Tanya* is the only nonhalakhic book written by RSZ himself. It consists of four parts, consecutively paginated, the last two added at various times after the publication of Part 1, *Sefer shel Benonim* (religious ethics), and Part 2, *Shaʿar ha-Yiḥud veha-Emunah* (theology), 1796. The last two parts are 3, *Igeret ha-Teshuvah* (tract on repentance), Zolkiew, 1799 (rev. ed., Shklov, 1806); and 4,

Igeret ha-Ḳodesh (scholarly, pastoral letters), with an appendix titled *Ḳunṭres Aḥaron* (kabbalistic explications), Shklov, 1814.

For a more complete publication history, see the appendix of any Kehot edition from 1954 onward. See also H. Glitzenstein's biography, *Sefer ha-Toldot RSZ* (New York, 1975), pp. 315–16. I have used and occasionally emended the translation of the Soncino (London, 1973) Hebrew-English edition. The translators are: Pt. 1, Nissan Mindel; Pt. 2, Nissan Mangel; Pt. 3, Zalman I. Posner; and Pt. 4, J. I. Schochet.

370. See the introduction.

371. For a brief but valuable historical survey of Jewish ethical thought, see Menachem Marc Kellner, "The Structure of Jewish Ethics," in *Contemporary Jewish Ethics,* ed. M. M. Kellner (New York, 1978), pp. 3–18.

372. And other mystics; cf. J. Leclercq, *The Love of Learning and the Desire for God* (New York, 1961), p. 91.

373. Both, as noted above, edited by R. Menaḥem Mendel, whose own discourses display the same pattern.

374. Cf. *Solomon Maimon,* p. 164: "Their sermons and moral teachings were not, as these things commonly are, thought over and arranged in an orderly manner beforehand. This method is proper only to the man who regards himself as a being existing and working for himself apart from God. But the superiors of this sect hold that their teachings are divine and therefore infallible only when they are the result of self-annihilation before God, that is, when they are suggested to them *ex tempore* by the exigence of circumstances, without their contributing anything themselves."

375. Cordovero, *Pardes,* p. 35b: מפורסם היות האדם צורותיו ותכונתו ואיבריו ועורקיו וגידיו דמות בבואה עליונה. והאדם צל עליון שנתגשם ונתעבה בעוה"ז. See also Joseph Ben-Shlomo, *Torat ha-Elohut shel R. Mosheh Kordovero* (Jerusalem, 1965), pp. 28–29 (hereinafter: *Cordovero*).

376. *Tanya,* p. 6a.

377. RSZ regularly uses the popular formula, "And from my flesh shall I behold God" (Job 19:26), as the basis for analogies to either the human body or the soul.

For the rich history and the ramifications of the *homo imago Dei* motif in medieval philosophy and kabbalah, see Alexander Altmann, "The Delphic Maxim in Medieval Islam and Judaism," in *Biblical and Other Studies,* ed. A. Altmann (Cambridge, Mass., 1963), pp. 196–222; on the use of the verse from Job, see p. 216f. See also Horowitz, *Shene Luḥot,* "Bet Yiśra'el."

On the interrelation between anatomy and philosophy, see E. Ruth Harvey, *The Inward Wits: Psychological Theory in the Middle Ages and the Renaissance* (Warburg Institute, University of London, 1975), p. 36.

On (Jewish) sources for RSZ's idea of the divine soul, see L. Jacobs, "The Doctrine of the Divine Spark in Man in Jewish Sources," in *Studies in Rationalism, Judaism, and Universalism,* ed. Raphael Loewe (London, 1966), pp. 87–115. Jacobs finds it in Philo, Baḥya, ibn Gabirol, the Zohar, Maimonides, Isaac Luria, Vidas, and Shabbetai Sheftel Horowitz's *Shefa Tal.* See also *Sefer Torot ha-Nefesh* (pseudo-Baḥya), ed. I. Broyde (Paris, 1896), p. 82; *Kuzari,* V. 16; Tishby, *Mishnat ha-Zohar,* II, 6, 9–11.

378. Thus, intuitive assumptions about even such complex phenomena as color are simply accepted as fact; *M* 5563, II, 533, version 2. See also this volume, pp. 82–84; *M Ket.*, I, 35f. (RSZ's theory of dreams); *M* 5562, II, 475, 477 (RSZ's rejection of the concept of gravity in favor of a kabbalistic theory).

379. See Scholem, *Sabbatai Ṣevi,* pp. 29–30: "No doubt the use of spatial concepts had introduced an alarmingly anthropomorphic quality into kabbalistic symbolism, and there is indeed no better illustration of the paradox of symbolism than Luria's doctrine of retraction. The kabbalists went on unabashed, neutralizing their daring utterances by a qualifying as it were or so to speak. With the aid of this formal reservation they attenuated their symbols in appearance but saved them in reality. All original kabbalistic thinkers, from the author of the Zohar in the thirteenth century to the great Hasidic *saddiqim* of the eighteenth, availed themselves of this approved method of taking the sting out of the sometimes shocking symbolism."

"As it were," however, could only be used to modify an entire idea and often did not appear until after the idea had been stated. Individual words or phrases with unsettling anthropomorphic implications continued to jar the reader's sensibilities. A far greater cushioning effect was produced by the use of the word *beḥinat* before each potential offender. Cordovero used it in a technical sense as well (Scholem, *Kabbalah,* pp. 114–15; cf. *MK,* 447), but RSZ makes it clear in *M* 5562, p. 285, that he understood the usage in Lurianic kabbalah as a superior form of "as it were," and it is in this sense—and as a substitute for inverted commas—that he uses it unstintingly. It is a signal that means: The following word or phrase should not be taken literally or in its usual sense.

A third device to blunt the effects of anthropomorphic symbolism is also worthy of mention: the (probably instinctive) shift to Aramaic whenever problematic symbols are mentioned. Parts of the body and other mundane things acquired a soothing otherworldly ring when referred to in Zoharic Aramaic. It was obvious, for example, that *dero*ʿ*a, resha,* or *gulgalta* could not possibly denote a *physical* arm, or head, or skull. Nor could the description of Ḥokhmah-Binah as "tren reʿin de-lo mitparshin" (*Sidur,* 129d) really mean "two inseparable friends." The language itself thus provided an additional reminder that this is only "as it were."

380. Scholem, *Kabbalah,* p. 99.

381. *Tanya,* 77b, 94b, 108a; cf. also 87a.

382. The locus classicus for both RSZ's basic explication of speech symbolism and his exposition of God's transcendent unity is *Tanya,* Pt. 2.

383. Scholem, *Sabbatai Ṣevi,* p. 29; Scholem, *Kabbalah,* pp. 143, 402–403.

384. Scholem, *Major Trends,* p. 268.

385. Scholem, *On the Kabbalah,* ch. 3.

386. Scholem, *Kabbalah,* p. 401.

387. See, e.g., *BZ,* 74a, 135a; *LT,* II, 38a; *M* 5568, p. 257; *BY,* 156; *M* 5564, p. 98; *M* 5567, pp. 26–27; *Igerot Ḳodesh,* p. 173; *MK,* 129; *M* 5562, II, 344; *M* 5569, p. 85–86.

388. Also reflected in RSZ's habitual use of the words "shenehem emet" (or their Yiddish equivalent) when reconciling apparent or real contradictions: *BZ,* 47d, 49b; *M* 5562, pp. 11, 187, 272; *M* 5568, pp. 177, 484; *Shene ha-Me*ʾ*orot,* p. 15a;

M 5566, p. 293; *EL,* 246; *M* 5564, p. 71; *M* 5563, I, 296–97, II, 558, 628, 704, 756; *M* 5568, II, 662; *M Par.,* I, 80, 132–33, II, 615, 644, 649; *M Iny.,* pp. 175, 418; *M Raz.,* p. 146; *M Nev.,* p. 92; *M Ket.,* I, 223, II, 173.

389. See *M* 5568, p. 108; *Sidur,* 105d; *MK,* 313; and infra, Chapter 4.

390. R. J. Z. Werblowsky, *Joseph Caro, Lawyer and Mystic* (Oxford, 1962).

391. David H. Freeman, *Logic: The Art of Reasoning* (New York, 1967), pp. 284–91. See, e.g., *BZ,* 40a, 114d, 115a, cf. 47a, 88b; *EL,* 93, 242, 245–46, 252; *M* 5562, pp. 87, 242; *M* 5566, pp. 44, 122, 239; *M* 5568, pp. 12–13, 115–16, 329, 373, 393, cf. pp. 320 and 403.

392. Hilman, *Igerot Baʿal ha-Tanya,* p. 97. Vital's own views, however, are far from sacrosanct; see *Sidur,* 75d. On contradictions in *ʿEts Ḥayyim,* see *M* 5563, p. 135.

393. Scholem, *Kabbalah,* p. 101; *TO,* 3a; *LT,* IV, 12d; *M* 5570, p. 62; *M* 5562, II, 373, 425. The dynamism of the sefirot was particularly stressed in Lurianic kabbalah.

394. Inanimate, flora, fauna, man.

395. A typical characteristic of the medieval (Jewish) intellectual; see Davidson, "Study of Philosophy," p. 55: "He has a completely static view of history. He cannot even imagine that people in Biblical times and rabbinic times looked at the universe differently from the way he looks at the universe. And by the same token, he never questions that the schools of Greek philosophy had achieved, definitively, the most accurate description of the universe possible for the unaided human intellect."

Chapter 2. Man in God's World

1. Scholem, *Kabbalah,* p. 95.
2. Ibid., p. 99.
3. Scholem, *Major Trends,* p. 223.
4. Ibid., p. 261.
5. Ibid., p. 263.
6. Scholem, *Kabbalah,* p. 131.
7. Scholem, *Major Trends,* p. 278.
8. Scholem, *Kabbalah,* p. 153.
9. Cf. David Ross, *Aristotle,* 5th ed. (London, 1964), p. 64: "What Aristotle finds common to all previous schools is that they recognize contraries as first principles."
10. Cordovero, *Elimah Rabati* (Jerusalem, 1966), pp. 6b, 10a–11b. See also Horowitz, *Shene Luḥot ha-Berit,* II, 66b, citing *Pardes Rimonim* on the obligation to believe in the existence of the sefirot in order to avoid philosophical dilemmas. See Cordovero, *Pardes, Shaʿar ʿEśer ve-lo Tesha,* viii–ix; *MK,* 516; *M* 5563, pp. 86, 318; *M* 5570, p. 54.
11. *Elimah,* p. 24d; *Tanya,* 26a, 68a, 72a, 129b; cf. *Tanya,* Pt. 2, chs. 7–8 and chs. 3–4; *LT,* IV, 26d; *RP,* 165, 167; *BZ,* 40a, 115a; *BY,* 174; *M* 5566, p. 316; *EL,* 92–93; *M* 5568, pp. 343–44; *MK,* 321–22, 330, 389.
12. *Tanya,* 44b note, 52b, 129a f., 156b; *TO* 79c, 93a; *LT,* III, 16a. For a detailed

explication of the kabbalistic concepts treated infra, see Scholem's *Major Trends,* chs. 6, 7; Scholem, *Kabbalah,* Pt. 1, ch. 3; Scholem, *On the Kabbalah,* ch. 3; Scholem, *Sabbatai Ṣevi,* pp. 22–66; and J. I. Schochet, *Mystical Concepts in Chassidism* (revised ed. in the Soncino edition of *Tanya* [London, 1973]).

13. *M* 5568, p. 408. See also *TO,* 10c, 103b–c; *BZ,* 16c; *BY,* 62; *Tanya,* 86a–87a; *M* 5563, p. 319. The double-perspective approach is also found in Cordovero; see Ben Shlomo, *Cordovero,* pp. 165, 168, 173–74. Cf. *TO,* 107d.

14. See Aristotle, *Metaphysics,* 1043a 10–20, and *Physics,* III, 201a; Ross, *Aristotle,* pp. 65–66; Maimonides, *Guide,* introduction to Pt. 2, no. 24; II, 14, pp. 287–88; II, 18.

15. *M* 5562, II, 355; *BZ,* 89a, 103b; *M* 5562, pp. 33, 150; *M* 5568, p. 546. These discourses differ on how much one can actually discern in the sperm; as did eighteenth-century savants. See Joseph Needham, *A History of Embryology* (Cambridge, Mass., 1934), p. 183f.; Arthur W. Meyer, *The Rise of Embryology* (Stanford University, 1939), ch. 5.

16. *Sidur,* 48a f.; *LT,* II, 46d, 52c f., V, 9b; *EL,* 252; *BZ,* 89a, 139d; *M* 5562, pp. 150, 256; *M* 5566, p. 316; *M* 5568, pp. 319, 329, 382; *M* 5567, pp. 24–26, 45, 114; *M* 5563, pp. 86, 236, 259 (cf. 347); *M Par.,* I, 64–68, 107, 201; *M Iny.,* pp. 59, 83. The decision to reveal, which apparently constituted a change of divine will, is dealt with at length by Cordovero; RSZ breaks no new ground on the issue. Indeed, here, as elsewhere, RSZ does not approach Cordovero's thoroughness or philosophical sophistication. See Ben Shlomo, *Cordovero,* pp. 194f., 326.

17. *M* 5568, p. 325.

18. *M* 5562, p. 42. Cf. *RP,* 167; *BZ,* 115a; *M* 5566, p. 121; *M* 5568, p. 86 (citing and disputing Cordovero); Ben Shlomo, *Cordovero,* pp. 92, 208–11.

19. *M* 5568, p. 342. See also *M Par., I,* 88, 140.

20. *M* 5568, pp. 343–44; *M* 5566, p. 35; *TO,* 93a; Ben Shlomo, *Cordovero,* pp. 64–67, 92, 204–11. See also *M Ket.,* I, 97.

21. As it was in Cordovero's; see the citations in Ben Shlomo, supra n. 20; *M* 5570, p. 77; *M* 5565, II, 832, 960–61, 980.

22. *Encyclopaedia Britannica* (Chicago, 1971), XXIII, p. 979.

23. He does not adopt Cordovero's striking "asymptotic" approach; see Scholem, *Kabbalah,* p. 402.

24. *M* 5562, p. 252; *BY,* 65; *Sidur,* 48c–49d, 244d.

25. Ross, *Aristotle,* pp. 64–65; Scholem, *Kabbalah,* p. 107; J. Guttman, *Philosophies of Judaism,* trans. D. W. Silverman (New York, 1964), p. 97.

26. *BY,* 61; *TO,* 93a, 109a; *M* 5562, II, 531; *M* 5565, II, 923–24, 980; *M Iny.,* pp. 191, 283, 347, 374; *M Raz.,* p. 256; *M Nev.,* p. 204; *M. Ket.,* II, 116, 121. An intermediary is necessary between Atsilut and the lower worlds as well; *M* 5564, p. 65; LT, III, 68c; *M* 5570, pp. 76–77. Cf. *TO,* 14 a–c.

For other examples of RSZ's frequent use of the intermediary principle, see *M* 5563, II, 647; *M* 5568 II, 669; *M Par.,* I, 10, 110 (angels as intermediaries), 161 (intermediaries between good and evil), 388, II, 531, 603, 607–608; *M Nev.,* p. 143.

27. *TO,* 24b, 52a, 76c, 98b, 114b; *Sidur,* 179d; *LT,* III, 37c–d, 52b; *M* 5562, II, 436, 462; *M* 5563, p. 158, II, 529, 532; *M Par.,* I, 196–99. See also *M Iny.,* p. 283.

28. *LT,* III, 75c, II, 4d, V, 29c, IV, 21a; *M* 5566, pp. 121–22; *M* 5562, p. 126, II, 349; *M* 5563, pp. 9, 44, II, 529–30.

29. *Tanya,* 67b–68; *LT,* V, 40c; *M* 5566, p. 312; *M* 5562, II, 398; *M* 5565, II, 731; *M Par.,* II, 512; cf. *M Ket.,* I, p. 106.

30. *LT,* III, 52b; *M* 5562, p. 242; *Sidur,* 98b; *TO,* 76c, 22a; *M* 5564, pp. 104–105; *MK,* 279; *M* 5562, II, 475–76; *M* 5565, II, 823. It is noteworthy that, at the beginning of *ʿEts Ḥayyim,* Vital added several diagrams that depict sovev (the original light in which the first tsimtsum occurred [*Tanya,* 67a]) as a circle. Cf. Aristotle, *Physics,* 266a21; Ross, *Aristotle,* p. 94; Maimonides, *Guide,* II, 14, pp. 286–87.

31. *M* 5568, p. 382; *M* 5562, p. 227.

32. *EL,* 78.

33. *LT,* II, 16a; IV, 58c; *RP,* 140; *M* 5563, p. 9. Cf. *MK,* p. 412, for a direct contradiction. See also *M* 5563, pp. 162–63, version 2, 166, version 2, II, 521.

34. *RP,* 128, 168–69; *TO,* 87a; *LT,* III, 1a.

35. *RP,* 169.

36. Ibid., 156; *LT,* IV, 99a.

37. *TO,* 92b.

38. *RP,* 147; *Tanya,* 68a–b, 83b–84a; *TO,* 91c; *M* 5570, p. 63.

39. *TO,* 91c, 92b–d; *RP,* 136, 147; *M* 5563, p. 357, version 1.

40. *LT,* IV, 20d, 99a; *RP,* 156, 165; *M* 5566, p. 121; *M* 5562, II, 324; *Tanya,* 77b; and previous citations. See, however, *M* 5563, II, 546, version 1.

41. Nevertheless, they do not appear in *Tanya,* which, as noted above, is a religio-ethical, not a theosophical, work.

42. *TO,* 114c. The interpretation is cited, however, not directly from Naḥmanides' Pentateuch commentary (p. 12 in Chavel's edition) but from the more authoritative *ʿEts Ḥayyim* in his name and in the name of *Sefer ha-Bahir.*

43. *Sidur,* 179b; *TO,* 9c, 10d, 52a, 114b–c; *BZ,* 143d; *M* 5565, II, 787.

44. The most extensive discussion is in the first discourse of *M* 5568. See also *TO,* 51d f.; *LT,* II, 37c f., III, 87a f.; *M* 5563, p. 191; *M* 5568, II, 690. Cf. I. Tishby, *Torat ha-Ra veha-Ḳelipah be-Ḳabalat ha-Ari* (Tel Aviv, 1942), p. 82f.

45. *Bereshit Rabah,* XII, 15; *Shemot Rabah,* XXX, 3; *Shoḥar Tov,* 34; *TO,* 9c; *M* 5565, II, 908. Cf. Vital's *Mevo Sheʿarim* (Jerusalem, 1960), I, 1, 1, p. 3.

46. *BY,* 177.

47. *BY,* 109.

48. See Tishby, *Torat ha-Ra,* pp. 41–42; Vital, *Mevo Sheʿarim,* V, 1, 2, pp. 184–85. According to *M Iny.,* p. 160, the Shevirah took place to provide the admixture of good and evil necessary for the struggle of Service, without which there could be neither reward nor punishment; see also p. 256.

49. *M* 5568, p. 257; *M Par.,* I, 37–38; Vital, *ʿEts Ḥayyim,* IX, 9.

50. *Sidur,* 107a; *TO,* 24d; *BY,* 118, 163; *M* 5566, p. 3; *M Par.,* I, 68; *M Nev.,* pp. 65–66; and the citations supra, n. 44. However, see *M Iny.,* p. 322; *M* 5563, II, 542, version 2, where RSZ, citing the Maggid, attributes the uncooperativeness of the Tohu vessels to an overabundance of self-nullification. Cf. Vital, *ʿEts Ḥayyim,* IX, 8, XI, 5.

51. *Sidur,* 74a, 217c; *TO,* 24d; *LT,* II, 23d, 38a; *M* 5568, pp. 6–13, 255f; *M* 5564, p. 193; *MK,* 545; *M* 5565, II, 719–20.

RSZ has no corresponding character trait for the increase in the *number* of vessels. Luria explains that this increased the distance between the lower seven and the En Sof, thereby reducing the intensity of light they had to sustain; *Sha'ar Ma'amre Rashbi* (Jerusalem, 1961), p. 162, and *Sha'ar ha-Hakdamot* (Jerusalem, 1961), p. 160. RSZ naturally preferred to avoid such spatial symbolism; see *M* 5567, pp. 95–96, and *M* 5570, p. 174.

52. *M* 5567; *M* 5570; see also Tishby, *Torat ha-Ra,* pp. 53–55.

53. *Ḥesed le-Avraham* (Warsaw, 1883), pp. 8a, 14a–b, 15a, 16b, 19b, 25a, 30b (a and b denote recto and verso of the page; not the column).

54. Or through the vessel that synthesizes opposites: Tif'eret; *LT,* II, 23c; *BZ,* 38c; *M* 5568, p. 13; *M Iny.,* pp. 422, 427–28. Ḥohkmah is the white knight in R. Abraham's theosophy as well; see *Ḥesed le-Avraham,* pp. 16b, 23b–26a, 33a, 34a.

55. *MK,* 169; *M* 5568, pp. 10–13, II, 671; *M* 5562, II, 440; cf. *LT,* II, 37d–38a, III, 87a–b.

56. See *M* 5568, p. 11.

57. *M* 5563, II, 542, 547, 727; *M Iny.,* pp. 424, 429; *M Raz.,* p. 325.

58. *BZ,* 143d; *TO,* 10d, 24c–d, 51d–52a, 97b; *LT,* III, 37d; *M* 5563, p. 167.

59. *LT,* III, 37c–d; *M* 5562, II, 436–37, 441–43; see also *M* 5564, p. 42; *M Par.,* I, 27–28, 145–46; *M Iny.,* pp. 63–71, 346, 349; *M Ket.,* II, 62–63, 132–33.

60. See Ben Shlomo, *Cordovero,* ch. 2.

61. E.g., *LT,* II, 51c, V, 7d.

62. *Elimah,* II, 17, p. 16a. Ben Shlomo, *Cordovero,* pp. 98–99, does not deal with this passage.

63. *Tanya,* 79a–b, 129a f.; *BZ,* 40a, 135a; *Sidur,* 166a. See also *M* 5568, pp. 407–408, 564; *M* 5567, pp. 32–33; *M* 5562, II, 343, 440–44; *M* 5563, pp. 342–44; *M* 5569, p. 218; *M* 5564, p. 1.

64. *Tanya,* 52b, 69a; *LT,* IV, 26d; *M* 5566, p. 35; *EL,* 92–93; *BZ* 41c; *M* 5568, pp. 343–44; *M* 5567, pp. 23–24; *M* 5563, p. 194; *M* 5570, p. 61; *M* 5565, II, 604, 886.

65. *Tanya,* 52b.

66. See infra, pp. 73–75.

67. *Tanya,* 79a–b; *BZ,* 135a; *Sidur,* 135d; *LT,* V, 31a. See also *M* 5563, p. 280.

68. Netsaḥ, Hod, Yesod are merely offshoots of these three and rarely play a significant role in RSZ's thought. See, however, *M* 5563, II, 659–60; *M Par.,* I, 420; *M Ket.,* II, 216–18.

69. *Tanya,* 152; *LT,* III, 25b, 65a, V, 49d; *TO,* 107b; *Sidur,* 247a, 76a–b, 258a; *M Par.,* I, 287; *M Ket.,* I, 11; *EL,* 126; *BZ,* 130c; *M* 5562, I, p. 4, II, 332, 364; *M* 5568, pp. 542–43; *M* 5564, pp. 132–33; *M* 5563, pp. 147, 255, 300–302; *M* 5570, pp. 158, 171; *M* 5569, p. 80; *M* 5565, II, 843–46; R. Menaḥem Mendel's *Be'ure ha-Zohar,* I, 362, II, 793.

70. Scholem, *Sabbatai Ṣevi,* p. 31. Cf. *M* 5567, p. 105; *M Par.,* I, 333; *M Iny.,* p. 447.

71. *M* 5566, p. 44. Cf. *EL,* 14; *M* 5568, pp. 542–43; *BY,* 169; *M* 5562, p. 164; *MK,* 329; *M* 5563, II, 753; *M Par.,* I, 138; *M Iny.,* p. 127; *M Ket.,* I, 64.

72. *RP,* 56; *BZ,* 86b, 130c; *M* 5563, p. 191; *M* 5568, II, 690; *M* 5562, II, 344, 376; *M* 5569, pp. 85–86; *M* 5565, II, 927–28. Cf. Ben Shlomo, *Cordovero,* pp. 95–98.

73. *TO,* 19a–b, 26d, 87c, 96d, 109a; *LT,* III, 28a, 43d, IV, 5a–d, 12d, 57a, V,

47d; *BY,* 61–62; *Sidur,* 47c, 59a–b, 83a, 104d, 129d–131a, 156a, 158b, 217b–c, 265a; *Tanya,* 149d; *M* 5564, p. 196; *M* 5568, II, 664–65, 671; M 5565, II, 612; *M* 5563, I, p. 190, II, 593, version 2; *M* 5570, p. 133; *M Par.,* I, 85, 342; *M Iny.,* p. 58; *M Ket.,* II, 120. See also *M* 5563, II, 498, version 2; *M Par.,* I, 342, *M Ket.,* II, 173; and infra, p. 102. Here and elsewhere I personify the sefirot to reproduce RSZ's (and Luria's) common mode of explication.

74. *Tanya,* 144d, 148a, 159b–160a; *TO,* 5c, 26b, 96d, 110d; *LT,* III, 54b; *M* 5563, II, 549, 728; *M* 5565, II, 863, 869; *RP,* 24; *M* 5566, p. 277; *M* 5564, p. 55; *M Par.,* I, 85–88, 134–35. See also *M* 5563, p. 368; *M* 5568, II, 630, 670, 688. Daʿat, not surprisingly, is occasionally portrayed as possessing the same qualities; e.g., *TO,* 26b, and *Sidur,* 65a–b, 257c.

75. Cf., Vital, *ʿEts Ḥayyim,* X, 1; *Mevo Sheʿarim,* I, 1, 2, II, 2, 3; *Tanya,* 6a–7a, 8b, 23b–24a, 44b, 85b, 144b, 149b, 159b–160a; *TO,* 90a, 93a; *Sidur,* 44d, 83a, 86a, 87c, 200d; *M* 5564, p. 64; *LT,* V, 33a; *M* 5562, II, 425; *M* 5563, pp. 185–86, 368; *M* 5568, II, 630, 688; *M* 5565, II, 863, 869, 923–24, 980.

76. *LT,* IV, 57b, V, 22d, 26a; *TO,* 70a; *Sidur,* 173c, 217a, 259b; *RP,* 51; *BZ,* 88d, 126c; *M* 5566, pp. 138, 377; *M* 5568, p. 526; *M* 5562, I, pp. 46, 96, II, 411; *EL,* 188; *MK,* 393–94; *M* 5563, pp. 94, 149, II, 695, 729, 788.

77. In several discourses, however, RSZ explains that occasionally pleasure is contingent on will, since one may refuse to derive pleasure from the ordinarily pleasurable; *M Par.,* I, 407–408; *M* 5562, p. 217. Cf. *M* 5568, p. 47; *M* 5563, p. 190, II, 686; *MK* 538; *M Raz.,* p. 20; and esp. *M Nev.,* pp. 217–18.

78. *Tanya,* 149b; *LT,* III, 38c, 48b, IV, 49d; *Sidur,* 130c; *BZ,* 47a, 88b, 126c; *M* 5568, pp. 526, 568; *RP,* 51; *M* 5564, p. 186; *M* 5563, II, 686, 729; *M Ket.,* I, 202–203, 212.

79. *M* 5568, p. 542. See also *M* 5562, p. 128; *M* 5563, II, 579, version 2, 705; *M* 5566, p. 185; *M Par.,* I, 159.

80. *M* 5562, pp. 96–97, 100–101, II, 631, 680.

81. Philip Wheelwright, *The Presocratics* (New York, 1966), pp. 77, no. 98, p. 78, no. 109. Cf. also no. 26: "all things come to pass through the compulsion of strife;" no. 31: "It throws apart and then brings together again; it advances and retires"; no. 108: "The way up and the way down are one and the same"; no. 114: "day and night . . . are one"; no. 117: "People do not understand how that which is at variance with itself agrees with itself. There is a harmony in the bending back, as in the cases of the bow and the lyre"; no. 118: "Listening not to me, but to the Logos, it is wise to acknowledge that all things are one."

82. *Tanya,* 132b; *LT,* III, 38b, 43d. See also *TO,* 33a, 43c–d.

83. *LT,* III, 38b.

84. Reflecting the Aristotelian idea that the celestial spheres are arranged in concentric circles, and motion is communicated through their "intellects" from outer sphere to inner. The encompassing sphere and its intellect was thus superior to the encompassed. See Ross, *Aristotle,* pp. 181–82; *Mishneh Torah, Hil. Yesode ha-Torah,* III, 1–2, 9, 10, II, 6; *Guide,* II, 4, p. 257, II, 10, p. 271, II, 11, pp. 274–75; *Tanya,* 129b; *Sidur,* 240c–d, 296a, 104a.

85. *Sidur,* 97c–d.

86. *TO,* 52a; *Sidur,* 231b.

87. *M* 5564, p. 126, where RSZ states that this principle derives from the teachings of the Besht and the Maggid; *LT,* II, 34c, 39c, III, 38b, 73d, et passim with variations. *M* 5565, II, 731, 741, links the concept expressed by this principle with the dictum in *Sefer Yetsirah.* Cf. *Sidur,* 303c.

88. *BY,* 165. Cf. *M* 5569, pp. 101–102 and *MK,* 290, for a different explanation. See also *M Par.,* I, 91. The Maggid's association of the "higher" with the more incomprehensible is echoed in a number of early discourses; e.g., *MK,* 111, 332. See infra, note 213.

89. *M Par.,* I, p. 19.

90. See supra, n. 88; *LT,* III, 13b, 37a, 39c, IV, 5c, V, 35b; *M* 5562, pp. 121, 237, 247 (cf. *RP,* 130), II, 443; *BZ,* 123d; *M* 5568, pp. 108, 393; *TO,* 4a–b; *Sidur,* 242a, 262a; *M* 5564, p. 189; *M* 5567, p. 259; *M* 5563, pp. 3, 40, II, 733; *M* 5570, pp. 67, 74–75, 121, 173–74; *M* 5565, II, 637–38, 741, 764 (cf. 955), 894; *M Par.,* I, 129.

91. See *TO,* 27c–d, 61a; *LT,* III, 82c, IV, 13a; *M* 5568, pp. 260, 278; *M* 5563, pp. 370–71; *M Raz.,* p. 448. Cf. Tishby, *Torat ha-Ra,* pp. 41–42.

92. See *Tanya,* 10b. The terms *siṭra aḥra, kelipot, ḥitsonim, śarim, goyim, elohim aḥerim* are generally used synonymously. See, e.g., *Tanya,* 8a, 10b, 11a, 12b, 27b–28a, 29b, 139b; *TO,* 12b; *LT,* III, 80a; *Sidur,* 69d; *MK,* 251; *M* 5563, p. 88.

93. *Tanya,* 97a, 103b; *LT,* II, 21c–d, 28b, III, 90a, 91b; *Sidur,* 68c, 163d; *M* 5568, p. 461; *MK,* 424; *M* 5563, p. 38.

94. *Tanya,* 13b, 37b–38a.

95. *TO,* 20b; *M* 5565, II, 645.

96. *Sidur,* 62b, 158c, 200c, 203a; *M* 5568, p. 146. Cf. *Shene ha-Meʾorot,* 22b. See also *M Par.,* II, 828; *M Raz.,* pp. 224–25 (on the need to appease the siṭra aḥra).

97. See the sources cited in notes 92 and 94; *M* 5565, II, 1016.

98. *M* 5566, p. 293. See also *RP,* 17; *LT,* II, 21a–d; *M* 5563, I, 6 (cf. p. 261), II, 727.

99. Ben Shlomo, *Cordovero,* pp. 13, 290–91. Cf. *Tanya,* 39b; *TO,* 11d, 26b, 109a; *LT,* II, 21a, III, 56c, 69b, 90a, V, 18c; *Sidur,* 9a, 65a–b, 143d, 163d, 257c; *MK,* 1 (cf. *Degel Maḥneh Efrayim,* p. 131), 9, 299, 379, 413, 528; *Igerot Ḳodesh,* p. 118; *M* 5563, p. 261, II, 700–701.

100. *M* 5564, pp. 25, 84; *TO,* 4b, 21b; *LT,* II, 34c, III, 38b; *EL,* 233; *M* 5562, p. 121, II, 351; *M Par.,* I, 86, 90; *M Iny.,* pp. 392–93 (cf. pp. 385–86); *M Ket.,* II, 71; *M* 5566, p. 185; *M* 5567, pp. 222–23; *MK,* 48, 75; *M* 5563, pp. 133, 370, 377; *M* 5570, pp. 121, 134.

See *M Nev.,* pp. 129 and 132, where RSZ warns his followers not to take the highest-lowest principle to its logical conclusion by sinning for the purpose of redeeming evil through repentance, thereby drawing the highest—God Himself—into the lowest—evil itself. This, says RSZ, was the mistake for which both Temples were destroyed.

101. *M* 5568, p. 568, II, 631, 680; *MK,* 585–86; *M* 5562, II, 374; *M Par.,* I, 288; *M Ket.,* I, 129, 205, II, 139. See also *M* 5563, pp. 207, 392 (but cf. II, 695), 338; *M Par.,* I, 340, 408.

102. Scholem, *Kabbalah,* pp. 50, 61; E. Gottlieb, "Ha-Ramban ki-Meḳubal," in

Mehkarim be-Sifrut ha-Kabalah, ed. J. Hacker (Tel Aviv, 1976), pp. 88–96; Jacob Ḥayyim Tsemaḥ, *Nagid u-Metsaveh,* "Introduction," p. 4; Vital, *ʿEts Ḥayyim,* "Introduction," p. 4d.

103. *Guide,* II, 13, p. 282, II, 25. Naḥmanides' view appears on p. 12 of Chavel's edition.

104. Scholem, *Kabbalah,* p. 152; Scholem, *On the Kabbalah,* pp. 101–103. Alexander Altmann, "Creation and Emanation in Isaac Israeli: A Reappraisal," in *Studies in Medieval Jewish History and Literature,* ed. I. Twersky (Harvard University Press, 1979), pp. 1–16.

105. *LT,* IV, 95b; *Sidur,* 86b.

106. *TO,* 13a.

107. Ibid., 90b; *LT,* IV, 12d, 26d; cf. *Tanya,* 129b–130a.

108. *LT,* IV, 19d.

109. Ibid., 55a. See also *M* 5563, pp. 259, 296–97; *M Raz.,* p. 78.

110. *LT,* IV, 12d. See Scholem, *Kabbalah,* p. 110.

111. *Guide,* II, 6, pp. 262–64; *LT,* III, 46a; *Sidur,* 83d–84a (cf. 27a–b); *BY,* 65; *M* 5562, p. 40; *MK,* 482.

112. *LT,* V, 5b; *M* 5563, p. 268, II, 675; *Guide,* II, 4, p. 258, II, 6, p. 261, II, 7.

113. *Shemot Rabah,* XXXII, 7; *Va-Yikra Rabah,* XXIX, 2; Tal. B., *Sukah* 55b; *Sidur,* 114d; *LT,* III, 33d, 80a; *EL* 56; *M* 5568, p. 76; *Tanya,* 139b. Hilman, *Igerot Baʿal ha-Tanya,* p. 84; *MK,* 114, 423; *M* 5562, II, 374; *M* 5563, p. 266, II, 535; *M* 5564, I, pp. 138, 144. Maimonides does not mention these princes, but I believe he would have no difficulty accepting the notion. It is, after all, only a special case of his principle that God delegates His providence to intermediaries; *Guide,* II, 4, p. 259, II, 5, p. 261.

114. *Sidur,* 138b, 271b; *TO,* 42a.

115. *Sidur,* 63a, 73d; *Tanya,* 130a. Cf. *TO,* 75b; *LT,* V, 5b; *Tanya,* 51b–52a.

116. *M* 5563, p. 341; *TO,* 4b; *LT,* IV, 98a (cf. III, 40b); *M* 5566, p. 100; *Sidur,* 73d, 275d (citing Ramban), 276a–b (cf. *Tanya,* 67a).

117. *Sidur,* 133b.

118. *LT,* II, 36a; *Sidur,* 138b.

119. *Sidur,* 82c; *LT,* II, 41b; *MK,* 276.

120. As in the Midrash and Zohar.

121. *Sidur,* 73d, 133b; cf. 65d, 138b, 148c–d, 168c.

122. *TO,* 9d; *M* 5566, p. 367; *Tanya,* 133a; cf. *EL,* 118–24; *BY,* 65.

123. *LT,* III, 28c, IV, 77b; *Sidur* 227a; *M* 5562, p. 270; *RP,* 29; cf. *LT,* II, 15b.

124. *TO,* 9d; *M* 5564, pp. 101–102, 108–10.

125. *Tanya,* 54a, 155a; *TO,* 42b; *LT,* III, 11a, V, 32b; *Sidur,* 273a, 308c; *M* 5564, p. 128.

126. *MK,* 315; *TO,* 3b, 9d; *LT,* II, 41b; *BZ,* 114d–115a; *EL,* 113; *M* 5562, p. 255; *RP,* 28; *M* 5564, pp. 108–110; *Tanya,* 94a. Cf. *Tanya,* 130a; *Sidur,* 133b, 168c, 231d; *M* 5562, II, 418–19; *M* 5563, p. 341; *M* 5570, p. 60, 63; *M Par.,* I, 29; *M Ket.,* II, 63.

127. *M* 5566, p. 101, suggests that their song produces an audible, tumultuous din.

128. *TO,* 3b, 37a; *LT,* III, 11a–b, 40b; *BZ,* 99b.

129. *Sidur,* 133b; cf. *TO,* 86a; *LT,* III, 11b; *Sidur,* 65d, 73d–74a, 168c; *M* 5562, II, 409.

130. *LT,* III, 10b, 11a–b, IV, 77b; *Sidur,* 308c.

131. *Sidur,* 273d.

132. *Tanya,* 51b, 159a; *TO,* 30c, 37a–b, 75b; *EL,* 112; *M* 5562, II, 343. See also *Tanya,* 136b, 157a.

133. *RP,* 92. In *BY,* 131, the body is referred to as "impure and abominable." Neither source, of course, is necessarily a quotation, but there are a sufficient number of inimical references to the body in other discourses to make them significant. See *Tanya,* 41a; *EL,* 178; *M* 5564, p. 220; *M* 5567, pp. 148, 231; *BY,* 131; *MK,* 381; *M Iny.,* pp. 265, 302–303; *M Nev.,* p. 147.

134. *LT,* III, 40b.

135. *Mishneh Torah, Hil. Yesode ha-Torah,* III, 9, IV, 6–9; *Teshuvah,* VIII, 3; *Guide,* II, 4, 11, III, 54, p. 635.

136. *Sidur,* 74a, 148c–d.

137. See, e.g., *Tanya,* 81a, 139b; *LT,* IV, 64d; *M* 5562, pp. 40, 242, 260; *RP,* 135.

138. *TO,* 42d. See also *M* 5567, pp. 106–107, 225.

139. *Guide,* II, 5, p. 260.

140. *LT,* III, 33d, 41d, 46d, IV, 11b, 47d, 57b, V, 24d; *TO,* 56b; MK, 251; *M Par.* II, 856–57. Cf. *Tanya,* 13a; *MK,* 381, 401.

141. Supra, nn. 122, 123; *M* 5562, p. 260; *RP,* 135; *LT,* III, 80a; *EL,* 56, 227 (cf. *M* 5562, pp. 146–47); *BY,* 65; *M* 5566, pp. 25, 367; *Sidur,* 287c; *M* 5567, p. 251.

142. See *Guide,* II, 22, pp. 319–20.

143. Although RSZ occasionally cites the views of the philosophers, he generally does so disparagingly or at least condescendingly. See *M Par.,* I, 94, 106–107, II, 558, 560; *M Iny.,* pp. 167, 335; *M Nev.,* p. 149; *M Ket.,* II, 54–55. See also *M* 5562, II, 475, 477.

144. *Tanya,* 50b, 132b; *TO,* 4d, 43c; *LT,* II, 32b, 37c, III, 5a–b, 57d, V, 4d; *Sidur,* 33a; *EL,* 90; *BZ,* 142b; *M* 5568, pp. 130, 268; *M* 5565, II, 584; *BY,* p. 110; *M Par.,* I, 22–25; *M Nev.,* p. 242. Some discourses state that angels, like flora, fauna, and minerals, possess only a single category, the one corresponding to their one-sided nature; and that only man, the microcosm, contains all four and therefore rules over the other three; *LT,* II, 37c, III, 5a–b; *M* 5568, p. 256. Cf. *M* 5568, II, 679; *M* 5563, p. 360.

145. RSZ owned these books (Hilman, *Igerot Ba'al ha-Tanya,* p. 149). He also studied David Gans's *Neḥmad ve-Na'im* (1743); see *M* 5562, p. 293. For Delmedigo on Copernicus, see *Elim* (Odessa, 1864), p. 27.

146. A. R. Hall, *The Scientific Revolution, 1500–1800* (Boston, 1962). It is noteworthy that half a century later, in the 1840s and 1850s, after virtually all astronomers had accepted Copernican astronomy, after the existence of a new planet (Neptune) had been predicted on the basis of Newton's explanation of Kepler's Laws, and telescopes had found it to be within a degree of the position predicted by Newtonian theory (Kuhn, *Copernican Revolution,* pp. 227, 261–62), R. Menaḥem Mendel wrote *Sefer ha-Ḥakirah* (New York, 1955), a scholastic philosophical treatise

based on the same principles (and works) of medieval astronomy and cosmology accepted by RSZ.

147. *Guide,* II, 4, p. 257. See *M* 5564, p. 127.

148. *M* 5562, I, 293, II, 475–79; *M Par.,* I, 15.

149. *Sidur,* 303a; *M* 5562, II, 479–80. See also *M Iny.,* p. 334.

150. *Mishneh Torah, Hil. Yesode ha-Torah,* II, 10; *Sidur,* 273c–d. Cf. *M* 5565, II, 585, where RSZ strikes a compromise: Air is presently higher, but fire will be higher "in the future."

151. *M* 5566, p. 44; *M* 5564, p. 161. See also *M* 5567, p. 35, on the spiritual mechanism responsible for rain.

152. *BY,* 109.

153. *BZ,* 8a. See also *MK,* 333.

154. *Sidur,* 137d. Cf. *M* 5558, pp. 147, 171.

155. *BY,* 109.

156. *M* 5562, p. 232.

157. *TO,* 97d; *BZ,* 65d; *BY,* 179; *M* 5566, p. 33; *M Iny.,* p. 433.

158. *M* 5566, p. 109; *MK,* 376; *M* 5563, p. 204. See also *M* 5562, II, 413.

159. *Sidur,* 130d; *M* 5568, pp. 367, 526; *LT,* III, 38c, V, 28d, 33d, 48a, 49c; *BZ,* 126c; *M* 5562, p. 139; *M* 5564, p. 121; *M* 5567, pp. 162, 184, 220; *MK,* 394; *M* 5563, II, 502; *M Par.,* I, 142, II, 701, 732; *M Ket.,* II, 97. Cf. *BZ,* 138b. According to *M* 5562, p. 245, not only the brain but man's entire animal soul is sustained by the taste of the food he eats. Cf. *M* 5562, II, 413.

See also *Sidur,* 97d, where RSZ maintains that an apple's sweetness is more closely akin to divine Pleasure than is intellectual pleasure. All this glorification of physical taste seems diametrically opposed to the position, cited supra (pp. 81–82 and n. 140), that all physical pleasure—including, of course, the taste of food (*TO,* 56b)—descends from supernal refuse. However, the contradiction is easily resolved by the highest-lowest principle: As a result of the Shevirah, Pleasure, the highest divine power, descended to the lowest level of the upper worlds, their refuse, and eventually materialized as physical pleasure. See *M* 5562, II, 413. Discourses with a more ethical thrust emphasize the invidious comparison between physical pleasure—that is, pleasure after its "fall"—(see, e.g., *M* 5567, p. 67) and the spiritual pleasure of Gan ʿEden. Discourses concentrating on theosophy or psychology tend to underscore pleasure's potency and significance.

160. *M* 5562, pp. 162, 230; *M* 5568, p. 248; *BZ,* 27c–28c; *M Par.,* I, 219, 251, 330.

161. *M* 5566, p. 262.

162. *Tanya,* 54a, 69a, 72a; *EL,* 178.

163. *Tanya,* 10b (cf. 30a).

164. *Tanya,* 45b–46b (cf. *M* 5568, pp. 88, 435); *BZ,* 127a; *LT,* II, 29d, III, 50a, et passim; *MK,* 130, 272–73; *M* 5563, p. 338, II, 697; *M Par.,* II, 576, 624, 738, 759–60, 706–707.

The idea that God created the world because He desired an abode "below," articulated in a paraphrase of *Midrash Tanḥuma* (*Naśo,* 16; cf. ibid., *Beḥuḳotay,* 4; *Bamidbar Rabah,* XIII, 6), *nitʾaveh ha-Ḳadosh barukh Hu liheyot Lo dirah be-taḥtonim,* is one of the central and most characteristic tenets of RSZ's Hasidic thought. It combines his belief in a theocentric world with his faith in *physical* man's indispensable role in it.

165. *Tanya,* 125b.

166. Ibid. Cf. *M* 5570, p. 65; *M* 5565, II, 772–73.

167. *TO,* 20a, 54b–c, 96a; *M* 5568, p. 52; *Tanya,* 46a; *M* 5564, p. 143; *MK,* 353, 574; *M* 5563, pp. 202, 231; *M* 5568, II, 687, 713–14 (cf. 697), 715; *M* 5565, II, 918; *M Raz.,* pp. 494–95; *M Nev.,* p. 61; *M Ket.,* II, 15, 228, 235; *M Par.,* I, 325.

168. Chavel, *Kitve,* II, 294f.; LT, II, 15c, III, 54b–c, IV, 7b, V, 4b, 29d, 48a, 50a; *TO,* 46b, 96a; *Sidur,* 238c; *M* 5568, pp. 52, 434; *M* 5570, p. 59; *Tanya,* 106b–107a.

169. *TO,* 73b, 96a; *LT,* II, 17a; *M* 5562, p. 152; *M* 5563, pp. 56, 201–202, II, 511; *M* 5564, p. 138; *Bereshit Rabah,* XCVI, 5: "The dead of the Land of Israel will be the first to be resurrected in the days of the Messiah." Cf. *Sidur,* 144d; *M* 5562, p. 274; *M* 5568, p. 180.

170. *Tanya,* 149a (cf. 46b, 48a, 104a).

171. Ibid., 80a.

172. *Sidur,* 34b, 236c, 245b; *Tanya,* 52a, 80a, 106b–107a, 125b, 150b; *TO,* 73b; *LT,* II, 31b, IV, 6b–c, 84d; *M* 5565, II, 960.

173. *Tanya,* 125b; *LT,* III, 75d, V, 29d; *TO,* 20a, 54c, 96a; *M* 5562, p. 152. Cf. *M* 5566, p. 259; *M* 5567, p. 222.

174. See *M* 5564, pp. 103, 105.

175. *Tanya,* 46b. Cf. *M* 5568, II, 688.

176. See *Sidur,* 238c (there, however, the Messianic Era equals the post-Resurrection era); *EL,* 81. Cf. *M* 5562, p. 274.

177. *Tanya,* 143a f.; *M* 5562, p. 152; *M* 5565, II, 641; *M* 5568, II, 688; *M Par.,* I, 261; *M Nev.,* p. 4; *M Ket.,* II, 5.

178. *M* 5568, p. 181; *M* 5562, p. 152.

179. *BY,* 23.

180. *EL,* 81.

181. *Tanya,* Pt. 1, ch. 37; *MK,* 112; *LT,* IV, 7c, 40d; *M* 5564, pp. 214, 233. See *Mishneh Torah, Hil. Teshuvah,* VII, 5.

182. *M* 5568, p. 181. But cf. note 188, infra.

183. *RP,* 121. See also Wilensky, *Ḥasidim u-Mitnagdim,* I, 295.

184. *LT,* IV, 16c; *M Nev.,* p. 95. See also *M* 5565, II, 1021, where RSZ pointedly identifies "Jerusalem below" (Tal. B., *Taʿanit,* 5a) not as the city but as Malkhut.

185. *M* 5564, p. 228.

186. *M* 5568, pp. 433–34.

187. *M* 5566, p. 102.

188. *M* 5567, p. 63. Discourses identifying exile with economic or political subjugation include *MK,* 178, 196, 221; *M* 5568, II, 681, 687. See also *M Iny.,* p. 86.

189. *M Par.,* I, 422. This was 1,775 years (see Exodus 38:28) after 68 C.E., the traditional date of the Temple's destruction. It is noteworthy that the decade beginning in 1840 saw a concerted English effort, instigated primarily by Lord Shaftesbury (then Lord Ashley), "to plant the Jewish people in the land of their fathers" (*The London Times,* August 17, 1840). Shaftesbury saw this as a necessary prelude to

the fulfillment of Biblical prophecy and the redemption of mankind. Barbara W. Tuchman, *Bible and Sword* (New York, 1956), pp. 175–223.

190. *Tanya,* Pt. 1, ch. 37.

191. *M Par.,* I, 340. See Deut. 13:4; R. Meir Simḥah ha-Kohen, *Meshekh Ḥokhmah,* Deut. 32:20.

192. *M* 5562, pp. 96–97; *Shene ha-Me'orot,* 10a–11a; *MK,* 175–76, 230, 260–61, 288, 488, 551; *M* 5563, II, 687, 731. See infra, Chapter 3, n. 75, regarding free will. A similar image of man as God's puppet or toy is found in Plato's *The Laws,* 644c f., 803c, 804b3. See also Jaeger, *Paideia,* III, 253.

193. *M. Par.* I, 339–40; *M* 5563, II, 692–93. See also *M Ket.,* I, 47.

194. *M Raz.,* pp. 141–43.

195. See infra, Chapter 3, note 7.

196. See Tal. B., *Soṭah,* 48a f.

197. *Tanya,* 96a; *TO,* 5a; *LT,* III, 85a, IV, 40a, 77c–d; *Sidur,* 137c; *EL,* 232; *M* 5562, p. 59; *BY,* 172; *MK,* 222, 362; *M* 5564, p. 243; *M Nev.,* II, 51.

198. *M* 5565, II, 774; *M* 5566, p. 367; *LT,* III, 85d–86a. Cf. *M* 5569, p. 230, where RSZ characteristically insists that the Jews of the first Temple period did not actually worship idols but rather engaged in such idolatrous practices as sorcery while remaining essentially faithful to God and His (other) commandments. Cf. *M* 5565, II, 737–38.

199. *M* 5565, II; *M* 5566; *LT,* III; *M* 5568, p. 447; *M* 5570, p. 64; *M* 5566, pp. 292–95; *MK,* 255, 326, 452, 539.

200. *M* 5567, pp. 309–10, 314–18; *M* 5565, II, 639. Cf. *TO,* 74b; *M* 5564, p. 60.

201. *Tanya,* 96a; *BY,* 172; *TO,* 5a, 50c; *BZ,* 90c; *LT,* IV, 77c–d, III, 85a; Hilman, *Igerot Ba'al ha-Tanya,* pp. 85–86. Cf., however, *MK,* 114.

202. *TO,* 56d, 74b, 49a; *M* 5565, II, 595, 639, 641; *M Par.,* I, 236.

203. *M* 5568, p. 433.

204. *Sidur,* 67d; *MK,* 438–39; *M Iny.,* p. 105; *M Raz.,* p. 316; *M Ket.,* II, 52–53.

205. *BZ,* 22d.

206. *TO,* 93a. Cf. *M* 5562, II, 339.

207. *M* 5564, p. 244; *MK,* 352. See also *M* 5564, p. 25.

208. *Sidur,* 220b, 271c. Cf. *TO,* 50b.

209. *M* 5566, p. 278; Tal. B., *Soṭah,* 49b; *TO,* 8d.

210. *TO,* 41a; *MK,* 508; *M Par.,* I, 39, 317, II, 696; *M Raz.,* p. 56. Cf. Tal. B., *Shabat,* 112b, *'Eruvin,* 53a, *Yuma,* 9b, *Berakhot,* 20a.

211. *Sidur,* 163a.

212. *M* 5563, II, 690, 774–75.

213. *Sidur,* 115d. See also *M* 5564, p. 228. It is an axiom of Maggidic thought that, contrary to Aristotle, the potential—that is, the still hidden (e.g., Ḥokhmah)—is always greater and purer than the revealed and actual (e.g., Binah). Related to this are the ideas that the yet unknown—and certainly the unknowable—is ontologically superior to the known, the simple (= yet undifferentiated) is superior to the complex. At the root of these value judgments is the belief that the Divine Ayin is superior to the subsequent yesh, since it is, in the Maggid's view, pure, unlimited potentiality. See *MK,* 380, 387.

214. *MK,* 395, 474, (but cf. the following discourses): *M* 5563, pp. 7–8; *M* 5565, II, 780–82; *M* 5564, p. 50; *M* 5567, p. 369; *EL,* 40–41; *BZ,* 81a; *M* 5568, pp. 277–78, 540; *Sidur,* 16b; *M* 5566, p. 372.

215. *TO,* 5a.

216. *EL,* 37; *M* 5565, II, 701.

217. *Tanya,* 151b–152a; *M* 5567, p. 211; *M Ket.,* II, 134; cf. *RP,* 93.

218. *Tanya,* 5b–6a, 7b; *Sidur,* 156a; *BZ,* 99a–b; *EL,* 229; *M* 5562, p. 96; *M* 5564, p. 5; *M* 5567, p. 130. Cf. *M* 5566, p. 388; *Tikune Zohar,* XVIII, 35; Zohar, I, 263b; *Shevile Emunah* (Warsaw, 1887), pp. 56b, 98b; *Sha'ar ha-Shamayim* (Roedelheim, 1801), p. 45b; *Elimah,* 139d; cf. also *BZ,* 138b. RSZ, following the Zohar, uses a similar line of thought to explain the supposed difference in intelligence between inhabitants of different locations: It depends on the water they drink, for Ḥokhmah is materialized in water; *MK,* 2–3; *M* 5563, II, 664. See also *MK,* 152.

219. *LT,* III, 31c et passim; *EL,* 136; *M* 5563, p. 351; *M* 5565, II, 889; *M* 5568, p. 125; *BY,* 167; *Tanya,* 122a–123a; introduction to *Tikune Zohar.*

220. *M* 5564, pp. 102, 193; *M* 5567, p. 33; *TO,* 92b; *M* 5562, p. 242. But cf. *M* 5565, II, 580.

221. *EL,* 56; *M* 5564, p. 120; *M Par.,* I, 413.

222. *RP,* 92.

223. *Tanya,* 5b–6a, 13b, 28a, 36a (cf. *BY,* 168), 71a–b; *LT,* V, 13d, III, 11a; *M* 5562, pp. 129, 213; *M* 5564, p. 66; *M* 5568, p. 125; *Sidur,* 203a–b; *EL,* 84; *BZ,* 82c, 123b; *MK,* 59.

224. *Tanya,* 131a; *LT,* III, 48b, IV, 49c, V, 22d et passim; *M* 5568, pp. 237–38; *M* 5562, pp. 211, 229; *BZ,* 69d, 127c–d. Cf. *LT,* V, 46c, IV, 38c–d, 76d; *Sidur,* 42a, 55a, 83d. Tears, too, are described as an overflow of *moḥin* (intellect, brain matter); *M* 5568, p. 535; *M* 5566, pp. 121–22; *M* 5565, II, 841; *M* 5562, II, 352; *M Ket.,* II, 150.

225. *LT,* II, 28d; *BZ,* 69d, 37d; *M* 5567, p. 61; *M* 5563, p. 290; *Sidur,* 57c. Cf. *M* 5562, p. 138; *BZ,* 104c; *M Ket.,* II, 187.

226. *BZ,* 37a–c; *EL,* 87, 213; *M* 5564, p. 34; *M* 5568, p. 444; *M* 5562, p. 245; *M* 5563, p. 114.

227. *M* 5564, p. 34. Cf. *Tanya,* 71b.

228. *M* 5568, pp. 71, 116, 118, 308, 375; *BZ,* 14c–15a; cf. *M* 5562, II, 370. See also *M* 5563, II, 688.

229. *M* 5565, II, 767; *M* 5566, p. 30; *M* 5562, pp. 222–23, and cf. p. 119; *M* 5563, I, 36, 281–82, 288, II, 532.

230. *EL,* 229, 234–35; *M* 5568, p. 292; *BY,* 146, 157; *BZ,* 113c; *M* 5562, p. 57; *RP,* 20. See also *M* 5563, pp. 216–17. When immersed in the subject, the intellect is said to be clothed in it; once the subject is *apprehended* (from the Latin *apprehendere,* to grasp, which connotes enveloping) the intellect is said to clothe it. See *Tanya,* Pt. 1, ch. 5; *M* 5565, II, 713.

231. *M* 5562, p. 173; *M* 5566, p. 296; *EL,* 93, 144, 242; *M Par.,* II, 625. See also *MK,* 227.

232. *BZ,* 122a–123b; *M* 5566, p. 389; *M* 5565, II, 812. Cf. *LT,* III, 77d.

233. *TO,* 15c, 74a, 117c; *Sidur,* 97d, 101a; *M* 5562, p. 238; *LT,* II, 13b; *Shene ha-Me'orot,* 13a.

234. *Sidur,* 203a–b; *BZ,* 137a; *M* 5564, p. 140; *M Raz.,* p. 315.

235. *TO,* 15d, 65d–66a, 124b; *LT,* II, 13b, 15c (cf. *TO,* 78c), 38c, III, 41d, 94a, V, 13d; *Sidur,* 101a, 203a–d. Cf. *M* 5562, p. 238.

236. *LT,* II, 13b.

237. *Tanya,* 71a–b. It is arguable, however, that this passage refers to the body when it is engaged in fulfilling a commandment. See also *MK,* 114.

238. *BY,* 167; *LT,* III, 80a.

239. *Tanya,* 69b–70.

240. *LT,* III, 40c, II, 38b; *M* 5562, p. 269, II, 331; *M* 5566, p. 165; *M* 5568, p. 542; *M* 5565, II, 849, 1007.

241. *TO,* 86b; *LT,* IV, 49c, V, 49b; *BZ,* 110b; *M* 5562, II, 413–14; *M* 5565, II, 824–28, 832, 859–60, 880; *M Ket.,* II, 174, 275.

242. *M* 5568, pp. 227, 320, 403, 406; *M* 5570, p. 33; *LT,* III, 15d–16a. Cf. *EL,* 69, 79; *M* 5566, p. 29; *MK,* 333, 338, 449, 494.

243. *Tanya,* 60b; *M* 5562, p. 242; *M* 5568, pp. 320, 403; *M* 5566, p. 30; *M* 5567, pp. 248–49; *TO,* 13c. Cf. *Guide,* III, 12, p. 445.

244. *Tanya,* 50a; *TO,* 29b, 30b; *LT,* IV, 34a; *BY,* 138; *M Par.,* II, 829–30. See also *Tanya,* 159a; *LT,* III, 65b–d, IV, 1a; *TO,* 4d; *M* 5564, p. 102. Cf. *Degel Maḥne Efrayim,* p. 96.

245. *Tanya,* 148b–149a; *TO,* 16a, 16c; *LT,* III, 51d; *M* 5563, II, 628, version 2. See also *BZ,* 43d, where RSZ cites Luria's view that these garments require purification because Adam's sin sullied them.

246. *TO,* 24d, 39c–d, 63c, 71c; *LT,* III, 38d, 73d, IV, 75b; *M* 5565, II, 776. See also *TO,* 63a, 71a; *LT,* III, 67d, IV 25a; *M Par.,* II, 516. Note the contradictions among *LT,* III, 40b, *Sidur,* 287a–d, and *LT,* III, 67d, on whether or not the soul was originally united with the Godhead. Cf. also *LT,* IV, 69a, II, 16c; *EL,* 113; *BZ,* 115a; and *LT,* III, 67d, IV, 27a; *TO,* 26d; *Tanya,* 148b–149; *BY,* 136; *M Iny.,* pp. 255, 408, 422, 428.

247. *TO,* 32d–33a.

248. These garments (*levushim*) should not be confused with the 613 Lurianic soul-garments, which RSZ discusses in *TO,* 16c, and elsewhere; or with the *levush* discussed in *Tanya,* 7a. On the two souls and the three garments, see *Tanya,* Pt. 1, chs. 1–13; *M Par.,* I, 140–41.

249. *Tanya,* 18a; *M* 5569, p. 69.

250. Ibid., 18b. Cf. Zohar, III, 224a.

251. *Tanya,* 24b.

252. However, at least one discourse, (assuming it is correctly attributed to RSZ) identifies nature with the rational and the true. According to *M Raz.,* p. 91, in the natural and rational order of things, most individuals would never deliberately choose their predestined spouses, for uniting a couple in a lasting marriage requires a power transcending reason and nature—the power of God Himself (see *Bereshit Rabah,* 68:4) as mediated by the matchmaker, who misleads reason and contravenes nature by lying religiously.

253. *Tanya,* 23b.

254. Ibid., 24b. According to Mindel, *R. Schneur Zalman,* vol. 2, p. 189 n. 3, "this passage does not mean extinction of the soul; only its cessation as a *distinct*

entity." This is borne out by Rabbi Menaḥem Mendel's gloss in *LT,* III, 45c. Since, according to such mystics as Cordovero, the Maggid, and RSZ, God is the only absolutely real existent, the soul could be said truly to exist only when completely submerged in Him. See also Chapter 3, n. 60.

255. *Tanya,* Pt. 1, chs. 9, 12, 16–18, 25.

256. Ibid., 25a.

257. Ibid., 16b–19a, 59a–60a. See also *M Par.,* II, 654; *M Nev.,* pp. 203–204; *M Ket.,* I, 35.

258. See E. Urbach, *Ḥazal: Pirḳe Emunot ve-De'ot* (Jerusalem, 1969), pp. 415–27; Julius Guttmann, *Philosophies of Judaism,* trans. David W. Silverman (New York, 1964), pp. 23–29; *Kuzari,* I, 27, 95, II, 44, 54, V, 16.

259. *Hil. Yesode ha-Torah,* IV, 8–9. On the correspondence of the animal soul with the yetser ha-ra, see Zohar, I, 79b.

260. *LT,* II, 46, 47c; *M* 5566, pp. 31, 163; *EL,* 210; *M* 5568, p. 116; *TO,* 39c.

261. *EL,* 75; *Tanya,* 122a; *M* 5568, p. 405; *Tanya,* 123a.

262. *LT,* III, 40c.

263. *Tanya,* 12b, 14b, 35a; *TO,* 38b; *Shene ha-Me'orot,* 1–3b. Cf. *Tanya,* 45a. See also *MK,* 123.

264. *Tanya,* 12b, 14b. See also *MK,* 302, 382.

265. *M* 5562, p. 273; *M* 5566, p. 68; *LT,* III, 56d.

266. See *Tanya,* Pt. 1, ch. 12. Cf. also *LT,* III, 42b, 91a. At least one discourse apparently maintains that a *Tsadiḳ* may occasionally succumb to thoughts that according to Tanya would classify him as a *Rasha* (a "wicked man"); see *M* 5563, II, 675 and cf. *Tanya,* 15b–16a, 33b–34a, 35a, although the wording of these passages suggests a distinction between merely idle thoughts and positively sinful thoughts.

267. *LT,* III, 29d, 92a; *M* 5562, p. 242; *M* 5563, pp. 41, 117; *BZ,* 99b, 106b, 114d, 115a; *M* 5568, pp. 4, 13; *Shene ha-Me'orot,* 34b; *BY,* 83.

268. See supra, n. 246.

269. *LT,* III, 79d; *TO,* 71b–c; *EL,* 75, 122–23, 188; *M* 5562, pp. 155, 194, 209–10, 212, 255; *BY,* 83; *M* 5564, pp. 34, 135, 186; *MK,* 32, 40–41, 99, 501–502, 511; *M* 5568, II, 670; *M* 5563, II, 621–23.

270. *EL,* 169; *M* 5562, pp. 209–10; *M* 5563, pp. 197, 313, II, 517, version 2, 604, version 2, 737, 761, 787; *M* 5565, II, 699–700; *M* 5568, pp. 4, 13, 323; *M* 5564, pp. 135, 151; *M* 5567, p. 207; *LT,* IV, 54b, 56d, V, 13d; *Sidur,* 130c, 161b, 234d; *TO,* 75a; *BZ,* 75b; *M Par.,* I, 161, 180–81, 188; *M Raz.,* p. 56. Cf. *Tanya,* 105a–106a, 161a–b; *MK,* 179.

Yeḥidah is occasionally identified as the transcendent aspect of the soul; see supra nn. 241, 242; cf. *M* 5564, p. 5; *MK,* 484.

271. *EL,* 75; *Tanya,* 7b, 59b, 66b, 123a, 124a; *TO,* 19a–b, 75a, 88a; *LT,* II, 29b, III, 28a, IV, 5a–b, 19c, V, 39b; *M* 5568, p. 292; *M* 5567, p. 182; *MK,* 324, 487; *M* 5563, pp. 197, 313. Note that in *M* 5565, II, 770, 951, Da'at is defined as the faculty responsible for self-consciousness and self-knowledge. Cf. *MK,* 484–85. See also *M Par.,* I, 342; *M Raz.,* p. 450; *M Ket.,* II, 173.

272. *Tanya,* 7a, 10a, 123a; *BZ,* 31d.

273. *EL,* 57.

274. *BZ,* 47d–48a, 103d. Cf. *EL,* 212; *M* 5562, p. 87.

275. E.g., *TO,* 19a–b. See also *LT,* V, 30b, 46d, III, 19b, 23a, IV, 58d; *BZ,* 47d, 54b; *M* 5563, p. 149.

276. *M* 5568, I, pp. 2–4, 6, 9, 388. See also *Sidur,* 272b; *LT,* V, 47c; *M* 5563, pp. 216–17; *M* 5562, II, 508; *M Par.,* II, 629; *M Iny.,* pp. 418, 420, 426; *M Raz.,* p. 324; *M Ket.,* I, 208.

277. *BZ,* 106b; *M* 5568, I, 427, II, 637; *M* 5562, p. 129, II, 388–89; *M* 5568, II, p. 405; *EL,* 212; *M* 5564, p. 66; *TO,* 38b.

278. *EL,* 213, 218; *Sidur,* 52d, 264a; *M* 5562, p. 245; *BZ,* 34a–b, 137c; *M* 5568, pp. 79, 444; *EL,* 87, 213; *TO,* 93b; *MK,* 13.

279. *M* 5568, p. 427; *M* 5565, II, 856, 889; *M* 5567, p. 207. Cf. *EL,* 258; *MK,* 179.

280. *TO,* 42b; *Tanya,* 76b–77b, 79b, 84a–85a, 88a–90a, 107a–b; *LT,* II, 36a, 45d, 52d–53a, III, 58a, V, 6b, 32d; *BY,* 151; *Sidur,* 52d, 57c, 270b–271a; *M* 5562, pp. 108, 112, 189; *EL,* 115–16; *BZ,* 98d, 104c, 113c, 122c, 139d; *MK,* 320; *M* 5563, p. 141. See also *Tanya,* 79b, 130b; *Sidur,* 181a; *LT,* IV, 39b.

281. Cf. *TO,* 71a; *LT,* III, 45d–46b, 52d, V, 4b, and Rabbi Menaḥem Mendel's gloss, V, 1c; *Sidur,* 181a, 245a, 272d; *M* 5568, pp. 118, 429, 562. See also *M* 5563, pp. 310–11.

282. *EL,* 105, 108, 170, 175; *LT,* II, 16d.

283. *M* 5562, p. 35; *M* 5568, pp. 484, 548. Cf. *LT,* II, 28d; *M* 5568, p. 474.

284. *M* 5562, p. 4; *M* 5565, II, 890. See also *EL,* 175.

285. Supra, n. 267; *Tanya,* 6a, 77b, 88a–90a, 93b–95a, 107b–109b, 122a–b, 130b, 139a; *LT,* II, 41b, III, 57c–d, 67d, 92a, IV, 24d, 39b, 69a, V, 25c; *Sidur,* 181a, 270d–271a; *EL,* 258; *BZ,* 91c, 99a; *M* 5568, p. 247; *M* 5566, p. 389; *TO,* 16a.

286. *LT,* II, 50d, III, 11c, 12d, 29b; *Sidur,* 260a, 264a, 309d.

287. Tal. B., *Sanhedrin,* 34a, *Bamidbar Rabah,* XIII, 15 (cf. Tal. B., *Shabat,* 88b); Zohar, I, 47b, 54a, III, 160a, 216a; *Tanya,* 5b, note; *LT,* IV, 94a; Max Kadushin, *The Rabbinic Mind* (New York, 1965), pp. 115–30; Scholem, *On the Kabbalah,* pp. 60–65.

288. See, e.g., *BZ,* 107a, 129d. RSZ's view may, however, have been similar to Naḥmanides'. See Elliot R. Wolfson, "By Way of Truth: Aspects of Naḥmanides' Kabbalistic Hermeneutics," *AJS Review* 14 (1989): 125–52.

289. E.g., *LT,* V, 4b.

290. See *Tanya,* 6a–b, 19a, 21a (note), 23b–24a, 25b, 118a; R. Menaḥem Mendel's gloss, *LT,* III, 73c; *Sidur,* 181c; *RP,* 28; *BZ,* 99a–b, 106b, 114d.

291. *LT,* II, 16c, III, 15b, IV, 13c; *Tanya,* 62a–63b, 94a, 119a–b; *EL,* 61, 150, 216, 246; *TO,* 23c, 74c–d, 77a; *M* 5562, p. 274, II, 384; *M* 5566, p. 54; *MK,* 27, 123, 309, 384; *M* 5563, p. 129; *M Nev.,* p. 1.

292. *Tanya,* 20b.

293. Ibid., 7a.

294. Ibid., 6b–7a. See also *MK,* 114; *M* 5562, II, 365.

295. *EL,* 36; *M* 5568, p. 26; *M* 5566, pp. 102, 114.

296. *Tanya,* 11a; *M* 5563, p. 88; *BY,* 79; *M Par.,* I, 194, II, 793, 681. Nevertheless, the evil inclination of Jews is greater than that of gentiles, for "whoever is greater than his fellow has a greater [evil] inclination"; *M* 5563, II, 734; Tal. B., *Sukah,* 52a.

297. *LT,* III, 43a.

298. *BY,* 130 (four versions of this discourse appear in *M Nev.,* pp. 127–42); *Tanya,* 13a–b; *M* 5566, p. 25; *MK,* 232; *M* 5563, pp. 274–75.

299. *Tanya,* 81a, 114a; *M* 5565, II, 644; *M Par.,* I, 388.

300. *MK,* 258.

301. *BY,* 2.

302. *Sidur,* 142c; *M Iny.,* p. 383. See also *TO,* 61a; *LT,* III, 80a.

303. *BY,* 173; *MK,* 123; *LT,* III, 80a; *M Par.,* I, 390, 403. Cf. *Sidur,* 284c; *RP,* 18.

304. *MK,* 133.

305. *Sidur,* 303a, 305a; *M Par.,* II, 585. Cf. ch. 8 of Maimonides' introduction to *Avot, Shemonah Peraḳim* (p. 399 in Ḳafiḥ's edition of Maimonides' Mishnah commentary [Mosad ha-Rav Kuk, Jerusalem, 1963–1968]): **ובזה חולקים המדברים, לפי ששמעתים אומרים שהרצון בכל דבר הוא בכל עת ועת. ולא כן אמונתנו אנו, אלא הרצון היה בששת ימי בראשית, ושכל הדברים ינהגו לפי טבעיהם תמיד, כמו שאמר: מה שהיה הוא שיהיה ומה שנעשה הוא שיעשה ואין כל חדש תחת השמש**. This idea is repeated in his commentary to *Avot,* V, 5, and in *Guide,* II, 29.

Here, as in many other instances, RSZ was undoubtedly aware of Maimonides' view but chose to ignore it—or perhaps to reinterpret it in "the Hasidic manner"—since it conflicted with the views of the Besht and Maggid (and usually also of Luria, Cordovero or both). See *Tanya,* 76b–77a.

Continuous creation was also taught by Halevi; *Kuzari,* III, 11.

306. *Sidur,* 133a. See also *MK,* 178, 213, 256, 268, 270, 274, 310, 444–45; *M Par.,* II, 653–57.

307. *M* 5566, p. 106; *M* 5563, II, 536, version 2.

308. *LT,* 80a, 89b; *Sidur,* 142c; *Tanya,* 28a.

309. *Tanya,* 46a; *LT,* III, 89c; *BZ,* 24c. See also *BY,* 51.

310. *M* 5563, II, 539, version 2; *M Par.,* II, 515.

311. *M Par.,* I, 150.

312. *LT,* III, 40c.

313. *Sidur,* 146b; *EL,* 51; *M Ket.,* II, 185.

314. *LT,* III, 43a. Until then, however, fulfilling a commandment has no effect whatsoever on a gentile's soul; *M* 5563, II, 755, 780.

315. *MK,* 102–103.

316. *Tanya,* 140a; cf. 27b.

317. See ibid., 25a, 27b; *BY,* 79; *MK,* 251.

318. *EL,* 227; *M Par.,* I, 208.

319. *Tanya,* 140a; supra, pp. 90–91.

320. *Sidur,* 69c; *TO,* 61a; *M* 5562, pp. 146–48; *M* 5565, II, 776, 786–89; *M* 5563, I, 88, II, 543; *M* 5570, p. 36; *MK,* 330; *M Par.,* I, 71, 74, 93–94; *M Ket.,* II, 52–53.

Chapter 3. Ethical Ways and Means

1. See e.g., *M* 5562, II, 397; *M* 5563, II, 490, 769; *M Par.,* I, 174, 251, 289, II, 510–11; *M Iny.,* pp. 333, 424; *M Nev.,* p. 251; *M Ket.,* I, 32, 239.

2. *Tanya,* 20b, 38b, 126b (top); *LT,* III, 42c.

3. *TO,* 51b. Cf. *M* 5562, p. 34.

4. *Sidur,* 56c; *M* 5562, p. 169; *Tanya,* 58a; *BY,* 46, 99; *EL,* 127; *MK,* 10, 411.

5. *M* 5563, II, 774–75; *M Par.,* pp. 248–49; *M Ket.,* I, 121, 239.

6. For the Maggid, see Schatz, *Ha-Ḥasidut ke-Misṭikah,* pp. 26–30 and the index to her edition of *Magid* under *biṭul bi-metsiut; Or Torah,* 45b et passim. For R. Abraham, see *Ḥesed le-Avraham,* 9a, 21a, 30b, 33a et passim. For R. Menaḥem Mendel, see *Peri ha-Arets,* 15, 33, 36, 38, 44, 47, 55, 59 et passim.

7. *LT,* II, 37a, IV, 14d, 67b, V, 29c; *RP,* 102; *TO* 96b; *Sidur,* 146b.

8. *BY,* 15, 150, 170; *MK,* 97–98; *M* 5567, pp. 246–47; *Tanya,* 62a (note the repetition of the word *mamash*), 78a–b (cf. 42a); *M Par.,* I, 27, 402, II, 759–60, 847, 873; *M Iny.,* p. 272.

9. *BY,* 105; supra, Chapter 2, note 192.

10. *LT,* III, 87a, V, 29c.

11. *Tanya,* 79a–82b; *LT,* III, 88c–d, IV, 23d–24a, 56a–b, 67c; *Sidur,* 240c–241a; *MK,* 272–73, 389, 485, 491; *M* 5563, pp. 347–48.

12. *TO,* 11a, 96b.

13. *LT,* II, 42c, IV, 55c; *M* 5562, p. 251; *M* 5564, p. 8; *M* 5567, p. 153.

14. *M* 5568, p. 379.

15. *RP,* 149; *TO,* 68b, 119c; *M* 5562, pp. 45, 251, 284; *LT,* III, 16b; *Tanya,* 44b, note; *Sidur,* 83a, 87c; *MK,* 305–306; *M* 5563, pp. 324, 368.

16. *Sidur,* 116a; *TO,* 45c; *M* 5565, II, 714; *EL,* 262. See also *M* 5562, p. 274; *M* 5564, p. 238; *MK,* 40–41.

17. *LT,* III, 40d–41a, IV, 55c; *M* 5562, p. 264; *M* 5568, p. 437; *M* 5567, pp. 305–306; *BZ,* 16a–b; *Tanya,* 28b, 47b.

18. *LT,* III, 1b, 2a, 24c, 62d, IV, 20a, 55c, V, 37a; *M* 5567, p. 358; *BY,* 72, 178; *MK,* 195; *EL,* 109, 261; *M* 5562, I, 175, 251, 277, II, 350, 362, 365, 381; *M* 5566, pp. 102, 315; *BZ,* 141a; *M* 5563, II, 519, version 2, 624, 705; *M Par.,* I, 403, 418, II, 620; *M Iny.,* p. 232; *M Nev.,* p. 86; *M Ket.,* II, 16, 129, 140, 142.

19. *LT,* IV, 67b.

20. *Kuzari,* II, 26, 48, 60, III, 53; Maharal's *Tifeʾret Yiśraʾel,* chs. 6 and 15; Kleinberger, *Ha-Maḥshavah,* pp. 101–102, 112, 117–18, 181; A. Altmann, ed., *Three Jewish Philosophers* (New York, 1979), Pt. 2, pp. 44–46, 113–14; *Guide,* III, 12, 25–26, 31; *Mishneh Torah, Hil. Meʿilah,* VIII, 8.

21. *M* 5564, p. 130; *M* 5567, p. 358; *BZ,* 82d, 83b; *MK,* 121–22; *M* 5562, II, 473.

22. *LT,* III, 40a, IV, 54a. See also *M Nev.,* p. 7. RSZ's definition of *ṭaʿame ha-mitsvot* will be discussed in Chapter 4.

23. *BY,* 46; *TO,* 17b; *BZ,* 82d; *M* 5568, pp. 500–501; *M* 5563, II, 505; *M* 5562, pp. 114, 169, 277; *M Ket.,* II, 3. See also *BY,* 56.

24. See *Tanya,* 56a–57a, 60b; *LT,* III, 55b, IV, 29b–c; *TO,* 78d–79a; *M* 5564, p. 130; *EL,* 189; *M* 5562, pp. 114, 277, 279; *M* 5566, pp. 371–72; *BZ,* 81a; *MK,* 408, 490; *M* 5565, II, 780–82; *M* 5567, p. 367; *Or Torah,* 102b; *M Par.,* I, 130; *Peri ha-Arets,* 11, 20, 38, 45, 68; *Ḥesed le-Avraham,* 4a–b, 25a, 30b; *Meʾor ʿEnayim,* pp. 224, 234; *Ḳedushat Levi,* pp. 6, 141, 186 (cf. pp. 213–14). Cf. *Or Torah,* 101a; *Peri ha-Arets,* 65; and *Ḳedushat Levi,* p. 12, where Love is linked with Ḥokhmah and/or Ayin; and *Keter Shem Ṭov,* nos. 38, 177, 180, 207; *M Par.,* I, 390; *M Iny.,* p. 48.

See also Tishby, *Mishnat ha-Zohar,* II, 294–97; A. Altmann's review in *Ḳiryat Sefer* 34 (1959): 52. RSZ's approach will be discussed in more detail in Chapter 5.

25. *M* 5562, pp. 180, 263; *BY,* 99, 101, 115, 124, 170; *EL,* 184; *M* 5568, p. 163. In *MK,* 32, RSZ echoes the Maggid (see supra, p. 27) in stating that God can be "apprehended" not through intellect but only through suprarational desire. See also *M* 5570, p. 124, where RSZ states that contrary to the belief of philosophers and (other) heretics, God transcends intellect and can be truly apprehended only through faith.

26. *Shene ha-Me'orot,* 4b; *BY,* 93, 98; *Tanya,* 13b–14a.

27. *BY,* 106, 120, 122, 133; *EL,* 119, 128, 190, 219; *M* 5562, pp. 204, 218. Cf. *Keter Shem Ṭov,* 243.

28. *Tanya,* 31b, 116a–b; *MK,* 259, 526. These concepts are discussed further infra.

29. *MK,* 119, 237.

30. *BY,* 51; *MK,* 171–72, 175–76, 518; *TO,* 20b; *Igerot Ḳodesh,* p. 183; *EL,* p. 98.

31. Hilman, *Igerot Baʿal ha-Tanya,* p. 85; *M* 5570, p. 178; *M* 5562, p. 235.

32. *MK,* 342–43, 526, 555; *M* 5563, p. 129.

33. *BY,* 50, 71, 89–90, 130; *M* 5562, p. 169; this point is discussed further infra.

34. *EL,* 34, 115.

35. *M* 5562, p. 377; *M Par.,* II, 773, 837.

36. *TO,* 29b, 36b, 61b, 98a–99b; *LT,* III, 69a, IV, 11c, 25a, 46c–d, 74a, V, 1a, 42b; *M* 5562, pp. 175, 209; *BY,* 72, 89–90; *EL,* 109; *MK,* 99, 122, 165, 167, 302; *M Nev.,* pp. 139–40. Cf. Tishby, *Mishnat ha-Zohar,* II, 290–91, 297.

37. Tal. B., *ʿAvodah Zarah,* 11a; *M* 5566, p. 134; *LT,* II, 26b, IV, 54b. Cf. Maharal, *Netivot ʿOlam* (Jerusalem, 1971), *Teshuvah,* ch. 8.

38. See *EL,* 127; *TO,* 25a; *LT,* III, 55b, V, 36b; *Tanya,* 62b.

39. *M* 5562, pp. 13, 58; *M* 5563, p. 367; *M* 5566, pp. 102, 354; *Tanya,* 24a, 31b–32a, 58a; *TO,* 105d, 124d; *LT,* II, 3d; *Sidur* 26a; *MK,* 99, 109, 439. The value of actively desired martyrdom is also supported by reference to R. Joseph Karo's frequent allusions to it in *Magid Mishnah; M* 5566, p. 134.

Here, as in the value of self-mortification (see infra), the mystic's quest for biṭul and unio led him along the same path taken by Ḥaside Ashkenaz for different reasons. See S. Spiegel, "Me-Agadot ha-ʿAḳedah," *Sefer ha-Yovel Alexander Marx* (New York, 1958), pp. 534–37. RSZ's approach should also be distinguished from R. Akiva's desire to fulfill *be-khol nafshekha* ("with all your soul"; Deut. 6:5) by suffering martyrdom (Tal. B., *Berakhot* 61b). There the motive was undoubtedly not self-annihilation but self-dedication even to the extent of self-sacrifice, for as Max Kadushin, *Worship and Ethics* (New York, 1963), p. 180, has noted: "There is no self-naughting of any kind" in rabbinic worship. Rabbinic acts of worship "are emphatically not a means of communion or fusion with the divine. . . . What is experienced in all the forms of Jewish worship considered here is not communion but God's nearness." Thus, while RSZ the mystic extolled self-annihilation, RSZ the Talmudist insisted on self-dedication through the fulfillment of the commandments in this world. Indeed, "the purpose of this world's creation is that the Holy One, blessed be He, desired to have an abode in the lower worlds" (*Tanya,* 45b). And this abode is prepared through the fulfillment of the commandments (*Tanya,* 46b–49b;

MK, 130, 272–73). It follows that R. Akiva's desire was predicated on the fact that, under certain conditions, martyrdom is part of the commandment to love God, and, as the wording for the passage implies, he was concerned lest these conditions never materialize, thereby depriving him of giving his last full measure of devotion. The mystic, on the other hand, including RSZ in the discourses cited, sees martyrdom as the highest form of self-annihilation and as therefore transcending the commandments.

40. *LT,* III, 85a, IV, 44a, 76b, V, 37a; *BY,* 33, 57, 48, 145; *M* 5567, p. 262; *M* 5562, p. 239.

41. See infra for further discussion.

42. See Maharal, *Netivot ʿOlam, Yisurin,* chs. 1, 2; E. Underhill, *Mysticism* (New York, 1911), Pt. 2, ch. 3.

43. *LT,* V, 35d; *TO,* 61b; *BY,* 89–90; *MK,* 85, 106, 163–64, 192, 229, 425, 483; *M* 5563, p. 110; *M* 5567, p. 148; *M* 5570, pp. 35–37, 41.

44. *Tanya,* 34a. Cf. ibid., 38b; *LT,* I, 3a–d, III, 36b, V, 32a–b; *BY,* 145. See also *BY,* 56, 78–79.

45. *M* 5564, p. 130; *LT,* III, 55b, IV, 29b; *RP,* 160; *BZ,* 134a; *MK,* 371, 436; *M* 5565, II, 780–82; *M Par.,* I, 130.

46. *LT,* V, 36b. See also *M* 5565, II, 514; *M* 5567, p. 262 (where sovev is linked with asceticism).

47. *LT,* V, 26b–c.

48. *Guide,* III, 32, p. 526f.

49. *Igerot Ḳodesh,* pp. 40–41. See also *EL,* 219; and infra n. 50.

50. *Tanya,* 64a, 96b, 98a, 109b, 161b; *TO,* 24a, 51a; *LT,* II, 26c, III, 35b, IV, 13c, 41a, V, 49c; *M Par.,* I, 399, II, 894–95; *M Iny.,* pp. 311, 460; *M Raz.,* pp. 18, 92, 96; *M Nev.,* pp. 108, 112, 126 (cf. pp. 135, 138), 155, 251; *M Ket.,* I, 32–33, 239. Cf. *Sidur,* 227c; *MK,* 49–50.

51. *TO,* 46c, 56d; *LT,* III, 78c; *BY,* 126–27; *Tanya,* 21b–22a, 53b, 56a–59a, 63b.

52. See *BY,* 77, 111, 115, 122, 129, 133; *MK,* 293; *EL,* 102, 119, 189–90; *M* 5562, pp. 218, 239. But cf. *M Ket.,* II, 175.

53. *Tanya,* 38b, 59b; *LT,* III, 70c.

54. *LT,* III, 67d, 71b, 88d, IV, 77b; *BY,* 96; *MK,* 122; *M* 5563, pp. 236–37.

55. *LT,* III, 86a, 88d. Cf. *Tanya,* 135a; *LT,* III, 67d, 71b, IV, 77b; *BY,* 56; *MK,* 520; *M* 5563, II, 635, version 2.

56. *Tanya,* 24a, 31b; *TO,* 99b; *LT,* III, 61b, IV, 46c–d; *BY,* 99; *EL,* 128; *M* 5562, pp. 114, 170; *MK,* 40–41, 99, 411.

57. *M* 5566, p. 377; *M* 5568, p. 363; *BZ,* 59b; *M* 5562, p. 51; *M Par.,* I, 320, 342; *MK,* 474, 522. Cf. *Liḳuṭim Yeḳarim,* 278; *Tsavaʾat ha-Ribash,* 32.

58. E.g., *M Raz.,* pp. 88–89, a discourse apparently delivered around 1812.

59. *Tanya,* 29a–b, 46b; *BY,* 89, 101, 113, 139, 143; *TO,* 31d.

60. Which, according to R. Menaḥem Mendel's gloss in *LT,* III, 45c, does not mean self-extinction but self-vitalization through union with the divine Source of vitality. See also *M Nev.,* p. 212; *M Ket.,* p. 184. Cf., however, *LT,* II, 20a–b, 40c–d; *Tanya,* 24b; *M Raz.,* pp. 20, 220–21; *M Par.,* I, 240.

61. See, e.g., *MK,* 503; *M* 5562, II, 350–52; *M Par.,* I, 359; *M Nev.,* p. 251; *M Ket.,* I, 239.

62. *BY,* 36, 45, 129; *M* 5562, p. 142; *Tanya,* Pt. 1, chs. 26–33, introduction to Pt. 2, 76a. Cf. *Sefer ha-Yashar* (Jerusalem, 1967), p. 76.

63. *M* 5562, p. 164; *MK,* 53; *M* 5563, pp. 172–73. Cf. *RP,* 160.

64. *TO,* 18a, 21c, 25d; *LT,* III, 20a, V, 20c, 37a; supra, Chapter 2, pp. 73, 77, 88–89.

65. Guttman, *Philosophies of Judaism,* p. 176.

66. Supra, Chapter 1, p. 19.

67. See, e.g., *M Ket.,* I, 183–84. And see Chapter 5, pp. 185–86 and n. 42.

68. E.g., *Tanya,* 7b, 20b–21b, 25b–27a, 42a, 56a–b, 59b, 60b, 62a, 67a–70a, 109b–110a, 126b–127a; *M* 5565, II, 820; *M* 5562, p. 218; *BY,* 56; *MK,* 389, 468–69, 472–73, 519.

69. *Tanya,* 36b–37a, 39a, 40a–b, 65a–b, 97a–98a; *BY,* 36, 106, 114, 129, 133; *EL,* 128, 190; *M* 5562, p. 219.

70. *Tanya,* 42a, 61a, 61b; *M* 5564, p. 208; *M* 5567, pp. 72, 246–47; *Shene ha-Me'orot,* 38b; *BY,* 15, 89–90, 98, 129, 170; *M* 5570, pp. 44–47. Cf. *Degel Maḥneh Efrayim,* p. 18.

71. *LT,* IV, 4a; *Sidur,* 284c; *M* 5563, pp. 176, 356; *M* 5565, II, 729. Cf. *Degel Maḥneh Efrayim,* p. 234; *M Raz.,* p. 95; see I. Efros, *Studies in Medieval Jewish Philosophy* (Columbia University Press, 1974), p. 14, that for Saadya the idea of God is as self-evident as mathematical and logical axioms.

72. *Igerot Ḳodesh,* p. 88; *Tanya,* 60b; 141b; *TO,* 6a, 11a; *M* 5564, pp. 90–91; *LT,* IV, 4a, 46c; *Sidur,* 237b; *MK,* 256, 268; *M Nev.,* p. 149 (faith is required to buttress reason and prevent it from falling into error).

73. *Tanya,* 33a.

74. Ibid., 116b.

75. *MK,* 198, 201. RSZ maintains that sovev, or *Da'at 'Elyon* (Higher Knowledge) transcends free will, which operates only within the parameters of memale, or *Da'at Taḥton* (Lower Knowledge) (*TO,* 15a–b; cf. *M* 5563, II, 731). Ultimately, in other words, man does not have free will; nevertheless, he is held responsible for his actions. Two early discourses describe this as a paradox beyond human understanding (*MK,* 380, 491. See also *Tanya,* 82b–83a, concerning the incomprehensible nature of God's knowledge [cf. *Mishneh Torah, Hil. Teshuvah,* V, 5] and, by implication, of man's free will.) A third explains that since the power man has to refrain from sinning—that is, to choose good over evil—is identical with the emanation of the Shekhinah that resides in him, he is not really a free agent (*MK,* 423).

Note that for RSZ, man's (apparent) free will (i.e., his ability to choose evil over good) is a liability, because it impedes his ability to achieve constant and total self-nullification (see *M Par.,* II, 681). In this respect, domesticated animals, with their instinctive submissiveness, are superior to man. Nevertheless, free will is also a potential asset, because it permits man to achieve freely chosen self-nullification based on reason (*M* 5563, II, 733–34; *M Par.,* II, 578–79).

76. *LT,* IV, 79d, 84a, 88d; *Sidur,* 45c–d, 103a, 135a, 137b–138a, 281d. Joy is also related to biṭul, because the truly humble man harbors no unrealized expectations and is therefore never disappointed or dismayed. See *M* 5562, p. 52; *LT,* IV, 43a, 47d.

77. *TO,* 20b, 46c, 61d, 64c; *LT,* II, 20c, III, 18a–b, 33d, V, 24b, 42b; *M* 5562, pp. 51, 54; *M Par.,* I, 348–49, 376; *M Iny.,* p. 202.

78. *Tanya,* 32b.

79. Ibid., 33a, 116a–b.

80. Ibid., 33b.

81. Ibid., 39b–40a.

82. Ibid., 37a–b (*Nefesh ha-Bahamit* here is more or less synonymous with yetser ha-ra).

83. Ibid., 33b–35a, 42b–43a; *MK,* 437–38, 555.

84. *Tanya,* 96b–97a; *Sidur,* 152a–b; *LT,* III, 30b, 78c. According to advice RSZ gave to one of his followers, however, the ideal time for self-abasement sessions was immediately upon arising in the morning, when one's mind is still muddled with sleep and therefore more susceptible to melancholy thoughts (*M Par.,* II, 830).

85. *Tanya,* Pt. 1, ch. 29. Cf. *M Par.,* I, 359.

86. *M* 5562, II, 397; *Tanya,* 36a–39a, 37a (וגם בעיונו בספרים); *Igerot Ḳodesh,* p. 41, where specific sections of *Reshit Ḥokhmah* are recommended. (On the influence of this work, see M. Pachter, "Sefer *Reshit Ḥokhmah* le R. Eliyahu de Vidas ṿe-Ḳitsuraṿ," *Ḳiryat Sefer* 47 (1971–1972): 686f. It was also recommended by the Maggid; see Gries, "ʿArikhat," p. 198.

The musar works mentioned in *Tanya* are: *Sefer Ḥaredim* (cited on p. 41b), *Sefer Ḥasidim* (59b, 91a), *Reshit Ḥokhmah* (93b, 126b, introduction to Pt. 2), Vital's *Shaʿar ha-Ḳedushah* (5b), and *Sefer Roḳeaḥ* (91b).

87. *Igerot Ḳodesh,* pp. 40–41; *Tanya,* 98a.

88. *Tanya,* 32b–33a; *LT,* IV, 43a; *M* 5562, II, 350.

89. *Tanya,* 40a–b.

90. Ibid., 41b–42a.

91. Ibid., 39b. See also *MK,* 476.

92. *Tanya,* 39b; *M* 5562, p. 218; *EL,* 219; *MK,* 291.

93. *Tanya,* 37a–38a. The Maggid, of course, also stressed self-abasement; *Keter Shem Ṭov,* 243.

94. *Tanya,* 99b. But see *M Raz.,* pp. 41, 45, 55; *M Par.,* II, 642–43.

95. *Tanya,* 100b–101a, 43b, 35a, 5a; *BY,* 123; *MK,* 395–96.

96. *Sidur,* 128c.

97. *M* 5566, p. 378; see also *TO,* 113c; on pleasure, see *LT,* III, 19b.

98. *LT,* II, 9c.

99. *BZ,* 134c.

100. *M* 5562, II, 48. See also *M Par.,* I, p. 250.

101. *TO,* 7c; *LT,* III, 77c, IV, 98a, V, 1c; *Sidur,* 278c; *M* 5562, II, 482.

102. But see *LT,* I, 5c, and cf. *TO,* 62c (שהם כעין בחינת נגינה) indicating that they are not necessarily to be sung.

103. *Sidur,* 128c.

104. *M* 5565, II, 924; *Tanya,* 136b; *MK,* 213–14. But see *M* 5711, p. 243. See also *S* 5704, p. 97.

105. See Wilensky, *Ḥasidim u-Mitnagdim,* II, 293; Mindel, *R. Schneur Zalman,* pp. 136–37, 244–49; *Keter Shem Ṭov,* Appendix, nos. 167, 168.

106. *Igerot Ḳodesh,* pp. 53, 68–70, 75–79, 103–105.

107. Ibid., letters nos. 1, 3–7, 9, 11–12, 16, 21, 25, 27, 30, 33, 62, 66–68, 73, 75–76, 143.

108. Ibid., no. 24, pp. 123–24; *Tanya,* 146a–147b. The discourses did occasionally reflect external concerns. See this volume, pp. 127–28; Tali Loewenthal, "Early Hasidic Teachings—Esoteric Mysticism or a Medium of Communal Leadership," *JJS* 37 (1986): 58–75.

109. *EL,* 36; *BY,* 4, 61; Mindel, *R. Schneur Zalman,* pp. 70–74.

110. *Tanya,* 147a.

111. *Igerot Ḳodesh,* no. 24, p. 55. *Keter Shem Ṭov,* 133, also discourages over-reliance on the Zaddik. A number of early discourses, however, do reflect the Zaddikism of R. Jacob Joseph of Polonnoye and others; see *MK,* 58, 130, 149–50, 314, 403, 535.

112. *Igerot Ḳodesh,* p. 124. See also ibid., pp. 98–99, 113, 141; *Tanya,* 8a, 53a–b, 56a.

113. Tal. B. *Berakhot,* 63a, according to the reading of *ʿEn Yaʿaḳov.*

114. *Igerot Ḳodesh,* pp. 123–24; title page of *Tanya.* See also *MK,* 233.

115. For the following two paragraphs, see Hilman, *Igerot Baʿal ha-Tanya,* pp. 105–13, 168–69, 171. See also ibid., p. 54; Mindel, *R. Schneur Zalman,* pp. 222–26.

116. A paraphrase of *Devarim Rabah,* XI, 6.

117. This was indeed the thrust of quite a few Lyozna discourses. See, e.g., *MK,* 51–52, 65–67, 69, 77, 84–86, 137, 155–56, 158–59, 183–84, 200–202, 208–209, 215, 220, 225–27, 230, 236, 242, 293, 330, 419–20, 522.

118. Hilman, *Igerot Baʿal ha-Tanya,* p. 109.

119. Ibid.

120. Ibid., p. 172.

121. It is unclear whether or not *Shene ha-Meoʾrot,* 38b, is an interpolation of R. Dov Baer.

122. On the exact date, see R. Elior, "Ḳunṭres ha-Hitpaʿalut le-R. Dov Baer Shneerson," *Ḳiryat Sefer* 54 (1979): 384–88, and S. D. Levin's note in ibid., pp. 829–30.

123. *LD,* I, 111; *M* 5562, p. 116; *LT,* II, 41a, III, 17d, 86b, IV, 36a; *Keter Shem Ṭov,* Appendix, nos. 165, 166; see *Tanya,* 5b–6a. For R. Menaḥem Mendel, see his *Peri ha-Arets,* 76–77; for R. Menaḥem Naḥum, *Meʾor ʿEnayim,* p. 26; for Vital, *Shaʿare Ḳedushah,* Pt. 1, *Shaʿar* 2. See also R. Zeʾev Wolf, *Or ha-Meʾir,* 16b, 111a, 117a.

124. See, however, *M Raz.,* p. 140.

125. It is arguable that this is because rabbinic Judaism does not recognize ethical values that are independent of halakhah, and therefore ethical traits are valuable only because they lead to religious (i.e., halakhic) perfection. Cf. A. Lichtenstein, "Does Jewish Tradition Recognize an Ethic Independent of Halakhah?" in *Contemporary Jewish Ethics,* ed. M. M. Kellner (New York, 1978), pp. 102–23.

126. This contrasts with Maimonides' view that certain commandments are intended to foster certain ethical traits; see *Guide,* III, 38, 39, 48. Cf. also *Sefer ha-Ḥinukh,* nos. 22, 216, 218, 220, 294, 596.

127. See *Tanya,* 17a, 37b; Pt. 1, ch. 17; *BY,* 24; *Keter Shem Ṭov,* Appendix, no. 243.

128. *MK,* 504.

129. *LT,* V, 48c; *M* 5567, pp. 187–88 (see also p. 361); *M* 5565, II, 820; *BY,* 13; *MK,* 56, 62, 77, 79, 113. In *MK,* 218, it is pointed out that this approach applies only to the evil lurking in one's character traits that does not give rise to actual sin. Otherwise, turning away from evil through traditional acts of teshuvah (renouncement, remorse, confession, resolution) is an indispensable prerequisite for future Service. Cf. *Tanya* 23a, and see infra.

130. *M Par.,* I, 414.

131. Cf. Baḥya, *Ḥovot ha-Levavot,* (Warsaw, 1875), 113b–114b, 123b–124a.

132. *M* 5565, II, 655–56, 722; *M* 5568, p. 169; *BY,* 122; *M* 5562, p. 145; *M Ket.,* II, 51.

133. *BY,* 52, 101, 112, 121; *MK,* 86, 521, 523; *M Par.,* II, 513.

134. *M Nev.,* p. 108.

135. *M Par.,* I, 302, 306–307, 416.

136. *Sidur,* 80a; *EL,* 91; *BY,* 23, 50, 132; *TO,* 45d; *M* 5562, pp. 169, 239; *M* 5565, II, 828; *M* 5568, pp. 67, 169; *LT,* IV, 37c, V, 25d; *MK,* 56; *M Par.,* I, 242, 406.

137. *M* 5565, II, 855.

138. *BY,* 4.

139. *TO,* 51b; *M* 5568, p. 169; *M* 5565, II, 651, 655–56; *MK,* 530–31. One discourse, however, citing a well-known Talmudic dictum, rather reluctantly admits that industriousness can merit wealth, but only, it adds, when coupled with prayer; *M* 5562, p. 143. Another discourse echoes the rabbinic view (Tal. B., *Shabat,* 63a) that wealth and honor are merited through Torah-study; *MK,* 110. Cf. the Vilna Gaon's view in H. H. Ben Sasson, "Ishi'uto shel ha-Gra ve-Hashpa'ato ha-Hisṭorit," *Zion* 31 (1966): 67, 69.

140. *BY,* 72.

141. *TO,* 8c–10a; *M* 5568, pp. 67, 76. See also *M* 5564, p. 132; *LT,* IV, 43a.

142. *M* 5564, p. 169.

143. See *Tanya,* 93a–b, 124b; *TO,* 102c; Hilman, *Igerot Ba'al ha-Tanya,* p. 238; *Igerot Ḳodesh,* nos. 7, 16, 18, 22, 25, 26, 78.

144. *Tanya,* 116a–b.

145. Tal. B., *Shabat,* 55a. There are, of course, exceptions, as the Talmud indicates; ibid., 55b; *Berakhot,* 5a; *Sanhedrin,* 39a, 93b; *Ḳidushin,* 40b.

146. *Tanya,* 134b. See also ibid., 90b; *MK,* 364–66, 451; *M Raz.,* p. 235.

147. *TO,* 31c; *LT,* IV, 19b–c.

148. *BY,* 33; *MK,* 16.

149. *TO,* 72b.

150. *BY,* 33; *Tanya,* 35b–36a, 97a; *M* 5567, p. 148.

151. *M* 5564, p. 132; *MK,* 316.

152. *Ḳidushin,* 40b; *M* 5565, II, 650.

153. *Tanya,* 116a–b. On the midrashic dictum "no evil descends from above" (*Bereshit Rabah,* LI, 3), see *MK,* 1 (cf. *Degel Maḥneh Efrayim,* p. 131), 9, 299, 379, 413, 528; *Igerot Ḳodesh,* p. 118.

154. *Tanya,* 116b. See also *MK,* 10, 163, 216; *M* 5563, II, 769; *M Par.,* I, 370, 413; *M Iny.,* pp. 265, 302–303; *M Nev.,* pp. 147–48; *M Ket.,* II, 129. Cf. Vital's *Sha'are Ḳedushah,* Pt. 3, p. 4.

155. See, e.g., Baḥya's *Sha'ar ha-Biṭaḥon* in *Ḥovot ha-Levavot;* and *Sefer ha-Biṭaḥon,* ch. 1 (in Chavel's edition of *Kitve ha-Ramban,* II, 353f.).

156. *BZ,* 37d.

157. *Reshit Ḥokhmah* (New York, 1965), 111a, 114a, 119c, 121a; Horowitz, *Shene Luḥot ha-Berit, Masekhet Ta'anit,* 122a, 154a, 156a–162, 174a. See also Maharal, *Netivot 'Olam, Teshuvah,* ch. 7.

On the asceticism of Baḥya's *Ḥovot ha-Levavot,* which strongly influenced both Vidas and Horowitz, see A. Lazaroff, "Bahya's Asceticism and Its Rabbinic and Islamic Background," *JJS* 21 (1970): 11–39.

158. *Sha'ar Ruaḥ ha-Ḳodesh* (Tel Aviv, 1963), pp. 50, 63; see also pp. 39–40; Jacob Ḥayyim Tsemaḥ, *Nagid u-Metsaveh,* pp. 181–92.

159. *Reshit Ḥokhmah,* 118b, 119c.

160. Horowitz, *Shene Luḥot ha-Berit, Yuma,* 174a, 173b.

161. Ibid.

162. Ibid., 171af.; *Reshit Ḥokhmah,* 110c, 125d. See also *Ḳitsur Shaloh* (Jerusalem, 1960), pp. 97, 135, 136, 207.

163. *Keter Shem Ṭov,* 219, 231. But cf. *Tsava'at ha-Ribash,* 11, 13, 14, 18. It is probable that these are teachings of the more ascetically inclined Maggid.

164. *Igerot Ḳodesh,* no. 17; *LT,* IV, 62a. Cf. *M Nev.,* pp. 139–40.

165. See *Tanya,* 91b–92a.

166. Ibid., 92a.

167. Ibid.; cf. *MK,* 259.

168. Supra, n. 157.

169. *Tanya,* 91b; cf. *MK,* 299–300.

170. *Tanya,* 93a. The basic concept of redeeming fasts through charity was well known. See, e.g., Isserles' glosses to *Shulḥan 'Arukh Oraḥ Ḥayyim,* 334:26, and *Yoreh De'ah,* 185:4.

171. *MK,* 79, 85, 106, 299, 300, 360, 364–66, 586–87; *M Iny.,* p. 302; *Tanya,* 101a; *BY,* 35–36; *LT,* IV, 36c. See also *Tanya,* 36a.

172. According to the first edition of *Igeret ha-Teshuvah,* the regimen of fasts prescribed in these sources was divinely inspired (Hilman, *Igerot Ba'al,* p. 82). This edition appeared in the *Tanya* published in Zolkiew in 1799. The second and final edition, which appeared in 1806 (Shklov), is an expanded more scholarly, and more scholastic version but contains no substantial doctrinal or conceptual changes. However, because its approach is somewhat more kabbalistic and less Hasidic, it tends toward greater asceticism and a stronger emphasis on Tiḳun Ḥasot (which the first edition does not mention at all, although it is mentioned in *Tanya,* 32b).

173. *LT,* IV, 9d. Cf. *BY,* 35–36, 52. See also *M Iny.,* p. 311.

174. Zohar, III, 122a–123a, 216a; Tiḳ. Zohar, XXI, 59b–60a; *Reshit Ḥokhmah,* 106b–c; *Tanya,* 93b; Hilman, *Igerot Ba'al ha-Tanya,* p. 86; *M* 5565, II, 774.

175. *Tanya,* 93b–95a, 98b; *MK,* 54, 257; *LT,* IV, 27a, 35c–d, 45d, 60d–61a, 62c, 71c–d; *M* 5563, p. 191, II, 742; *M* 5565, II, 586, 833 (cf. *MK,* 238); see supra, p. 97.

176. Supra, p. 98; *LT,* IV, 72c.

177. *Tanya,* 40a, 98b–99a, 113a; Hilman, *Igerot Ba'al ha-Tanya,* pp. 86–87; *LT,* II, 25c, IV, 39a (cf. 36c, 45d), 60d, 61a, 66c, V, 49a; *TO,* 45a, 86b; *MK,* 584; *M* 5563, II, 737.

178. See *LT,* III, 71a, IV, 33a, 40c, 66c, 71d, 72b–c; *Sidur,* 226a; *TO,* 45a, 121a; *Tanya,* 40a; *MK,* 584; *M* 5562, p. 233; *M* 5563, II, 737; *M* 5564, p. 237; Hilman, *Igerot Ba'al ha-Tanya,* p. 83.

179. *Tanya,* 23a, 95a–b; Hilman, *Igerot Ba'al ha-Tanya,* pp. 84–86; *LT,* IV, 52a, 64d, 68c–d, 69d; *MK,* 359; *EL,* 207; *M* 5570, pp. 177–80; *M Raz.,* p. 134. See also *M* 5563, p. 93; *MK,* 102–103.

180. *Tanya,* 95a–96b; Hilman, *Igerot Ba'al ha-Tanya,* pp. 84–86; *LT,* IV, 40d, 62c; *M* 5564, p. 225; *MK,* 305. See also supra, p. 105.

181. *Tanya,* 23a, 97a.

182. Ibid., 23a–b, 96b.

183. See the citations in note 175 supra.

184. *Tanya,* 96b–99b; Hilman, *Igerot Ba'al ha-Tanya,* p. 87; *LT,* II, 26d, III, 73b–75a, IV, 40d–41a, V, 3d–4a; *MK,* 146, 169, 180, 225 (version 1), 246, 359, 586–87; *BY,* 4, 34, 53; *EL,* 202; *M* 5562, pp. 38, 233, 236, 239–40, 278; *M* 5565, II, 833, 857–58, 922; *M Raz.,* p. 448; *M Nev.,* p. 146; *M* 5570, pp. 177–80; *M* 5563, II, 741, 752, 771; supra, p. 101.

185. Hilman, *Igerot Ba'al ha-Tanya,* pp. 90–91 (cf. *M* 5562, p. 120); *Tanya,* 40a–b; *MK,* 146, 149 (version 1).

186. *LT,* IV, 33c, 39a, 45c–d, 52a, 54a–b, 58b, 60d–61a, 69d, 72c, 80d–81a, V, 49a; *Sidur,* 115a, 226d; *TO,* 86b, 121a; *Tanya,* 12a; *MK,* 146; *M* 5563, pp. 290–91, II, 680, 742, 771, 799; *M* 5564, p. 233; *M* 5567, pp. 221–22; *M* 5565, II, 587, 880.

187. See supra, note 177; infra, Chapter 4, note 253.

188. Tal. B., *Shabat,* 153a; *Tanya,* 40a, 100b (last line); *LT,* IV, 33a; *Sidur,* 226a; *MK,* 227; *M Par.,* I, 180–82, II, 763; *M Raz.,* 18.

189. *M Ket.,* I, 60.

Chapter 4. Torah and Commandments

1. *HTT,* I, 4; *Tanya,* 148b, 159b; *LT,* II, 30d; *M* 5567, p. 359; *MK,* 496.

2. In fact, there is probably only one such source (as *LT,* II, 30d suggests): *Sifre* to Deut. 11:22; see *HTT,* I, 4. RSZ's view contrasts with that of such scholars as Joseph ibn Kaspi, who maintained that many parts of the Torah are required study for judges only; and with that of Maimonides, who believed that no man can memorize all the *halakhot* contained in both Talmuds and the Beraitot; see Abrahams, *Ethical Wills,* p. 138; *Ḳovets Teshuvot ha-Rambam,* ed. A. L. Lichtenberg (Leipzig, 1859), p. 26a. Note that mastery for RSZ meant perfect memorization; *HTT,* II, 3.

3. Although in *HTT,* I, 4–6, RSZ cites Maimonides and R. Meir Abulafia as sources for this view, neither really supports it. *Mishneh Torah, Hil. Talmud Torah,* I, does not spell out the quantitative extent of one's Torah-study obligation with respect to Talmud, and Abulafia's statement (cited in *Ṭur, Yoreh De'ah,* 245, and *Shulḥan 'Arukh, Yoreh De'ah,* 245, 6) does not make it a Biblical obligation for every father. See also *Ḳunṭres Aḥron* to *HTT,* I, 1, where RSZ labors mightily and brilliantly to prove his view, and Y. M. Epstein's critique in *'Arukh ha-Shulḥan, Yoreh De'ah,* 245, 3–4.

4. *HTT,* I, 4; *Ḳunṭres Aḥron* to III, 1 (p. 843b in New York, 1968, edition of RSZ's *Shulḥan ʿArukh*); *HTT,* IV, 2–3.

5. *HTT,* II, 1.

6. Ibid., II, 3.

7. Ibid., II, 4. On the eternal validity of the Torah, cf. *Degel Maḥneh Efrayim,* p. 231, in the name of the Besht.

8. *Ḳunṭres Aḥron* to *HTT,* III, 1. Unlike MYT, which is fulfilled passively after one has mastered and memorized the Torah, this second aspect of the commandment is fulfilled by actively studying, articulating, and understanding. See infra.

9. Ibid. and *HTT,* III, 1, IV, 3.

10. *HTT,* III, 1–3 and *Ḳunṭres Aḥron.*

11. *HTT,* IV, 2–3.

12. Ibid.

13. *Ḳunṭres Aḥron,* p. 843a–b.

14. See Tal. Y., *Shabat,* I, 2, 7a; Mishnah, Tal. B., ibid. and commentary of R. Obadiah and Meiri; Meiri (*Bet ha-Beḥirah*) on *Sukah,* 38a; *Riṭba* on Tal. B., *Shabat,* 9b; *Ṭur* and *Shulḥan ʿArukh Orah Ḥayyim,* 106 and commentaries; *Levush.*

15. *Hilkhot Tefilah,* VI, 8.

16. *HTT,* IV, 5; RSZ's *Shulḥan ʿArukh, Oraḥ Ḥayyim,* 106, 4. See also *M Raz.,* p. 57; *M Ket.,* I, p. 184.

17. Tal. B., *Shabat,* 10a.

18. Maimonides' approach to the question of prayer for *mi she-torato umanuto* is questioned by R. Aryeh Leib b. Asher Gunzberg in *Shaʾagat Aryeh,* no. 14. RSZ took Maimonides' lead on this issue despite the fact that he disagreed with him on the Biblical status of prayer (see his *Shulḥan ʾArukh, Oraḥ Ḥayyim,* 106, 2) and could have therefore more consistently and more authoritatively cited one of the reasons offered in Tal. Y. for exempting a full-time scholar from prayer; viz., Torah-study is, but prayer is not, a Biblical obligation. This is the reason cited by R. Mordecai Yaffe, Meiri, Ritba, and others.

19. *HTT,* IV, 3. On Ashkenazic halakhah when R. Asher disagrees with Maimonides, see *Encyclopedia Talmudit,* IX, 336–38 and notes 370–71, 386, 391; Malachi b. Jacob ha-Kohen, *Yad Malakhi* (Berlin, 1857), pp. 130b, no. 36, 129d, no. 30; R. Dov Baer's introduction to RSZ's *Shulḥan ʿArukh:* והעיקר בהאשר״י. ולחזור על פסקי הדינין היוצאים מהרא״ש בפנים.

20. *HTT,* IV, 5, 6, Cf. *M Raz.,* p. 335.

21. This is clear from the discussions in Tal. B., *Berakhot,* 11a; *Sukah,* 25a–26a; and is explicitly affirmed by Meiri, *Bet ha-Beḥirah* (Jerusalem, 1966) on *Sukah,* p. 80a–b.

22. *HTT,* IV, 4. Still elsewhere RSZ identifies MYT with (the higher form of) Teshuvah; *Tanya,* 98b–99a; Hilman, *Igerot Baʿal ha-Tanya,* p. 86.

23. *Mishneh Torah, Hilkhot Talmud Torah,* III, 3.

24. *Shaʿar Ruaḥ ha-Ḳodesh,* p. 34; also cited by Jacob Ḥayyim Tsemaḥ, *Nagid u-Metsaṿeh,* p. 73.

25. *Shaʿar Ruaḥ ha-Ḳodesh,* pp. 34–36; *Shaʿar Ha-Mitsṿot* (Tel Aviv, 1962), pp. 78–83; introduction to Vital's *ʿEts Ḥayyim,* pp. 1d, 2a.

26. See Rashi, Tal. B., *Berakhot,* 17a, s.v. *ha-ʿośeh she-lo li-shemah.*

27. *Sha'ar Ma'amre Rashbi* (Tel Aviv, 1961), p. 32; *Sha'ar ha-Mitsvot,* p. 79.

28. *Peri 'Ets Ḥayyim* (Lemberg, 1864), 49d, 50b–c.

29. See Tishby, *Mishnat ha-Zohar,* II, 375f.

30. Introduction to Vital's *'Ets Ḥayyim,* pp. 1–3; *'Ets ha-Da'at Ṭov, Ḥuḳat.*

31. Cordovero, *Or Ne'erav,* III, 1, I, 6.

32. Cordovero, *Pardes,* XXVII, 1, p. 59c.

33. Cordovero, *Or Ne'erav,* III, 1.

34. Ibid., V, 1, 2. Cf. Zohar, I, 185a, III, 96a.

35. Cordovero, *Or Ne'erav,* III, 3–4, I, 6.

36. Ibid., V, 2.

37. See *Keter Shem Ṭov,* 96, 142, 204, 426; *Peri ha-Arets,* pp. 55, 63, 73; *Me'or 'Enayim,* pp. 63–64, 106, 111–112, 171, 182–183, 303 (but cf. p. 81); *No'am Elimelekh,* p. 54; *Or ha-Me'ir,* p. 187a.

38. *Magid,* p. 87.

39. *Or Torah,* p. 47b.

40. See *Or ha-Me'ir,* pp. 4a, 17a, 38b, 58b–59a, 105a, 113a, 121a, 160b, 187a, 201b–202a–b, 214a, 216a.

41. *Ḳedushat Levi,* pp. 112, 209, 212, 218–219, 7. Cf. *Magid* (1990 ed.), p. 394.

42. *Me'or 'Enayim,* p. 302; Ben Sasson, "Ishi'uto shel Ha-Gra ve-Hashpa'ato," 19. They also shared the view that *Torah li-shemah* is a level that can be achieved only by first studying *lo li-shemah.* See *Me'or 'Enayim,* pp. 171, 182; Ben Sasson, p. 28. N. Lamm's statement to the contrary (*Torah li-Shemah* [Jerusalem, 1972], p. 183) is untenable.

43. *Me'or 'Enayim,* p. 66, cf. p. 183.

44. Ibid., p. 352; cf. *Or Torah,* 91b, 16a.

45. *Me'or 'Enayim,* pp. 184, 287.

46. *Peri ha-Arets,* pp. 33–34, 63–64, 73; cf. *Keter Shem Ṭov,* 3.

47. *Keter Shem Ṭov,* 167; *Liḳuṭim Yeḳarim,* 29, 59; *Tsava'at ha-Ribash,* p. 7 (see variants, p. 9).

48. *Magid,* p. 27; cf. *Keter Shem Ṭov,* 203.

49. See p. 357, n. 82. *Magid,* p. 149; cf. *Keter Shem Ṭov,* 96.

50. *Liḳuṭim Yeḳarim,* 132.

51. Ibid., 51. Cf. *Degel Maḥneh Efrayim,* p. 108.

52. *Keter Shem Ṭov,* 142, 426.

53. Ibid., 3.

54. See *M* 5563, I, 42, 44–45.

55. The interpretation of this Mishnah is an interesting example of the power Maimonides had over subsequent Jewish thought. The context of the passage cited, as well as the Gemara's discussions in Tal. B., *Ḳidushin,* 39b and *Shabat,* 127a–b, indicate that this clause compares the reward for Torah-study with the reward for the acts mentioned previously as coming under the category of "things for which a man enjoys the fruits in this world while the principal remains for him in the world to come": honoring one's parents; acts of charity; and making peace between man and his fellow man. Our clause states only that the reward for Torah-study equals the combined rewards for these acts. Maimonides, however, in his Mishnah com-

mentary and *Mishneh Torah* (*Hil. Tal. Torah,* III, 3, 4) apparently combined this clause with the Talmud's conclusion in *Ḳidushin,* 40b, that "study is greater than action, for study leads to action," and pronounced Torah-study to be equal in value to all the other commandments combined. This view, which is supported by one opinion in Tal. Y. (*Pe'ah,* I, 1, 4a), was adopted in *Ṭur, Shulḥan ʿArukh* (*Yoreh Deʿah,* 246), and subsequent halakhic and ethical works. Its validity is called into question, however, by Tal. B., *Megilah,* 3b, which concludes that Torah-study is superseded by the Temple service. It is at least arguable that the halakhic context of this conclusion in Tal. B. makes it more authoritative than the single opinion expressed in an aggadic context in Tal. Y., and that *Ḳidushin* 40b, has no bearing on the Mishnah in *Pe'ah.* But no one to my knowledge made this argument.

See also H. Z. Reines, *Torah u-Musar* (Jerusalem, 1954), p. 78f., who argues that Torah-study achieved axiological supremacy over other commandments only after the destruction of the second Temple.

56. *Tanya,* 10a, 29a; *TO,* 82a; *LT,* I, 3c, III, 71b; *Sidur,* 25c; *M* 5567, pp. 370–372. Cf. *M* 5567, II, 611, version 2 and *M* 5562, II, 355.

57. *Tanya,* 10a. See Zohar, III, 29b, 239b.

58. Aristotle, *De Anima,* Book III, 5, 430a20. In *Metaphysica* 1075a Aristotle adds that this applies (only?) to the "theoretical sciences"; i.e., metaphysics.

This concept was the basis of the Aristotelian doctrine of the immortality of the acquired intellect, and of its corollary—that immortality depends on the level of metaphysical knowledge attained. Immortality was thus possible (1) only for the intellectual part of the soul and (2) only for philosophers. Maimonides, while adopting Aristotelian psychology, could not accept this last limitation and was forced to "burst the bounds of his own system." See Guttmann, *Philosophies of Judaism,* pp. 139–40, 178–79, 223, 235–37, 243. The kabbalists, who adopted Maimonides' doctrine of immortality by simply substituting kabbalah for metaphysics as the knowledge that confers eternal beatitude, accepted neither limitation. Such inconsistencies are particularly noticeable in "conceptual" kabbalists such as Cordovero and RSZ, who try to intellectualize kabbalistic symbolism by infusing it with philosophical concepts.

59. *Tanya,* 28b–29a.

60. Ibid., 160a.

61. *LT,* I, 3c, II, 4c; *Sidur,* 25c.

62. *TO,* 7a, 27b, 38d–39b, 49c, 56a, 71a–b, 82a, 83b, 108c; *LT,* II, 27a, III, 27a, 57a, IV, 46d, 74a, 79c; *Sidur,* 15c; *M* 5563, I, 324; *M* 5564, p. 8; *M* 5566, pp. 221, 225; *M* 5562, pp. 141, 251, 284; *M* 5570, pp. 48, 57.

63. *LT,* III, 13a–b, IV, 84b; *M* 5565, II, 687; *M* 5568, pp. 384–85.

64. *MK,* pp. 370–72. Cf. *M* 5568, pp. 334–35.

65. *Tanya,* 49a–b; *LT,* III, 13a–b; *M* 5567, p. 314; *M* 5565, II, 787; *RP,* p. 138; *M* 5568, pp. 160–61, 230; *BZ,* p. 25b; *MK,* pp. 236, 265; *M* 5563, II, 626–27, version 2.

66. *M* 5568, pp. 334–35, 345, 351–52, 397; *M* 5562, pp. 259, 271; *MK,* pp. 370, 372; *LT,* III, 17b, 39c, 92d, IV, 99b; *M* 5566, p. 250; *M* 5563, II, 525, version 1, 699.

67. *Tanya,* 48b, 155a; *MK,* p. 265; *M* 5570, p. 49.

68. *RP,* pp. 157–58.

69. *Tanya,* 114a (cf. 155a); *Sidur,* 23a; *M* 5567, p. 309; *M* 5562, pp. 45–46.

70. *M* 5564, p. 8; *EL,* p. 107; *MK,* pp. 311, 456.

71. *LT,* III, 17a–b; IV, 23b, 33d, V, 22c; *Sidur,* 228b; *RP,* p. 146; *M* 5570, p. 62. See also *M* 5568, pp. 346–48, 500; *Tanya,* 131a; *M* 5567, p. 313.

72. *LT,* II, 27a, III, 49b, V, 38d; *BY,* p. 37.

73. *Tanya,* 155a; *M* 5564, p. 36; *BY,* p. 91; *MK,* pp. 303, 442, 562; *M* 5562, pp. 262–63; *M Par.,* II, 747.

74. *MK,* pp. 310, 496.

75. *M* 5567, p. 218; *BY,* p. 37; *M* 5563, I, 338–39; cf. *MK,* p. 564; *M Par.,* I, 28, 40, II, 696.

76. *TO,* 43c; *LT,* IV, 23b, V, 18b, 44b; *M Par.,* I, 412.

77. *LT,* II, 5a, 22d, IV, 29a, 74a, V, 18c, 20c, 41d, 43b; *M* 5566, p. 138; *RP,* pp. 168, 172; *EL,* p. 107; *MK,* p. 564; *M* 5563, I, 131, 134, 165; *M* 5570, p. 48; *M Par.,* II, 643, 700, 762; *M Iny.,* p. 51; *M Raz.,* p. 53.

78. *EL,* p. 100; *LT,* II, 49c; *MK,* p. 208, version 1; *M* 5570, p. 47; *M* 5563, II, 582, version 2.

79. *LT,* IV, 84b.

80. *LT,* V, 38d.

81. See, e.g., *LT,* IV, 57b–c.

82. *Sidur,* 75a–b; *M* 5564, p. 36; *M* 5562, p. 141; *MK,* p. 562; *M* 5563, I, 142; *M* 5570, p. 48.

83. Soloveitchik, "Three Themes," 343–46; see also pp. 353–54.

84. Tal. B., *Yevamot,* 109b.

85. *TO,* 7a; *LT,* II, 5a, 40c, III, 54c, IV, 14a, 74a, V, 18b, 44b; *Sidur,* 132d; *BY,* p. 12; *MK,* pp. 174–75, 347; *M* 5570, p. 48; *M* 5563, II, 580–81, version 2; *M Nev.,* p. 92.

86. *BY,* p. 12. See also *MK,* p. 298.

87. See *M* 5568, II, 682, and infra. But cf. *M Iny.,* pp. 445, 447.

88. *TO,* 7a, 20a, 36d, 38d–39b, 40d, 51b, 56a, 67b, 71a–b, 83b, 108c; *LT,* II, 4c, 5a, 27a–b, 40c, III, 27a, 57a, 86d, IV, 46d, 74a, 79c, 94b–c; *Sidur,* 15c (purpose of study is biṭul); *M* 5564, pp. 8, 149, 168; *M* 5566, pp. 221, 225; *RP,* p. 168; *M* 5568, p. 230; *M* 5562, pp. 141, 251, 284; *M* 5567, p. 153; *MK,* pp. 113, 131, 134, 142, 324 (purpose of study is biṭul); *M* 5570, pp. 47–49, 57; *M* 5563, II, 580–82, version 2; *M Par.,* I, 189.

89. *MK,* p. 570; *Tanya,* 10a.

90. *MK,* p. 142; *Sidur,* 128a.

91. *LT,* III, 57a–b, II, 27a–b, III, 27a; *M Ket.,* I, p. 204.

92. *HTT,* II, 12; *Tanya,* 47a, 150b.

93. *LT,* II, 27a–b, III, 27a, V, 41a, d; *M* 5567, p. 153; *M* 5563, II, 582, version 2; *TO,* 27b, 49c, 56a; *M* 5564, p. 8; *M* 5562, pp. 251, 284.

94. *M* 5566, p. 221; *LT,* IV, 76a, V, 40b; *Sidur,* 277c; *M* 5565, II, 784; *RP,* p. 168; *M* 5568, p. 31; *BY,* 104; *MK,* p. 308. Cf. Zohar, III, 179a and Kadushin, *Worship and Ethics,* p. 86.

95. *M* 5564, pp. 39, 149 (based on the sources cited in M. Schneerson, *Likuṭe Siḥot,* IV (New York, 1964), p. 1088, n. 11); *TO,* 67b; *M* 5570, p. 48. See G. Scholem,

"Revelation and Tradition as Religious Categories in Judaism," in his *Messianic Idea,* pp. 282–304.

96. See, e.g., *MK,* p. 267; *BY,* p. 1: *Tanya,* 144b; *M* 5562, pp. 30, 103. Cf. Zohar, I, 4b, 8b, 9a, III, 185a, 243a.

97. *LT,* IV, 11a, 22a, 81c, 84b.

98. *LT,* II, 23a; *Sidur,* 19a; *M* 5564, p. 39; *M* 5566, p. 324; *M* 5562, p. 272; *MK,* pp. 268–69, 571; *M* 5563, I, 158, 306–307. See also *LT,* II, 33a; *Sidur,* 85b.

99. *Tanya,* 47a. Cf. Zohar, III, 39a–b.

100. *M* 5568, p. 400; *M* 5562, p. 208. See also *EL,* p. 117.

101. Cf. Maharal, *Netivot ʿOlam* I, 23: **כאשר הוא עוסק [בתורה] במחשבה בלבד כאילו אין האדם עצמו עוסק בתורה, כי אין המחשבה הוא האדם רק הדיבור.**

102. *Tsavaʾat ha-Ribash,* no. 29, 43. See also no. 41, 133. But cf. no. 30; *Keter Shem Ṭov,* 167, 399. See also *MK,* pp. 310, 354–55.

103. *Tanya,* 8b, 9b, 49b; *LT,* IV, 43a; *Sidur,* 128a; *M* 5562, pp. 219, 252; *BY,* pp. 92, 129, 173; *MK,* p. 570; *M* 5564, p. 65. Cf. Zohar, III, 36a.

104. *Sidur,* 128d.

105. *LT,* V, 3a (cf. *TO,* 62c–63d, regarding the letters of prayer); *M* 5567, pp. 40–41; *BY,* p. 112 (cf. p. 87).

106. *MK,* p. 232.

107. E.g., *M* 5567, p. 41.

108. *M* 5562, p. 219; *TO,* 63a; *MK,* p. 232, and cf. the sources cited supra, n. 105; *TO,* 63a; *LT,* V, 3a; *BY,* pp. 67, 112; *M Ket.,* I, 232; *M Raz.,* p. 495.

109. *EL,* pp. 2–3.

110. *Tanya,* 159b; *TO,* 1a, 7a, 38d, 43c, 77c, 82c–d; *LT,* II, 33a; IV, 46a, 67a, V, 17a, 18b–c, 19d, 20c, 25b–d; *Sidur,* 15c, 27d; *M* 5568, pp. 31, 66; *M* 5570, p. 57; *M Par.,* I, 393, 418.

111. Rashi, Tal. B., *Berakhot,* 17a, s.vv. *ha-ʿośeh she-lo li-shemah*; R. Asher's commentary to Tal. B., *Nedarim,* 62a, s.vv. *ṿe-daber bahen li-sheman.*

112. *Tanya,* 10a.

113. Ibid., 53b. Cf. Zohar, I, 142a.

114. See *Tanya,* 53a, 154b.

115. See *M* 5568, p. 31.

116. *TO,* 82c–d; *LT,* III, 47c, 86b, IV, 46d, 73d, V, 17a, 18b–c, 26c; *Sidur,* 27d, 128a; *M* 5567, p. 267; *M* 5566, p. 296; *BZ,* 20d, 25b; *BY,* p. 60; *MK,* p. 83.

117. See supra, n. 42; *Sidur,* 128a; *MK,* p. 192, version 2. Cf. *BY,* p. 60.

118. *MK,* pp. 51–52. That at least a conscious *desire* for deveḳut is a prerequisite for achieving *li-shemah,* or a lower level of *li-shemah,* is hinted at in *Tanya,* 57a–59a. The discourses, as usual, go further and occasionally require *attaining* deveḳut ("attachment" to the Or En Sof).

119. *MK,* p. 570.

120. *Sidur,* 28b.

121. *BY,* p. 44.

122. *LT,* V, 21a, 32d; *Sidur,* 28b; *Tanya,* 155a.

123. *M* 5562, p. 144.

124. *MK,* p. 391.

125. *Tanya,* 58b.

126. See ibid., 159a; *TO,* 36c–d; *M* 5565, II, 981; *M* 5563, I, 44–45; *LT,* V, 25b.

127. *TO,* 77c; *LT,* II, 33a; *M Par.,* I, 416; *M* 5563, II, 755.

128. *LT,* V, 41d; *TO,* 36d.

129. *BZ,* 19d.

130. *TO,* 31d; *LT,* III, 86c; *EL,* pp. 105–106; *Tanya,* 160b. Cf. Zohar, I, 134b, 185a, 207a, III, 9b, 11b.

131. See *Tana Deve Eliyahu Rabah,* beginning of ch. 18; *Yalḳut Shimʿoni,* 1035.

132. See, e.g., *M* 5566, p. 221.

133. See *TO,* 16b; *LT,* IV, 46a, 76a, 81c; *Sidur,* 27d, 77a; *M* 5565, II, 784; *M* 5568, p. 66; *RP,* p. 168; *M* 5562, p. 272. Cf. Zohar, III, 179a.

134. *LT,* II, 41a–b, IV, 46d, 96b, V, 16d, 18b, 19d, 20a, 39d; *Sidur,* 143c; *M* 5566, pp. 128–30, 299; *M* 5562, p. 252; *BY,* p. 60. See also R. Menaḥem Mendel's discussion in *LT,* V, 26d.

135. *LT,* II, 24c, III, 16b; *M* 5568, p. 230; *MK,* p. 11. *Shulḥan ʿArukh ha-Ari* (Jerusalem, 1961 or 1962), p. 93. See also *Tanya,* 3b; LT, IV, 46a.

136. *LT,* III, 16b. Cf. *Tanya,* 29a.

137. For divine Will, see *Tanya,* 8b–9b, 29a, 102b, 158a; *LT,* III, 7a; *TO,* 88b. Cf. *Elimah* (Jerusalem, 1966), p. 130c.

For *Keter,* or Ḥokhmah of Keter (*Ḥokhmah Setimaʾah* or *Moaḥ Setimaʾah* of ʿAtik or Arikh Anpin), see *TO,* 11c, 39c, 88b, 91b, 108c; *LT,* II, 5b, 28d–29a; III, 7a, 27c, IV, 20b, 33d, 95c, 96b, V, 10d, 22c, 23b, 48a; *Sidur,* 40c, 130d–131c, 228b, 231a; *M* 5568, pp. 397, 503; *M* 5563, I, 150, 329, 333, II, 501, 582; *M Par.,* I, 89; *M* 5562, p. 259; *M* 5570, p. 62. Cf. *Elimah,* 16c, 27b, 28c, 33b, 34c, 53a, 54a, 63a, 109c; Zohar, III, 128b, 130b, 131b, 288a, 290a, 292b.

For the Or En Sof, or for the Godhead (ʿAtsmut), see *Tanya,* 160b; *TO,* 42c; *Sidur,* 287b; *M* 5565, II, 848; *M* 5568, p. 408.

For Adam Ḳadmon or some aspect of it, see *TO,* 87c; *Sidur,* 136a; *M* 5566, p. 377; *M* 5562, II, 418.

For Ḥokhmah, see *Tanya,* 8b–9b, 29a, 128a, 158a, 159b; *TO,* 6d, 11c, 88b; *LT,* III, 7a; V, 19b, 20c; *M* 5570, p. 57; *M* 5562, II, 357. Cf. Zohar, II, 62a, III, 183a.

For the "outer," or lower, aspect of Ḥokhmah, see *LT,* IV, 94b, V, 26c; *M* 5564, pp. 115–16; *M* 5566, p. 128; *MK,* p. 307; *M* 5563, I, 130, 264; *BZ,* 25b; *Tanya,* 128a.

For Binah, see e.g., *M* 5563, I, 118; *TO,* 59b. Cf. Zohar, II, 85a.

For Zeʿir Anpin, or one aspect of it, see *LT,* V, 19b; *Sidur,* 75b, 282a; *M* 5563, I, 41.

For Malkhut, see *Tanya,* 144b; *TO,* 6d; *Sidur,* 87c, 274d; *M* 5568, p. 400; *BZ,* 20b; *MK,* p. 120; *LT,* IV, 15c. Cf. *Elimah,* 130d.

For maḳif or sovev, see *Tanya,* 29a; *TO,* 63a, 67b; *LT,* IV, 11a, 22a; *BY,* p. 117.

For penimi or memale, see *TO,* 25a, 92b; *LT,* III, 49b.

For the idea that Torah transcends creation (including Atsilut), see *TO,* 1a, 71a–b; *M* 5567, p. 295; *M* 5568, p. 160.

The sources cited for the first four levels above, and those for maḳif/sovev and the transcendence of Torah, belie N. Lamm's assertion—and the conclusions drawn from it—that, unlike RSZ, R. Ḥayyim of Volozhin located the Torah's supernal source above Atsilut (*Torah li-Shemah,* p. 78f.). Indeed, many of the positions Lamm attributes to R. Ḥayyim in contradistinction to RSZ may just as validly be attributed to RSZ and may, in fact, have originated with him. This applies, e.g., to the relationship of Torah-study to the other commandments cited from R. Ḥayyim on p. 120, and to Lamm's statement on p. 90 that R. Ḥayyim's view leads to a synthesis between the worlds of halakhah and kabbalah. On the latter point see infra.

138. I say "theoretically" because certain issues—e.g., the relative values of Torah-study and prayer—were determined for RSZ by halakhic and aggadic sources, and the kabbalistic factors were actually used to buttress predetermined conclusions.

139. Supra, p. 108.

140. *Sidur,* 63c.

141. Cf. *M* 5567, p. 269; *MK,* p. 481, and the sources cited supra, n. 137, for the lower aspect of Ḥokhmah.

142. *M* 5568, p. 258.

143. *M* 5570, p. 182, Cf. *HTT,* III, 7.

144. *M* 5562, p. 102.

145. *MK,* p. 480.

146. Zohar, III, 257a, 153a.

147. *Shaʿar ha-Kelalim,* I; *Nahar Shalom* (Jerusalem, 1910), p. 47c. See also *Mevo Sheʿarim,* II, 3, 6.

148. Cordovero, *Pardes,* XXXIII, *ʿErke ha-Kinuyim,* ch. 22.

149. *Tanya,* 151a; *TO,* 6d, 31b, 57d, 59b–c; *LT,* III, 84b, IV, 14d, 15c, 85b, 94a, V, 40a; *RP,* p. 63; *M* 5563, I, 47, 118–20; *M* 5564, pp. 3–4, 252.

150. *LT,* I, 1a, IV, 60d, 73b, V, 11b, 28b; *TO,* 1c, 6c–d, 40b, 80a, 88c; *M* 5562, p. 34; *Sidur,* 132c–134b.

151. Zohar, III, 149b, 152a, II, 217b. See Tishby, *Mishnat ha-Zohar,* II, 368–69.

152. *M* 5567, pp. 355, 361; *M* 5568, p. 162; *LT,* II, 5b; *BY,* pp. 55, 116.

153. *TO,* 57d–59a; *Sidur,* 35d; *M* 5564, p. 40; *M* 5568, pp. 162, 409; *BY,* pp. 49, 67, 69, 112; *M* 5563, I, 111; *LT,* II, 5b; *MK,* p. 599.

154. *Tanya,* 49b; *TO,* 57d–58a, 63a, 77c; *LT,* IV, 12c, 23a, 67a, V, 28a; *Sidur,* 164a; *M* 5568, p. 66; *BY,* p. 40; *HTT,* II, 12–13.

155. Zohar, II, 254b. Cited in *Tanya,* 144b, 148a.

156. *Tanya,* 102b, 144b, 151a; *TO,* 17b, 36c–d, 39b, 49b; *Sidur,* 16c, 35d, 44d, 134b; *BY,* p. 69; *Shene ha-Meʾorot,* 15a; *M* 5562, pp. 214, 253–59; *M* 5563, I, 111, II, 561, second version; *BZ,* 98b; *LT,* IV, 30b; *M* 5568, pp. 251, 400, 503; *EL,* p. 117; *MK,* p. 115.

157. Supra, p. 141.

158. *Sidur,* 66c; *M* 5567, p. 359; *M* 5562, p. 177; *M* 5569, p. 104; *MK,* p. 571. Cf. *LT,* IV, 12c. See esp. *M* 5567, pp. 370–72, where, in direct opposition to *HTT,* RSZ states that recitation is greater than MYT, and that it is concerning *this* aspect of the commandment that the Mishnah rules: "ṿe-talmud Torah ke-neged kulam."

159. *HTT,* II, 13; *Tanya,* 47a, 150b; e.g., *Sidur,* 35d; *BY,* p. 69; *M* 5563, I, 111; *LT,* II, 5b, V, 28a; *EL,* p. 161; *MK,* p. 563.

160. Tal. B., *Sanhedrin,* 24a.

161. *Tanya,* 144b; *TO,* 17b, 49a–c, 51b; *LT,* II, 40d, III, 64b, V, 32c, 37c, 41c; *Sidur,* 28b, 98c–d; *M* 5568, p. 400; *M* 5562, pp. 30, 214; *BZ,* 91c; *BY,* p. 1; *Shene ha-Me᾿orot,* 5b; *MK,* pp. 267, 573; *M* 5563, II, 561.

162. *TO,* 38d–39b, 49c; *M* 5567, p. 149; *RP,* p. 166; *M* 5570, p. 48.

163. *BZ,* 20b; *M* 5563, II, 716; *Tanya,* 119a.

164. *RP,* p. 164; *BY,* p. 107.

165. *M* 5568, p. 386; *M Ket.,* II, 66.

166. *TO,* 25a; *Sidur,* 40c, 273b; *M* 5562, p. 214.

167. *MK,* p. 313 (the Patriarch Jacob, who was a "chariot" for Atsilut, was therefore permitted to marry two sisters). Cf. *MK,* p. 335; *Sidur,* 105d–106a (incestuous relations were permitted to Adam).

168. *M* 5562, p. 30.

169. *LT,* III, 86c.

170. *TO,* 25a.

171. *LT,* IV, 80a–b, V, 44d (cf. *TO,* 31b); *Sidur,* 268d–269a; *M Raz.,* p. 277. See also *M Ket.,* II, 70.

172. *M Raz.,* p. 491.

173. *M* 5564, pp. 3–4.

174. *RP,* p. 63; *M* 5568, p. 408; supra, n. 149.

175. *M* 5562, p. 34.

176. Despite several discourses to the contrary; cf. supra, nn. 162 and 149; *BY,* p. 120.

177. *LT,* II, 5a–b; *RP,* p. 177; *M* 5568, p. 409. Cf. *MK,* pp. 307, 354; *Tanya,* 55b (note), 109a, 73b; *M* 5566, p. 227; *M Ket.,* I, 9. This principle—what is higher descends lower—is thus used to explain both the superiority of the Written Torah and the superiority of the Oral Torah. See also *TO,* 52d and *M Nev.,* p. 125, where RSZ argues that because the Oral Torah is higher, it *cannot* descend to the level of written letters.

178. *BY,* p. 49.

179. *EL,* p. 128. Regarding the nullification of halakhah, see *Tanya,* 142a–145b; *M* 5562, p. 152.

180. *EL,* p. 168.

181. Cf. *MK,* p. 73, 355; *M* 5563, I, 119.

182. Cf. *Tanya,* 55b (note), 73b, 109a, 144a–b, 158a–159a; *M* 5566, p. 227; *MK,* 73, 307, 354–55; *M* 5563, I, 119; *RP,* pp. 173–74; *LT,* V, 42b; Vital, *Sha῾ar ha-Mitsvot,* p. 83.

183. *LT,* II, 5a; *TO,* 90d; *Sidur,* 75a–76c, 202c; *M* 5567, p. 159; *M* 5563, II, 641, second version; *LT,* IV, 6b, V, 41b–42d; supra, n. 182.

184. *Tanya,* 9a–b, 28b, 142a–145b, 156b; *LT,* II, 5a, IV, 6c; *MK,* p. 393; *M* 5563, I, 323.

185. *BZ,* 3a.

186. *EL,* p. 232; *LT,* II, 41a, IV, 6b–c; *Sidur,* 3d, 5d, 86d–87a, 98c–d; *M* 5568, pp. 40, 140, 334–35; *M* 5562, p. 186; *M* 5570, pp. 52, 59, 62; *M* 5563, II, 561, first version, 568, second version; Hilman, *Igerot Ba῾al ha-Tanya,* p. 82; *M Raz.,* p. 113–14.

187. *M* 5563, II, 573, second version.

188. *Tanya,* 128a; *TO,* 17b; *LT,* III, 49b, IV, 93d, V, 1c, 22c, 41c, 48a; *Sidur,* 28b, 128b (e.g., of Taᶜame Torah), 131a–132a, 143d; *M* 5562, II, 411; *EL,* pp. 40, 232; *BY,* pp. 69, 92; *BZ,* 2c–3d, 19d–20a; *M* 5563, I, 266; *M* 5565, II, 768; *M* 5568, pp. 140, 334–35, 350–52, 376, 384–85, 503, 527; *M* 5570, p. 52; *M Par.,* I, 263, II, 582; *M Nev.,* p. 4; *M Ket.,* I, 212–14, II, 188.

189. *LT,* II, 41b–c, IV, 23a, V, 48a; *Sidur,* 130d–131a; *M* 5563, I, 265; *MK,* pp. 174–76, 390, 393; *M* 5567, p. 355; *M* 5568, pp. 351–52; *BY,* p. 72; *M Par.,* II, 761–62; *M Raz.,* pp. 113, 170, 494–95; *M Nev.,* p. 61.

190. *Tanya,* 125b; *TO,* 98c; *LT,* II, 41b–c, IV, 6c, V, 22c; *M* 5565, II, 768, 982 (e.g., of Gan ᶜEden study; see also *LT,* II, 23a–24d; cf. *RP,* p. 156); *M* 5562, p. 186; *M* 5570, p. 52; *EL,* p. 168; *M Ket.,* II, 64.

191. *BZ,* 2c. See *M Iny.,* pp. 410–11; *M* 5566, p. 27; *M* 5562, p. 104f.; *BZ,* 55a, for examples.

192. *M* 5568, p. 165; *EL,* p. 127.

193. *MK,* p. 354. Similarly, every verse of the Bible has 600,000 valid interpretations; *TO,* 43c. See also *LT,* IV, 94a; *EL,* p. 40; *Shulḥan ᶜArukh ha-Ari,* pp. 93–94.

194. See *HTT,* II, 1.

195. Ibid., 9. Cf. *Sefer Ḥasidim,* ed. R. Margoliot (Jerusalem, 1960), no. 1011.

196. *HTT,* II, 8–10. See also *M Raz.,* pp. 335–36.

197. *HTT,* II, 11.

198. *LT,* II, 5c, V, 3c. See also *BZ,* 3a.

199. *HTT,* II, 1; *LT,* II, 5c.

200. *Peri ᶜEts Ḥayyim, Shaᶜar Hanhagat ha-Limud; Shaᶜar ha-Mitsvot,* p. 83.

201. In his introduction to the Kopys, 1816, edition of RSZ's *Shulḥan ᶜArukh* (reprinted in subsequent editions).

202. *MK,* p. 571 (Cordovero's statement regarding the value of reading Zohar even without comprehension is repeated there); *M. Par.,* II, 831–32.

203. Cf. *MK,* p. 514, where RSZ advocates studying *Ets Ḥayyim, Hekhal* 7, and the Zohar from beginning to end. Needless to say, familiarity with Lurianic kabbalah was indispensable for a full appreciation of RSZ's discourses.

Torah was to be studied and taught in Yiddish ("Ashkenaz"), in order to elevate that language; *M* 5568, p. 77.

The question of where to subsume kabbalah in the Scripture-Mishnah-Gemara triad was answered in very concrete terms by one of RSZ's successors. In accordance with the categorization of the discourses and with RSZ's personal schedule (supra, p. 46), R. Shalom Dov Baer Schneersohn of Lubavitch decreed in 1904 that the students of his newly founded yeshiva, Tomkhe Temimim, should devote two-thirds of their study time to Talmud and cognate works, and one-third to Hasidism (which by then had completely supplanted the study of kabbalah per se among virtually all Ḥabad Hasidim. The roots of this development may be traced to the Besht; see *Keter Shem Ṭov,* Appendix, p. 12a n. 26). See H. Glitzenstein, *Sefer ha-Toldot Admor Moharshab* (New York, 1981), pp. 176–80.

204. *Tanya,* 28a, based on *Tikune Zohar,* XXX, 74a.

205. See, e.g., *TO,* 34d, 63c, 64c, 67d, 87b; *LT,* II, 47b, III, 13a, IV, 22d, 23c, 67b, 72d, V, 16b; *Sidur,* 74b; *M* 5562, II, 444; *RP,* p. 15; *M* 5562, p. 41.

206. Tal. B., *Makot,* 23b, *Ohalot,* I, 8. See G. Appel, *A Philosophy of Mitzvot* (New York, 1975), p. 26 and notes.

207. *Tikune Zohar,* LXX, 130b; XXI, 76a. See R. Menaḥem Mendel's gloss, *LT,* III, 17b–c.

208. *Tanya,* 47b; *TO,* 52c; *LT,* V, 11c; Vital, *Likuṭe Torah* (Vilna, 1880), p. 15a, on Ṭaʿame ha-Mitsyot; Meir Ibn Gabbai, *ʿAvodat ha-Kodesh* (Warsaw, 1883), I, 25, p. 45.

209. *Tanya,* 111a–b; *LT,* II, 45c, 47b, 48a, III, 13a, IV, 23c, 27b, V, 16b; *Sidur,* 17a; *M* 5562, II, 444; *M* 5565, II, 587; *RP,* p. 15; *M* 5562, pp. 31, 271; *M* 5566, p. 333; *M* 5564, pp. 112, 228, 236.

210. Other sefirot are also occasionally associated with the supernal source of the commandments, but all are explicitly or implicitly related to Keter. See *Tanya,* 58a, note, 131a; *TO,* 16a, 55b, 104a, 112a; *LT,* II, 47d, III, 5c, 9c, 14b–c, 62b–c, IV, 10c, 50c, 99b–c; *Sidur,* 20d, 228b; *M* 5563, II, 520, second version, 624, second version; *M* 5565, II, 582, 591; *M* 5562, pp. 204, 211; *M* 5566, p. 256.

211. *TO,* 96a; *LT,* I, 1d, III, 18a–b, IV, 49c; *M* 5563, II, 520, second version, 624, second version; *M* 5562, p. 211; *M* 5568, pp. 346–47; *M* 5564, pp. 5–6, 34; *M* 5567, p. 220; *M Nev.,* p. 99; *M Ket.,* I, 212.

212. *TO,* 32c–d; *LT,* III, 18a–b; *M* 5562, p. 272; *M* 5568, pp. 346–47; *M* 5566, p. 184. See also *M* 5563, II, 505, 610, 623.

213. *M* 5562, II, 473; *LT,* II, 47d, III, 18a.

214. *Tanya,* 104a, 111a–b, 149b, 150b; *TO,* 2a, 16d, 38c, 42c, 46c, 53c, 75d, 87b; *LT,* II, 29a (cf. *TO,* 42c), 33a, 45c, 48a, III, 43d, 78b, 91c, IV, 23c, 27b, 40d, V, 16b, 17b; *Sidur,* 25c, 74b; *BY,* pp. 27, 117, 161; *M* 5565, II, 582, 587, 793; *RP,* p. 26; *M* 5566, pp. 247–48, 333, 354–55; *M* 5564, pp. 42, 112, 228, 234, 236; *M* 5563, I, 364; *M* 5562, p. 31.

215. *M* 5562, I, p. 266, II, 358, 468.

216. Cf. *Tikune Zohar,* XVIII, 37b.

217. Who fulfilled all the commandments spiritually; see *BY,* p. 6 (= *MK,* p. 327); *BZ,* 16a–b; *M* 5566, p. 206; *LT,* III, 38b, V, 9b; *TO,* 11d, 68a, 73d, 96c.

218. According to some discourses, however, they foster conscious Love, Fear, and faith; see *LT,* III, 5d, IV, 20a; *Sidur,* 133a; *MK,* p. 178; *M* 5565, II, 794.

219. See supra, p. 85.

220. Cf. *LT,* III, 92c; *Sidur,* 131d; *EL,* p. 94; *M* 5562, p. 192; *BZ,* 141c; *M* 5563, I, 229; *M Nev.,* pp. 84, 95. Even the prohibition of murder is rooted not in social benefit but in the need to elevate the fallen sparks; *BZ,* 141a.

221. *Tanya,* 28a–b, 45a–51b, 66a. Cf. *TO,* 54d–55a; *MK,* p. 456; *RP,* p. 57; *M* 5568, p. 16; *M* 5567, p. 170.

222. Cf. *Tanya,* 145a–b; *TO,* 46d, 74b, 76c; *LT,* II, 47b, IV, 59d; *BY,* p. 47; *M* 5564, pp. 93–94; *M* 5563, I, 238; *M Ket.,* I, 223.

223. *TO,* 52c; *MK,* pp. 279, 36d–37a; *LT,* III, 38b, 69d, 78b, 81c, IV, 27b, V, 22c–d; *M* 5563, II, 624, second version. See also *LT,* III, 17b–c; *Tanya,* 153b–154a; *M Par.,* I, 129.

224. *M* 5563, II, 752.

225. *Tanya,* 49b–51a, 55b. Cf. *M Nev.,* p. 221; *M Ket.,* I, 83.

226. See *Tanya,* 46b–49a.

227. Ibid., 51a–52b, 55a. Cf. *MK,* p. 382.

228. *Tanya,* 50b.

229. Ibid., 51a–52b; *Avot,* IV, 2. Cf. *Tanya,* 104a; *TO,* 81c, 110b; *LT,* IV, 23c; *BY,* p. 33; *MK,* pp. 161, 456; *M* 5563, II, 505 (cf. *TO,* 96b; *M* 5568, pp. 366, 377; *M* 5566, p. 333); *M* 5566, p. 322; *M Par.,* II, 774. The discourses in parentheses maintain that the value of fulfilling the commandments in this world exceeds the value of their reward in the next. As *M* 5563, II, 504, explains, this is a corollary of the cause-effect relation that exists between the commandments and the reward they generate. For a more precise analysis of the relation between intellectual and natural love, see infra, pp. 179–83.

230. Cf. *TO,* 96a; *LT,* III, 70d, IV, 10c, 49c, 55c, 69c, 83b; *MK,* p. 382; *M* 5563, II, 568–70, second version; *M* 5568, p. 517; *M* 5566, pp. 254, 349; *M* 5564, p. 130; *M* 5563, I, 8; *M* 5570, p. 150.

231. *LT,* III, 39a, IV, 54a, 55c; *Sidur,* 234c; *M* 5566, pp. 247, 254 (cf. p. 326); *M* 5567, p. 367.

232. *LT,* III, 39a; *M* 5566, p. 254. See also *LT,* IV, 49c.

233. On Love and Fear in Maimonides' two major works, see *Mishneh Torah, Hil. Yesode ha-Torah,* II, 1–2, IV, 12; *Guide,* III, 29, p. 518, III, 51, pp. 621, 627–28, III, 52, pp. 629–30.

234. Cf. *LT,* III, 71a, IV, 10c, 54a, 69c; *M* 5563, II, 442; *M* 5566, p. 254; *M* 5564, p. 112. Cf. *M* 5563, II, 710.

235. E.g., *TO,* 35c.

236. *MK,* p. 391. Cf. *Guide,* III, 44.

237. *TO,* 20b.

238. *TO,* 53b; *LT,* III, 92b; *M* 5563, II, 504; *M* 5566, p. 348. See also *M Ket.,* II, 7, 28, 29.

239. *M* 5563, II, 710.

240. See, however, *M* 5566, p. 349.

241. See *Guide,* I, 58.

242. Thus, kaṿanah, birkhat ha-mitsṿah, the positive commandments, and the negative commandments are all identified, in different discourses, as generators of sovev. On the negative commandments, see *TO,* 52c; *LT,* IV, 68c, 75a, V, 45c; *Sidur,* 16b, 17a; *MK,* p. 364; *RP,* pp. 131–32, 135; *M* 5568, p. 505; *M* 5564, p. 55; *M Nev.,* p. 125; *M Ket.,* II, 52, 53, 69–70, 140.

243. *Tanya,* 149b; *TO,* 8b, 96a; *LT,* II, 47b, IV, 10c, 50c, V, 16b.

244. *M* 5564, pp. 51, 56; *LT,* I, 6d. See also *TO,* 53b; *LT,* III, 85a, IV, 80b, V, 7a.

245. *TO,* 52c; *LT,* IV, 80b.

246. *Sidur,* 269b; *M* 5563, I, 30.

247. *M* 5563, I, 30.

248. Tal. B., *Yevamot,* 3b, 7a, *Shabat,* 132b, *Betsah,* 8b.

249. *M* 5562, p. 266.

250. *TO,* 52b.

251. See *Igerot Ḳodesh,* p. 524, for the complete list.

252. Glitzenstein, *Sefer ha-Toldot RSZ,* p. 270.

253. *Tanya,* 48b, 125a; *LT,* III, 91c, V, 22a, 44b; *Sidur,* 16a; *BY,* p. 135; *RP,* p. 57. See also *BY,* pp. 5, 136; *MK,* pp. 326, 535; *M* 5566, p. 271; *M* 5567, pp. 323–24; *M* 5562, p. 183.

Chapter 5. Love and Fear

1. See introduction to Part 2, p. 76a, of *Tanya,* where RSZ promises to explain the concept of reciprocal Love in more detail "in its place." This place is obviously not *Sha'ar ha-Yiḥud,* where it is not mentioned, but *Sefer shel Benonim,* ch. 46. One can only speculate as to why RSZ changed their order.

2. *Tanya,* p. 75b, 76a. Cf. 146b: "The life of the Tsadiḳ is not a physical life but a spiritual life consisting of faith, Fear, and Love." Like Saadya, Baḥya, Maimonides, and others, RSZ held that faith should be based on heuristic knowledge—one must understand God's unity as far as possible before one can truly believe in it. See, e.g., *MK,* pp. 444–45, 468–69, and infra.

3. Chs. 1–17, of *Sefer shel Benonim,* in addition to frequently touching and occasionally dilating on Love and Fear, lay the groundwork for this exposition, which is primarily contained in chs. 18–25, 38–44, and 46–50. Most of the remaining chapters deal with methods for promoting joyous Service and combating depression. Cf. *Kuzari,* III, 50, where the three foundations of Service are identified as Fear, Love, and joy; *'Iḳarim,* III, 31–36.

4. For an overview of Jewish thought on the subject, see G. Vajda, *L'Amour de Dieu dans la théologie juive du Moyen Age* (Paris, 1957), and A. Altmann's review of same in *Ḳiryat Sefer* 34 (1958–1959): 52–54.

5. Specifically, *Mishneh Torah, Hil. Yes. ha-Torah,* II, 1–2; *Hil. Teshuvah,* X; *Guide,* I, 39, III, 28, 44, and esp. 51 (cf., e.g., p. 621 and *Tanya,* 59a–b); *Sefer ha-Mitsvot,* Positive Commandments 3–5; Mishnah Commentary, *Avot,* I, 3.

Specific citations of RSZ's other sources, or possible sources, are given infra.

6. I. Twersky, *Introduction to the Code of Maimonides* (Yale University Press, 1980), p. 262 n. 49; see also p. 216 n. 63 and p. 363.

7. *Tanya,* 53a–57b. Cf. *Igerot Ḳodesh,* pp. 174–75. The quotation is from *Tiḳune Zohar* X, 25b, and is cited or alluded to in *Tanya,* 22a–b, 53b, 55a–b, 153b; and in the Maggid's teachings, e.g., *Liḳutim Yeḳarim,* no. 93, 163; *Or Torah,* 85b.

8. *Tanya,* 8a. Cf. Maimonides' Mishnah Commentary, *Avot,* I, 3; *Reshit Ḥokhmah,* 50c–d; Tishby, *Mishnat ha-Zohar,* II, 287.

9. *Tanya,* 55b. See also *M Par.,* I, 5; *M Iny.,* pp. 236, 260–61, 262, 267; *M Raz.,* p. 450.

10. For Maimonides, see supra, n. 6; for the Maggid, *Or Torah,* 44c, 72b. See also Albo's *'Iḳarim,* III, 35.

In the discourses RSZ occasionally emphasizes the reverse relation: Love and Fear are attained by the proper fulfillment of the commandments (cf. *Kuzari,* III, 11; *'Iḳarim,* III, 31; Baḥya, *Ḥovot ha-Levavot,* X, 3; Twersky, supra, n. 6). See *TO,* 47b–c; *LT,* III, 16b, 38d, 63a, 96c, IV, 45a; *MK,* pp. 203, 205, 209, 275, 316; *RP,* p. 71. Generally, however, the types of Love and Fear discussed in these discourses are not identical with those described in *Tanya* as being the foundations of Service; see infra.

11. *Tanya,* 8a.

12. Ibid., 1c, 21b, 98b.

13. Ibid., 56a, 28a–b, 45a, 65b, 9a. Cf. RSZ's exegesis of Ps. 145:18 in *Tanya,* 49b, and the Maggid's exegesis in *Or Torah,* 55a (= 77b).

14. *Tanya,* 62a; see also 23a.

15. Ibid., 14a.

16. Ibid., 13b–14b, 19b–20a, 62a, 126a–b. Cf. Zohar, I, 11b, III, 263b; *ʿIḳarim,* III, 36.

17. *Tanya,* 21a.

18. Cf. ibid., 98b, 126b, 162a; see also 63b–64a, where RSZ stretches the Zoharic-philosophical concept of intellectual Love-Fear (cf. *Tanya,* 22a–b, 51b–53b) to include certain forms of Innate Love. This reflects RSZ's general attempt to bring Maimonides' elitist intellectualism and the kabbalists' elitist mysticism within reach of every man.

19. Cf. *Sefer Ḥasidim,* 28.

20. *Tanya,* 62b–63b, 65a–66a.

21. Ibid., 64a.

22. Ibid., 70b; cf. 12a.

23. Ibid., 56a–62b. Cf. *Igerot Ḳodesh,* pp. 172–75, 460–63; *Ḥovot ha-Levavot,* X, 6; *ʿIḳarim,* III, 32; *ʿAvodat ha-Ḳodesh,* I, 25–28; Zohar, I, 7b, 11a; *Tiḳ. Zohar,* introduction, 5b; *Sefer Roḳeaḥ* (Jerusalem, 1967), pp. 5–6; *Reshit Ḥokhmah,* 6d–7a, 8d, 13d, 51c–52d; *Or Torah,* 53a, 60a–b, 68b–69a, Appendix, no. 48, 49.

24. *Tanya,* 21a–24a, 31a–b, 53a–b, 56b–58a, 59a–60b, 62b–64a, 65a. See also *M Raz.,* p. 96.

25. E.g., *Tsavaʾat ha-Ribash,* 36, 135; *Or Torah,* 53a, 60a, 68a–69a. Cf. *Peri ha-Arets,* 58.

26. See *TO,* 47a (cf. 18b, 25c, 39c), 47d, 77a, 82c, 87c; *LT,* II, 20a, III, 30a–b, 38d, 42c, 66b, 67c, 84a, 94a, 96c, IV, 13b, 16d, 78d; *M* 5563, II, 605; *MK,* pp. 203, 218, 294, 316, 333; *BY,* p. 48; *M* 5562, pp. 116–18, 176–77 (on the Love of be-khol meʾodekha, which, as previous citations indicate, is often synonymous with Ahavah Rabah), 221, 250; *RP,* pp. 70, 71.

27. *TO,* 47a; *LT,* I, 5b, III, 30a–b, 42c, 66b, IV, 13b; *MK,* pp. 203, 218, 294; *EL,* p. 42; *M* 5568, p. 538; *RP,* p. 139. Cf. *Tanya,* 14a, 62a.

28. *MK,* p. 182.

29. On the axiological standing of Love vs. Fear, see *LT,* III, 96c; *MK,* pp. 417–18; *M* 5565, II, pp. 780–82; *M* 5564, pp. 50, 237; *M* 5567, p. 369; *BY,* p. 66; *EL,* pp. 40–41; *BZ,* 81a; *M* 5562, p. 277; *M* 5568, p. 540. On Ahavat ʿOlam vs. Ahavah Rabah, see *TO,* 47b, 73a, 86c–d; *LT,* III, 42c, 66b, IV, 16d, 78d; *Sidur,* 152a; *MK,* pp. 203, 260, 294, 341–42, 433; *M* 5562, p. 221; *M* 5563, II, 770; *M Par.,* II, 510–11. Cf. *LT,* III, 29c–d, 63a; *M* 5562, p. 221, on the Love of Abraham vs. the Love of Aaron; see *TO,* 25b–c, 60d, 111c; *LT,* II, 40c–d, III, 63a, 84a, IV, 26b, 43a; *MK,* pp. 260, 475; *BZ,* 132d–134b; *M* 5562, pp. 96, 116, on the Love "like fire" vs. the Love "like water." These three pairs of Love-types are interrelated, but, like the

hierarchical standing within each pair, the relation varies according to the discourse.

30. Note the various definitions of *ḥolat ahavah* in *Tanya,* 70b; *MK,* p. 275; *M* 5564, p. 64; of re'uta de-liba and/or the Love of the "inner" vs. the "outer" heart in *Tanya,* 22b, 52a, 63b, 105a; *TO,* 7b; *LT,* III, 67c, IV, 45a, 78d; *M* 5563, pp. 183, 321; *M* 5567, pp. 358, 363, 365; *BY,* p. 59; *EL,* p. 187; *M* 5562, p. 276; and the combinations, contradictions, or variations of *Tanya* Love-types: in *Tanya,* 126b, *TO,* 25c, *LT,* V, 24d, *M Par.,* I, 413, II, 861, *M Nev.,* p. 32; *MK,* pp. 322–23, Love of life; in *M* 5567, p. 369, *Shene ha-Me'orot,* 25a, *M* 5562, p. 251, *BY,* p. 48, filial Love; in *TO,* 60d, *MK,* pp. 185, 203, *BY,* pp. 37, 96, reciprocal Love; in *LT,* II, 40a, III, 88d (cf. IV, 2c, 86d), *Sidur* 231c, *M* 5563, II, 692, *M Par.,* I, 390–93; *M Ket.,* II, pp. 24–25, 28–29, *MK,* pp. 70, 209, 218, 316, *BY,* pp. 27, 48, 97, *EL,* pp. 10, 50–51, Innate (= "hidden," or "natural") Love.

31. *BY,* p. 13; *M* 5562, p. 20; *RP,* p. 160; *Sidur,* 152b; *MK,* p. 217; cf. *M* 5569, p. 96.

32. See *Reshit Ḥokhmah,* 40d–41c; Zohar, I, 11b; Baḥya, *Ḥovot ha-Levavot,* X, 6.

33. *MK,* p. 105; cf. *'Avodat ha-Ḳodesh,* I, 25.

34. *Igerot Ḳodesh,* pp. 172–75; *TO,* 79a; *LT,* III, 89a, IV, 19d; *Sidur,* 151c–152a, 188a; *MK,* pp. 67, 267, 277, 357–58, 489, 500, 520; *M* 5566, p. 146; *M* 5563, p. 320.

35. E.g., *TO,* 47d, 56c, 78d, 86b, 87c; *Sidur,* 152a–b; *BY,* p. 96; *EL,* pp. 139, 187.

36. See, e.g., *MK,* pp. 387–88; *EL,* pp. 127–29.

37. *MK,* p. 438; *M Iny.,* p. 24.

38. *M* 5562, pp. 17–18; *M* 5568, pp. 538–40; *MK,* pp. 95, 275, 371, 436; *M* 5565, II, 480–82; *Tanya,* 103b; *M Par.,* I, 129–30, 247.

39. See *Tanya,* 50b, 53b, 155b–156b; *Igerot Ḳodesh,* p. 461; *EL,* p. 173; and infra.

40. I am referring to the dispute between RSZ's son, R. Dov Baer, and R. Aaron of Starosielce. See L. Jacobs, *Hasidic Prayer* (New York, 1973), pp. 100–103; L. Jacobs, *Seeker of Unity* (London, 1956), pp. 12–13, 128–29; R. Elior, "Ha-Maḥloket 'al Moreshet Ḥabad," *Tarbiz* 49 (1979–1980): 167–86, esp. 175–85. The passages Elior quotes from R. Dov Baer's *Ḳunṭres ha-Hitpa'alut,* along with the rest of the work, have been translated by L. Jacobs in *Tract on Ecstasy* (London, 1963), which also contains a valuable introduction and helpful explanatory notes.

41. See *Tanya,* 19a–20b, 57a–58a.

42. *TO,* 78d–79a; *Sidur,* 152b; *MK,* pp. 26, 123, 185, 387–88, 395; *M* 5563, p. 127; *M* 5567, p. 256; *BY,* pp. 96, 173; *EL,* pp. 139, 249, 251; *M* 5568, p. 84; *Igerot Ḳodesh,* pp. 461–63; Y. I. Epstein, *Ma'amar: Shene ha-Me'orot* (New York, 1971), p. 60; *M Par.,* I, 173, 306, 366, 418, II, 833; *M Iny.,* pp. 62, 134, 279; *M Raz.,* p. 94; *M Nev.,* p. 223; *M Ket.,* I, 105. Cf., however, *M* 5562, p. 216.

That the fulfillment of the commandment to love God requires, primarily or only, intellectual immersion and dedication of one's will rather than emotional arousal is also evident from *Tanya,* 76a; *LT,* III, 26b, 29c–d; *M* 5563, II, 698; *MK,* p. 407; *M* 5567, p. 356; *BY,* pp. 38, 143; *M* 5568, p. 217; *RP,* p. 139. Cf. *M* 5568, p. 516.

On the relation of Love, Fear, and (the desire for) biṭul, see *Tanya,* 18b, 19a,

24b; *TO,* 25c; *LT,* II, 20a, III, 63a; *MK,* p. 98; *M* 5566, pp. 312–13; *M* 5564, pp. 8–9; *BY,* p. 48; *BZ,* 83d; *M* 5568, p. 555.

43. *Tanya,* 16b, 102b, 112a–113b, 162a; *TO,* 7d, 85c, 111c, 122d; *LT,* III, 5d, 13d, 61d, IV, 29a, 42d, 78d, V, 5c, 28c–29a; *Igerot Kodesh,* pp. 33–34; *MK,* p. 362; *M* 5565, II, 583; *M* 5563, p. 360; *M* 5564, p. 64; *M* 5567, pp. 292, 319; *RP,* p. 73. See Zohar, II, 109b, 202b.

44. See Scholem, *Major Trends,* ch. 4.

45. *Tsava'at ha-Ribash,* no. 32, 35–36, 38, 40, 42, 62, 66–68, 87, 105, 135. *Keter Shem Tov,* no. 216, 259, 421; *Magid,* pp. 73, 81, 85, 184, 186–87, 330, 1990 ed., p. 400, and p. 13a in the Kehot edition; *Or Torah,* 37b, 83a, 97b, 105a; *Degel Maḥneh Efrayim,* p. 282 (cf. *Tsava'at,* no. 41; *Keter Shem Tov,* 197, 219); *Kedushat Levi,* pp. 42, 73, 199; *Or ha-Me'ir,* 14a, 35a, 116a–118b, 130a, 132b, 173b, 191b, 213a–b, 246b, 280b. See Zohar, II, 200b; *Tik. Zohar,* LXX, 122a, on praying with "Fear and Love," i.e., with religious fervor; and Zohar, II, 178a, on the spiritual ascendency of a relatively unlearned man who prays with all the kavanot (cf. *Tsava'at ha-Ribash,* 41; *Keter Shem Tov,* 197); Tishby, *Mishnat ha-Zohar,* II, 260, 291; Scholem, *Major Trends,* pp. 275–77. See also R. Schatz, "Contemplative Prayer in Hasidism," in *Studies in Mysticism Presented to Gershom Scholem* (Jerusalem, 1967), pp. 207–26.

It should be noted that Schatz's attributions of certain teachings to the Besht (see "Contemplative Prayer," p. 211, n. 3; p. 213; p. 214, n. 13) are improbable.

46. *TO,* 29c, 65b, 111c; *LT,* III, 2c, 66a, 70d, IV, 34c, V, 28c, 43a; *Sidur,* 19c–d, 22c; *MK,* pp. 273–74; *M* 5562, p. 267; *M* 5563, pp. 177, 362; *M* 5564, p. 179; *M* 5567, p. 263; *M* 5568, pp. 31–32, 403, 441; *M* 5570, pp. 51, 83; *RP,* p. 73; *BY,* p. 29; *Tanya,* 155a, 162a, 163a; *Igerot Kodesh,* pp. 33–34, 115–16.

47. *TO,* 1c, 122c–d; *Sidur,* 24a; *MK,* pp. 123, 322; *M* 5566, p. 372; *M* 5568, p. 84; *M* 5570, pp. 51, 83; *M* 5563, p. 8; *BY,* p. 38; *BZ,* 71a; *Igerot Kodesh,* pp. 462–63.

48. *LT,* II, 40c, III, 13d, 79d; *M* 5563, I, p. 362; *M* 5563, II, 605; *M* 5568, p. 31; *RP,* p. 73. See Zohar, III, 192b; Tishby, *Mishnat ha-Zohar,* II, 297.

49. *Sidur,* 281d.

50. *M Iny.,* p. 51; *M Par.,* II, 700; *Shulḥan ʿArukh, Oraḥ Ḥayyim,* 155:1.

51. *LT,* V, 16d–17a; *M* 5563, II, 668; *M* 5570, p. 83; *M* 5564, pp. 7, 34; *M* 5567, pp. 36, 292; *BZ,* 71a. On the etymology of *tefilah,* see *TO,* 79d–80a; *ʿAvodat ha-Kodesh,* II, 6, p. 57; *Peri ha-Arets,* 20; *Magid,* pp. 70, 248; *Or Torah,* 75b; *Kedushat Levi,* p. 205.

52. *M* 5566, p. 21; *Sidur,* 56a. See also *Tanya,* 29a; Zohar, II, 213b, 238, III, 20a.

53. *LT,* I, 2d, III, 5d.

54. *Peri ʿEts Ḥayyim, Shaʿar ha Tefilah,* ch. 1.

55. *M* 5564, p. 70; *TO,* 45c, 47b, 56c; *LT,* IV, 42d, V, 43d; *Igerot Kodesh,* pp. 33–34; *M Par.,* II, 641–42.

On the function and contemplative themes of *Pesuke de-Zimrah,* see *TO,* 1d, 56c; *LT,* I, 5c, II, 35b–c, 47d, III, 2c, 20d, 28b, 32d, V, 16d, 45b; *MK,* p. 404; *M* 5570, p. 50; *Igerot Kodesh,* p. 462; *M* 5566, p. 183; *M* 5563, p. 177; *M* 5568, p. 370. Cf. *Or Torah,* 78b; *Or ha-Me'ir,* 148a.

On *Birkhat Keri'at Shema,* see *Tanya,* 69b–70a, 98b, 162a; *TO,* 30b, 56c, 122d–123a; *LT,* III, 28c–d, IV, 34d, V, 42b; *Igerot Kodesh,* pp. 33–34; *MK,* p. 405.

On Ḳeri'at Shema, see *TO,* 1a, 30b, 38c–d, 82c, 84d; *LT,* V, 43c; *Sidur,* 19c, 56a; *Igerot Ḳodesh,* p. 462; *MK,* p. 407; *EL,* p. 140; *M Par.,* II, 728.

On *Shemoneh ʿEśreh,* or the ʿAmidah, see infra.

56. Zohar, I, 266b, III, 306b. See *TO,* 88a; *LT,* III, 26b–d, IV, 97a, V, 28c; *M* 5566, pp. 333, 372.

57. See *TO,* 1d, 8a, 60d; *MK,* pp. 53, 260, 305, 371, 409; *M* 5565, II, 622; *M* 5563, I, 8; *M Par.,* I, 28; *M Ket.,* II, 178; *EL,* p. 129; *LT,* III, 83d–84a, IV, 35a; *RP,* p. 73; cf. *Tanya,* 70b–71a; *Sidur,* 66a; *TO,* 25b; *M* 5567, p. 36; *M* 5564, p. 64.

The upshot of these citations is that the ratso-shov relation applies or should apply to: (1) the continually fluctuating emotional states of the worshipper during each of the first three stages and possibly during the ʿAmidah as well; (2) these three stages (ratso) vis-à-vis the ʿAmidah (shov); and (3) prayer as a whole (ratso) vis-à-vis Torah-study (shov).

58. See, e.g., *M* 5570, p. 51.

59. *Tanya,* 14a, 18b, 162a–b; *Sidur,* 23b; *TO,* 29c, 111c–d; *LT,* III, 74d, IV, 78d; *M* 5563, p. 177; *M* 5562, p. 267; *M* 5568, p. 441; *EL,* p. 132.

60. See supra, Chapter 4, pp. 153, 173.

61. *LT,* II, 41a, III, 71a, V, 43b; *MK,* p. 496; *M* 5562, p. 187; *Igerot Ḳodesh,* p. 178.

62. *LT,* V, 43c; *Sidur,* 273a; *BZ,* 119a; *M* 5568, pp. 44–45, 50. Cf. *Reshit Ḥokhmah,* 166a; Zohar, II, 58a, 201b–202a, I, 167b.

63. *Tanya,* 35a–b; *LT,* II, 49a–b; *TO,* 31a–b, 55a–b; supra, Chapter 3, p. 115.

But cf. *MK,* p. 189, which appears in MS no. 1174 (among others) and was therefore probably delivered before 1798 (see *MK,* p. 599). RSZ apparently abandoned the Besht's doctrine on the elevation of profane thoughts sometime in the 1790s. See also *M Par.,* I, 206, 249; *M* 5563, II, 490; *M Raz.,* p. 226.

64. *Mishneh Torah, Hil. Teshuvah,* X, 2.

65. Tal. B., *Berakhot,* 20b.

66. Ibid., 28b–35a. See also *Tiḳ. Zohar,* XVIII, 32b.

67. *ʿAvodat ha-Ḳodesh,* introduction, II, 2, 6, 8, 10, p. 286 et passim. See also Horowitz, *Shene Luḥot,* I, 48a, 52b.

68. *Keter Shem Ṭov,* 395; *Tsava'at ha-Ribash,* 123. See also *Magid,* p. 324.

69. Cf. Zohar, II, 133a; III, 255a; *Tiḳ. Zohar,* L, 86a; Tishby, *Mishnat ha-Zohar,* II, 254–55, 267, 270–74; Scholem, *Major Trends,* pp. 271, 275–77.

70. See *Keter Shem Ṭov,* 20, 61, 80, 126, 138, 176, 182, 214, 268; *Magid,* pp. 25, 51–53, 183, 257; *Or Torah,* 19b, 74b; *Degel Maḥneh Efrayim,* pp. 130, 253; *Peri ha-Arets,* 48, 57, 91; *Ḳedushat Levi,* pp. 73, 143, 193, 206; *Or ha-Me'ir,* 7b, 8b, 34b, 36a–b, 43b, 70b, 92b, 173b, 250a, 269b–270a.

L. Jacobs summarizes most of the basic interpretations in *Hasidic Prayer,* pp. 23–31.

71. *Tanya,* 57b–58a; cf. *LT,* IV, 88c. Although Luria's Shekhinah was relatively personalistic (see Scholem, *Major Trends,* pp. 275–76), it was less so than the Shekhinah of the Besht and Maggid.

72. *LT,* III, 70d, 71c, IV, 38b, 97a, V, 28d–29a; *Sidur,* 22c, 25d, 85d; *M* 5563, I, p. 363; *M* 5563, II, 715; *M* 5562, II, 487; *M* 5566, pp. 21–23, 372; *M* 5564, p. 145; *BY,* p. 155; *M Par.,* II, 738–39, 761–62.

73. *TO,* 45c, 103a; *LT,* IV, 79c, V, 43c–d; *Sidur,* 16b, 116a, 128c, 273b–c; *M* 5563, I, 8, II, 716; *M* 5568, pp. 44–45; *EL,* pp. 140, 210.

On reciting the ʿAmidah inaudibly, a requirement RSZ links with biṭul (in several of the above citations), see Zohar, I, 210a, II, 202a.

74. Cf. Zohar, I, 45b; II, 63b, 261b.

75. *LT,* III, 70d; *Sidur,* 22c; *M* 5562, II, 487; *M* 5563, II, 715; *M* 5566, pp. 21–23.

76. *BY,* p. 85.

77. *M Iny.,* p. 252; Tal. B., *Sukah,* 52a, *Ḳidushin,* 30b.

78. *TO,* 38c; *LT,* III, 26c, 79d, IV, 34c–d, 35c; *M* 5566, p. 236; *M Nev.,* pp. 122.

79. *LT,* III, 72a, 79d; *MK,* pp. 302–303; *M* 5566, p. 166. Cf. *Sidur,* 116c; *BY,* p. 38.

80. *Tanya,* 103a; *TO,* 9a, 47c, 52d–53a, 65b, 87c–88b; *EL,* p. 3; *M* 5562, p. 34; *RP,* p. 60; *Sidur,* 173c–d, 211c–d; *MK,* p. 152; *BY,* p. 10; *M* 5568, pp. 32–33; *LT,* III, 72a–b, IV, 72c, V, 19a, 24b; *M* 5567, p. 257.

81. The practices include: (a) engaging in frivolity before prayer (see Wilensky, *Ḥasidim u-Mitnagdim,* II, 102, 273; *Magid* [Kehot ed.], 13b); (b) praying at great length, or after the optimum or required halakhic times (Wilensky, *Ḥasidim u-Mitnagdim,* I, 38, n. 19, 54, 87, 118, 126, 138, 317, II, 103, 195, 207, 235, 246, 273, 302, 348; Jacobs, *Hasidic Prayer,* ch. 4); (c) praying with shouts and wild gesticulations (Wilensky, *Ḥasidim u-Mitnagdim,* I, 41 and n. 27, 54, 59 and n. 15, 87, 102, 125, 138, 151, 156, 205, 208, 227, II, 90–92, 102, 142, 192, 302; Jacobs, *Hasidic Prayer,* ch. 5); (d) praying in separate congregations (Wilensky, *Ḥasidim u-Mitnagdim,* I, 40–41 and n. 36, 62, 102, 139, 151, 156, 178, 193, 224, 323, II, 155, 236); (e) adopting the Lurianic liturgy (Wilensky, *Ḥasidim u-Mitnagdim,* I, 45 and n. 10, 47–48, 53, 67–68, 102, 112, 118, 124, 139, 151, 156, 178, 193, 208, 224, 227, 330, II, 57, 86–87, 90–92, 235, 248–49; Jacobs, *Ḥasidic Prayer,* ch. 3).

82. Supra, Chapter 2, p. 109.

83. *Tanya,* 59b–60b, 63b, 103a, 135a, 162a–b; *LT,* III, 32d, IV, 38b, 42d, V, 2c; *Sidur,* 163a–b; *Igerot Ḳodesh,* pp. 11, 33–34, 177–79; *M* 5562, II, 679, 692; *MK,* pp. 93, 362, 403; *M* 5565, II, 400–401; *M* 5566, p. 187; *M* 5570, p. 50; *EL,* p. 139; *M Par.,* II, 696; *M Nev.,* p. 139. On the proper minimum duration of the Morning Prayer, cf. *Tanya,* 103a; *Igerot Ḳodesh,* p. 11; and *MK,* p. 404.

84. RSZ maintained that there was no valid halakhic objection to this change; see *Igerot Ḳodesh,* no. 81.

85. *Tsava'at ha-Ribash,* 33; *Keter Shem Ṭov,* 166, 226 (cf. *Or ha-Me'ir,* 5b, 68b–69a; *Sefer Ḥasidim,* 57, 768, 820); *Igerot Ḳodesh,* p. 33; *M* 5564, p. 70.

On the value of melodious prayer, see *MK,* pp. 6–7; *M* 5562, II, 342. Cf. Jacobs, *Hasidic Prayer,* p. 68; *Sefer Ḥasidim,* 156.

86. *MK,* p. 398; *EL,* p. 24. Cf. *Tsava'at ha-Ribash,* 16, which states that the Besht was extremely scrupulous in adhering to the optimum halakhic time for the Morning Prayer and exhorts the reader to do likewise.

87. The adoption of this essentially Sephardic liturgy should not be confused with the use of Lurianic kavanot. RSZ's masters and colleagues taught that the value of these kavanot was outweighed by the value of emotionalistic, ecstatic prayer. In justifying this shift of values, they were able to fall back on the standard

position, shared by the Mitnagdim, that only full-fledged kabbalists were qualified to pray with these kavanot (whereas all were able and therefore obligated to pray with some degree of hitlahavut; *Or Torah,* 97b). See *Tsava'at ha-Ribash,* 123; *Or Torah,* 37c; *Or ha-Me'ir,* 14a, 173b, 213a.

RSZ characteristically adopted a middle, antielitist course and advocated the use of kavanot by all, but only during the ʿAmidah; *Sidur,* 85d; *M* 5566, pp. 21–23. This approach is reflected in his recension of the Prayer Book, *Seder Tefilot mi-kal ha-Shanah ʿal pi Nusaḥ ha-Arizal* (Shklov, 1803; reprinted twice in Kopys during RSZ's lifetime). It combines elements of the Ashkenazic and Sephardic liturgies according to four general criteria for selection: (1) prayers and recensions included in the Talmud, Midrash, and Zohar; (2) those included in the works of R. Hai Gaon; (3), those in Lurianic works that RSZ considered authoritative, provided these prayers or recensions were appropriate for the general public (not only for kabbalists); and (4) correctness of grammar and usage. (According to one discourse, however, RSZ did not consider this to be a universally important criterion, since, in his view, no one, "not even the Ari and the Besht," could claim to know the Holy Tongue perfectly. Nevertheless, the kavanot of these luminaries ensured that once their prayer-letters ascended, they would be properly edited and fully effective; *M* 5570, p. 53. Presumably, therefore, it was only for the less potent prayer-letters of the common man that a considerable degree of grammatical accuracy was vital.)

88. *Tanya,* 103a, 135a, 136b, 162a–b; *Igerot Kodesh,* nos. 8, 15, 42, 82–84.

89. See supra, pp. 120–22.

90. *Berakhot,* V, 1.

91. Tal. B., *Berakhot,* 31a: **אין עומדין להתפלל . . . אלא מתוך שמחה של מצוה.**

92. See pp. 121–22.

93. Tal. B., *Berakhot,* 31a: **אין עומדין להתפלל . . . אלא מתוך הלכה פסוקה.**

94. *MK,* p. 94.

95. *Tanya,* 19a; *LT,* III, 30b, 71c, IV, 43b–c; *Sidur,* 19c, 22c, 24a, 152b; *MK,* pp. 305, 433; *M* 5570, p. 51; *BY,* p. 96; *EL,* p. 34; *M* 5562, p. 149. See also *M Par.,* II, 591–92.

Glossary

Expressions are defined in accordance with the way they are used in this study.

Adam Ḳadmon. "Primordial Man," the initial configuration of divine light after the tsimtsum (q.v.)

Aggadah (pl. aggadot). S.v. Midrash

Ahavah Rabah. The "great love" sometimes bestowed by God as a gift for Service

Ahavat ʿOlam. Love generated by contemplation

ʿAḳudim. The original, undifferentiated ("bound-together") lights of Adam Ḳadmon (q.v.)

ʿAmidah. Lit. "standing"; the principal prayer of the liturgy, consisting on weekdays of nineteen blessings recited silently while standing

Amoraim. Rabbinic teachers of the Gemara (q.v.) who succeeded the Tannaim (q.v.)

Arikh (Anpin). The lower of the two aspects of Keter (q.v.), corresponding to the faculty of will

ʿAśiyah, (ʿOlam ha-). The lowest of the four supernal worlds

ʿAtiḳ (Yomin). The higher of the two aspects of Keter (q.v.), corresponding to the faculty of pleasure

Atsilut. The highest of the four supernal worlds, each of which is comprised of a complete series of ten sefirot (s.v. Sefirah)

ʿAtsmut. (1) The Godhead; (2) divine "substance"; that is, lights or emanations contained and channeled by kelim (q.v.)

Ayin. The divine "Nothingness," the unrevealed essence of God, so called because it is unknowable and therefore, from man's perspective, virtually nonexistent

Benoni. The "intermediate man" in *Tanya*; i.e., between the Tsadiḳ (q.v.) (Righteous) and *Rashʿa* (Wicked); one who can be tempted to sin but never succumbs

Beraita. A compilation of Tannaitic teachings not included in the Mishnah and therefore of secondary authority

Berakhah. The blessing preceding the fulfillment of a commandment

Beriʾah. The second, in descending order, of the four supernal worlds

Binah. "Understanding"; the second sefirah (q.v.) (counting from Ḥokhmah); closely allied with its source, Ḥokhmah ("Wisdom"); the second of the intellective triad of sefirot (s.v. Ḥabad); develops and ramifies the intellective "point" generated by Ḥokhmah

Birur. Sifting or separation of good from evil

Biṭul. Self-nullification

Daʿat. "Knowledge," the third sefirah (counting from Ḥokhmah), which synthesizes its two predecessors and constitutes the third sefirah of the intellective triad, Ḥokhmah, Binah, Daʿat; considered the outer or lower aspect of Keter; corresponds to the faculty of intellectual concentration, or "attachment" to the idea that has been grasped by Binah

Deveḳut. Clinging or cleaving to God (from Deut. 4:14, 11:22, 13:5)

Din. "Strict judgment"; the divine attribute corresponding to, or identical with, the sefirah (q.v.) of Gevurah (Power)

En Sof. "Infinite [Being]," the unrevealed and unknowable essence of God

Gan ʿEden. The "Garden of Eden," the supernal paradise for souls

Garments. (1) The faculties of thought, speech, and action in which the soul "clothes" itself; (2) the "filters" created for the soul through the fulfillment of the commandments that enable it to assimilate and enjoy the divine light of Gan ʿEden (q.v.) without being overwhelmed

Gemara. Commentary to the Mishnah comprising the traditions, discussions, interpretations, rulings, and homilies of the Amoraim and their immediate successors, the Savoraim

Gevurah. "Power," fifth sefirah (q.v.) (counting from Ḥokhmah), opposed to Ḥesed (Loving-kindness); source of divine self-limitation

Gilui. "Revelation," the complementary opposite of heʿelam (hidden); the actualization of the potential

Ḥabad. Acronym consisting of the initials for the Hebrew words Ḥokhmah, Binah, Daʿat (q.v.)

Halakhah. Jewish law as formulated in the two Talmuds, Tosefta, midreshe halakhah, commentaries, codes, and responsa literature

Heʿelam. "Hidden," potential; complementary opposite of gilui (revelation)

Ḥesed. "Loving-kindness," the fourth sefirah (q.v.) (counting from Ḥokhmah); first of the six emotive sefirot; source of divine beneficence; opposed to Gevurah, which delimits that beneficence

Hod. "Majesty," the seventh sefirah (q.v.) (counting from Ḥokhmah); third of the left triad of sefirot comprising Binah, Gevurah, and Hod

Ḥokhmah. "Wisdom," the first sefirah (q.v.) (when Keter is not counted) and first of the three intellective sefirot, comprising Ḥokhmah, Binah, Daʿat; corresponds to the faculty that generates the first flash of intellect before it is fully understood and developed by Binah; it is the epitome of biṭul (self-nullification)

Ḥurban. Destruction of the Temple and beginning of exile

ʿIgulim. Circular, concentric emanations; related to, or identified with, (or) maḳif (q.v.) and sovev (kol ʿalmin) (q.v.); complemented by yosher—linear emanations

Ḳabalat ʿol (malkhut shamayim). "Acceptance of the yoke (of the Kingdom of Heaven)"; heteronomous devotion to God

Ḳavanah (pl. kavanot). Intention, meditative devotion; the concentrated thought accompanying prayer or the fulfillment of a commandment. Whereas rabbinic kavanah consisted essentially of concentrating on the meaning of the words of prayer and/or the intention to fulfil the commandment at hand, kabbalists emphasized the importance of specific, technical, kabbalistic kavanot

Ḳedushah. "Holiness," the side of good, as opposed to ḳelipah (q.v.), or the siṭra aḥra (q.v.)—the "other side"

Kelim. The "vessels" containing, limiting, and channeling the orot (lights)

Ḳelipah (pl. ḳelipot). "Shell" or "husk"; the supernal realm opposed to ḳedushah (q.v.) that dims or blocks the holy emanations. Three ḳelipot are considered completely evil, whereas Ḳelipat Nogah, the Translucent Shell, is neutral and serves as an intermediary between good and evil

Ḳelipat Nogah. S.v. Ḳelipah

Ḳeriʾat Shema. The obligatory twice-daily reading of three Biblical sections beginning with the words *Shema Yiśraʾel* (Deut. 6:4) and representing the contemplative crescendo of the morning liturgy

Keter. "Crown," often counted as the first sefirah; comprising ʿAtiḳ (Yomin) (q.v.) and Arikh (Anpin) (q.v.), which correspond to the faculties of pleasure and will

Lights. Divine emanations that fill and are channeled by the vessels; the vessels themselves are actually "thickened" lights

Malkhut. "Kingdom," the last sefirah (q.v.); immediate instrument of creation and providence; source of the faculty of speech; known as Ḥokhmah Tata'ah (Lower Ḥokhmah) to indicate its relation to the first sefirah, which is the original sefirotic source of creation and speech; identical with Shekhinah (God's indwelling presence) and *Keneset Yiśra'el* (the Congregation of Israel, the supernal source of the Jewish people); the feminine aspect of Divinity

Maḳif ([or] maḳif). Encompassing emanation; related to, or identical with, ʿigulim (q.v.) and sovev (kol ʿalmin) (q.v.); opposed to penimi (q.v.)

Maskil (pl. Maskilim). Adherent of the Haskalah movement, the Jewish reflection of the Enlightenment; generally an intellectual who sought to disseminate Western culture among Jews and favored some form of Jewish assimilation into modern society

Maṭi ve-lo maṭi. Emanations that "reach and do not reach"; that oscillate between egression and regression and hover over their vessels without permeating them; related to, and sometimes identified with, ratso (q.v.) ve-shov (running and returning)

Memale (kol ʿalmin). "Filling (all the worlds)"; the immanent emanation of Divinity permeating the vessels and worlds, as opposed to sovev (kol ʿalmin) (q.v.), the transcendent emanation

Mesirat nefesh. Self-sacrifice; surrender of one's will to God

Midot. Emotive attributes or faculties, as opposed to moḥin (q.v.)

Midrash. Compilation of rabbinic homilies and homiletic interpretations. Its subject matter, particularly when found in the Talmud, is known as *agadah* (or aggadah); individual passages of aggadah are often referred to collectively as aggadot.

Mitnagdim. Opponents of Hasidim

Mitsvah. A commandment; specifically, one of 613 halakhically defined Biblical imperatives or one of seven halakhically defined rabbinic imperatives

Moḥin. Intellective attributes or faculties, as opposed to midot (q.v.)

Musar. Religioethical exhortation

Neḳudim. Individualized "points" of light emitted by Adam Ḳadmon (q.v.) that succeeded ʿaḳudim (q.v.)

Netsaḥ. "Lasting Endurance," the sixth sefirah (q.v.) (counting from Ḥokhmah); third of the right triad of sefirot comprising Ḥokhmah, Ḥesed, Netsaḥ

ʿOlam ha-Ba. "The World to Come"; the post-Messianic and/or post-Resurrection world

Or En Sof. "The Infinite Light" emanated by the En Sof, the Infinite Being

Or ḥozer. "Reflected light," as opposed to or yashar, the direct light

Or yashar. The direct light, as opposed to or ḥozer, returning or reflected light

Orot. Lights, the infinite emanations that were eventually limited and channeled by the kelim (q.v.)

Penimi ([or] penimi). "Inner," permeating light that can be assimilated by its vessel; as opposed to (or) maḳif, encompassing light that transcends its vessels

Peshat. Plain meaning of a text based on language, grammar, syntax, context, and literary genre

Pesuḳe de-Zimrah. "Verses of Praise"; the section of the morning liturgy preceding *birkhot* Ḳeriʾat Shema, the blessings before Ḳeriʾat Shema (q.v.)

Pilpul. Halakhic dialectics, often sophistic

Ratso. (1) Egression or emanation, as opposed to shov, regression or return; (2) the ecstasy of prayer that brings the soul close to expiring with desire, as opposed to its forced, self-disciplined containment in a body devoted to Service on earth

Sefirah (pl. sefirot). One of ten primary emanations from the En Sof (q.v.), corresponding to ten divine attributes

Shekhinah. God's indwelling presence; s.v. Malkhut

Shevirat ha-Kelim; Shevirah. "The breaking of the vessels"; the planned primordial cosmic catastrophe giving rise to the mixture of good and evil on earth and to man's mission to separate and select the former from the latter

Shov. S.v. Ratso.

Siṭrʾa aḥra. The "other side"; the metaphysical realm of the ḳelipot (q.v.) and evil, as opposed to the side of ḳedushah (holiness)

Sovev (kol ʿalmin). "Encompassing (all worlds)"; the encompassing, transcendent light of the En Sof, as opposed to memale (kol ʿalmin), the immanent emanation permeating the vessels and worlds

Ṭaʿame mitsyot. The esoteric reasons for the commandments, often synonymous with ṭaʿame Torah

Ṭaʿame Torah. S.v. Ṭaʿame mitsyot

Talmud Torah. The study of Torah in such a manner as to fulfil the mitsṿah (q.v.)

Tannaim. Rabbinic teachers of the Mishnaic period (to ca. 250 C.E.)

Teshuvah. Return to God through repentance and Service

Tif'eret. "Beauty," the fourth sefirah (q.v.) (counting from Ḥokhmah); the third of the main triad of emotive sefirot, which synthesizes its two predecessors, Ḥesed and Gevurah, and is thus related to the synthesizing sefirah of Daʿat

Tiḳun, (ʿOlam ha-). The metaphysical World, or Realm, of Melioration, rectification, and order; successor to (ʿOlam ha-) Tohu, the World of Chaos. Tiḳun exists to make possible the Service that alone can redeem the fallen "sparks" of Tohu.

Tiḳun Ḥatsot. The Midnight Liturgy of the kabbalists

Tohu, (ʿOlam ha-). The World of Chaos, in which the Shevirah (q.v.) occurred, giving rise to (ʿOlam ha-) Tiḳun

Torah li-shemah. Torah-study for its own sake

Tsadiḳ. The Righteous (Man), who, according to the definition of *Tanya*, is incapable of sinning

Tsedaḳah. (1) The commandment to act righteously by providing pecuniary aid to the needy; usually translated as "charity"; (2) the act or aid itself

Tsimtsum. Contraction or condensation of the Or En Sof (q.v.) that made creation possible

Vessels. S.v. Kelim

Yesod. "Foundation," the ninth sefirah (q.v.) (counting from Ḥokhmah); last of the six emotive sefirot

Yetsirah. Third, in descending order, of the four supernal worlds

Yiḥudim. Necessary supernal unions effected through specific kaṿanot (q.v.)

Yosher. Linear emanations, as opposed to ʿigulim (q.v.), circular concentric emanations

Zaddik. A saintly Hasidic leader

Zeʿir Anpin. "The Small Face"; a metaphor for the six emotive sefirot, Ḥesed through Yesod

Selected Bibliography

Noteworthy secondary works on, or relating to, the first three generations of Hasidism (ca. 1740–1815) include:

Baumbinger, S. "Le-Igeret ha-Besht." *Sinai* 58 (1971): 170–98.

Ben Ezra, A. "Le-Toldot Hitnagdut ha-Gra le-Ḥasidut." *Tarbiz* 46 (1977): 133–40.

Chitrik, A. Note. *Sinai* 73 (1972): 190.

Dinur, B. Z. *Be-Mifneh ha-Dorot.* Jerusalem, 1955, pp. 83–227.

Dresner, S. *The Zaddik.* New York, 1960.

Dubnow, S. *Toldot ha-Ḥasidut.* Tel Aviv, 1944.

Elior, R. "Ḳunṭres ha-Hitpaʿalut le-R. Dov Baer Schneerson." *Ḳiryat Sefer* 54 (1979): 384–92; and S. D. Levin's Note, pp. 829–30.

Etkes, I. "ʿAliyato shel R. Shneur Zalman mi-Liadi le-ʿAmadat Manhigut." *Tarbiz* 54 (1985): 429–41.

———. "Darko shel R. Shneur Zalman mi-Liadi ke-Manhig shel Ḥasidim." *Zion* 50 (1985): 321–54.

———. Review of N. Lamm's *Torah Lishmah. Ḳiryat Sefer* 50 (1975): 638–48.

———. "Shiṭato u-Faʿalo shel Rabi Ḥayyim mi-Volozhin ki-Teguvat ha-Ḥevrah ha-Mitnagdit le-Ḥasidut." *PAAJR* 38–39 (1970–1971): Heb. section, 1–47.

Green, A. *Tormented Master: A Life of Rabbi Nahman of Bratslav.* University of Alabama Press, 1979.

Gries, Z. "ʿArikhat Tsaṿaʾat ha-Ribash." *Ḳiryat Sefer* 52 (1976–1977): 187–211.

———. "Sifrut ha-Hanhagot ha-Ḥasidit ke-Bitui le-Hanhagah ve-Etos." Thesis, Hebrew University, 1979.

———. "Sifrut ha-Hanhagot ha-Ḥasidit me-ha-Meḥtsah ha-Sheniyah le-Me'ah ha-18 ve-ad li-Shenot ha-Sheloshim le-Me'ah ha-19" *Zion* 46 (1981): 198–236, 278–305.

Hallamish, M. "Mishnato ha-ʿIyunit shel R. Shneur Zalman mi-Liadi." Thesis, Hebrew University, 1975.

Hasidism: Continuity or Innovation? Ed. B. Safran. Cambridge, Mass., 1988.

Heschel, A. *The Circle of the Baal Shem Tov.* Ed. S. Dresner. Chicago, 1985.

Hisdai, Y. "Eved Hashem be-Doram shel Avot ha-Ḥasidut." *Zion* 47 (1982): 253–92.

Jacobs, L. "The Doctrine of the Zaddik in the Thought of Elimelekh of Lizensk." University of Cincinnati, 1978.

———. *Hasidic Prayer.* New York, 1973.

———. *Seeker of Unity.* London, 1956.

———. *Tract on Ecstasy.* London, 1963.

Katz, J. *Tradition and Crisis.* New York, 1961, last chapter.

Kupfer, E. "Teʿudot Ḥadashot bi-Devar ha-Maḥloket ben Rashaz mi-Liadi u-ven R. Avraham mi-Ḳalisḳ." *Daʿat* 1 (1978): 121–41.

Lamm, N. "The Letter of the Besht to R. Gershon of Kutov." *Tradition* 14 (1974): 110–25.

———. *Torah li-Shemah.* Jerusalem, 1972.

Lieberman, H. *Ohel Raḥel.* New York, 1980.

Liebes, Y. "Ha-Tiḳun ha-Kelali shel R. Naḥman mi-Braslav ve-Yaḥaso le-Shabta'ut" *Zion* 45 (1980): 201–45; critique by Y. Mondshein. *Zion* 47 (1982); reply of Liebes. *Zion* 47 (1982): 224–31.

Loewenthal, N. *Communicating the Infinite: The Emergence of the Ḥabad School.* University of Chicago Press, 1990.

Migdal ʿOz. Ed. Y. Mondshein. Kefar Ḥabad, 1980.

Mindel, N. *R. Schneur Zalman of Liadi.* New York, 1971.

———. *R. Schneur Zalman of Liadi.* Vol. 2: *The Philosophy of Chabad.* New York, 1973.

Nigal, G. "ʿAl Meḳorot ha-Deveḳut be-Sifrut Reshit ha-Ḥasidut." *Ḳiryat Sefer* 46 (1971).

———. "ʿAl R. Aharon Shemuel ha-Kohen, mi-Talmide ha-Magid mi-Mesritch." *Sinai* 78 (1976): 255–62.

———. "Ḥeṭ Tokhaḥah u-Teshuvah be-Mishnat R. Elimelekh mi-Lizensk." *Bar Ilan* 12 (1976): 234–49.

———. "Maḳor Bilti Noda be-Sifrut Hanhagot ha-Ḥasidit." *Kiryat Sefer* 48 (1973): 154–84.

———. "Maḳor Rishoni le-Sifrut ha-Sipurim ha-Ḥasidit ʿal Sefer Keter Shem Ṭov u-Meḳorotav." *Sinai* 79 (1976): 132–46.

———. "Mishnat ha-Ḥasidut be-Kitve Rabi Elimelekh mi-Lizensk u-Vet Midrasho." Thesis, Hebrew University, 1972.

———. "Moro ve-Rabo shel R. Yiśraʾel Baʿal Shem Ṭov." *Sinai* 71 (1972): 150–59.

———. *Torot Baʿal ha-Toldot.* Jerusalem, 1974.

Peraḳim be-Torat ha-Ḥasidut. Ed. A. Rubinstein. Jerusalem, 1978.

Piekarz, M. *Bi-Yeme Tsemiḥat ha-Ḥasidut.* Jerusalem, 1978.

———. "Radiḳalism Dati bi-Yeme Reshit Hitpashṭutah shel ha-Ḥasidut be-Ispaḳlaryat Kitve R. Tsevi Hirsh mi-Galina." *Tarbiz* 54 (1985): 263–89.

———. "Ha-Teʿudah ha-Rishonah bi-Defus le-Torat ha-Ḥasidut." *Molad* 35–36 (Winter 1975): 183–87.

Rabinowitz, Z. M. "Meḳorot u-Teʿudot le-Toldot ha-Ḥasidut be-Polin." *Sinai* 82 (1978): 82–86.

Rafael, Y. "Genizat Ḥerson." *Sinai* 81 (1977): 129–50.

Rubinstein, A. "ʿAl Rabo shel ha-Beshṭ ve-al ha-Ketavim she-mehem Lamad ha-Beshṭ." *Tarbiz* 48 (1978–1979): 146–58.

———. "ʿAl Sheloshah Sipurim be-Sefer Shivḥe ha-Beshṭ." *Sinai* 90 (1982): 269–79.

———. "Ḥasidim ve-Ḥasidut be-Varsha." *Sinai* 75 (1974): 61–84.

———. "Igeret ha-Beshṭ le-R. Gershon mi-Ḳutov." *Sinai* 67 (1970): 120–39.

———. "ʿOd le-ʿInyan Igerot ha-Beshṭ." *Sinai* 72 (1973): 175–80.

Schatz-Uffenheimer, R. *Ha-Ḥasidut ke-Misṭiḳah.* Jerusalem, 1968.

———. "Martin Buber, Master of Hasidic Literature." *Judaism* 9 (Summer 1960): 277–82.

Schneersohn, J. I. *Igerot Ḳodesh meʾet . . . Rabenu Yosef Yitsḥaḳ.* New York, 1982.

———. "Ḳovets Mikhtavim." Appendix to *Sidur Tehilat Hashem,* 14th ed. New York, 1966.

———. *Ḳunṭres Biḳur Chicago.* New York, 1957.

———. *Ḳunṭres 18 Elul 5703.* New York, 1955.

———. *Ḳunṭres Limud ha-Ḥasidut.* New York, 1947.

———. *Ḳunṭres u-Maʿayan mi-Bet Hashem.* New York, 1958.

———. *Ḳunṭres Torat ha-Ḥasidut.* New York, 1946.

———. *Liḳuṭe Diburim.* New York, 1957.

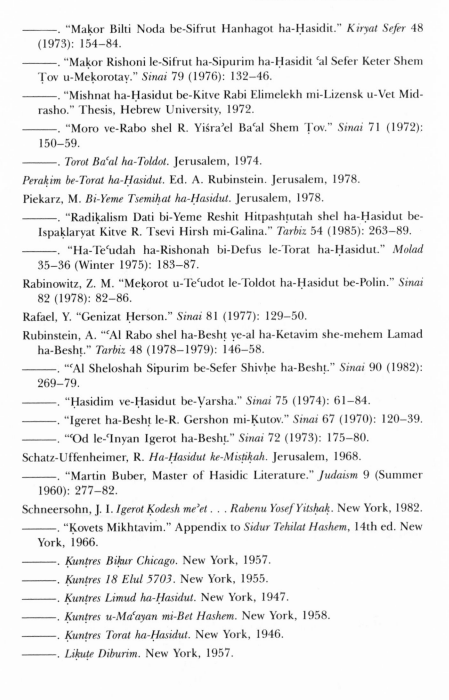

———. *Sefer ha-Śiḥot, Ḳayits 5700*. New York, 1961.

———. *Sefer ha-Śiḥot 5701*. New York, 1964.

———. "Vikuaḥ Minsk." In R. Elior's article in *Meḥḳare Yerushalayim be-Maḥshevet Yiśraʾel* 4 (1982): 208–35.

———. Articles in *Ha-Tamim* (q.v.).

Schneersohn, S. D. *Sefer ha-Śiḥot Torat Shalom*. New York, 1982.

Schneerson, M. *Ha-Yom Yom*. New York, 1961.

Schochet, J. I. *The Great Maggid*. New York, 1974, ch. 15.

Scholem, G. "Ha-Bilti Muda u-Muśag—Ḳadmut ha-Śekhel be-Sifrut ha-Ḥasidit." In *Hagut* (Hugo Bergmann Festschrift). Jerusalem, 1944.

———. *Major Trends in Jewish Mysticism*. New York, 1972.

———. "Martin Buber's Conception of Judaism." In *On Jews and Judaism in Crisis*, ed. W. J. Dannhauser. New York, 1976.

———. *The Messianic Idea in Judaism*. New York, 1974, pp. 176–251.

———. *On the Kabbalah and Its Symbolism*. New York, 1974.

Sefer ha-Ḳan. Jerusalem, 1969.

Seltzer, Robert M. "Coming Home: The Personal Basis of Simon Dubnow's Ideology." *AJS Review* 1 (1976): 283–301.

Solomon Maimon, An Autobiography. Trans. J. Clark Murrey. Boston, 1888.

Szmeruk, H. "Mashmeʿutah ha-Ḥevratit shel ha-Sheḥitah ha-Ḥasidit." *Zion* 20 (1955): 47–72.

Ha-Tamim, 2d ed. Kefar Ḥabad, 1971.

Teitelbaum, M. *Ha-Rav mi-Liadi u-Mifleget Ḥabad*. Warsaw, 1913.

Tishby, I. "Ḳitrugo shel R. Yiśraʾel mi-Shklov ʿal ha-Ḥasidim." *Ḳiryat Sefer* 51 (1976): 300–303.

———. "Ḳudsha Berikh Hu, Oraita ve-Yiśraʾel kula Ḥad: Maḳor le-Imrah be-Perush Idra Rabah le-Ramḥal." *Ḳiryat Sefer* 50 (1975): 480–92, 668–74.

Weinryb, B. D. *The Jews of Poland*. Philadelphia, 1973, ch. 12 and Appendix 4.

Weiss, J. *Meḥḳarim be-Ḥasidut Braslav*. Ed. M. Piekarz. Jerusalem, 1974.

Zucker, M. "Ḳetav Yad me Reshit ha-Ḥasidut." *Ḳiryat Sefer* 49 (1973): 224–35, and G. Nigal's Note, pp. 451–52.

Noteworthy editions of primary works or material include:

R. Elimelekh of Lyzhansk, *Noʿam Elimelekh*. Ed. G. Nigal. Jerusalem, 1978.

Ḥasidim u-Mitnagdim. Ed. M. Wilensky. Jerusalem, 1970.

Igerot Baʿal ha-Tanya u-Bene Doro. Ed. D. Z. Hilman. Jerusalem, 1953.

Igerot Ḳodesh. Ed. S. D. Levin. New York, 1980.

R. Jacob Joseph of Polonnoye, *Sefer Ketonet Pasim*. Ed. G. Nigal. Jerusalem, 1984 or 1985.

———. *Tsafnat Paneaḥ*. Ed. G. Nigal. Jerusalem, 1989.

Keter Shem Ṭov. Kehot Publication Society, New York, 1982.

Liḳuṭim Yeḳarim. Ed. A. I. Kahn. Jerusalem, 1974.

Magid Devarav le-Yaʿaḳov. Ed. A. I. Kahn. Jerusalem, 1971.

Magid Devarav le-Yaʿaḳov; Or Torah. Kehot Publication Society, New York, 1972.

Magid Devarav le-Yaʿaḳov. Ed. R. Schatz-Uffenheimer. Jerusalem, 1976; 2d ed., Jerusalem, 1990.

R. Menaḥem Mendel of Vitebsk, *Peri ha-Arets*. Jerusalem, 1987.

R. Menaḥem Naḥum of Chernobyl, *Upright Practices: The Light of the Eyes*. Trans. A. Green. New York, 1982.

Shivḥe ha-Beshṭ. Ed. Y. Mondshein. Jerusalem, 1982.

R. Shneur Zalman of Lyady, *Tanya*. Soncino Press, London, 1973.

Tsavaʾat ha-Ribash. Ed. J. I. Schochet. New York, 1975.

Unless otherwise indicated, references in the notes are to the following editions:

Degel Maḥneh Efrayim. Jerusalem, 1963.
Ḥesed le-Avraham. Warsaw, 1883.
Ḳedushat Levi. Jerusalem, 1946 (= Berditchev, 1908).
Keter Shem Ṭov. Kehot, 1982.
Liḳuṭim Yeḳarim. Ed. A. I. Kahn, 1974.
Magid Devarav le-Yaʿaḳov. Ed. R. Schatz-Uffenheimer, 1976.
Meʾor ʿEnayim. Jerusalem, 1968.
Noʿam Elimelekh. Ed. G. Nigal, 1978.
Or ha-Meʾir. New York, 1954.
Or Torah. Kehot, 1972 (in one volume with *Magid Devarav le-Yaʿaḳov*).
Peri ha-Arets. Lublin, 1928 (= Jerusalem, 1965).
Tanya. Soncino Press, 1973.
Toldot Yaʿaḳov Yosef. Lvov, 1863.
Tsavaʾat ha-Ribash. Ed. J. I. Schochet, 1975.

Citations for *EL*, *MK*, and *RP* refer to page numbers. Citations for *Peri ha-Arets* refer to the Arabic numeral pagination.

Index

Aaron Samuel ha-Kohen, 43
Aaron of Staroselye, 185
Abraham Kalisker, 37, 47, 48, 125–26
Abraham "ha-Malakh" (b. Dov Baer), 9, 46–47, 48, 67, 72, 110
Abulafia, Abraham, 18, 187
Acosmism, 15, 89, 110–11, 178
Adam, 63, 94
Adam Ḳadmon, 62, 73
Aescoly, A. Z., 204
Aggadah, 29
ʿAḳudim (ʿOlam ha-), 62, 66, 69
Alkabetz, Solomon, 142
ʿAmidah, 111, 147, 188, 189–91
Amoraim, 97
Angels, 79–81, 253 (n. 144)
Anthropomorphism, 55, 245 (n. 379)
Antinomism, 16, 56
Arikh (Anpin), 71, 73, 156
Aristotle, 28, 32, 83, 108, 189, 273 (n. 58)
Asceticism, 4, 13, 25, 31, 114, 132–33
Asher b. Yeḥiel, 139, 152
Ashkenazi, Zevi Hirsch, 6–7
ʿAśiyah (ʿOlam ha-), 71, 73, 76
ʿAtiḳ (Yomin), 71, 72, 73, 156, 170
Atsilut (ʿOlam ha-), 64, 65, 66, 69, 70, 76, 84, 94, 106, 111, 156, 161, 170, 171, 173
ʿAtsmut (the Godhead), 65, 66, 70, 73
Ayin, 27, 58, 71–72, 78, 187, 256 (n. 213)

Bacharach, Yair Ḥayyim, 6
Bahya ibn Pakuda, 18, 31, 181, 269 (n. 157)
Benomi, 101, 110, 120, 121, 174, 182
Ben Sasson, H. H., 3, 5
Beriʾah (ʿOlam ha-), 80, 106, 173
Besht, ix, x, 5, 9, 10–48 passim, 124, 125, 132, 142, 144–45, 151, 159, 178, 182, 187, 189, 190, 195, 196, 199, 201, 204, 207, 208, 209–11, 230 (n. 106), 236 (n. 241)
Bible: study of, 17–18, 142–43, 158–59, 162–63, 167–68
Binah, 70, 71–72, 79, 92, 94, 102, 104, 105, 119, 134, 136, 141, 158, 162
Birur, 93, 97, 159–60, 164
Biṭul, 15, 21, 33, 68, 72, 80, 92, 110–18, 130–31, 146, 148–50, 171–72, 186, 188, 263 (n. 39)

Body (human), 80–81, 86, 93–97, 253 (n. 133)
Buber, Martin, 203–4

Charity. *See* Tsedaḳah
Commandments. *See* Mitsṿah; Mitzvah-fulfillment
Contemplation, 28, 182, 183, 185–88. *See also* Meditation
Cordovero, Moses, 55, 59, 60, 63, 69, 72, 76, 87, 142, 230 (n. 109), 247 (n. 16)
Creation ex nihilo, 58, 78–79
Crescas, Hisdai, 146

Daʿat, 59, 70, 71–72, 102, 103
Dan, Joseph, 39
Dancing, 15, 123
Delmedigo, Joseph Solomon, 5, 6, 8, 82–83, 225 (n. 43)
Depression, 24, 117, 119–22
Deveḳut, 9, 12, 16–22, 27, 136, 144–45, 149–50, 151–52, 153, 179, 186–87, 191, 199, 275 (n. 118)
Din (Gevurah), 61, 66–67
Dinur, B. Z., 2, 14, 42, 228 (n. 76)
Dov Baer b. Shneur Zalman, 42, 49, 50, 51, 52, 168, 169
Dov Baer of Mezhirech. *See* Maggid
Dubnow, S., 2–4, 9, 195

Eating, 96–97
Ecstasy, 185–86
Eliezer b. Durdaya, 113–14
Elijah of Vilna (the Vilna Gaon), 5, 8, 9, 118, 144, 231 (n. 119)
Elimelekh of Lyzhansk, 37
Emden, Jacob, 3, 7, 206, 210
En Sof, 58, 59, 61, 62, 64, 65, 66, 68, 86, 88
Ethical traits, 67, 127, 267 (n. 125)
Ethical works, 3, 4–5, 194, 266 (n. 86)
Evil, 67, 73, 75–77, 88–89, 109, 119, 120, 200; Besht and Maggid on nature of, 22–24, 33. *See also* Ḳelipot
Exile and redemption, 87, 89–93
Eybeschutz, Jonathan, 7, 8, 210, 225 (n. 33)

Faith, 118–19, 124–26, 282 (n. 2)
Farbrengen, 123, 198
Fasting. *See* Asceticism
Fear (of God), 181–82, 184. *See also* Love and Fear
Fortitude, 116
Free will, 265 (n. 75)

Galen, 93, 96
Gan ʿEden, 85, 86, 142, 146, 163–64, 166–67, 170, 172, 173, 180, 182
Gans, David, 5, 7
Gemara, 163, 164, 167. *See also* Talmud
Gentiles, 25, 82, 84, 86, 90–91, 97, 108–9, 118, 157, 260 (n. 296)
Geonim, 92
Gevurah, 32, 61, 66, 67, 70–71, 76, 84, 109, 122, 157, 161–62, 175, 181
Gilgulim, 98, 172
Graetz, H., 2
Gries, Z., 12, 13, 14, 195, 228 (n. 74)
Guttman, Julius, 117

Ḥabad (the term), ix
Halakhah, 137–46, 151, 153, 158, 159–61, 194
Hallamish, M., 52–54, 217–20
Ḥaside Ashkenaz, 4, 114, 132, 148
Hasidism: ix, 43, 48; study of, 2–37, 195–96, 203–6, 209–11; and Sufism, 14–16; and romanticism, 35–36; paradox of, 116; Mitnagdic criticism of, 287 (n. 81)

Ḥayyim of Volozhin, 276 (n. 137)
Heʿelam and gilui, 64–65
Hegel, F., 56
Heilman, H. M. (*Bet Rebi*), 44–45
Heraclitus, 32, 56, 73
Heschel, A. J., 235 (n. 220)
Ḥesed, 32, 61, 70–71, 84, 95, 105, 109, 128, 144, 157, 161–62, 175, 181
Hierarchy, 31, 57, 80–81, 94, 114, 155–56, 161–64, 175–76, 183
Highest-lowest relation, 74–77, 86, 162, 173, 176, 251 (n. 100), 278 (n. 177)
Hilman, D. Z., 41
History, RSZ's conception of, 89–93
Hitlahavut, 17, 21, 187
Ḥokhmah, 59, 64, 68, 70, 71–73, 75, 78, 79, 83, 92, 93, 94, 99–100, 101, 102, 104, 105, 106, 111, 112, 119, 141, 146, 149–62 passim, 164, 165, 180, 257 (n. 218)
Horodetsky, S. H., 2, 203
Horowitz, Isaiah (*Shene Luḥot ha-Berit*), 4, 5, 45–46, 132, 133
Ḥurban, 80, 92. *See also* Exile and redemption

Ibn Gabbai, Meir, 5, 189–90
ʿIgulim (and yosher), 65, 66, 69, 83
Intellect and emotion, 95, 99–100, 102–4, 185–86, 257 (n. 230)
Intermediary, concept of, 65, 79
Introspection, 115, 118, 120–21
Israel, land of, 87, 91–92, 201
Israel Baal Shem Tov. *See* Besht
Israeli, Isaac, 78, 79

Jacob Joseph of Polonnoye, 10, 11, 12, 17, 34–35, 37
Jacobs, Louis, 39–40, 284 (n. 40), 286 (n. 70)
Joy, 115, 119, 121, 122, 131, 265 (n. 76)
Judah Halevi (*Kuzari*), 32

Kabbalah: Lurianic, 8, 9, 13, 20, 53, 55, 60–63, 65, 67, 72, 76, 81, 83, 98–99, 106–7, 137, 139, 141–42, 146, 155, 159, 160, 161, 164, 173–74, 188, 190, 193, 198, 199; early, 18, 59, 78; study of, 163–69, 230 (n. 109), 279 (n. 203). *See also* Ethical works
Kahn, A. I., 12
Ḳaṭnut-gadlut, 33
Katz, Jacob, 3
Kavanah, kavanot, 4, 13, 20, 21, 80, 85, 173–75, 187, 189, 190, 287 (n. 87)
Ḳelipat Nogah, 22, 91, 108, 109, 120, 159, 171, 172, 176, 191
Ḳelipot, 22, 72, 76, 84, 90–91, 108, 109, 118, 119, 134, 135, 141, 150–51, 172, 175. *See also* Evil
Ḳeriʾat Shema, 80, 149, 190
Keter, 27, 59, 60, 65, 66, 70, 71–72, 75, 93, 101, 104, 105, 156, 170, 172–73, 175
Keter Shem Ṭov, 11

Lamm, N., 272 (n. 42), 276 (n. 137)
Letters: and deveḳut, 16–20; soul's production of, 104–5; arrangement of Torah's, 143
Levi Isaac of Berditchev, 37, 47, 126, 143–44
Lights and vessels. *See* Orot and kelim
Liḳuṭim Yeḳarim, 11, 21
Livelihood, the need to earn one's, 128–30, 268 (n. 138)
Love (of God): hidden, or Innate, 99–103, 173, 180–81, 183, 185; be-khol meʾodekha, 129, 136; Ahavat ʿOlam, 179–85, 186; Ahavah Rabah, 179–84; other types of, 181. *See also* Love and Fear

Love and Fear (of God), 13, 17, 21, 38, 80, 81, 102, 112, 114–15, 123, 124, 140, 144, 151, 153, 154, 173, 174, 178–79, 182–87, 189, 192–94, 197, 199, 282 (n. 10), 283 (n. 18). *See also* Love; Fear
Luria, Isaac, 19, 22, 78, 85, 114, 119, 132. *See also* Kabbalah: Lurianic

Maggid (of Mezhirech), ix, x, 1, 9–48 passim, 52, 67, 68, 72, 73, 74, 89, 104, 106, 112, 124, 125, 131, 142–45, 151, 154, 178, 182, 184, 187–88, 190, 195, 196, 201, 211, 212–13, 215, 256 (n. 213)
Maharal of Prague, 5, 112, 133
Maimonidean controversy, 4–5
Maimonides, Abraham, 31
Maimonides, Moses, 8, 18, 22, 28–30, 65, 78, 79, 81, 83, 84, 86–87, 100, 106, 112, 115, 117, 137, 139, 166, 168, 174, 178, 189, 197, 198, 199, 232 (n. 160), 237 (n. 270), 252 (n. 113), 261 (n. 305), 267 (n. 126), 271 (n. 18), 272 (n. 55), 273 (n. 58)
Makif, or, 62, 65, 66, 69, 76, 150, 151, 156, 170, 171
Malkhut, 66, 70, 75, 79, 81, 88, 92, 105, 120, 134, 148, 154, 156, 158, 162
Martyrdom, 263 (n. 39)
Meditation, 117–22, 126, 127, 132, 194. *See also* Contemplation
Memale (kol ʿalmin), 65–66, 95, 175
Menaḥem Mendel of Bar, 34–35
Menaḥem Mendel of Lubavitch, 42, 49–50, 51, 52, 69, 242 (n. 340), 248 (n. 358), 253 (n. 146)
Menaḥem Mendel of Przemyslany, 11–12, 207–9
Menaḥem Mendel of Vitebsk, 9, 47, 48, 49, 110, 126, 144
Menaḥem Naḥum of Chernobyl, 9, 126, 144
Mendelssohn, Moses, 7
Meshullam Feivush of Zbaraz, 12, 208–9
Mesirat nefesh, 113–14, 151, 188, 190, 263 (n. 39)
Messianic Era, 85–88, 91–92, 165, 166, 172, 173, 192, 155 (n. 189)
Mindel, N., 40
Mishnah, 152, 163, 167, 168, 169–70
Mitnagdim, 118–19, 197, 200, 202, 287 (n. 81)
Mitsṿah, mitsṿot, 18, 22, 85–88, 98–99, 112, 135, 138–40, 142, 145–48, 164–65, 169–77, 180–81, 188, 200–201
Mitzvah-fulfillment, 3, 4, 27, 63
Moaḥ Setimaʾah, 73
Mordecai b. Samuel (*Shaʿar ha-Melekh*), 24–26
Moses, 38, 107

Naḥmanides, Moses, 66, 78, 85, 159
Nature, natural phenomena, 81–84, 99, 258 (n. 252)
Neḳudim (ʿOlam ha-), 62, 66, 68, 69
Netsaḥ and Hod, 93, 105
Nigal, G., 43

ʿOlam ha-Ba, 28, 85, 86, 130
Oppenheim, David, 6, 7
Opposites (complementary First principles), 63, 70
Or En Sof, 58, 61, 64, 67, 68, 72, 81, 85, 88, 97, 98, 145–55 passim, 160, 161, 163, 166, 171, 172, 173, 176, 190
Orot and kelim, 66–70
Or yashar and or ḥozer, 62, 74

Patriarchs (of the Bible), 110, 111, 118, 143, 172

Penimi, or, 62, 65, 156
Philosophy, study of, 2, 263 (n. 25). *See also* Secular studies
Piekarz, M., 14, 20, 195, 225 (n. 70)
Pinḥas of Korets, 9, 12, 208
Plato, 28–29, 103
Pleasure: divine, 23–24, 27–28, 77, 88–89, 111, 117, 120, 164–65, 170, 192, 200; human, 28, 72–73, 82, 84, 93, 116, 119, 123, 179–80, 185, 250 (n. 77), 254 (n. 159)
Poland (and Lithuania), 3, 5–8
Prayer, 2, 13, 15, 19–22, 46, 92, 100, 139–40, 147–48, 186–94, 199, 287 (n. 87). *See also* Love and Fear
Profane thoughts. *See* Thought
Providence, 66

Rabbis of Poland-Lithuania, 3–8
Raḥamin, 66–67, 115
Ratso and shov, 71, 74, 91, 114–15, 117, 148, 184, 189, 286 (n. 57)
Reason, 73. *See also* Intellect and emotion
Repentance. *See* Teshuvah
Reshimu, 62
Resurrection, 85–88, 172, 173
Reward and punishment, 85–89, 172–73. *See also* Gan ʿEden; Messianic Era; Resurrection
Rubinstein, A., 20, 195, 211

Saadya Gaon, 112
Sabbath (Shabbat), 2, 25, 110, 192
Sabbatianism, 4, 8, 9, 13, 16, 20, 24, 35, 43, 209–12
Schapiro, D., 40
Schatz(-Uffenheimer), Rivkah, 9, 12, 14, 39, 196, 206–7, 212–15, 285 (n. 45)
Schneersohn, Joseph Isaac, 41–42, 44–45
Schneersohn, Shalom Dov Baer, 279 (n. 203)
Schneerson, Menaḥem M., 51
Schochet, J. I., 40–41, 216
Scholem, Gershom, 9, 16, 42, 55, 58, 59, 60, 63, 71, 195, 211–12, 236 (n. 241)
Scripture. *See* Bible
Secular studies, 2, 108, 112, 157, 206, 226 (n. 50), 253 (n. 146). *See also* Philosophy
Sefer Roḳeaḥ, 4, 132, 133
Sefirah, sefirot, 19, 58–63, 68, 93, 162. *See also* individual sefirot
Self-nullification. *See* Biṭul
Self-pity and self-abasement, 115, 120–22, 189, 266 (n. 84)
Service, 22, 32–33, 80–81, 92, 97, 101, 107, 112, 113, 114, 116–17, 119, 121, 123, 127, 129, 130, 136, 178–82, 184, 186, 187–88, 189, 197, 200, 201–2
Shekhinah, 21, 85, 91, 98, 120, 134, 189–90
Shevirat ha-Kelim (Shevirah), 55, 62, 63, 66, 72, 97, 109, 159, 248 (n. 48)
Shivḥe ha-Besht, 42–43
Shneur Zalman of Lyady: ix, x, 10; relationship to Besht and Maggid, 1–2; view of simple Jew, 38–47; previous scholarship on, 38–45, 52–54, 217–20; intellectual biography of, 45–51; transcriptions of discourses of, 50–52; general characteristics of discourses, 52–57, 196, 267 (n. 108); view of history, 89–93; exegesis of, 105–6; biographies of, 216–17
Shulḥam ʿArukh: of Joseph Karo, 17, 168, 197, 202; of RSZ, 45, 47, 137, 168–69
Simeon b. Yohai, 129, 147–48
Sin, 24, 134–36
Song, 123

Soul(s), 63, 72, 79–81, 94, 97–102, 104–8, 155–56, 170–73, 179–80, 182, 191, 192, 197–98, 244 (n. 377), 258 (nn. 246, 254)
Sovev (kol ʿalmin), 65–66, 73, 85, 94, 146, 170, 171, 172, 175, 248 (n. 30), 281 (n. 242)
Sparks (in Lurianic kabbalah), 20, 22–23, 62, 86, 172
Speech: divine, 55, 59, 105, 134, 162; human, 104–6, 162
Steinsaltz, A., 40
Striving, 110, 113, 116
Suffering, 4, 109, 119, 128, 130–31
Sufism, 14–16
Szmeruk, H., 42

Ṭaʿame Torah, 164, 166
Talmud, Talmud study, 141–45, 160–61, 165–66, 174, 184, 194, 198, 199
Tannaim, 92
Tanya, 39, 40, 49, 53, 54, 88, 99–102, 107, 114, 118, 122, 123, 125, 134, 140, 145, 146, 147, 149, 152, 154, 160, 171, 172–86 passim, 190, 199, 218–19, 243 (n. 269), 269 (n. 172), 282 (n. 3)
Taste, sense of, 72, 84
Teitelbaum, M., 38–39
Temple period, 80, 87, 89–92, 135, 192–93, 256 (n. 198)
Teshuvah, 27, 98, 115, 133–36, 268 (n. 129)
Tetragrammaton, 105, 134, 135, 158
Thought: elevation of profane thoughts, 9, 12, 19–20, 189, 286 (n. 63); act of thinking, 96
Tifʾeret, 70, 72
Tiḳun (act of), 55, 63, 107
Tiḳun, ʿOlam ha-, 66–69, 71, 74, 75, 80, 81, 94, 97, 104, 109, 162
Tiḳun Ḥatsot, 120, 122, 194
Tishby, Isaiah, 9, 39, 195, 209–11
Tohu, ʿOlam ha-, 62, 66–69, 74, 75–76, 80, 81, 90, 93, 97, 104, 109, 162
Toil, 116
Torah, 72; source of, 156–57; Written and Oral, 157–63; exoteric and esoteric, 163–69
Torah-study, 3, 4, 12, 13, 17–18, 21, 22, 27, 46, 80, 134, 200–201; scope and importance of, 137–45, 270 (nn. 2, 3); and prayer, 139–40, 147–48, 188, 194; and other commandments, 145–49, 272 (n. 55), 277 (n. 158); and biṭul, 149–50; must be oral, 150–51; and deveḳut, 151–52, 179; li-shemah, 141–45, 149, 152–54, 272 (n. 42), 275 (n. 118); power of, 155–56; order and method of, 167–69, 230 (n. 109), 279 (n. 203)
Trust in God, 131
Tsadiḳ, 90, 92, 100, 101, 107, 134, 164, 174, 182, 189, 193, 259 (n. 266)
Tsavaʾat ha-Ribash, 11
Tsedaḳah, 108, 134, 176–77, 201
Tsimtsum, 55, 60–62, 64, 69
Tuvia b. Moses Cohen, 6, 8

Vidas, Elijah de (*Reshit Ḥokhmah*), 4, 132, 133, 266 (n. 86)
Vital, Ḥayyim, 8, 23, 126, 141, 168, 199

Weiss, Joseph, 9, 12, 42, 43, 207–9
Will: divine, 66, 72, 102, 111, 146, 156, 170, 171, 172–73, 174, 179, 188, 190, 200; human, 100, 101–2, 103, 111, 136, 188, 190, 191, 250 (n. 77), 265 (n. 75)

Worlds, supernal, 61, 63, 70, 188

Yesod, 105
Yetsirah (ʿOlam ha-), 71, 173
Yiḥuda ʿIlaʾah and Tataʾah, 111
Yiḥudim, 19, 112, 173, 188
Ysander, Torsten, 204

Zaddik, 9, 12, 124–26, 143–44, 267
(n. 111); fall of, 33–35; relationship with his followers, 35–38
Zeʾev Wolf of Zhitomir, 10, 143
Zohar, 13, 19, 21, 22, 23, 25, 58, 60, 72, 76, 78, 83, 85, 96, 114, 126, 135, 142, 157, 158, 159, 164, 167–68, 169, 178, 182, 184, 188, 189, 190, 198, 199, 230 (n. 109)
Zweifel, E., 2, 203

ABOUT THE AUTHOR

Roman A. Foxbrunner is a Postdoctoral Fellow, Harvard University Center for Jewish Studies. He received his B.A. from Queens College and his M.A. and Ph.D. from Harvard University.